booksonline

Read SAP PRESS online also

With booksonline we offer you online access to leading SAP experts' knowledge. Whether you use it as a beneficial supplement or as an alternative to the printed book – with booksonline you can:

- Access any book at any time
- Quickly look up and find what you need
- Compile your own SAP library

Your advantage as the reader of this book

Register your book on our website and obtain an exclusive and free test access to its online version. You're convinced you like the online book? Then you can purchase it at a preferential price!

And here's how to make use of your advantage

1. Visit www.sap-press.com
2. Click on the link for SAP PRESS booksonline
3. Enter your free trial license key
4. Test-drive your online book with full access for a limited time!

Your personal **license key** for your test access including the preferential offer

w39h-egtk-8djz-bpca

SAP® Interface Programming

SAP PRESS

SAP PRESS is a joint initiative of SAP and Galileo Press. The know-how offered by SAP specialists combined with the expertise of the Galileo Press publishing house offers the reader expert books in the field. SAP PRESS features first-hand information and expert advice, and provides useful skills for professional decision-making.

SAP PRESS offers a variety of books on technical and business related topics for the SAP user. For further information, please visit our website: *www.sap-press.com*.

Dominik Ofenloch, Roland Schwaiger
Getting Started with Web Dynpro ABAP
2010, app. 480 pp.
978-1-59229-311-7

Alfred Barzewski, et al.
Java Programming with SAP NetWeaver
2008, 696 pp.
978-1-59229-181-6

Horst Keller, Sascha Krüger
ABAP Objects, 2nd ed.
2007, 1080 pp.
978-1-59229-079-6

Jens Stumpe, Joachim Orb
SAP Exchange Infrastructure
2005, app. 288 pp.
978-1-59229-037-6

Michael Wegelin and Michael Englbrecht

SAP® Interface Programming

Galileo Press

Bonn • Boston

Galileo Press is named after the Italian physicist, mathematician and philosopher Galileo Galilei (1564–1642). He is known as one of the founders of modern science and an advocate of our contemporary, heliocentric worldview. His words *Eppur se muove* (And yet it moves) have become legendary. The Galileo Press logo depicts Jupiter orbited by the four Galilean moons, which were discovered by Galileo in 1610.

Editor Maike Lübbers
English Edition Editor Kelly Grace Harris
Translation Lemoine International, Inc., Salt Lake City, UT
Copyeditor Julie McNamee
Cover Design Jill Winitzer
Photo Credit Fotolia/Aleksandr Lukin
Layout Design Vera Brauner
Production Editor Kelly O'Callaghan
Assistant Production Editor Graham Geary
Typesetting Publishers' Design and Production Services, Inc.
Printed and bound in Canada

ISBN 978-1-59229-318-6

© 2010 by Galileo Press Inc., Boston (MA)
1st Edition 2010
1st German edition published 2009 by Galileo Press, Bonn, Germany

Library of Congress Cataloging-in-Publication Data
Wegelin, Michael.
 [SAP-Schnittstellenprogrammierung. English]
 SAP interface programming / Michael Wegelin, Michael Englbrecht. -- 1st ed.
    p. cm.
 Includes bibliographical references.
 ISBN-13: 978-1-59229-318-6 (alk. paper)
 ISBN-10: 1-59229-318-2 (alk. paper)
 1. SAP R/3. 2. User interfaces (Computer systems) 3. Information resources management. I. Englbrecht, Michael. II. Title.
 QA76.9.U83W38713 2010
 005.4'37--dc22   2009037259

All rights reserved. Neither this publication nor any part of it may be copied or reproduced in any form or by any means or translated into another language, without the prior consent of Galileo Press GmbH, Rheinwerkallee 4, 53227 Bonn, Germany.

Galileo Press makes no warranties or representations with respect to the content hereof and specifically disclaims any implied warranties of merchantability or fitness for any particular purpose. Galileo Press assumes no responsibility for any errors that may appear in this publication.

"Galileo Press" and the Galileo Press logo are registered trademarks of Galileo Press GmbH, Bonn, Germany. SAP PRESS is an imprint of Galileo Press.

All of the screenshots and graphics reproduced in this book are subject to copyright © SAP AG, Dietmar-Hopp-Allee 16, 69190 Walldorf, Germany.

SAP, the SAP-Logo, mySAP, mySAP.com, mySAP Business Suite, SAP NetWeaver, SAP R/3, SAP R/2, SAP B2B, SAPtronic, SAPscript, SAP BW, SAP CRM, SAP Early Watch, SAP ArchiveLink, SAP GUI, SAP Business Workflow, SAP Business Engineer, SAP Business Navigator, SAP Business Framework, SAP Business Information Warehouse, SAP inter-enterprise solutions, SAP APO, AcceleratedSAP, InterSAP, SAPoffice, SAPfind, SAPfile, SAPtime, SAPmail, SAPaccess, SAP-EDI, R/3 Retail, Accelerated HR, Accelerated HiTech, Accelerated Consumer Products, ABAP, ABAP/4, ALE/WEB, Alloy, BAPI, Business Framework, BW Explorer, Duet, Enjoy-SAP, mySAP.com e-business platform, mySAP Enterprise Portals, RIVA, SAPPHIRE, TeamSAP, Webflow and SAP PRESS are registered or unregistered trademarks of SAP AG, Walldorf, Germany.

All other products mentioned in this book are registered or unregistered trademarks of their respective companies.

Contents at a Glance

1 Basic Principles of SAP Interface Programming 13

2 Remote Function Call with ABAP 95

3 Remote Function Call with C 145

4 Remote Function Call with Java 217

5 IDocs and ALE 271

6 Service-Oriented Architecture Protocol 311

7 SAP NetWeaver Process Integration 347

A Bibliography 391

B The Authors 393

Contents

Preface 11

1 Basic Principles of SAP Interface Programming 13

1.1 SAP NetWeaver Application Server 13
    1.1.1 SAP Solutions and SAP NetWeaver 13
    1.1.2 SAP NetWeaver Application Server ABAP 16
    1.1.3 SAP NetWeaver Application Server Java 29
1.2 Security 32
    1.2.1 Security in Heterogeneous Landscapes 32
    1.2.2 User Management Engine 36
    1.2.3 KeyStores: Authentication, Signatures, Encryption 38
    1.2.4 Authentication and Authorization 40
1.3 Programming SAP NetWeaver AS ABAP 57
    1.3.1 ABAP Dictionary 58
    1.3.2 Authentication and Authorization 63
    1.3.3 Number Ranges 64
    1.3.4 Function Modules 64
    1.3.5 Update Modules 67
    1.3.6 Application Functions and User Interfaces 68
1.4 Overview of SAP Interface Technologies 70
    1.4.1 File Interface 70
    1.4.2 Remote Function Call 72
    1.4.3 BAPIs 82
    1.4.4 Application Link Enabling 84
    1.4.5 SOAP 90
    1.4.6 XI SOAP 92

2 Remote Function Call with ABAP 95

2.1 RFC Function Modules in ABAP 95
    2.1.1 Function Modules for Reading 95
    2.1.2 Call via sRFC 98
    2.1.3 Function Modules for Deleting and Changing ... 101

2.2	Transactional RFC		106
2.3	Queued RFC		111
	2.3.1	qRFC with Outbound Queue	112
	2.3.2	qRFC with Outbound and Inbound Queue	115
2.4	Business Objects and BAPIs		118
	2.4.1	Developing Business Objects	118
	2.4.2	Developing BAPIs	119
	2.4.3	"Helpvalues" Business Object	141

3 Remote Function Call with C ... 145

3.1	C RFC Library		145
	3.1.1	RFC Software Development Kit	146
	3.1.2	Connection Tests	148
	3.1.3	Compiling and Linking	152
3.2	Simple RFC Clients and RFC Parameters		153
	3.2.1	Structure of an RFC Client Program	154
	3.2.2	Simple Parameters	164
	3.2.3	Structured Parameters	167
	3.2.4	Table Parameters	171
3.3	More Complex RFC Clients		174
	3.3.1	Calling BAPIs	174
	3.3.2	Transactional RFC	177
	3.3.3	Queued RFC	188
3.4	RFC Server		189
	3.4.1	Logon to Gateway	192
	3.4.2	Installing and Executing Functions	194
	3.4.3	Dispatching	202
	3.4.4	Transactional RFC	205

4 Remote Function Call with Java ... 217

4.1	SAP Java Connector		217
	4.1.1	Installation	217
	4.1.2	Architecture of SAP Java Connector	218
	4.1.3	Programming with SAP Java Connector	220
	4.1.4	Processing Tables and Structures	229
	4.1.5	Transactional RFC	232

	4.1.6	Queued RFC	234
	4.1.7	Metadata Processing	236
4.2	Enterprise Connector		237
	4.2.1	Generating Proxy Classes	238
	4.2.2	Programming the Client	243
4.3	RFC Server		244
	4.3.1	Server-Side and Client-Side Repository	245
	4.3.2	Programming a Simple JCo Server	247
	4.3.3	Registering a Function Handler	249
	4.3.4	Managing Transactions	251
4.4	JCo RFC Provider Service		252
4.5	SAP NetWeaver Portal Connector Framework		256
	4.5.1	Java Connector Architecture	257
	4.5.2	System Landscape of the Portal	258
	4.5.3	Introduction to Programming in the Portal	261
	4.5.4	Application Example of the Connector Framework	264

5 IDocs and ALE 271

5.1	IDocs		272
	5.1.1	Developing IDocs	272
	5.1.2	Creating IDocs	275
	5.1.3	Inbound Processing of IDocs	279
5.2	ALE		284
	5.2.1	ALE Configuration	284
	5.2.2	Testing and Monitoring	290
	5.2.3	ALE Interface for BAPIs	292
5.3	IDoc Programming with the C RFC Library		296
	5.3.1	IDoc Receiver	297
	5.3.2	IDoc Sender	300
5.4	IDoc Programming with Java and JCo		302
	5.4.1	Preparation for the Use of IDoc Libraries	302
	5.4.2	Client Application for IDocs	303
	5.4.3	IDoc Server	307
	5.4.4	Configuration for the Dispatch of IDocs	310

6 Service-Oriented Architecture Protocol ... 311

6.1 Web Services and Clients with SAP NetWeaver AS ABAP ... 311
   6.1.1 ABAP SOAP Web Service ... 311
   6.1.2 ABAP SOAP Web Client ... 319
6.2 Web Services and Clients with SAP NetWeaver AS Java ... 323
   6.2.1 Web Service Infrastructure in SAP NetWeaver AS Java ... 323
   6.2.2 Web Service Provider with J2EE ... 326
   6.2.3 Web Service Clients ... 333
   6.2.4 Adaptive Web Service with Web Dynpro ... 338
6.3 SOAP Programming with Java ... 338
   6.3.1 Java API for XML Web Services ... 338
   6.3.2 Implementing a Web Service Client ... 340
   6.3.3 Implementing a Web Service Provider ... 341
6.4 SOAP Programming with C# ... 342

7 SAP NetWeaver Process Integration ... 347

7.1 SAP NetWeaver Exchange Infrastructure 3.0 ... 347
   7.1.1 System Landscape Directory ... 349
   7.1.2 Integration Repository ... 352
   7.1.3 ABAP XI Proxies ... 356
   7.1.4 Java XI Proxies ... 360
   7.1.5 Integration Directory ... 366
7.2 SAP NetWeaver Process Integration 7.1 ... 372
   7.2.1 Service Interfaces ... 372
   7.2.2 ABAP SOAP Proxies ... 374
   7.2.3 Java SOAP Proxies ... 383

Appendices ... 391

A Bibliography ... 391
B The Authors ... 393

Index ... 395

Preface

In this book on SAP interface programming, you will find detailed technical information on how SAP systems communicate with each other and with external systems. This information is illustrated in executable and coded programming examples, which you can download from the book's page at *www.sap-press.com*.

The target group of this book includes developers who want to integrate their programs with SAP systems, technical consultants who want to recommend integration options to their customers, and SAP customers who want to gain a profound insight into integration programming.

Detailed instructions and programmed examples facilitate the implementation in real life. Here, we incorporate our experience as trainers and interface developers and consider the four important programming languages: ABAP, C, Java, and C#.

Chapter 1, Basic Principles of SAP Interface Programming, starts with an overview of the whole topic and introduces the sample application that is used throughout the book. This sample application is used to manage orders of booksellers to wholesalers and from wholesalers to publishing companies.

Chapters 2 to 4 deal with the Remote Function Call (RFC), an SAP interface technology that you can use to call function modules in other systems. **Chapter 2**, Remote Function Call with ABAP, discusses this topic from the ABAP perspective, **Chapter 3**, Remote Function Call with C, describes the programming using C, and **Chapter 4**, Remote Function Call with Java, outlines die programming using Java. The development and use of Business Application Programming Interfaces (BAPIs) is also described in these chapters.

Chapter 5, IDocs and ALE, describes Application Link Enabling (ALE). This SAP technology enables applications to exchange information in the form of Intermediate Documents (IDocs). It is based on RFC.

Preface

Following the SAP RFC and ALE technologies, **Chapter 6**, Service-Oriented Architecture Protocol, deals with the Service-Oriented Architecture Protocol (SOAP). This open web standard enables applications to exchange information in the form of XML documents (Extensible Markup Language) via HTTP (Hypertext Transfer Protocol) or other protocols. Today, it is supported in virtually all development platforms as it is demonstrated based on the C# example.

Chapter 7, SAP NetWeaver Process Integration, details how you can develop new applications in the outside-in approach using SAP NetWeaver Exchange Infrastructure 3.0 (SAP NetWeaver XI) or SAP NetWeaver Process Integration 7.1 (SAP NetWeaver PI). For this approach, you first describe the interfaces, generate the classes that implement the technical communication from the interface description, and then use these classes for the implementation of the application.

This book is based on many freely accessible sources of SAP: the online help at *http://help.sap.com*, as well as the blogs, discussion forums, and white papers of the SDN (*SAP Developer Network*) at *http://sdn.sap.com*. The SAP NetWeaver Development Subscription was also a major help for us because all examples were created on an SAP NetWeaver Application Server from this subscription. At this point, a big thank-you goes to SAP AG for the great software and its developers and those who helped to develop it.

Special thanks are also due to our editors, Stefan Proksch and Maike Lübbers, from Galileo Press. Stefan Proksch encouraged us to write this book, and Maike Lübbers ensured that it can also be read and understood by other people apart from the authors.

I, Michael Wegelin, thank Vera, Tabea, and Benedict for your support and patience. The life I share with you is exciting, funny, and simply wonderful.

I, Michael Englbrecht, thank Michaela, Domenik, and Sophie for your thoughtfulness and patience. Without you many things wouldn't be possible and everything only half as good.

The Authors
Michael Wegelin and **Michael Englbrecht**

This chapter summarizes the basic knowledge you will need for SAP interface programming: information about the SAP NetWeaver Application Server architecture, structure of ABAP programs, and supported application protocols.

1 Basic Principles of SAP Interface Programming

This first chapter provides an overview of the SAP NetWeaver Application Server architecture (SAP NetWeaver AS) and focuses in particular on the components responsible for communicating with external systems. It gives you a brief introduction into programming with ABAP and Java and presents the ABAP Workbench and SAP NetWeaver Developer Studio (NWDS) tools. This is followed by an initial listing of the interfaces supported by SAP NetWeaver AS and also a description of the libraries and connectors for the C, Java, and C# programming languages required for interface programming.

1.1 SAP NetWeaver Application Server

In this section, we introduce you to the SAP NetWeaver AS architecture. We will concentrate here on components particularly important for interface programming. These include application layer components responsible for executing ABAP and Java programs.

1.1.1 SAP Solutions and SAP NetWeaver

SAP NetWeaver AS is the basic SAP NetWeaver module of the SAP infrastructure platform. SAP NetWeaver consists of a range of servers that provide different infrastructure services within an SAP system landscape:

- **SAP NetWeaver Application Server**
  Platform for other SAP NetWeaver servers and for business applications

- **SAP NetWeaver Business Warehouse**
  Data warehouse for integrating and analyzing data from an entire company

- **SAP NetWeaver Exchange Infrastructure**
  Integration platform for A2A and B2B scenarios

- **SAP NetWeaver Master Data Management**
  Platform for guaranteeing data consistency in application systems

- **SAP NetWeaver Mobile**
  Platform for mobile solutions

- **SAP NetWeaver Portal**
  Web portal that provides users with role-specific, company-wide access to relevant data and applications

Role of SAP NetWeaver AS

As you can see, SAP NetWeaver AS Server plays a key role within an SAP system landscape: It is the technology platform not only for infrastructural SAP NetWeaver servers but also for all SAP business applications such as SAP Customer Relationship Management (SAP CRM), SAP ERP Financials, SAP ERP Human Capital Management (SAP ERP HCM), SAP Product Lifecycle Management (SAP PLM), SAP Supplier Relationship Management (SAP SRM), and SAP Supply Chain Management (SAP SCM).

SAP NetWeaver AS is a portable application server that runs on many different hardware, operating system, and database platforms. It supports applications written in ABAP or Java. In principle, it therefore consists of two application servers that can either be installed separately (*single stack*) or together (*double stack*).

Client-server architecture

SAP NetWeaver AS forms the middle layer of a classic three-layer client-server architecture. This architecture comprises the data layer, application layer and presentation layer, as illustrated in Figure 1.1.

The *data layer* is composed of a relational database, for example, Oracle or Microsoft SQL Server. Business master data, transaction data, and system data are stored in database tables. The schemas for the ABAP and Java part are strictly separated from each other within the database. This means that ABAP applications cannot directly access data in the Java part of the database, and vice versa.

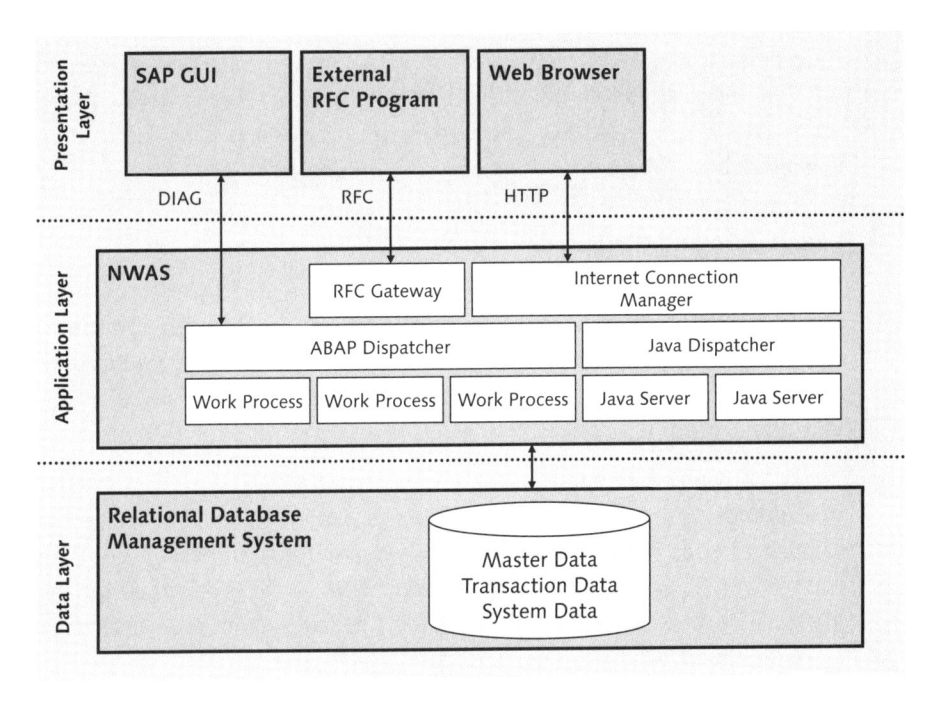

Figure 1.1 Three-Layer Architecture of an SAP System

The *application layer* is made up of processes that execute the application programs written either in ABAP or Java. Graphical user dialogs displayed by the presentation layer are also created in the application layer. SAP NetWeaver AS contains two technology stacks: the ABAP stack (light gray in Figure 1.1) and the Java stack (white in Figure 1.1). When installing SAP NetWeaver AS, you can either install only the ABAP stack (SAP NetWeaver AS ABAP) or the Java stack (SAP NetWeaver AS Java) or both stacks together (double stack system).

Application layer

The application layer results are displayed for the user on the *presentation layer*. This layer accepts the entries made by a user and forwards his commands to the application layer. The presentation layer is implemented using the *SAP Graphical User Interface* (SAP GUI) or an HTML browser. These programs are installed on the desktop PCs of users who want to work with the applications on SAP NetWeaver AS.

Presentation layer

1.1.2 SAP NetWeaver Application Server ABAP

The majority of and most important SAP solutions are implemented in ABAP, so it is particularly important to know the architecture and runtime behavior of SAP NetWeaver AS ABAP. If you have never worked with an SAP system before, in the next section, you will learn how to log on to the system and navigate between applications, in advance of then learning about SAP NetWeaver AS ABAP in detail.

Logging On and Navigating with the SAP GUI

To work interactively with an ABAP system, start the *SAP GUI* on your local work station. This is a Windows application that can communicate with SAP NetWeaver AS ABAP through the *Dynamic Information and Action Gateway* (DIAG) communication protocol. As well as SAP GUI for Windows, there is also SAP GUI for Java and SAP GUI for HTML.

User session — When you start the SAP GUI, it connects to a SAP NetWeaver AS ABAP of the application layer. During a *user session*, which begins with the logon and ends with the logoff, you always work with exactly one SAP NetWeaver AS ABAP of an entire system. This server is specified for the SAP GUI at the start, or it is allocated by the SAP system message server through a load balancing mechanism.

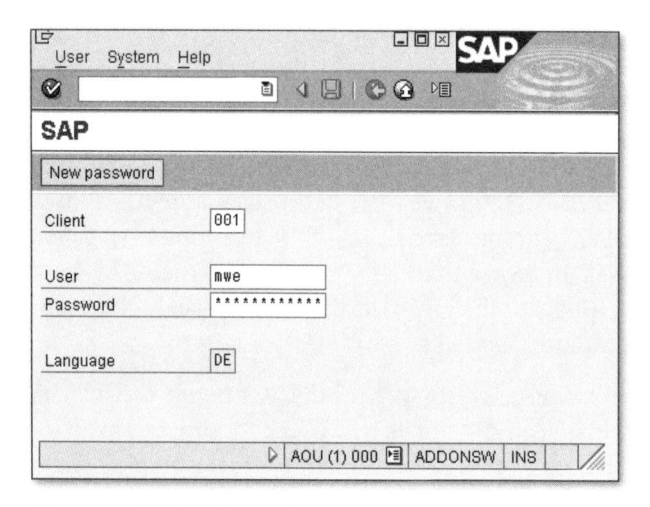

Figure 1.2 SAP GUI Logon Screen

After you start the SAP GUI, a logon screen like the one shown in Figure 1.2 appears. You must specify four pieces of information to log on:

Logon

1. **Client**
   SAP systems are *client-enabled*, which means that within an SAP system, you can store types of data that, from a business perspective, are independent of each other. This is achieved by the fact that the first column of every business table contains the three-digit client number. The database interface for SAP NetWeaver AS ABAP adds the current logon client of the user to the WHERE clause of each database query. This means that a user only ever sees and processes data belonging to the client he has used to log on. In practice, this is generally used on quality assurance and test systems to separate different test datasets from one another.

2. **User**
   To enable a user to log on to the system, a client-based user master record must be created for him. The user is identified by a unique user name within the client. The user enters this user name when logging on.

3. **Password**
   The logon will only be successful if the user has entered the valid password for the user.

4. **Language**
   SAP systems are multilingual. Developers can translate all texts displayed on the GUI into different languages. The language the user specifies when logging on will determine the language in which these texts are output.

The SAP Easy Access screen opens after the user logs on. As you can see from Figure 1.3, the screen is divided into different areas:

Screen layout

- **Menu bar**
  The top line of the screen contains dropdown menus used to execute application functions. This menu bar includes different functions for each application. Only the last two menu options, System and Help, are the same for all applications.

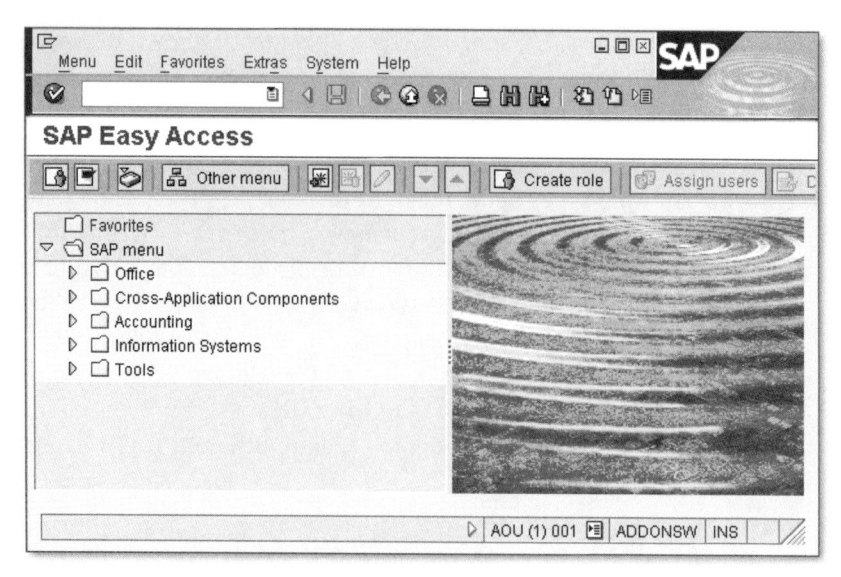

1 | Basic Principles of SAP Interface Programming

Figure 1.3 SAP Easy Access: Default Initial Screen

- **Standard toolbar**

    The standard toolbar underneath the menu bar is the same for all applications and provides access to important system functions like Entry Check, Command Input, Save, Return, Exit, Cancel, Print, Search and Scroll in Lists.

    The first icon in the standard toolbar, a white checkmark on a green ball, triggers a check on the entries made by the user. Incorrect entries will cause the incorrect input fields to be displayed in red, and an error message will appear in the status bar at the bottom of the screen.

Command field

The *command field* for entering commands directly is not generally displayed after the first logon, but the user can display it by clicking the small gray triangle in the standard toolbar. Transactions (ABAP programs) can be started and finished by entering commands in the command field. Table 1.1 lists the most important commands.

- **Title bar**

    The title of the program just executed is displayed under the standard toolbar.

- **Application toolbar**

  The application toolbar is located under the title bar. A mouse click can trigger the most important application-specific functions here.

- **Screen**

  The majority of the screen occupies an area where a user can enter data, choose functions, or view lists. The SAP Easy Access application has a logo in the right-hand window area. The left window area contains a tree, the SAP Menu, from which business programs can be started.

- **Status bar**

  The status bar appears at the very bottom. System messages (errors, warnings, and information) are displayed here. Other information such as the system ID, logon client, user name, transaction code of the application just executed, or host name of the application server are also provided there. This additional information may also initially be concealed behind a small gray triangle.

Command	Function
/n	Ends the running transaction.
/nxxxx	Ends the running transaction and starts Transaction xxxx.
/i	Deletes the current external mode.
/o	Lists all external modes. A new external mode can be started from the dialog box.
/oxxxx	Starts a new external mode with Transaction xxxx.

Table 1.1 Important Commands for Command Field in Standard Toolbar

During a user session, a user always communicates with the same SAP NetWeaver AS ABAP through the SAP GUI. The user can open up to six windows, or *external modes*, during a session. Different programs can run in these windows, between which the user can switch. SAP NetWeaver AS stores the entire user context within a session.

External mode

SAP NetWeaver AS ABAP Instance

Within an SAP system, there is only one single database process on the data layer, but on the application layer, there may be several SAP NetWeaver AS ABAP instances that execute ABAP programs. Each *instance* in turn consists of different processes that perform specifically limited tasks. An instance is uniquely identified by the specification of three parameters:

- **System ID**
  The system ID identifies an SAP system uniquely within a group of systems. The system ID is an identifier consisting of three characters (letters and digits), for example, SD1. The system ID is normally used as the name for an SAP system database.

- **Host name**
  All SAP instance processes run on the same host. However, there may be several SAP instances within a system that generally run on different hosts. The host name therefore has to be specified to identify an instance.

- **System number**
  Several SAP instances, however, can also run on a host. To distinguish different instances uniquely on the same host, a third specification is therefore needed, the two-digit system number. This system number can accept any value between 00 and 99. The system numbers of two SAP instances on the same host must be different, even if these SAP instances belong to different SAP systems.

An SAP instance name is therefore made up of three components: <SID>_<HOST>_<SYSNR>.

<SID> here is the three-character system ID, <HOST> is the host name of the application server, and <SYSNR> is the two-digit system number of the SAP instance.

Communication protocols

An SAP instance can communicate with external programs through different application protocols. These application protocols are transported through the *Transaction Control Protocol* (TCP). An SAP instance component opens a TCP port on its host for each application protocol. SAP Basis supports the following three protocols:

- **Dynamic Information and Action Gateway (DIAG)**
  DIAG is an application protocol used for communication between the SAP GUI and SAP instance. The SAP instance uses this protocol to send screens and lists to the SAP GUI and to accept user commands.

The *dispatcher* implements this protocol within the SAP instance. The dispatcher opens the TCP port with the number 32<*SYSNR*> on the host to communicate with DIAG. Because the port numbers must be unique, every instance on a host must have a different port number. In the services file of computers that want to communicate with an SAP instance through this port, the *sapdp<SYSNR>* service name is assigned to the port.

▶ **Remote Function Call (RFC)**
RFC is an SAP application protocol that external programs can use to call function modules in the SAP instance. In this case, parameters can be transferred to the function module and received by it.

RFC is implemented by the *gateway*. The gateway opens the TCP port with the number 33<*SYSNR*> on the host; the corresponding service name is sapgw<*SYSNR*>.

When the SAP GUI is being installed on a computer, the service names and relevant port numbers are automatically entered into the services file. The services file is located under <*WINDIR*>/system32/drivers/etc on Windows systems. Listing 1.1 shows an extract from this services file.

```
# Copyright (c) 1993-1999 Microsoft Corp.
#
# This file contains port numbers for
# known services in accordance with IANA.
#
# Format:
#
# <service name>   <port number>/<protocol>   [Alias...]
echo               7/tcp
echo               7/udp
discard            9/tcp         sink null
#...
sapdp00            3200/tcp
sapdp01            3201/tcp
sapdp02            3202/tcp
#...
sapgw00            3300/tcp
sapgw01            3301/tcp
sapgw02            3302/tcp
#...
```

Listing 1.1 Assigning Service Names to Port Numbers in Services File

1 | Basic Principles of SAP Interface Programming

- **Hypertext Transfer Protocol (HTTP)**
  Since Release 6.10, SAP Basis has provided an additional application protocol with HTTP. This protocol is implemented by the *Internet Connection Manager* (ICM). ICM accepts HTTP requests and forwards them to corresponding applications. The standard port for the HTTP service is 80, but an SAP system administrator can choose any other TCP port for this service.

Work processes
The dispatcher plays a key role within an SAP instance. It accepts requests and forwards them for execution to the next free work process.

> **Optimum Use of Resources by Dispatching to Work Processes**
>
> There are generally a great deal fewer work processes within an SAP instance than there are active user logons to this instance. This is because a considerable amount of time usually elapses between two requests from a user — from the perspective of the computer at any rate. During the time in which a user reads what is output on a screen to when he enters data, the work process can process a request from another user.
>
> Owing to the fact that only some work processes can process requests from many users, resources can be optimally used on the application server. Significantly fewer processes are run, and there are also considerably fewer connections to the database, as would be the case if a separate work process were assigned to each user.
>
> However, this also noticeably affects the transaction concept, as we will illustrate in this section under the heading, ABAP Transaction Concept.

Types of work processes
The types of work processes managed by an SAP instance dispatcher differ and are each identified by one of the letters D, B, S, U or E.

- **Dialog work processes (D)**
  These work processes execute ABAP programs in a user dialog and function modules called through RFC.

- **Background work processes (B)**
  These work processes execute ABAP programs that were scheduled for background processing. These ABAP programs do not conduct a user dialog, and the required entries are already specified at the time they are scheduled.

- **Spool work processes (S)**
  These work processes are responsible for printing lists.

- **Update work processes (U)**
  These work processes execute programs that write changes into business database tables. These programs are triggered from dialog programs, as we will discuss in more detail later.

- **Lock management work process (E)**
  These work processes are represented by the letter E from the term *enqueue* (which means to place a data item in a queue). There is exactly one instance with exactly one lock management work process within an SAP system. ABAP programs use this process to set and release data record locks. It is important that only one of the many dialog processes of the different servers can ever set a specific lock at a time. For this reason, there must only be one E process in the whole SAP system, and lock requests must be lined up in a single queue. We will look at this concept in more detail in this section under the heading, Lock Objects.

In addition to these work processes, an instance mainly has memory areas that all work processes can share:

Memory areas

- **Buffer area for database contents**
  Data that was read from a work process from the database can be stored in this buffer area and is then available for all work processes. This speeds up read access to this type of data.

- **Roll area for user contexts**
  The contexts of logged-on users are stored in this memory area. In particular, these include the statuses of programs that have just been executed for a user.

There is a specific instance in an SAP system that makes another central service available with the *message server*. The message server is used for communicating between dispatchers of all SAP instances in an SAP system. It is through the message server that work processes of an instance find the enqueue process responsible for lock management.

Load distribution through the message server

Another important message server task is distributing the load between SAP instances. The administrator can divide SAP instances of an SAP system into several logon groups. To distribute the load between SAP instances of a logon group, the SAP GUI can be configured to address the message server at the start so that it can be distributed to an SAP instance of a specific logon group. Owing to the periodic SAP instance messages to the message server through their momentary loading, the message server can select a suitable SAP instance from the requested logon group and assign it to the SAP GUI for logging on.

The SAP GUI and dispatchers also communicate with the message server through TCP. The SAP system administrator assigns a port number to the message server. The service name chosen and entered into the services files is *sapms<SID>*.

The SAP GUI and other client programs consequently have two options to connect with an SAP instance: directly by specifying the application server host name and the system number, or indirectly by specifying the host name and service name of the message server. These two options are summarized in Table 1.2.

Connection Type	Required Information
Without load distribution	▸ Host name or IP address of application server. ▸ System number of ABAP instance. ▸ The host name and service name of an alternative gateway can also be specified for RFC connections if the gateway of the specified application server is not to be used.
With load distribution	▸ Host name or IP address of message server of SAP system. ▸ Service name of message server. ▸ Logon group.

Table 1.2 Information a Client Must Provide to Connect to SAP NetWeaver AS ABAP

Firewalls and SAP Routers

Two connection options

External clients generally have no direct access to an SAP instance through TCP/IP. Instead, they are separated from the SAP instance by firewalls and at least one (though normally two) SAP routers, as shown in Figure 1.4.

An *SAP router* bundles client requests onto several SAP instances. This means that only the route to the IP address and the SAP router port must be released in the firewall before the SAP router. When installing the SAP router, the administrator usually chooses 3299/TCP as the TCP port. This is the highest possible port number for a dispatcher, so it is unlikely that this port is already being used by an SAP instance dispatcher.

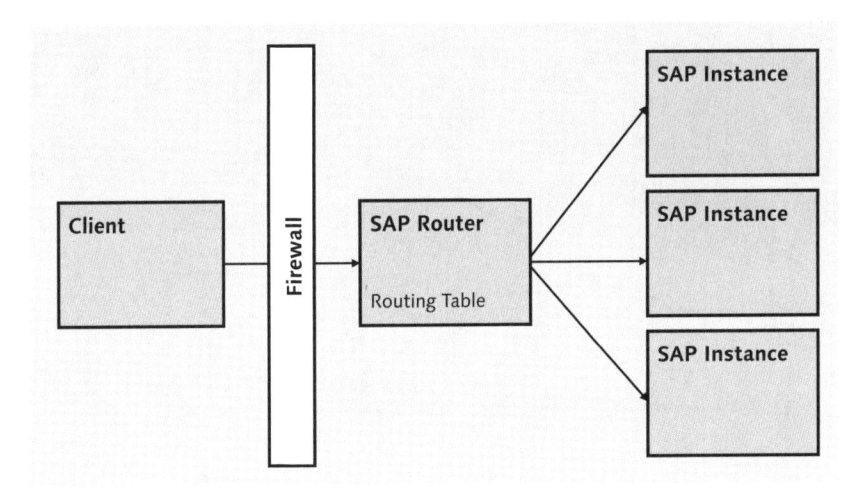

Figure 1.4 Firewall and SAP Router Ensure Access to SAP Instances

The SAP router contains a table where the administrator releases or locks routes from clients (identified by their IP address) to SAP instances (identified by their IP address and system number).

If a client wants to connect to an SAP instance, in addition to specifying the application server host name and instance system number, it must also indicate the host name or IP address of the SAP router and its port number. This information is specified in the *SAP router string*, which prefixes the application server host name:

/H/<routerhost>/S/<routerport>/H/   SAP router string

<routerhost> here is the host name or IP address of the SAP router, and <routerport> is its port number.

Dialog Processing

The diagram in Figure 1.5 shows the process flow of a *dialog transaction*. The user starts an SAP transaction on the SAP GUI by entering the transaction code in the command field on the standard toolbar.

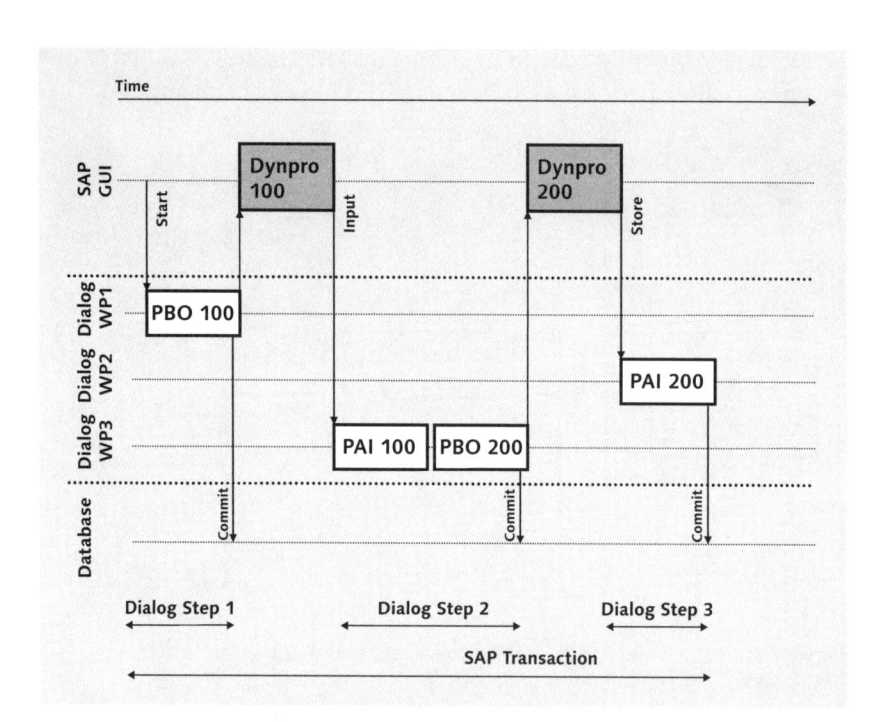

1 | Basic Principles of SAP Interface Programming

Figure 1.5 Dialog Transaction Process Flow

In the example shown in this figure, two screens are displayed for the user in the course of the Transaction: Dynpro 100 and Dynpro 200. User entries, such as the key for the data record to be processed, are made in Dynpro 100. The data record is changed, and its backup triggered in Dynpro 200.

Dialog steps

From the perspective of the application server, this SAP transaction is divided into three *dialog steps* that can be executed by three different dialog work processes. The flow logic is defined with the screen when dialogs are processed in SAP systems. *Process After Input modules* (PAI modules) are processed after the user has made his entries on the SAP GUI. *Process Before Output modules* (PBO modules) are processed before the screen is displayed on the SAP GUI. Therefore, a dialog step consists of the PAI modules of one screen and PBO modules of the next screen.

> **One Dialog Work Process for Many Users**
>
> After a dialog work process has processed a dialog step, it is immediately available again for the next user. This is possible because dialog work processes work very quickly compared to the speed at which a user works.
>
> As a result, many users can be dealt with on the application and database servers using a small number of dialog work processes and therefore a relatively low consumption of resources.

Because a work process carries out completely unrelated dialog steps consecutively, it must execute a commit on the database after every dialog step. This is triggered by SAP Basis without any further intervention from the ABAP developer. This means that database changes that were made in this dialog step are committed on the database after each dialog step without an explicit COMMIT WORK statement by the ABAP developer.

Implicit database commit

If the ABAP developer programs an explicit ROLLBACK WORK, this rollback will of course also be forwarded to the database. A rollback on the database is therefore only ever possible up to the beginning of the current dialog step. A rollback on the database across several dialog steps is not possible with database-related technology.

If a user transaction therefore stretches across several dialog steps, specific precautionary measures must be taken to ensure a rollback is possible if an error occurs or if the user cancels a transaction.

ABAP Transaction Concept

A user transaction that may stretch across several dialog steps is also known as an *SAP transaction* or *SAP Logical Unit of Work* (SAP LUW) and therefore differs from the database transaction or *Database Logical Unit of Work* (DB LUW). As we explained in the previous section, specific precautionary measures must be taken for an SAP transaction to ensure that a rollback is possible if the user cancels a transaction or if an error occurs. This applies in particular to changing transactions that create, change, or delete master or transaction data in the database.

A changing SAP transaction generally begins with the user selecting from the initial screen the data record he wants to change. In the first dialog step, the dialog work process sets a lock on this data record. To do this, it communicates with the enqueue work process, exactly one of which

Locks

runs in every SAP system. If a lock has not yet been set on the requested data record, the enqueue work process enters the lock in its lock table. If a lock is already set, the dialog work process must issue a corresponding error message to the user and cannot continue with the intended change.

In the subsequent dialog steps, the dialog work process in the dialog with the user collects the changes to be made to the data record. These changes are not carried out immediately but are collected and flagged for changing.

Asynchronous updating

SAP Basis provides *update function modules* technology for this purpose. These are function modules where the developer encapsulates changing the UPDATE, INSERT and DELETE database statements and which have been flagged by the developer as update function modules. While the changes are being collected, the dialog program calls these function modules and transfers the data to be changed to them through their interface. The SAP system does not execute these function modules straightaway but stores the name of the function module and transferred data in the update table for executing later.

Commit and rollback

This means the user can easily cancel the SAP transaction at any time. In this case, or if an error occurs during the SAP transaction, the dialog program simply has to execute the ROLLBACK WORK statement. The SAP system then rejects all entries in the update table and deletes the set locks.

If the user exits the SAP transaction with the request to save his or her data, the dialog program executes the COMMIT WORK statement. In this case, the SAP system starts a new task asynchronously in an update work process.

The update work process executes the flagged function modules in the sequence in which they were entered in the update table and, in doing so, transfers the data that was stored in the update table to them. Only now do the function modules actually implement the database changes.

If everything runs smoothly, the update work process executes a commit on the database and deletes the set locks. If an error occurs anywhere in one of the function modules, the update work process executes a rollback on the database and informs the user. Rollback is possible across several function modules because the update work process is working within a single database LUW.

1.1.3 SAP NetWeaver Application Server Java

The Java stack represents the second part of the application platform of the SAP NetWeaver infrastructure. SAP NetWeaver 7.0 implements the J2EE Version 1.3 specification developed by Sun Microsystems. Besides purely implementing the specification, SAP provides enhancements that simplify integration into SAP-based landscapes. Many known topics from the ABAP world are also integrated into the Java stack to produce a homogeneous landscape on both sides. The following section is a brief overview and is not intended to be an in-depth introduction to the individual aspects of the J2EE specification. We will return to some topics in the Java programming examples in Chapter 4, Remote Function Call with Java; Chapter 5, IDocs and ALE; and Chapter 6, Service-Oriented Architecture Protocol.

Java 2 Enterprise Edition (J2EE) was defined as the standard for developing large enterprise applications. The objective was to simplify the development of applications that require a well-built infrastructure. Reusing application components was also a key aim.

Introduction to J2EE

This was achieved by separating technical and specialist aspects. This is referred to as *separation of concerns*, whereby certain vertical aspects of an application or application infrastructure do not have to be implemented again every time by the relevant development team. The infrastructure undertakes the implementation and provision of technical aspects such as security, transactional processing, or similar important application components that require a high degree of knowledge and smooth implementation. Furthermore, the application server is also responsible for managing the different phases in the life of an application component.

The application components are called *Enterprise Java Beans* (EJB). The specification in Version 1.3 differentiates between three different component types:

Application components

- Session beans (SB)
- Entity beans
- Message-driven beans (MDB)

Session beans are differentiated in terms of whether they are stateful (*Stateful Session Beans*, SFSB) or stateless (*Stateless Session Bean*, SLSB). Session beans are used for implementing business functions.

The second component type, the *entity bean*, was defined to map persistence. Entity beans are provided as *container-managed* (CM) and *bean-managed* (BM) entity beans. The objective of CM entity beans is that the container itself implements the SQL-relevant aspects, and as a result, the developer only has to define declarative specifications at development time. Session beans, like entity beans, are called synchronously.

Message-driven beans in integration scenarios

In many infrastructures, particularly in integration scenarios, asynchronous communication is essential. The specification describes *message-driven beans* (MDB) for this purpose. As the name suggests, MDBs are based on the exchange of messages. However, the message generator is not (as is the case with session beans) directly in contact with the message receiver; rather, messages are delivered through the medium of *Message-Oriented Middleware* (MOM). There has been a proliferation of proprietary MOM implementations over the years, so Sun responded to this development and defined a standard. This standard is called *Java Message Service* (JMS). The JMS specification consists of an *Application Programming Interface* (API) specification and a *Service Provider Interface* (SPI) description. Senders and receivers of messages use the API part of the specification. The SPI part of the specification in contrast is implemented by the particular manufacturer of the JMS providers. This abstraction from a specific product or protocol for exchanging messages makes message-driven beans particularly appealing for integration scenarios.

Design by contract

All three components define their own lifecycle, which is nevertheless completely abstract for the developer. The developer can rely on the fact that the application server will handle the processing properly. The developer only comes in contact with the individual phases of the lifecycle to the extent the interface agreement stipulates for this between the application server and component. The interface agreement defines *hook methods* in this case. These methods represent the contract between the component and server. This is referred to as *design by contract*. Contracts control the interaction between the application components on the one hand and the application server on the other.

Problems with the current standard

At first glance, the benefits of separation of concerns and definition of contracts appear to be obvious. But if we look more closely at the separation of concerns in particular, it turns out only to be a shift of responsibilities for the application server that has to carry out most of the tasks. This significantly increases the complexity for the application server.

That is also precisely what happened with J2EE. At worst, applications that rely very heavily on this division of labor experience performance problems when the number of users increases.

One specific example of this is the persistence layer. If entity beans are used incorrectly, this can very quickly cause the performance of the application to deteriorate dramatically. This resulted in J2EE being used as the platform but without the use of EJBs.

Sun Microsystems could not ignore this development, and in the course of changing the Java language standard, the company also changed or completely restructured the J2EE standard at the same time. Due to the serious change, the standard was also given a new name. J2EE therefore became *Java Enterprise Edition* (JEE).

SAP also implemented this standard and released it for the first time with *SAP NetWeaver 7.1 Composition Environment* (SAP NetWeaver CE). SAP NetWeaver CE is the forerunner of SAP NetWeaver 7.2 but not its basis. SAP NetWeaver CE is a standalone platform. The aim of this infrastructure is to make it easy to implement composite applications and at the same time also provide an infrastructure for service orientation. This infrastructure supports you, like the development tool, in creating and managing an SOA landscape.

From the perspective of the JEE standard, the previous strong dependency of components on the application server was reduced. This is achieved by using annotations in the source text. Annotations supersede complex and error-prone XML configuration files (*Deployment Descriptors*).

But let's return to the SAP NetWeaver Java 7.0 architecture. The Java stack of an SAP system runs within the application layer (refer to Figure 1.1). The Java server itself is divided into three layers, as is also normally the case with other Java application servers.

Java stack layers

The top layer contains the *web container*. This is used as a runtime environment for executing applications based on servlets and JSPs (*Java Server Pages*). Both are technologies described within the J2EE specification and are ultimately used for dynamically programming web pages. In addition to the standard, the SAP web container provides a Web Dynpro runtime environment for Java applications.

The middle layer provides the environment for executing EJB components. The *EJB container* defines the runtime environment for the components. It contains session beans and entity beans as well as message-driven beans.

The lowest layer of the Java server is the *data access layer*. SAP searched very thoroughly here for an analogy to the ABAP world. When you use ABAP, you can trust that your application is completely database-independent — and so too the source code that accesses the database. This is guaranteed by using Open SQL. But because J2EE is a standard, and there is also a very much greater degree of freedom in the Java world in terms of accessing a database, SAP provides not just one technology but many technologies for accessing databases.

1.2 Security

Heterogeneous, integrative landscapes must offer a higher level of security. This is an important aspect when programming interfaces in particular. When you give external applications access to your SAP systems, you must make sure that these external systems only see the data and, above all, only change the data they are allowed to see and change. You must ensure that only correctly identified applications get access to your network.

Facets of security

The highest level of security can only be given if it consists of different facets. These facets include authenticating and authorizing users and encrypting messages. The following section describes how these facets look in theory, in order for us then to discuss how to implement security concepts.

1.2.1 Security in Heterogeneous Landscapes

In heterogeneous landscapes with a high degree of integration, security plays a very important role. Due to the nature of integration, however, one universal solution cannot be arrived at for security. We also have to understand that there is never 100 % security; all we can ultimately do is make it more difficult for attackers to achieve their objective.

There are two basic types of security in a company. One is *infrastructural security*. This is security that can be achieved through firewalls or backup concepts. It is less about the software and more about the hardware used to protect the data and the infrastructure.

The other is *application security*. This type of security is achieved by using programming tools to get the highest possible level of security. We want to concentrate on this security type in this section. Infrastructural and application security can of course also be combined. An example of this is access control in companies.

As with all systems, you can generally also describe certain security-relevant landscape requirements for integrative landscapes:

Requirements for security-critical systems

- **System security**
  Monitoring concepts.
- **Data security**
  Confidentiality, integrity, and non-repudiation of data.
- **Access security**
  User authentication and authorization.

This multilevel security shows that interaction from different components and concepts increases the level of security in the system.

Data Confidentiality

Data security contains concepts for data confidentiality, in other words, protection against unauthorized access to information exchanged between systems. This is guaranteed using encryption concepts. There are different concepts involved here. The two best-known concepts are *public-key cryptography* and *private-key cryptography*. They are also referred to as asymmetric and symmetric procedures.

Symmetric procedures work with only one cryptographic key. The key is used for encrypting and decrypting data. Symmetric procedures are very difficult to use directly, particularly for encrypting communication data, because the key must be exchanged before communication.

Symmetric encryption

Asymmetric procedures use two corresponding keys for cryptographic operations: a public key and a private key. All operations performed using one key can be undone or verified by the other key. Security is achieved by the fact that information can only be traced back from one of the keys to the other key in a very time-consuming way.

Asymmetric encryption

Besides purely symmetric or asymmetric cryptography, there are combinations of both options. One of the best known is *Secure Socket Layer* (SSL).

Data Integrity

Besides confidentiality, data integrity also plays an important role in integration scenarios. Data integrity basically means that data exchanged between two communication participants cannot be changed, or at least changes cannot be established, during transport.

Hash functions

> **Hash Functions**
>
> The *hash value* is used for data integrity. The hash value is the result of processing a *hash function*. Hash functions are used wherever abridged information, displayed as clearly as possible, is required. Hash functions are *one-way functions*. Information must not be able to be traced back from a hash value to the displayed abridged information.
>
> This now also raises the question of how the receiver can identify whether the data was changed when being transported. To detect a change, the actual status must be compared with the planned status. The information therefore actually has to be transferred twice. Before sending the information, the sender creates a hash value from the information to be transferred. The sender subsequently sends the information itself and then its hash value. The receiver can calculate the hash value from the data received and then compare it with the information received.

Non-Repudiation of Information

Finally, data exchanged between two communication participants must be non-repudiated. Non-repudiation of information can, as in real life, be guaranteed by a signature.

Digital signatures

Digital signatures are used in different ways in heterogeneous systems. Digital signatures are quite easy to create. The hash value is calculated for information that is to be digitally signed. The hash value together with the private key of the signer is used as an entry for an algorithm for the digital signature. Finally, the information together with the digital signature and hash value can then be transferred to the receiver.

In accordance with the basic principle of asymmetric cryptography, the receiver of a digital signature must verify this signature using the public key of the sender. This is not a security problem because the public key can be exchanged between communication participants without any cause for concern. However, for public keys to be exchanged without any problems, private keys must be kept absolutely secure. After all, what happens if the private key of the sender is compromised? An attacker could have obtained the private key and can now sign data in the name of another sender. Key management as central as possible therefore has to be established.

The term *key management* covers creating key pairs, managing *lock lists*, certifying keys, and providing a directory service. The key management area is the central point of contact for all services associated with the key material. It is also responsible for all communication partners being able to trust the key material. The keys of communication participants that were compromised are listed in the lock list. In integrative scenarios in particular, it is important that an incoming quotation actually comes from the sender specified on the quotation letter. This security can only be achieved if a common area responsible for the key material and corresponding infrastructure having a high level of security is set up. This central area must identify public keys from communication partners as being trustworthy. This is done using certificates.

Key management

Digital certificates are nothing other than proof that the public key belongs to a certain identity and only to this identity. Certificates can be issued for not only a natural person but also for computers or applications and therefore also represent an option for authentication. Through a certificate, the central management area uses a digital signature to confirm that a key belongs to an identity. The signature itself or its verification is problematic here. The receiver needs the public key of the signer to verify whether a signature is correct. As already mentioned, the receiver obtains this key using the certificate from the signer and must in turn check the signature of the signer of that certificate. This checking of public keys can be very complex and drawn out. For this reason, the communication participant or application decides the level of *trust* as of which the key can be classified as secure. Infrastructures that represent this type of trust and are responsible for managing certificates are called *public-key infrastructures* (PKI). We do not want to discuss PKIs in great detail here, but you should note that using them may involve a great deal of effort in a company. (For more information, refer to PKI: *Implementing & Managing E-Security* [McGraw-Hill Professional, 2003].)

Certificates

1.2.2 User Management Engine

Now that we have discussed the basic terms and security concepts, we will turn our attention to the SAP NetWeaver AS and implementing the said concepts.

The *User Management Engine* (UME) plays the principal role in SAP NetWeaver AS Java. The UME is a central service of the application server that is used to manage users, group affiliations, authorizations, and roles. Users and groups can be stored in different containers here and managed in databases, directory services (e.g., LDAP [*Lightweight Directory Access Protocol*]), or the ABAP stack itself.

Managing security identities

The type of installation can also affect the UME and the way security identities are stored. When a double stack is installed, the UME is automatically configured in such a way that the installed ABAP stack is used for saving users. Access to the J2EE stack is set to *read-only* by default. This means user data can only be read using the UME. The standard user SAPJSF is used for communicating between the UME and ABAP user management. If only the Java stack is installed, the UME can be configured through the *Visual Administrator* (VA) in such a way that users are retrieved from another ABAP system.

Using configuration files, the administrator basically has the freedom to manage security identities. He can change the configuration either using the J2EE Config tool or SAP NetWeaver Portal. The configuration here includes setting the data source and also defining which identity attributes (in addition to the ones defined in a system based on the X.500 ISO standard) are managed.

Figure 1.6 illustrates the basic UME structure. The *UME Persistence Manager* is responsible for communication between the UME and different data sources. It does not do this directly but instead uses suitable adapters for the relevant backend. Adapters therefore provide a very simple, flexible option to connect back-end systems from different manufacturers to the UME.

Principal API

At the core of the UME is the *principal API*. This programming interface gives the developer program-based access to identity information from the different connected systems.

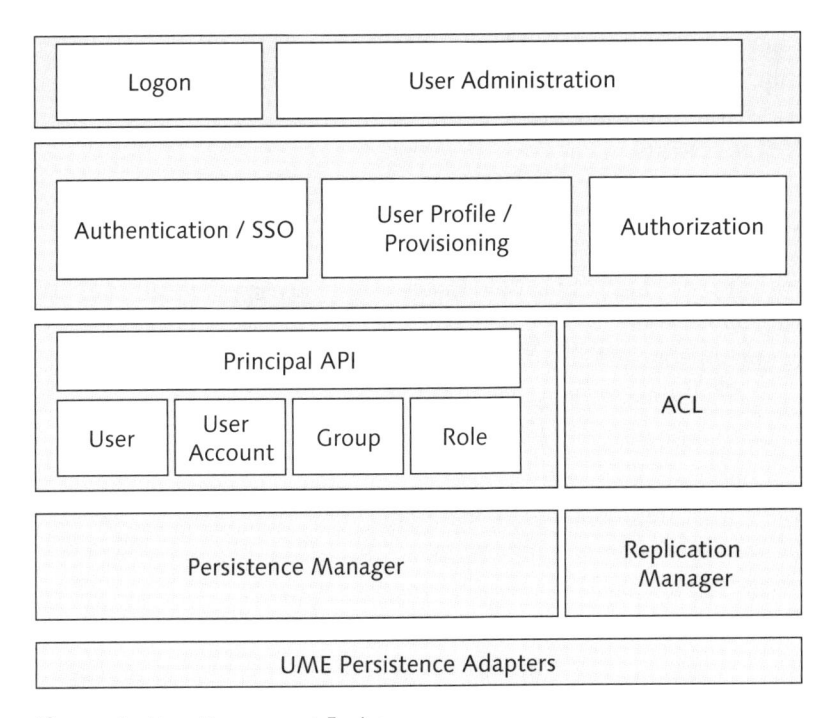

Figure 1.6 User Management Engine

```
┌─────────────────────────────────────────────────────────┐
│  Logon          User Administration                      │
│                                                          │
│  Authentication / SSO   User Profile /   Authorization   │
│                         Provisioning                     │
│                                                          │
│           Principal API                      ACL         │
│   User  User Account  Group  Role                        │
│                                                          │
│        Persistence Manager         Replication Manager   │
│                                                          │
│             UME Persistence Adapters                     │
└─────────────────────────────────────────────────────────┘
```

After you have logged on successfully to the Java stack, your identity is available as an `IUser` object. This interface contains all methods required for read access; however, write access to the identity through `IUser` is not possible. The `IUserMaint` interface (`Maint` stands for maintenance here) is available for write access. Separating the two access options was introduced for performance reasons. Write access would always result in a lock on the object, which would lead to the identity having to be locked in the backend every time a user was accessed. This restriction might be considered annoying, but write access is more of a rare case anyway. Write access on the *user datastore* is usually only used if users themselves can set up an account on the portal (*self-registration process*).

In addition to the principal API mentioned in the previous paragraph, the UME also provides interfaces for working with roles and groups. This means you can also easily access authorization structures for a user in your own applications and decide, based on these structures, whether a certain user should get the full range of application functions or only a version adapted to his authorization structure. The UME fits perfectly into the security requirements of the J2EE specification from Sun Microsystems.

1.2.3 KeyStores: Authentication, Signatures, Encryption

In Section 1.2.1, Security in Heterogeneous Landscapes, we already discussed some of the security concepts, but we did not specifically illustrate how they are used. In this section, we will now describe how security is used and implemented.

Providing key material

As already mentioned, the main focus when using cryptographic functions should be on managing and saving key material securely. Java itself provides an option to store key material and certificates using *KeyStores*. KeyStores are a type of database for keys, and besides their own key material, they can also contain confidential certificates. Access to a KeyStore is password-protected.

KeyStore contents are created by *cryptography providers*. Cryptography providers offer flexibility in using different implementations of cryptographic functions. The basis for implementing these types of providers are the *Java Cryptography Architecture* (JCA) and its *Java Cryptography Extension* (JCE). Both specifications are described by Sun Microsystems and implemented by the relevant provider. When KeyStore files are accessed, all the providers that were used for creating the files must be known in the Java runtime context. A provider can either be registered at runtime by transferring a parameter or statically by using a configuration file. Each cryptography provider can define its own format for saving KeyStore contents. Two different types are provided in the Java standard for representing KeyStore file contents:

- *JKS* is the KeyStore type supported by the Sun provider.
- *PKCS12* defines a transfer syntax for PKCS#12 key material.

The PKCS12 standard describes an option as to how content can be processed independently of a provider.

KeyStore tools

There are two options available in the standard version for processing KeyStore files. You can use the `java.security.KeyStore` Java class for access from Java applications. For administrative purposes, the Java installation provides the command line-based *keytool* that you can use to create and manage contents of a KeyStore file.

KeyStores and SAP KeyStores are naturally also used in the SAP Java stack. After the installation, a KeyStore file is created automatically the first time you start the Java stack. The file is called *verify.der* and contains the key material for the application server. This key material is used for creating the digital signature "under" the SAP logon ticket generated with each logon to the application server. The file is therefore the basis for managing trust between the SAP NetWeaver Java stack and other infrastructure components. If you now use the *keytool* on the *verify.der* file with the `-printcert` switch, you get the digital certificate information:

```
c:\keytool -printcert -file verify.der
```

The statement issued indicates the validity and issuer of the certificate. As mentioned, this information can be important for authentication and authorization, particularly when establishing trust. The public key of the certificate owner can also be used for encrypting and verifying digital signatures. It would be very awkward in this case if KeyStore files were stored unstructured on the server. SAP deals with this problem with a central service on the J2EE engine, the *J2EE KeyStore service*. The J2EE KeyStore service is used as a central service in the application server for saving and accessing all KeyStore files and their contents.

Displaying digital certificates

J2EE KeyStore Service — Single Sign-On in J2EE Server

The J2EE KeyStore service is available in the *Visual Administrator* (VA) and *SAP NetWeaver Administrator*. Here we will show you how to manage KeyStore files with the Visual Administrator.

After you log on to the VA, navigate to the Key Storage service by selecting the CLUSTER • SID • SERVER • SERVICES • KEY STORAGE path. In this view, you have a very detailed overview of the *verify.der* file contents (Figure 1.7).

As already mentioned, this KeyStore file was created and registered in the KeyStore service the first time the J2EE engine was started. You can also use the KeyStore service to connect other systems to the J2EE server securely. To define other trust relationships, all you have to do is add the corresponding certificate using the Load button. Click Load, and expand the Files of Type dropdown menu to get an idea of the range of functions of the service.

KeyStore service in VA

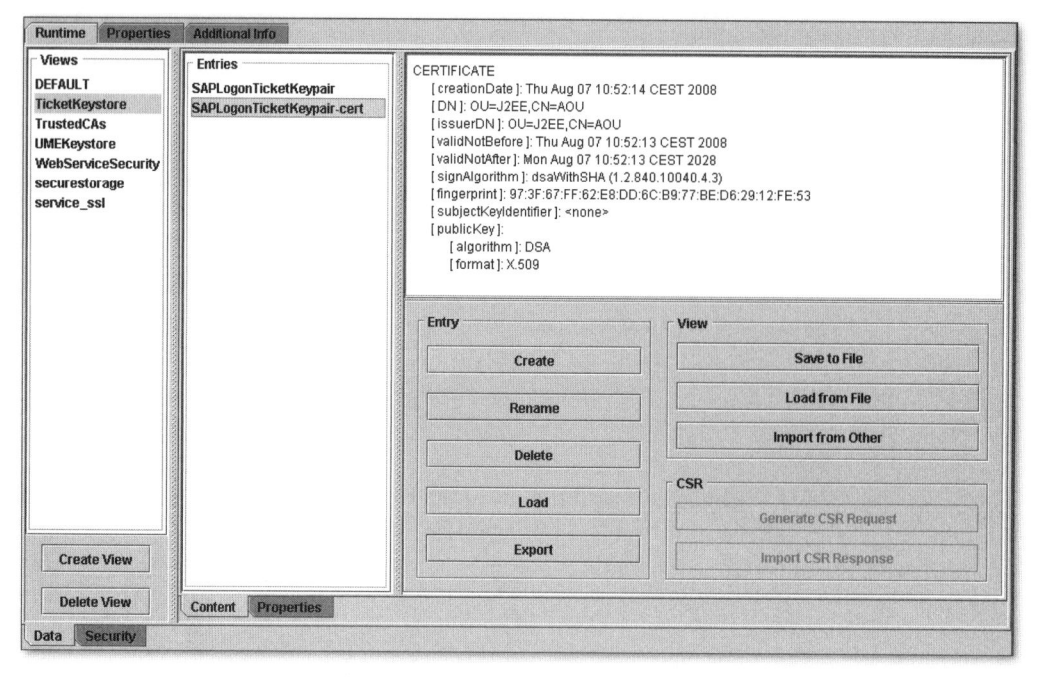

Figure 1.7 KeyStore Service in Visual Administrator

Not only is it able to include certificates, it can also act as a key management tool for cryptographic keys. As you can see, the KeyStore service is a similar concept to the STRUSTSSO2 ABAP transaction. You use this transaction to manage keys and certificates on the ABAP stack.

Personal Security Environment

SAP uses *PSE files (Personal Security Environment* files) to store key information. Like KeyStore files, PSE files contain a list of trustworthy certificates in addition to their own key information. The *sapgenpse* command line-based tool is used for working simply with PSE files. Access to contents is password-protected. The *sapgenpse* tool is hugely similar to the one known from the Java Development Kit, the *keytool*, which you will learn about in the next section.

1.2.4 Authentication and Authorization

After having now discussed the basics of key management, in this next section we turn our attention to the aspects of authentication and authorization we already addressed briefly in Section 1.2.1, Security in Heterogeneous Landscapes. We will discuss *Single Sign-On* (SSO) configuration between the SAP NetWeaver Portal and an ABAP system and configuring *Secure Network Communication* (SNC).

Particularly, but not exclusively, in heterogeneous and shared integration scenarios, only those identities that have been explicitly granted access rights are allowed to have access to information. The accessing identity must be authorized for access. To verify the authorization of the accessing identity, the first step involves authenticating it. Authentication and downstream authorization are two mechanisms that should not be missing in any system and must occur for every access attempt.

Authentication

Authentication concepts range from querying a combination of the user name and password to checking biometric characteristics. Which concept is used for authentication will depend on the existing infrastructure or products. Most systems offer not just one type of authentication but rather let the user choose the option that can best be integrated into the infrastructure. However, one problem persists with this range of options: with a heterogeneous, complex landscape, there is a risk that the user will be required to authenticate himself several times a day (whenever he wants to access another system). If the user also has different user IDs and passwords for the different systems, it is extremely difficult, or only possible by making notes of the access data, to keep track of everything.

Multiple sign-on

Using *single sign-on* can prevent you from having to log on repeatedly when switching systems. SSO solutions help, in that users only have to log on to one system, preferably the operating system when the system is started. If a user then switches systems in between, the central system delegates his identity. The user saves time by establishing a "relationship of trust" between the different systems.

Single sign-on to simplify the login procedure

Unfortunately, there are also disadvantages to SSO solutions. The first disadvantage related purely to the infrastructure is that user identities must be homogenized. User *mmayer* must have the same user ID on all systems, therefore, *mmayer* in this example. A second disadvantage is that this individual access permission is a security risk. If a potential attacker is in possession of the single access ID, all doors to the system are open to him. To sum up, it is therefore safe to say that a high level of security

Disadvantages of SSO solutions

can only be achieved by sensibly coupling different security functions. This also includes decisions about where and how SSO is used.

Single Sign-On with SAP NetWeaver Portal

We will take a closer look at an SSO scenario now. Let's assume a user wants to access an SAP NetWeaver AS ABAP from an SAP NetWeaver Portal. For this access, the user simply has to authenticate himself on the portal. Every other access from the portal does not require explicit user authentication. For this to be possible, a system first has to be declared as a *ticket issuer*. The ticket issuer is the infrastructure instance responsible for issuing SAP logon tickets. It is therefore also the root of a relationship of trust. In the scenario discussed here, the issuer is almost always the portal. The reason for this is that a *single-point-of-access strategy* is chosen with the portal integration. All applications are exclusively called through the portal for this type of strategy. An explicit call through the SAP GUI, for example, would not be welcome here. The ticket issuer signs all created logon tickets digitally and stores them as non-persistent cookies in the relevant browser session. The digital signature is verified against an external system for authentication. All systems addressed from the portal in this case need a relationship of trust to the ticket issuer. As already mentioned, a key pair consisting of a public and private key is required to create a digital signature. The key pair for the portal is automatically created when the portal server is started for the first time after the installation and then the private key for creating the digital signature is used "under" the SAP logon ticket.

Transferring the SAP logon ticket

If the user from the portal now calls a function module from the ABAP system, the SAP logon ticket is transferred to the ABAP system for each call. Unfortunately, it is not enough just to transfer the ticket — the ABAP system naturally also has to verify whether the user has system authorization, whether there is sufficient trust in the ticket, and lastly, whether the accessing system is authorized to access the client. This requires some configuration steps:

- Exporting the digital certificate of the portal server
- Configuring profile parameters to accept logon tickets
- Adding an ACL entry (*Access Control List*) to the ABAP stack for the portal server

- Importing the digital certificate of the portal server using Transaction STRUSTSSO2

We describe the configuration steps in detail in the next section.

Exporting the Certificate

The certificate is exported directly into SAP NetWeaver Portal. You must log on as a user with administrator rights for this purpose. Then navigate to the management view for the keys by selecting SYSTEM ADMINISTRATION • SYSTEM CONFIGURATION • KEYSTORE ADMINISTRATION. Choose the SAPLogonTicketKeypair-cert entry from the dropdown list here. Then click the Download verify.der File button, and save this on your hard drive. The file is saved as a ZIP file. Unpack the ZIP file.

Adding an ACL Entry to the ABAP Stack for the Portal Server

After you have exported the certificate, you can begin configuring the ABAP stack. To enable the portal server to be recognized as a system allowed to communicate with the ABAP stack, an ACL entry must be created for it. You make the ACL entry in the TWPSSO2ACL table. Start Transaction SM30 for the configuration, and enter the table name in the search field. Then add a new entry to the table with the following information:

- Portal system ID
- Client to be accessed
- Subject name
- Name of issuer of the certificates
  (SID of server containing the SAP logon tickets)

ACL maintenance using Transaction SM30

You can read this information from the KeyStore administration of your portal. To do this, select the ROLE SYSTEM ADMINISTRATION • SYSTEM CONFIGURATION • KEYSTORE ADMINISTRATION path. Then choose the SAPLogTicketKeypair-cert entry from the dropdown list.

Configuring Profile Parameters

To ensure the ABAP system can also accept and process SAP logon tickets, you must set two profile parameters. Start Transaction RZ10 to do this. If you execute the transaction for the first time, no profiles exist yet.

To change this, choose the Import Profiles of Active Servers option from the Utilities menu. The parameters are set in the instance profile of the server. Set the value of the `login/accept_sso2_ticket` parameter to 1. This parameter specifies that SAP logon tickets are accepted for authentication. Also set the value of the `login/create_sso2_ticket` parameter to 0. With this parameter, you signal to the server that it can also act as a ticket issuer.

After you have set both parameters, you must start the server again. You can then test the configuration in Transaction SSO2. To do this, you set the value in the RFC Destination field to NONE, and then press F8. The result should correspond to the screen shown in Figure 1.8.

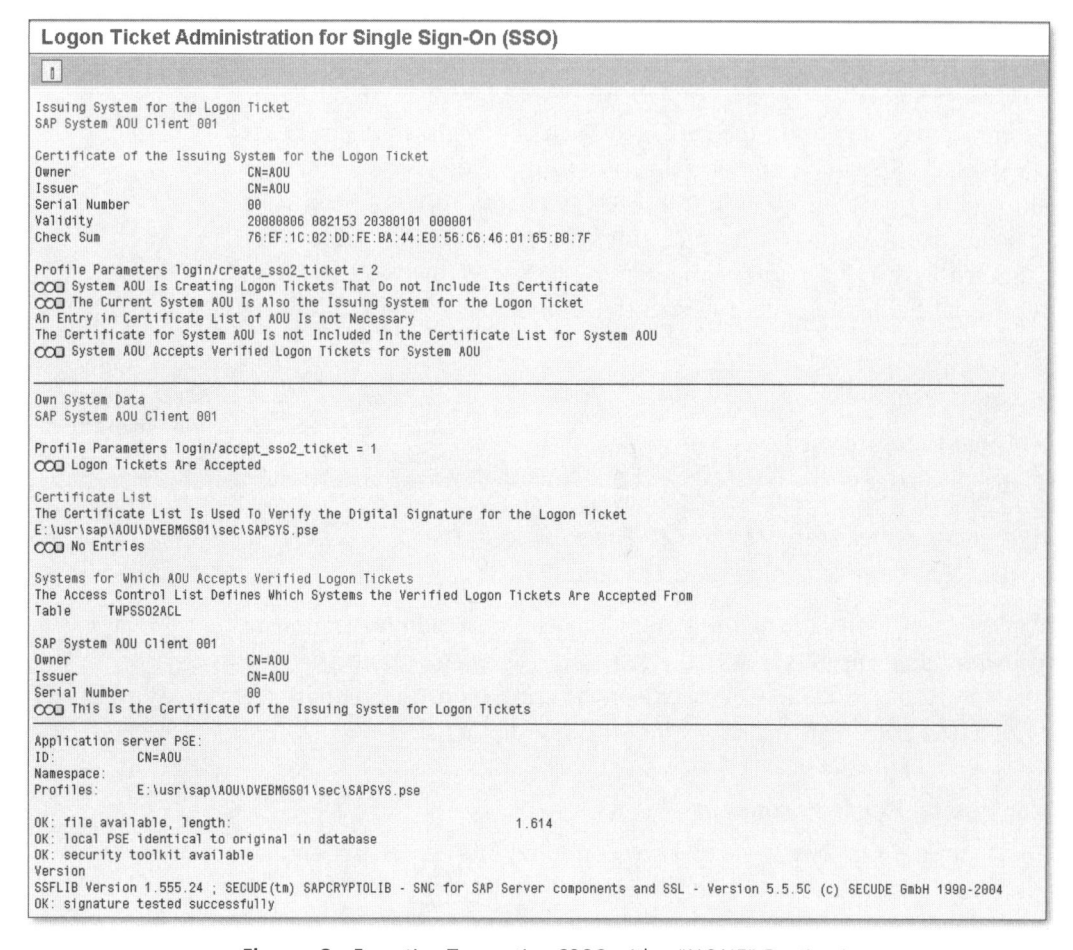

```
Logon Ticket Administration for Single Sign-On (SSO)

Issuing System for the Logon Ticket
SAP System AOU Client 001

Certificate of the Issuing System for the Logon Ticket
Owner                    CN=AOU
Issuer                   CN=AOU
Serial Number            00
Validity                 20080806 082153 20380101 000001
Check Sum                76:EF:1C:02:DD:FE:BA:44:E0:56:C6:46:01:65:B0:7F

Profile Parameters login/create_sso2_ticket = 2
OOO System AOU Is Creating Logon Tickets That Do not Include Its Certificate
OOO The Current System AOU Is Also the Issuing System for the Logon Ticket
An Entry in Certificate List of AOU Is not Necessary
The Certificate for System AOU Is not Included In the Certificate List for System AOU
OOO System AOU Accepts Verified Logon Tickets for System AOU

Own System Data
SAP System AOU Client 001

Profile Parameters login/accept_sso2_ticket = 1
OOO Logon Tickets Are Accepted

Certificate List
The Certificate List Is Used To Verify the Digital Signature for the Logon Ticket
E:\usr\sap\AOU\DVEBMGS01\sec\SAPSYS.pse
OOO No Entries

Systems for Which AOU Accepts Verified Logon Tickets
The Access Control List Defines Which Systems the Verified Logon Tickets Are Accepted From
Table    TWPSSO2ACL

SAP System AOU Client 001
Owner                    CN=AOU
Issuer                   CN=AOU
Serial Number            00
OOO This Is the Certificate of the Issuing System for Logon Tickets

Application server PSE:
ID:          CN=AOU
Namespace:
Profiles:    E:\usr\sap\AOU\DVEBMGS01\sec\SAPSYS.pse

OK: file available, length:                              1.614
OK: local PSE identical to original in database
OK: security toolkit available
Version
SSFLIB Version 1.555.24 ; SECUDE(tm) SAPCRYPTOLIB - SNC for SAP Server components and SSL - Version 5.5.5C (c) SECUDE GmbH 1998-2004
OK: signature tested successfully
```

Figure 1.8 Executing Transaction SSO2 with a "NONE" Destination

Importing the Certificate in the SAP System

You conclude the configuration by importing the portal certificate into the ABAP system and defining a relationship of trust between the systems. To do this, start Transaction STRUSTSS02. When you open the *System PSE* folder, you will see the dialog box displayed in Figure 1.9. Click the Import certificate button to start the dialog box for uploading the exported portal certificate. Choose Binary as the file format here. When you confirm the dialog box, you are directed back to the initial screen.

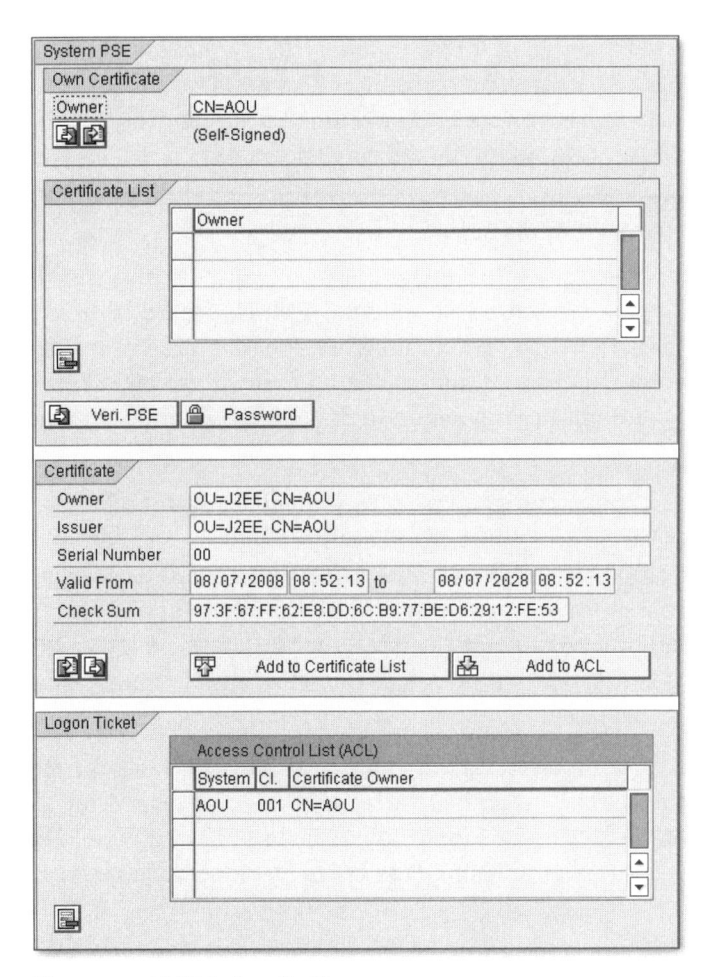

Figure 1.9 ABAP System KeyStore

The dialog box now shows an owner, issuer, and other information about the certificate. Click the Add to Certificate List button to import the portal certificate into the certificate list.

Using the logon ticket requires user IDs to be homogenized in all systems. In some cases, this may cause a considerable increase in the time and effort required to homogenize IDs. Another option in the context of the portal is to use user mapping: This involves connecting users within the different systems with each other through the UME. Similar to homogenizing user IDs, user mapping can result in a great deal of time and effort being required for very large systems. The issue of how authentication can be controlled across several systems through mapping has to be clarified. A process as to how users in the company obtain access to a corresponding system must also be defined.

Integrating External Systems Securely

After having discussed pure SAP integration, we will now look at the options for using systems from an external SAP landscape securely. The question that often arises when integrating these types of systems is how to perform the authentication. There are many different techniques ranging from pure configuration to programming authentication mechanisms.

Let's take a closer look at programming an authentication solution. We will assume that we are accessing an SAP Java stack application addressed on a J2EE application server from another manufacturer. This means that proprietary communication protocols are used throughout and direct communication is not possible. We will mainly focus on the question of how an SAP logon ticket can be validated. The actual application integration is irrelevant here.

We can use the SAP logon ticket very easily for authenticating a user in the infrastructure just described. After the user has logged on to the J2EE server, the ticket is created and can be used from now on for authentication. The challenge is simply to verify the ticket in an external application.

SAP provides two different libraries for verifying logon tickets. The *SAP Crypto Toolkit* is an API based purely on Java for using cryptographic functions within the SAP landscape. This also includes working with the SAP logon ticket. The `SAPSSOEXT` verification library provides similar functions to the SAP Crypto Toolkit, but you can use this API both from Java per JNI (*Java Native Interface*) and from C or C++. It is available for different platforms.

Which of the verification methods is used will ultimately depend on the technological platform. In mixed landscapes (with Java and ABAP and possibly other external programs), it is certainly wise to revert to the `SAPSSOEXT` library because then the same implementation of all components can be used. In pure Java landscapes, it is easier to use only the SAP Crypto Toolkit.

Step 1: Setting Up the Class Path

To begin with, download the toolkit from the SAP Service Marketplace. You will find it under the DOWNLOAD • SAP CRYPTOGRAPHIC SOFTWARE path. After you have unpacked the CAR archive, you will find a file with the extension *.sda* there. The extension stands for *Software Deployment Archive*, and Java applications are deployed on the SAP J2EE server using these types of files. Unpack the file, and you will find a number of Java archives (JAR). The central Java archive is called *iaik_jce.jar*. IAIK here stands for *Institute for Applied Information Processing and Communication*. One of the many types of work performed by this institute of the Graz University of Technology in Austria includes implementing Java-based cryptographic functions collectively referred to as *cryptography providers*. SAP uses these cryptography providers in its Java-based solutions. As well as the cryptography provider, you still need three other JAR files, which you will find under the following paths:

- *<drive>:\usr\sap\<SID>\j2ee\cluster\server0\bin\ext\com.sap.security. api. sda\com.sap.security.api.jar*

- *<drive>:\usr\sap\<SID>\j2ee\cluster\server0\bin\ext\com.sap.security.api. sda\com.sap.security.core.sda\com.sap.security.core.jar*

- *<drive>:\usr\sap\<SID>\j2ee\cluster\server0\bin\system\com.sap. security. api.sda\logging.jar*

Add these JAR files to the class path of your development environment. You can then continue with establishing the relationship of trust.

Step 2: Establishing a Relationship of Trust Using a KeyStore File

Integrating certificates

Like the ABAP infrastructure, the J2EE server certificate must be integrated into an external environment before the ticket can be verified. The most secure way to integrate certificates is to use KeyStores. As already mentioned, you can manage KeyStores using the `keytool` command-line tool. You can use the `-alias` parameter to find and address entries more easily in a KeyStore, and you can use `-storepass` to specify for the keytool call the password for protecting the KeyStore. The parameters in the following `keytool` call make it almost self-explanatory:

```
keytool -import -alias portal -file x:\verify.der
-keystore c:\demokeystore.pse -storepass mypassword
```

The certificate for the *verify.der* file is included in the *demokeystore.pse* KeyStore file. You can also see that not only the `sapgenpse` tool but also the `keytool` can process PSE files.

After you have imported the certificate into the KeyStore and as a result it is available for verifying logon tickets, you can begin implementing the ticket verification. This implementation basically consists of two steps: reading trustworthy certificates from the PSE file and verifying the SAP logon ticket.

Step 3: Implementing Java Functions

Reading trustworthy certificates

Listing 1.2 is a method for importing a PSE file. The call parameters the `loadCertsFromPSE` method receives include the full file path for the PSE file and the password used for accessing the file securely. As return parameters, the method delivers a list of trustworthy certificates that were read from the PSE file.

```
public stat-
ic X509Certificate[] loadCertsFromPSE(String pse, String pwd) {
  java.security.cert.X509Certificate[] certificates = null;
  char passwd[] = pwd.toCharArray();
  InputStream stream = null;
  ArrayList certs = new ArrayList();
  try {
    stream = new FileInputStream(pse);
    java.security.KeyStore store =
      java.security.KeyStore.getInstance("JKS", "SUN");
    store.load(stream, passwd);
```

```
    Enumeration enu = store.aliases();
    while (enu.hasMoreElements()) {
      String alias = (String) enu.nextElement();
      if (store.isCertificateEntry(alias)) {
        certs.add(store.getCertificate(alias));
      }
    }
    stream.close();
    if (certs.size() < 1) {
      System.out.println(
        "PSE does not contain any certificates");
    }
    certificates =
      (java.security.cert.X509Certificate[]) certs.toArray(
        new java.security.cert.X509Certificate[0]);
    return certificates;
  } catch (Exception e) {
  }
}
```

Listing 1.2 Importing and Exporting X509 Certificates

Because the trustworthy certificates are stored within the PSE file, you must first import the PSE file. You do this by creating a `FileInputStream`. As already mentioned, PSE files are an SAP interpretation of the KeyStore concept, so it is little wonder that we can also use the `KeyStore` class for processing PSE files. You create the KeyStore instance using the `getInstance` factory method. The call parameter this KeyStore instance gets specifies which type of KeyStore representation is to be created. In our case, we will use the JKS standard implementation from Sun (*Java Key Store*). The last step for creating the KeyStore object involves calling the `load` method. It initializes the newly created KeyStore object with information from the imported file. By specifying an alias, you can then access the content and, as a result, the certificates.

Importing a PSE file

You will remember that the logon ticket is stored as a cookie on the client. If you now call a function in an external Java-based system, the SAP logon ticket will be sent to the system as a string. The `getSSOTicket` method shown in Listing 1.3 receives the SAP logon ticket as a string and must be decoded for further processing. The `verify` method of the `Ticket` class performs the actual ticket verification. We create a class

Validating the ticket

instance for this and initialize it using the list of known certificates and the decoded ticket.

```
private Ticket getSSOTicket(String encodedTicket)
  throws Exception {
  try {
    String decodedTicket = URLDecoder.decode(
      encodedTicket, "UTF-8");
    decodedTicket = decodedTicket.replace(' ', '+');
    X509Certificate[] certificates =
      loadCertsFromPSE(keystorePath, "password");
    IAIK provider = new IAIK();
    Security.addProvider(provider);
    com.sap.security.core.ticket.imp.Ticket ticket =
      new com.sap.security.core.ticket.imp.Ticket();
    ticket.setCertificates(certificates);
    ticket.setTicket(decodedTicket);
    ticket.verify();
    return ticket;
  } catch (UnsupportedEncodingException uncodingEx) {
    // Process exception sensibly
  } catch (TicketVerifyException tvEx) {
    // Process exception sensibly
  }
  return null;
}
```

Listing 1.3 Creating and Verifying the SAP Logon Ticket

Prospects for Using the SAP Logon Ticket in Other J2EE Application Servers

JAAS

Creating and forwarding the ticket to the SAP system are recurring tasks, and using the SAP logon ticket in other J2EE servers is immensely important. The J2EE standard allows for this requirement in its specification by describing the authentication and authorization in a separate specification. The *Java Authentication and Authorization Service* (JAAS) describes how separate authentication and authorization concepts can be integrated into the J2EE server.

Pluggable authentication model

For this purpose, JAAS implements the *Pluggable Authentication Model* (PAM) usual for UNIX. Authentication and authorization are not hard coded in the application in this case but rather are provided through flexibly exchangeable modules. All JAAS modules have a standard interface.

This and the responsibilities of the modules are defined in the specification. You can therefore use JAAS to integrate your own concepts into the SAP NetWeaver AS and also implement authentication per SAP logon ticket into another J2EE server. You create authentication components using login modules. In increasingly greater service orientation, you can therefore use uniform security concepts across system boundaries so that communication between the portal and ABAP system and from there to a non-SAP J2EE server can be achieved. With Java-to-Java communication, for which the SAP logon ticket is used for authentication, the ticket verification could be implemented in login modules.

Security on the Transport Layer

The last sections dealt almost exclusively with authentication and authorization. These are two important aspects, but protected data access is not much use if their exchange occurs in "plain text." An attacker can then "eavesdrop" very easily on the network to access confidential information.

We will therefore now cover using security on the transport layer. This will encompass the authenticity of communication partners, data integrity, and data confidentiality. Two different security protocols are supported for securing communication between SAP NetWeaver components:

Transport security with SNC or SSL

- *Secure Socket Layer* (SSL) for securing HTTP
- *Secure Network Communication* (SNC) for securing RFC and DIAG

SSL and SNC both work on the basis of certificates. In the following section, we will look in more detail at using SNC and explain how its infrastructure is set up.

Introduction to Secure Network Communication

SNC is used for securing communication between two SAP NetWeaver communication partners. SNC actually only describes a layer in the SAP NetWeaver system architecture, which describes an interface for integrating external security products. To put it more specifically, the interface between the SAP system kernel layer and a library (implementation) of an external manufacturer is described via SNC. Library manufacturers must implement GSS-API V2 (*Generic Security Services Application Pro-*

gramming Interface Version 2) in this case. It is loaded dynamically during the SNC initialization phase. SAP provides its own implementation of this type of external library for using SNC: SAP Cryptolib. The SNC approach is very much similar to the previously mentioned PAM concept of the Java Authentication and Authorization Service (JAAS). As already mentioned, SNC addresses three areas of security:

Levels of security with SNC

- Authentication only
- Protection of integrity
- Protection of data through encryption

The SNC user can therefore achieve security at several levels. When authentication is used, the system merely secures the identity of the communication partner. However, to secure communication during transit between the communication partners, it is essential to use data integrity and data protection through encryption. This is configured using profile parameters in the instance profile of the application server.

As already mentioned, SNC works with certificates. The one communication partner must have the digital certificate of the other communication partner and extend him a certain amount of trust. The key information here must be in a form that is difficult to abuse. The *Personal Security Environment* (PSE) is used in saving key information. Besides a certificate list of those certificates that are trusted, PSE files also contain their own key information.

Strength of trust scenarios

The strength of trust is described within SNC using two scenarios:

- **All communication partners that communicate with the ABAP system via SNC use the same PSE.**
  The advantage of this scenario is that management in the ABAP stack is much easier. The time and effort required before secure communication can be achieved is also significantly lower. This is because a new PSE does not have to be created for every communication partner, and the certificate of the partner therefore does not have to be imported into the ABAP stack.

  However, the disadvantage of this scenario cannot be ignored: An attacker may get possession of the PSE file, and the time and effort required to close any security loops — depending on the number of communication partners — could turn out to be enormous. Also bear in mind that localizing communication problems for a partner is really complicated because it is very difficult to find out which SNC connection is faulty.

▶ **Every communication partner gets an individual PSE.**
The big advantage of scenario 1 becomes a big problem here: The initial administration effort is greater and spontaneous communication therefore impossible. Before communication can take place, both partners must export their digital certificate from the PSE and import the certificate of the other.

Combinations of both scenarios are also possible by forming several groups of systems and by each system group using the same PSE.

Combinations

Installing SAP Cryptolib

Before you can start configuring the SNC, you need SAP Cryptolib for the SAP NetWeaver AS ABAP. Follow the DOWNLOAD • SAP CRYPTOGRAPHIC SOFTWARE path under *http://www.service.sap.com/download* to download the library. You will find the libraries for all SAP-supported platforms as CAR files under this address.

Because the examples in this book were developed on Windows 2003, we have decided to use the Windows platform. In the file, you will find three folders for the relevant instance of a Windows platform. Each of these folders contains the *sapcrypto.dll* file and a version of the *sapgenpse.exe* tool. In addition to a number of text files, you will also find a file called *ticket*. This file provides the license certificate for creating your own certificates.

To install SAP Cryptolib, simply copy the files into the corresponding application server directories, *exe* and *sec*. The DIR_INSTANCE configuration parameter is important for the storage location of the files. It points to *<drive>\usr\sap\<SID>\<instance>* on Windows. The parameter is prefixed to all profile parameters to specify the installation directory of the server instance.

Installation path

Copy the *sapcrypto.dll* and *sapgenpse.exe* files into the directory specified in the DIR_EXECUTABLE profile parameter. On Windows, the parameter normally points to *DIR_INSTANCE\exe*.

Then store the file with the ticket in the *DIR_INSTANCE\sec subdirectory*. If there is already a file called ticket in this directory, create a subdirectory and store the file there.

SECUDIR environment variable

To complete the installation, set the SECUDIR environment variable of the operating system in the *sec* subdirectory where the ticket is stored — in other words, in *DIR_INSTANCE\sec* or in the subdirectory you created. You must bear in mind here that the environment variable is set under the user, under which the application server is to be executed later. By setting variables, you let the runtime environment know where to find trustworthy tickets.

Configuring the Application Server for Using SNC

Now that we have installed SAP Cryptolib, we will turn to configuring SNC. In the first part of the configuration, you must notify the application server of the required information about the process parameters for SNC. You do this using the instance profile. Start Transaction RZ10 for this. Then open the instance profile in Extended Maintenance mode. Press [Shift] + [F8] to switch to edit mode, and start adding the parameters. You can do this either by clicking the Parameter button or pressing the [F5] key. Table 1.3 shows the parameters to be set and their descriptions.

Parameter Name	Value	Description
snc/enable	»1«	Activates the use of SNC
snc/gssapi_lib	$(DIR_EXECUTABLE)\sapcrypto.dll	Refers to the GSS-API implementation
snc/identity/as	p:CN=AOU, OU=IT, O=ADO, C=DE	Unique application server identifier
snc/data_protection/max	»3«	Maximum security support
snc/data_protection/min	»1«	Minimum security support

Table 1.3 Overview of SNC Profile Parameters and Their Descriptions

Parameter Name	Value	Description
snc/data_protection/use	»3«	Security support to be used
snc/accept_insecure_cpic	»1«	Access without SNC per CPIC connection allowed
snc/accept_insecure_gui	»1«	1 = access without SNC allowed per SAP GUI
snc/accept_insecure_r3int_rfc	»1«	1 = SAP system-internal access without SNC allowed
snc/accept_insecure_rfc	»1«	1 = access via RFC also without SNC allowed
sec/libsapsecu	$(DIR_EXECUTABLE)\sapcrypto.dll	File name of SAP cryptographic API to be loaded when server started
ssf/ssfapi_lib	$(DIR_EXECUTABLE)\sapcrypto.dll	File name of SAP cryptographic library
ssf/name	SAPSECULIB	Specifies environment variables of operating system

Table 1.3 Overview of SNC Profile Parameters and Their Descriptions (Cont.)

As you can see from the Description field in the table, the parameters are set in such a way that unsecure communication with the ABAP system is still possible. To complete the configuration, set the value of the `snc/enable` parameter to 1. You should then restart the server.

Check the Installation and Settings Thoroughly

Make sure you only set the value of the `snc/enable` parameter to 1 after you are sure the SAP Cryptolib installation is complete and all parameters in Table 1.3 have been set properly. If the library has been installed and configured incorrectly, the application server will no longer start.

Creating the SNC PSE Container

After the server has uploaded successfully, you can begin completing the configuration in the server. Because SNC is based on public-key cryptography using digital certificates, each communication partner must produce a trustworthy certificate.

Start Transaction STRUSTSSO2 to configure a relationships of trust in the ABAP system. After you start the transaction, you will see an entry highlighted in red on the left of the screen in your system: SNC (SAP Cryptolib). Select the Create menu option from the context menu by clicking the entry. In the window that appears, specify the same value as the one in the `scn/identity/as` profile parameter. This will create a PSE file for your application server. After you have confirmed your entries, you will be requested to create a password for the SNC PSE entry just created. Click the Password button (Figure 1.10) to create a password that will be used to protect access to the PSE file.

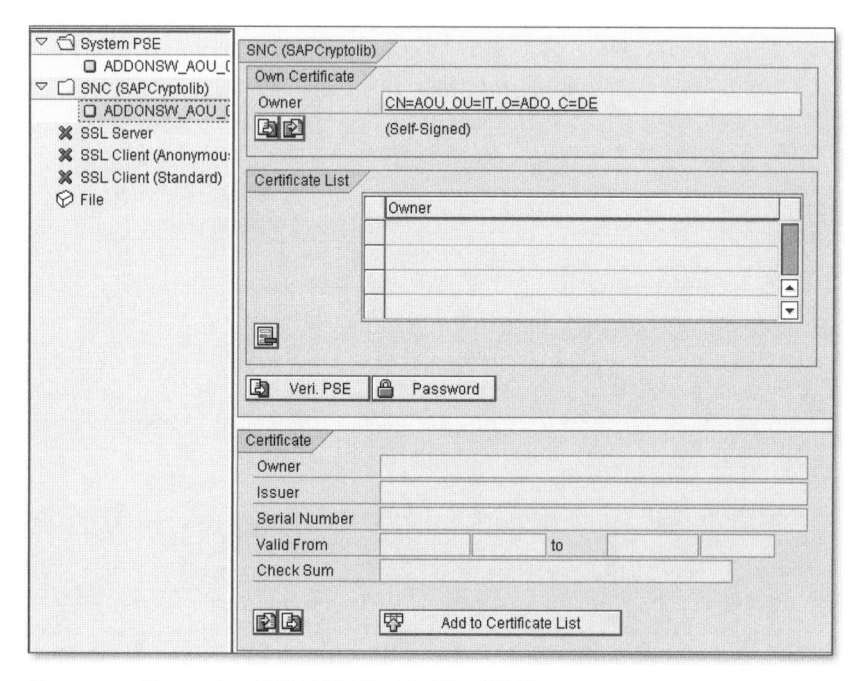

Figure 1.10 Transaction STRUSTSSO2 with SNC PSE File

Testing the Configuration

Unfortunately, there is no integrated way to test whether the SNC environment was installed and configured successfully. You would have to wait until the SNC environment was used from an RFC client. But if an error then occurs, the worst-case scenario is that you will not know what has caused the error: the configuration, the client itself or the client certificate.

However, SAP Notes 800240 and 912405 provide you with a program you can copy into your ABAP system using Transaction SE80. The program is called ZSSF_TEST_PSE.

Test program on the SAP Service Marketplace

1.3 Programming SAP NetWeaver AS ABAP

Next, we will develop a small application in ABAP that we will repeatedly use as an example in Chapter 2, Remote Function Call with ABAP, up to Chapter 7, SAP NetWeaver Process Integration. Our sample application will manage sales orders and vendor purchase orders for a book wholesaler. We will supply this application with inbound interfaces (for book store sales orders) and outbound interfaces (for vendor orders to publishing companies) in different interface technologies:

- *Remote Function Call* (RFC) in Section 2.1, RFC Function Modules in ABAP
- *Business Application Programming Interface* (BAPI) in Section 2.4, Business Objects and BAPIs
- *Application Link Enabling* (ALE) in Chapter 5, IDocs and ALE
- *Service-Oriented Architecture Protocol* (SOAP) in Chapter 6, Service-Oriented Architecture Protocol
- *XI Protocol* (SAP Exchange Infrastructure) in Chapter 7, SAP NetWeaver Process Integration

In Section 1.4, Overview of SAP Interface Technologies, we will take a closer look at the interface technologies listed here and explain them in the previously mentioned chapters using programmed examples. We will also program the corresponding outbound interfaces for book stores and inbound interfaces for publishing companies in C, Java, and C# programming languages. Figure 1.11 shows the systems involved.

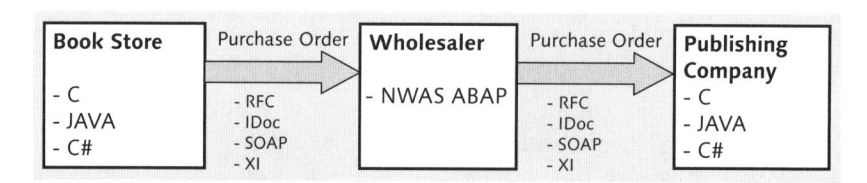

Figure 1.11 Sample Application

1.3.1 ABAP Dictionary

The application consists of two database tables with purchase order header data and item data:

- ZIFPORDER
  This table contains purchase order information.

- ZIFPORDERPOS
  This table contains information about purchase order items.

Sales orders and vendor purchase orders will be stored in the same tables in this case and will differ from each other by the content of the DOCTYPE field. This field contains the value SO for *sales order* entries and PO for *purchase order* entries.

Packages   We will assign all repository objects to the ZIFP package we will create using ABAP Workbench SE80. To do this, start Transaction SE80, and choose the Package entry from the dropdown list. Specify "ZIFP" as the name of the package, and click the button with the glasses icon to display the objects assigned to this package. Because the package does not yet exist, you are offered the chance to create it. Also create a new transport request at the same time for the new repository objects to be created.

Database Tables

After you have created the package, you can define the two transparent tables either directly from the Object Navigator or using Transaction SE11.

The fields for ZIFPORDER, their data elements (business data types), lengths, and descriptions are listed in Table 1.4, while the details about ZIFPORDERPOS are listed in Table 1.5.

Field	Data Element	Data Type	Length	Description
MANDT	MANDT	CLNT	3	Client
ORDERID	ZIFPORDERID	NUMC	10	Purchase order number
TYPE	ZIFPORDERTPYE	CHAR	2	Purchase order type
REFID	ZIFPREFID	NUMC	10	Reference number
BUYER	ZIFPBUYER	CHAR	50	Buyer
SELLER	ZIFPSELLER	CHAR	50	Vendor
DATE	ZIFPORDERDATE	DATS	8	Purchase order date

Table 1.4 ZIFPORDER Table Columns

Fields of sample tables

Field	Data Element	Data Type	Length	Description
MANDT	MANDT	CLNT	3	Client
ORDERID	ZIFPORDERID	NUMC	10	Purchase order number
ORDERPOS	ZIFPPOS	NUMC	5	Purchase order item
MATID	ZIFPMATID	CHAR	20	Material number
MATTEXT	ZIFPMATTEXT	CHAR	40	Material text
ORDERCOUNT	ZIFPCOUNT	INT4	–	Number
PRICE	ZIFPPRICE	CURR	8.4	Price
CURRENCY	ZIFPCURRENCY	CUKY	5	Currency

Table 1.5 ZIFPORDERPOS Table Columns

1 | Basic Principles of SAP Interface Programming

Figure 1.12 shows the definition of the `ZIFPORDERPOS` table in the *ABAP Dictionary* (DDIC).

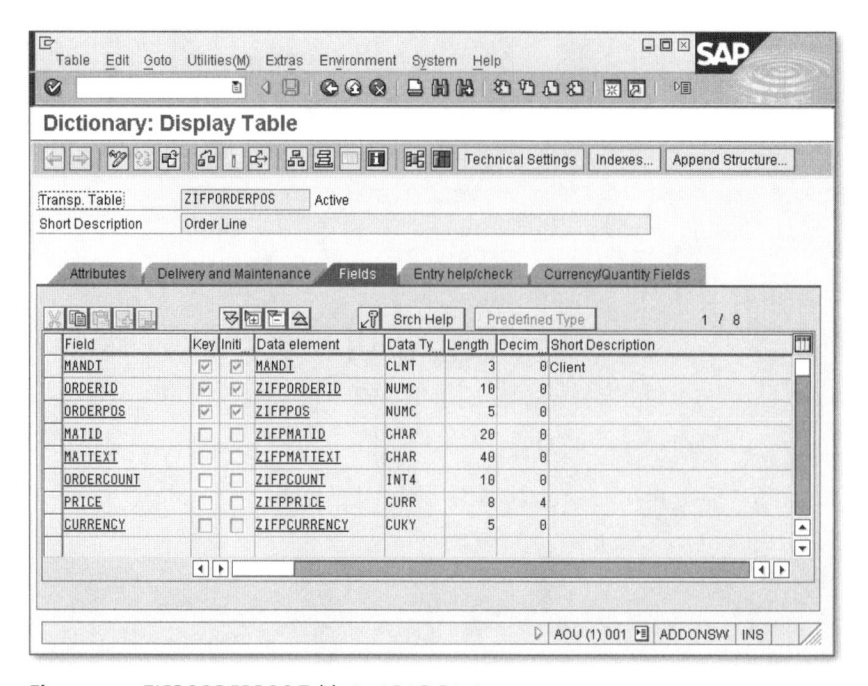

Figure 1.12 ZIFPORDERPOS Table in ABAP Dictionary

Foreign key

The key fields of the `ZIFPORDER` table are `MANDT` and `ORDERID`. In contrast, the key fields of the `ZIFPORDERPOS` table are `MANDT`, `ORDERID`, and `ORDERPOS`. The `MANDT` field in both tables is a check field with the `T000` check table that contains the clients. The `ORDERID` field of the `ZIFPORDERPOS` table is a check field with the `ZIFPORDER` check table. The foreign key in the `ZIFPORDERPOS` table, which uniquely defines an entry from the `ZIFPORDER` table, is made up of the `ZIFPORDER-MANDT` and `ZIFORDER-ORDERID` fields. The system can use these foreign key dependencies later to run automatic input checks on dynpros that use the check fields.

Table maintenance

When defining tables, you can select the relevant option from a drop-down list on the Delivery and Maintenance tab to specify whether table maintenance is allowed. Specify that this should be allowed, so that you will be able to maintain table contents using Transactions SE16 and SA16.

In the technical properties, which you can access by selecting the GOTO • TECHNICAL SETTINGS menu path, specify that both tables contain master and transaction data. Also set the size category in this dialog box to 0. Both tables contain transaction data, so they should not be buffered.

The corresponding database tables are created as soon as you activate the table definitions. You can now enter the first test data into the tables using Transaction SE16 or SA16.

Search Help

Because we will need the ZIFPORDER table when discussing the Helpvalues business object in Section 2.4.3, Helpvalues Business Object, we will create two elementary search help options and one collective search help for it:

- **ZIFPORDERA**
  This elementary search help is used for searching for purchase orders by the name of the buyer.

- **ZIFPORDERB**
  This elementary search help is used for searching for purchase orders by the name of the seller.

- **ZIFPORDER**
  This collective search help includes the ZIFPORDERA and ZIFPORDERB elementary search help options.

<small>Collective search help</small>

You create search help using the ABAP Dictionary (Transaction SE11). Search help is used to make it easier to design input help (F4 help) for displaying valid input values.

The ZIFPORDERA search help shown in Figure 1.13 obtains its data from the ZIFPORDER database table. This is the *selection method* of the search help that includes the four ORDERID, TYPE, BUYER, and SELLER search help parameters. These four parameters are shown on the search help hit list (in the LPos column in Figure 1.13). The first three of these parameters, ORDERID, TYPE, and BUYER, are displayed on the search help selection screen (in the SPos column in Figure 1.13). The search help selection screen is a user dialog where the user can specify selection criteria to limit the number of hits. If you want the search help to list only sales orders, enter the "SO" value into the Type selection field in the selection screen.

<small>Search help for purchase orders</small>

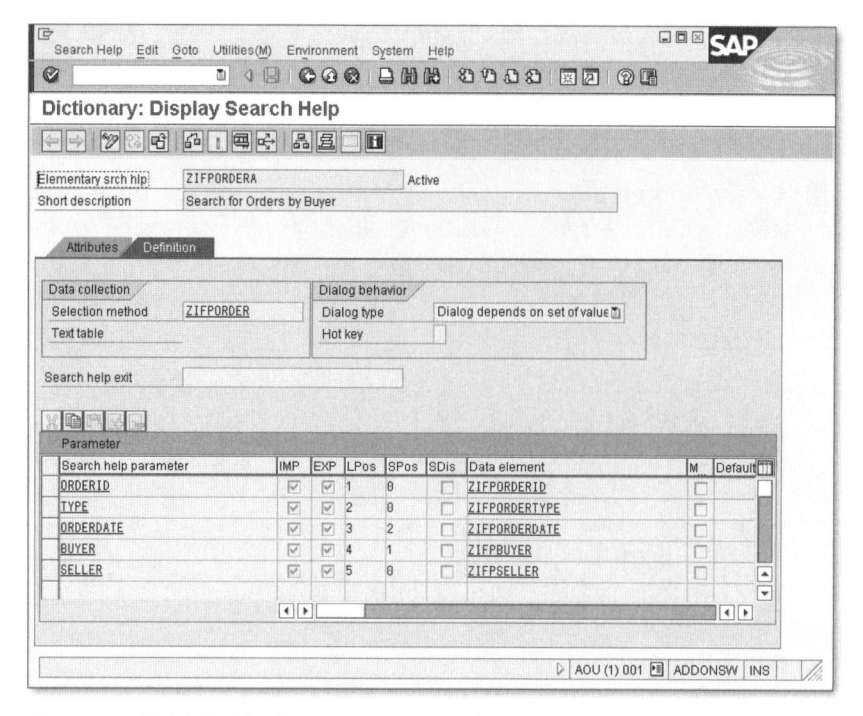

1 | Basic Principles of SAP Interface Programming

Figure 1.13 ZIFPORDERA Elementary Search Help

Attaching search help

You can attach search help to check tables, table fields, or data elements, although it is most often attached to check tables. When you request input help (F4 input help) on a check field with a check table, the search help attached to it is used. In our example, we will attach the ZIFPORDER search help to the ZIFPORDER check table. When you then search for a valid purchase order number in a check field of the ZIFPORDER check table, the system uses this search help.

The two elementary search help options, ZIFPORDERA and ZIFPORDERB, are included in the ZIFPORDER collective search help. This collective search help is attached to the ZIFPORDER check table and also to the ORDERID field of this table.

Lock Objects

When developing an ABAP application, you must make sure that many users can work with an SAP system simultaneously, so before you delete or change any data records, you must determine whether another user is currently working with the data record. First of all, you set an exclusive lock on the corresponding data record. If the lock cannot be set successfully because the data record is already being processed by another user, we must cancel the processing. If the lock can be set, we are free to delete or change the data record.

To be able to set locks, you develop a *lock object* in Transaction SE11 and an EZIFPORDER lock object with the ORDERID and ORDERPOS fields to enable you to lock all the items for a purchase order. The lock object relates to the primary ZIFPORDER table and secondary ZIFPORDERPOS table. Specify both of these tables when creating the lock object in Transaction SE11.

Developing lock objects

The two function modules, ENQUEUE_EZIFPORDER and DEQUEUE_EZIFPORDER, are generated when you activate the lock object. You can use them to set and remove locks. These two function modules have the ORDERID and ORDERPOS import parameters that you can use to uniquely determine from the ZIFPORDERPOS table, the data record to be locked. All items for a purchase order may also be locked generically, whereby nothing is transferred for the ORDERID lock argument. The remaining ENQUEUE_EZBOOK import parameters control the lock mechanism details but are prepopulated with default values sufficient for our purposes.

Lock modules

1.3.2 Authentication and Authorization

When logging on via the SAP GUI, a user is authenticated by specifying a user name, password, and client. These three details must match the data assigned when the user master data record is created in Transaction SU01. However, the application itself must establish whether an authenticated user is also authorized to perform certain actions. To do this, it uses the AUTHORITY-CHECK statement to compare whether authorizations with specific values defined by the application are stored in the profiles for the user.

We will create the ZIFPORDER *authorization object* with the ACTVT field (for "Activity") for this in the Object Navigator (SE80) or Transaction SU21. The values the ACTVT field can have are 01 (Add or Create), 02 (Change), 03 (Display), and 06 (Delete).

Authorization objects

To give a user authorization to display purchase orders, the administrator must create *authorization* for this authorization object in Transaction SU03 and set the value of the ACTVT field for this authorization to 03. In

Transaction SU02, the administrator then assigns this authorization to a profile that he subsequently assigns in turn to the corresponding users in Transaction SU01.

Authorization check

Before an application displays purchases orders for the user, it must check the user's profiles to verify whether the user actually has authorization for the ZIFPORDER authorization object where the value of the ACTVT field is set to 03. If this is not the case, the application is not permitted to display the data to the user. Listing 1.4 shows the corresponding ABAP source code for this check.

```
* Check display authorization
AUTHORITY-CHECK OBJECT 'ZIFPORDER' ID 'ACTVT' FIELD '03'.
CHECK SY-SUBRC EQ 0.
* Only proceed here if SY-SUBRC is = 0 .
* Display data.
```

Listing 1.4 Checking Authorization for Displaying Purchase Orders

1.3.3 Number Ranges

For order IDs to be created automatically for new purchase orders, you must create a *number range object* in Transaction SNRO (number range maintenance). The name you assign to this number range is ZIFPORDER. You use the ZIFPORDERDOM domain for the length of numbers of this number range object.

Number range intervals

After you create and save the number range object, you can create a corresponding *number range interval* for it. You do this on the initial screen of Transaction SNRO by clicking the Number Ranges button in the application toolbar. From there, you can create new intervals or change existing ones by clicking the Change Intervals button. An interval of this number range is displayed in Figure 1.14. You use the NUMBER_GET_NEXT function module to assign a number from this interval.

1.3.4 Function Modules

Function modules are modularization units of the ABAP programming language. They contain executable source code and can be called from ABAP programs using the CALL FUNCTION ABAP statement. They have a well-defined interface for transferring and receiving data. This interface defines the parameter types and transfer direction. Data can only be transferred to and received by the function module through this interface.

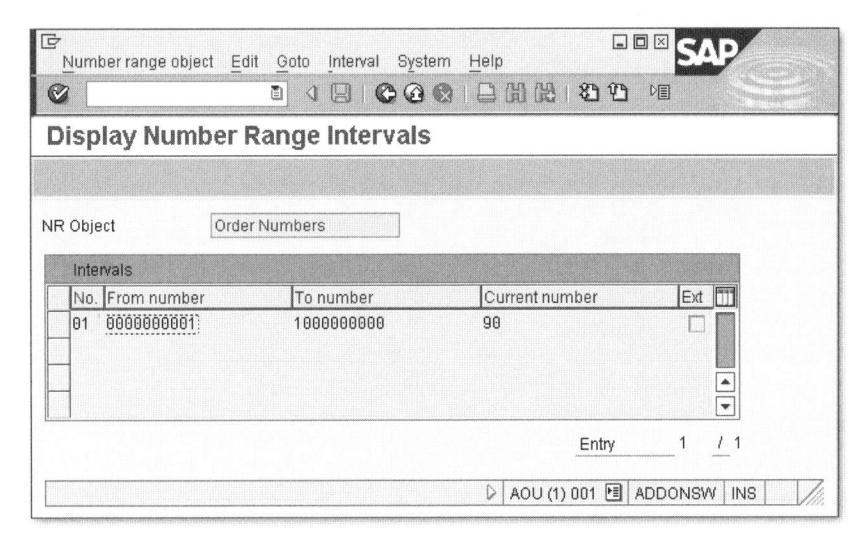

Figure 1.14 Number Range Interval of ZIFPORDER Number Range Object for Purchase Order Numbers

This section deals with features common to all function modules. We will come across specific function modules in the following sections, in particular in Sections 1.3.5, Update Modules, and 1.4.2, Remote Function Call, and in Chapter 2, Remote Function Call with ABAP.

The ABAP developer uses the *Function Builder* (Transaction SE37) to create function modules.

Function Builder

In addition to the source text, the Function Builder also defines the interface and properties for a function module.

Every function module is part of a *function group*. A function group is a program (F type) that can contain global data, dynpros, modules, and other components, like any other program. For example, the DDIF_FIELDINFO_GET function module is a member of the SDIFRUNTIME function group. This function group contains other function modules such as DDIF_NAMETAB_GET, DD_INT_UPDATE_DDFTX, and DDIF_FIELDLABEL_GET for accessing the ABAP Dictionary.

Function groups

Every function module of a function group can access the global data of this function group. A new instance of the global data for the function group is created in this case for every calling program; the global data contents of a function group therefore differ for every calling program. When a program calls two function modules of a function group, the first function module can write data into the global data of the function group that the second function module can then read and use. This is how function module calls can become stateful.

Function module interface

With the calling program, the function module can only exchange data through its interface. There are five parts to the interface:

- **Import**
  Data is transferred to the function module through import parameters. The function module cannot change the actual parameters here. Import parameters can be simple or structured and also flagged as optional. A default value is also identified in this case when the parameters are being defined.

- **Export**
  After it has been executed, the function module receives data through export parameters. Export parameters can be simple or structured.

- **Changing**
  Changing parameters are a combination of import and export parameters: Data can be transferred to the function module through changing parameters and then changed and returned again by this function module.

- **Tables**
  Import, export, and changing parameters may only be simple or structured up to Release 6.40. You use table parameters to transfer internal tables (*arrays*). Table parameters are always transferred by reference. They are therefore used to transfer data to the function module and return values from the function module. To find out which of these two functions are performed by a table parameter, you will have to refer to the function module documentation.

Exception statuses

- **Exceptions**
  Possible exception statuses are also defined in the function module interface. If an error occurs, the function module triggers one of the exceptions defined by the RAISE keyword. The caller is responsible

for evaluating the function module return code. If an exception has occurred, the return code will be a value not equal to zero.

Every function module has this type of interface. A function module has other properties besides the interface. The next section covers update modules, while Chapter 2, Remote Function Call with ABAP, deals with RFC modules.

1.3.5 Update Modules

Based on the transaction concept explained in Section 1.1.2, SAP NetWeaver Application Server ABAP, application programs should not program database changes directly using INSERT, UPDATE, and DELETE statements because these database changes are committed on the database by an implicit database commit immediately after each dialog step. Instead, the application programs should call special function modules with an IN UPDATE TASK statement. These function modules are identified in the properties as *update modules*. They are not executed directly when called but only when the application program triggers the COMMIT WORK command. It is only then that these update modules are executed asynchronously in a separate V-type work process and that they store the data transferred to them at the time of the call to the database. This concept also means that an SAP LUW consisting of several dialog steps can be canceled by a ROLLBACK WORK without committing the changed data to the database.

To begin with, update modules for creating data records should store the data transferred to them in an internal table within the function group and then use the ON COMMIT statement to call a subroutine that will perform the actual update with *array insert technologies*. You can create several objects efficiently within a transaction using update modules programmed in this way. The subroutine that performs the actual update is only executed once and saves all data records in a single database access. This is particularly important if mass data is to be read.

Mass updating

Listing 1.5 shows the z_ifp_v_create_order update module. It first writes the transferred parameters for header and item data into the internal it_orderheader_buffer and it_orderpos_buffer tables that were defined in the global data area of the ZIFP function group. Then it calls the buffersave subroutine using the ON COMMIT statement. Because of this statement, the subroutine is actually only executed once in the update process.

```
FUNCTION z_ifp_v_create_order.
*"----------------------------------------------------------
*"*"Update function module:
*"*"Local interface:
*"  IMPORTING
*"     VALUE(IM_ORDERHEADER) TYPE  ZIFPORDER
*"  TABLES
*"      IM_ORDERPOS STRUCTURE  ZIFPORDERPOS
*"----------------------------------------------------------
" Save the transferred data in the buffer table first
  APPEND im_orderheader TO it_orderheader_buffer.
  IF sy-subrc NE 0.
    MESSAGE a601(zifp) WITH im_orderheader-orderid.
  ENDIF.
  APPEND LINES OF im_orderpos TO it_orderpos_buffer.
  IF sy-subrc NE 0.
    MESSAGE a602(zifp) WITH im_orderheader-orderid.
  ENDIF.
  " Save entire table with commit
  PERFORM buffersave ON COMMIT.
ENDFUNCTION.
FORM buffersave.
  INSERT zifporder FROM TABLE it_orderheader_buffer.
  IF sy-subrc NE 0.
    MESSAGE a603(zifp).
  ENDIF.
  INSERT zifporderpos from table it_orderpos_buffer.
  IF sy-subrc NE 0.
    MESSAGE a604(zifp).
  ENDIF.
ENDFORM.                          "buffersave
```

Listing 1.5 z_ifp_v_create_order Update Module

1.3.6 Application Functions and User Interfaces

So far, you have programmed the data access layer for the sample application with transparent tables, search help, lock objects, authorization objects, and update modules. Next we would need to develop the application functions and user interface for our application. But this is not necessary for our purposes, and the procedure is adequately described in other books (e.g., *ABAP Objects* [SAP PRESS, 2007]), so we will only outline the rough procedure here.

For an application to be supplied with alternative user interfaces or be used by external programs through interfaces, it is useful to encapsulate the application functions in function modules. We will see this in Chapter 2, Remote Function Call with ABAP. We will use the function modules we develop there as the basis for ALE, SOAP, and SAP NetWeaver XI interfaces in Chapter 5, IDocs and ALE; Chapter 6, Service-Oriented Architecture Protocol; and Chapter 7, SAP NetWeaver Process Integration. If you want an application to be interface-enabled, the interprocess communication technology used is therefore less important than the sensible breakdown of application functions in elementary modules that can be used by different users.

Encapsulating functions

If the application functions are initially encapsulated in this way, it is also very easy to create graphical user interfaces using different techniques. There are at least four options to do this in ABAP:

Graphical user interfaces

- **Reports**
  Reports are type 1 ABAP programs that basically select data on the database and output it in the form of lists in the SAP GUI.

- **Module pools**
  Module pools are type M ABAP programs that consist of individual dynpros and are called through transaction codes.

- **Business Server Pages**
  Business Server Pages (BSPs) are HTML pages with embedded ABAP source code. These applications are not used through the SAP GUI but through a web browser (see *Web Programming in ABAP with the SAP Web Application Server* [SAP PRESS, 2005]).

- **ABAP Web Dynpro**
  ABAP Web Dynpro is a new framework for developing web applications. The interface here is not developed directly in HTML but rather described with graphical tools for the Web Dynpro runtime environment (see *Getting Started with Web Dynpro ABAP* [SAP PRESS, 2010]).

You can of course also develop user interfaces entirely without ABAP, for example, with Web Dynpro Java, Java Server Pages (JSPs), Java servlets, ASP.NET (*Active Server Pages*), and many other technologies.

Developing user interfaces without ABAP

1 | Basic Principles of SAP Interface Programming

1.4 Overview of SAP Interface Technologies

In this section, we will present the most important interface technologies used by ABAP programs:

- The *file interface* for reading and writing files (Section 1.4.1, File Interface)
- *Remote Function Call* (RFC) for calling function modules remotely (Section 1.4.2, Remote Function Call)
- *Business Application Programming Interfaces* (BAPIs), which provide an object-oriented view of application functions (Section 2.4, Business Objects and BAPIs)
- The ALE interface (*Application Link Enabling*) for exchanging messages asynchronously (Chapter 5, IDocs and ALE)
- The *Service-Oriented Architecture Protocol* (SOAP) based on the HTTP and XML Internet standards (Chapter 6, Service-Oriented Architecture Protocol)
- The *XI protocol* used by SAP NetWeaver XI/SAP NetWeaver PI (Chapter 7, SAP NetWeaver Process Integration)

In this section, we will explain the basic interdependencies and show you the most important transactions for managing interfaces.

1.4.1 File Interface

One method (which is also important in practice) to exchange data between two systems is to send it through a file system. The sending system writes data into a file that is then transported to a target system directory. This file is read by the target system and imported into the database. SAP systems already have completed programs for importing important types of data. However, these programs expect the file in a specific format. The file is read and the data written to one of three types in the database tables:

Import programs

- **Call transaction**
  The ABAP programming language knows the CALL TRANSACTION keyword that can be used to call an SAP transaction. The data to be entered is transferred to this transaction in the form of a *batch input table*. For every dynpro input field of the called transaction, the data

to be entered is available in the batch input table. The table also contains the function code to be used for every dynpro to complete an entry and navigate to the next dynpro.

A call transaction program reads the file with the data to be entered, creates a batch input table for every data record, and transfers this table to the SAP transaction using CALL TRANSACTION (which is normally executed online) to create a new data record. The called transaction is processed in the background, so the dynpros are not displayed. All input checks programmed in the SAP transaction naturally take place. This ensures that only valid and consistent data reaches the database through the call transaction technique.

- **Batch input**
  The first step with the batch input program runs like the call transaction program: The file with the data to be entered is read and a batch input table is created for every data record. However, this batch input table is not forwarded to the SAP transaction directly but is instead saved in a batch input session in the database. The batch input monitor (Transaction SM35) later reads this batch input session, and the batch input tables contained in it are transferred to the SAP transaction. We refer to this as "processing" the batch input session.

  During this processing, a protocol is created that can be analyzed later using the batch input monitor. If an error occurs, you can correct the data and process the session again. This option of controlling and correcting errors is the main advantage of the batch input procedure compared to the call transaction technique.

- **Direct input**
  The two preceding techniques may be too slow for mass data transfers in particular. Direct input programs therefore exist for some data types, particularly financial accounting documents. These programs read the file with the data to be entered, check the data, and store it directly in the database using UPDATE. Existing dialog transactions are therefore not used here for performance reasons.

These three techniques of program-driven data entry are sometimes encapsulated within function modules. The data to be entered is transferred through TABLES parameters of the function module in this case. The function module can then write the data to the database tables using

Batch input monitor

CALL TRANSACTION in function modules

CALL TRANSACTION or direct input or set up a batch input session for processing later. Using CALL TRANSACTION in a custom-developed function module is particularly useful if a suitable BAPI is not available.

1.4.2 Remote Function Call

You can also call ABAP function modules from external programs using the *Remote Function Call* (RFC) application protocol. RFC-enabled function modules are specifically identified in their properties as being remote-enabled. The properties for the DDIF_FIELDINFO_GET function module are displayed in Figure 1.15. It is identified as a remote-enabled function module in the Processing Type section, which means it can be called by external programs.

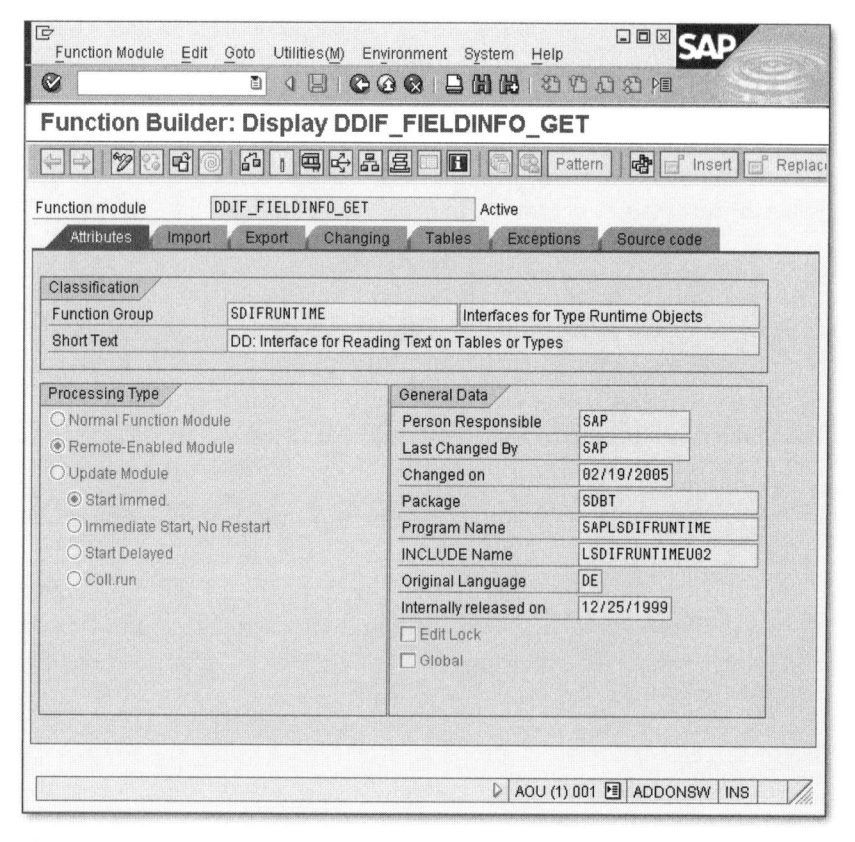

Figure 1.15 DDIF_FIELDINFO_GET RFC Function Module

All parameters with a reference to the ABAP Dictionary must be typed for remote-enabled modules, and the transfer type for import and export parameters must always be passed by vlaue. This means you must select the PASS VALUE selection field for all parameters. Only since Release 6.40 are remote-enabled function modules also able to have changing parameters.

Parameter typing

RFC Destinations

You call a function module from an ABAP program using the CALL FUNCTION command. If you want the function module to be executed in another system, you use the DESTINATION <dest> addition, whereby <dest> is a name maintained in Transaction SM59 (RFC Destinations). The technical information required by the calling system to reach the target system is maintained with the name in this transaction. We are particularly interested in two RFC connection types:

- Connection type 3: The target system is an SAP system.
- Connection type T: The target system is an external system.

If the target system is an SAP system, the technical information you maintain when creating an RFC destination includes details about the application host or message server, the gateway to be used, and the details for logging on to the target system.

ABAP target system

To create an RFC destination in Transaction SM59, click the Create button on the application toolbar. A dialog box then appears where you can enter the general destination attributes. These attributes include the name, a short description, and, in particular, the destination type.

To connect to an SAP system, choose Connection Type 3. As soon as you press Enter, the appearance of the screen changes (Figure 1.16). You can use the Yes/No fields of the Load Balancing option to choose whether the message server of the target system is to define an application server when the connection is being established or whether you want to communicate with a specific application server. In the first case, you must specify the host name or IP address of the message server, the system ID, and logon group; in the second, you specify the host name or IP address of the application server and the system number of the SAP instance.

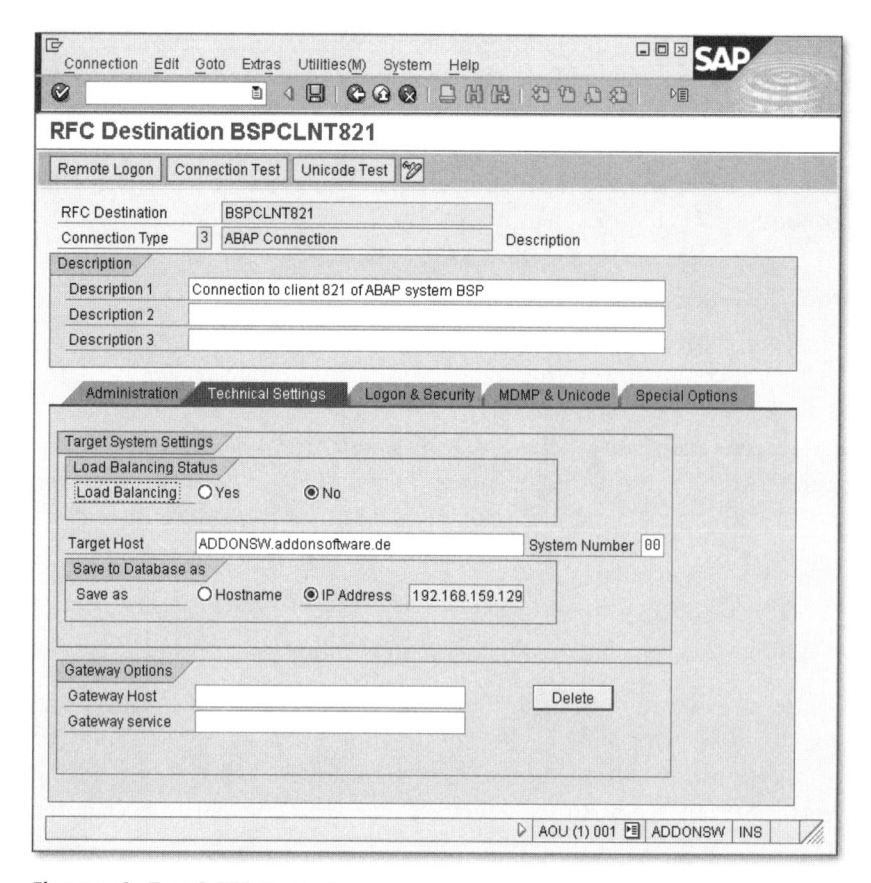

1 | Basic Principles of SAP Interface Programming

Figure 1.16 Type 3 RFC Destination

Lastly, you still have to specify the client, user and password, and language you want to use to log on to the target system. You can use the Connection Test button on the application toolbar to check whether a connection can be made to the other system. If you click the Remote Login button, a new SAP GUI session is started with the other system.

External target system

However, if the target system is an external system, in Transaction SM59, you must specify how this external system can be reached. An RFC destination to an external system is Connection Type T. As soon as you have entered the name, connection type, and description of the destination, press the [Enter] key. The screen will then look like the one shown in Figure 1.17.

There are four ways an external system can be reached:

- **Starting the program on the application server**
  You select the Start on Application Server option here. In the Program input field, you specify the path to an RFC server program on the application server. The program must be on the application server where the ABAP program that triggers the CALL FUNCTION command is executed. When called, the specified program is started on the application server and executes the required function.

- **Starting the program on an explicit host**
  You select the Start on Explicit Host option here. In the Target Host and Program input fields, you specify the host name and path to an RFC server program on this host. When called, the specified program is started on the specified host and executes the required function.

- **Starting the program on the presentation server**
  Here you specify the path to an RFC server program on the presentation server. For this, you select the Start on Front-End Work Station option. In the Program input field, you specify the path to an RFC server program on the frontend work station. The program must be on the work station of the user who executes the ABAP program using the CALL FUNCTION command. When called, the specified program is started on the work station of that user and executes the required function.

- **Registration**
  Here you specify a Program ID under which the external program is registered for an SAP gateway. The external program must therefore have already been started beforehand, irrespective of executing CALL FUNCTION. Like the destination name, the program ID is case-sensitive, so uppercase and lowercase spelling is important. It is also important that you specify the gateway on which the external program has been registered. To do this, you specify the name of the gateway host and gateway service in the two Gateway Host and Gateway Service fields. The gateway service is always called *sapgw<SYSNR>*, where *<SYSNR>* is the two-digit system number of the SAP instance to which the gateway belongs.

  Registering with the gateway

  In reality, the registration is probably the most important way and therefore also shown in Figure 1.17. The external program is started

1 Basic Principles of SAP Interface Programming

independently by a *Windows service* or a *UNIX daemon* and registered on a gateway under a program ID. You can use the external program functions from an ABAP program from this point onward.

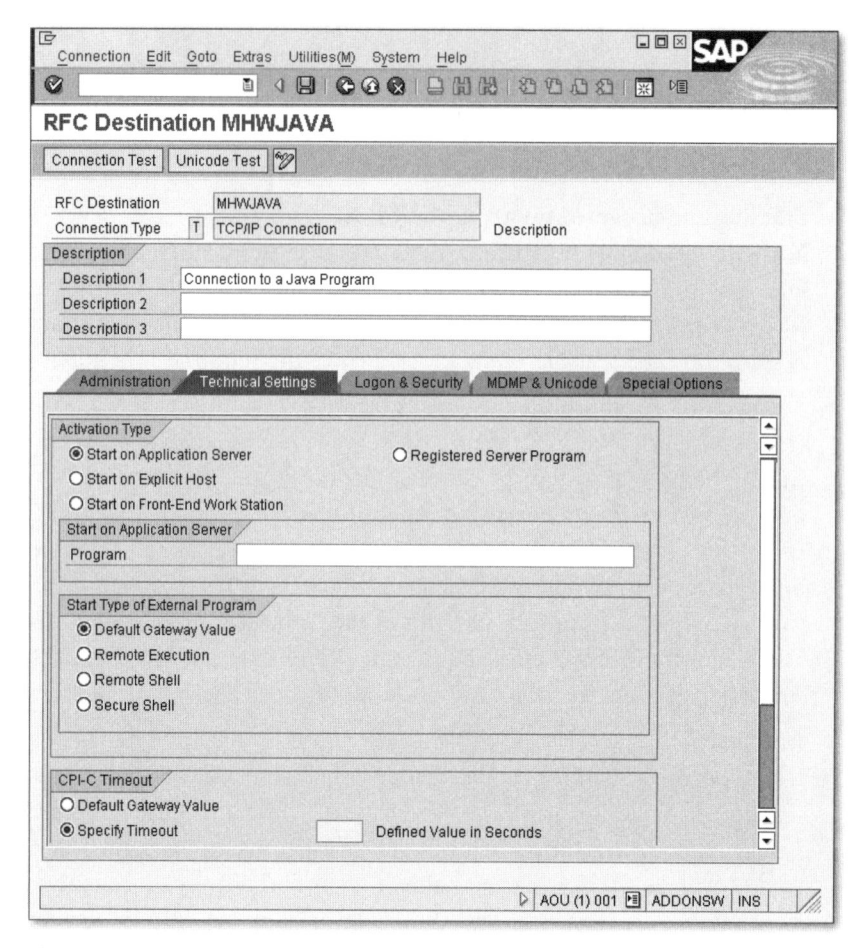

Figure 1.17 Type T RFC Destination with Registration

Specifying a destination when calling function modules

As soon as you have maintained a destination, and the connection test has been successful, you can use CALL FUNCTION ... DESTINATION ... to call function modules from an ABAP program. Follow the DESTINATION keyword with the name of the RFC destination as you maintained it in Transaction SM59.

Overview of SAP Interface Technologies | **1.4**

You can also test calling a function module in an external system using Transaction SE37, the Function Builder, without having to write an ABAP program. Enter the function module name in the initial screen of the Function Builder, and click the Test/Execute button ([F8]) on the application toolbar. In the next dialog box that appears for entering the transfer parameters, you can also enter the destination name. Be careful: This name is case-sensitive, so uppercase and lowercase spelling is also important here.

Testing in the Function Builder

RFC Types

Over time, SAP has developed four types of RFCs:

▶ **Synchronous RFC (sRFC)**
You use this normal RFC execution to read data in the called system.

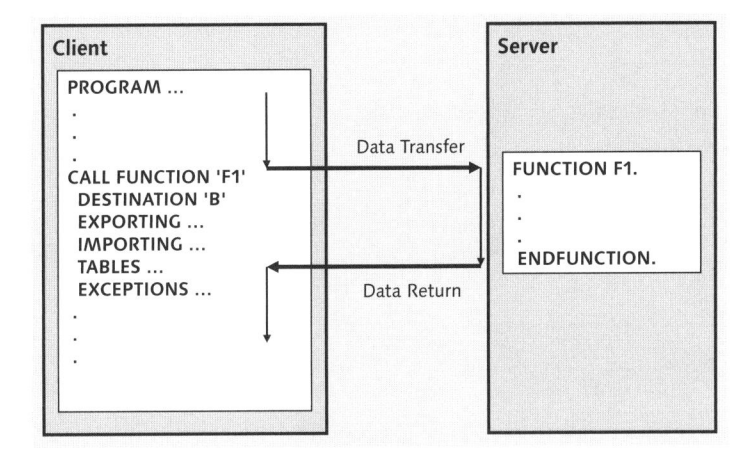

Figure 1.18 Synchronous RFC Process Schema

The synchronous RFC process schema is illustrated in Figure 1.18. The client calls the function module and waits until the function module has been processed. The client program then continues directly after the function module is called and can evaluate the exceptions and return parameters of the function module. An implicit database commit occurs in the client when the function module is called because the call begins a new dialog step and ends the old one. An implicit database commit also occurs in the target system after the function module is processed. The function module is therefore exe-

sRFC for reading data

77

cuted within a single database LUW. Synchronous RFC is normally used to read data.

- **Asynchronous RFC (aRFC)**
  Asynchronous RFC involves the client program continuing directly after the function module is called, without waiting for the called function module to be processed. This means tasks can be processed in parallel.

aRFC for load balancing

The asynchronous RFC process schema is illustrated in Figure 1.19. The client program continues directly after the function module is called, without waiting for the called function module to be processed. Therefore, neither the return parameters nor specific exceptions for the function module can be received and evaluated. When the function module is called, however, a FORM subroutine can be registered, which the system will call after the function module has been processed and where the return parameters for the function module can be received.

An implicit database commit also occurs here in the client after the function module is called, and the function module is also processed in a separate database LUW in the target system. Asynchronous RFC is used to process tasks in parallel. It is only available for ABAP programs, not external programs.

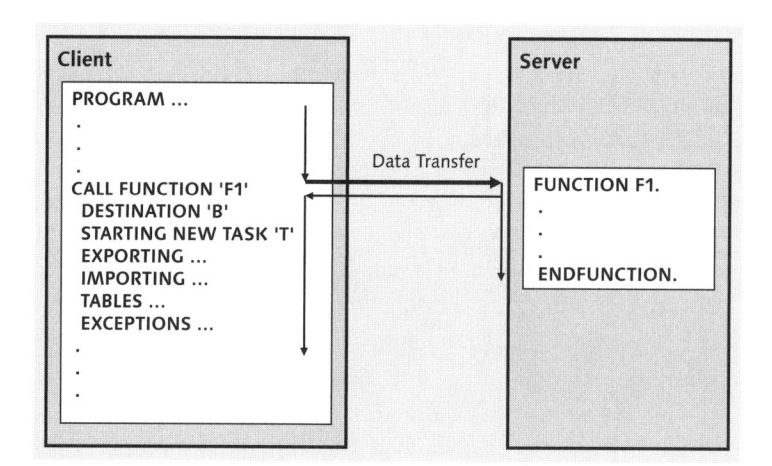

Figure 1.19 Asynchronous RFC Process Schema

▶ **Transactional RFC (tRFC)**
When the function module is called using import parameters with this type of RFC, a *transaction ID* (TID) is also specified. The function module is only executed specifically once on the server.

The transactional RFC process schema is illustrated in Figure 1.20. When the TID is received, the called system checks whether data has already been processed once with this TID. It will only execute the called function module if this is not the case. This ensures that data with the same TID is only processed once.

tRFC for writing data

If a system or connection error occurs, the client can save the data together with the TID and send it once again at a later stage. Even if the data on the called system had already been processed, for example, because a connection error only occurred when confirmation was being returned, the client can send the data with this TID any number of times. This guarantees that the data is only processed once.

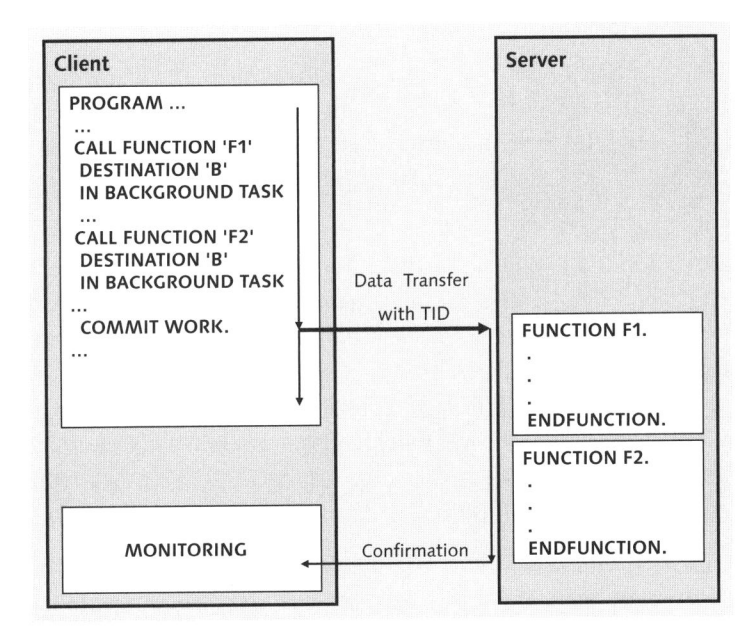

Figure 1.20 Transactional RFC Process Schema

Like asynchronous RFC, the client does not get back the function module return parameters here either. An implicit database commit is not executed when a function module is called on the client. The dialog step is only completed on the client when the explicit COMMIT WORK is executed. The called function modules are processed in a single database LUW on the server. tRFC is used to write or change data.

- **Queued RFC (qRFC)**
Queued RFC ensures that two tRFC packages that have been triggered in succession by the client are also processed one after the other by the server. The sender writes the tRFC packages into a queue for this purpose. The packages in this queue are then sent by tRFC to the receiver in the same sequence in which they were written in the queue. Using tRFC ensures that a tRFC package is also only specifically processed once if an error occurs. A package from the queue is only sent to the receiver when the receiver has safely received the previous package. This is the only way of guaranteeing that the processing sequence will be preserved.

Authorizations for RFC

Authorization checks occur within function modules, as they also do within every other ABAP program. This check verifies whether the user who executes the function module has *authorization* with the necessary field contents in one of the profiles assigned to his user master data record.

Authorization object

An authorization is an instance of an authorization object. The *authorization object* defines fields and possible values for these fields. For example, an authorization object field could be called ACTVT (for "activity") and its possible field contents could be 01 for displaying, 02 for creating, and 03 for changing data. Another field could be called BUKRS, and its possible field contents might be company code numbers. So if the user has authorization where 01 is set as the value for the ACTVT field and 1000 is set for BUKRS, he is allowed to display data for company code 1000.

Within his program, the ABAP programmer uses the AUTHORITY CHECK ABAP statement to check whether the user has the necessary authorization to perform the required action. If so, the program will continue; otherwise, it will terminate with an error message.

As well as authorization checks that occur in the function module, the ABAP runtime system also checks the S_RFC authorization object. This authorization object contains three fields:

Authorization object for function groups

- **RFC_NAME**
  This field contains the name of a function group.

- **ACTVT**
  This field can only have value 16 (Execute).

- **RFC_TYPE**
  This field always contains the FUGR (function group) value.

The S_RFC authorization object can be used to control whether an RFC user is allowed to execute function modules of a particular function group. Unfortunately, a limitation on specific function modules of a function group is not currently possible.

RFC users should only be given the authorizations absolutely necessary for them to be able to execute the function module(s) required for the task, so under no circumstances should they be assigned the SAP_ALL authorization profile. To find out which authorizations are required for a specific interface scenario, you can set the value of the auth/authorization_trace profile parameter in the SAP instance profile file to "y." Selecting this setting means the system will write the performed authorization checks and their result into the USOBX table. This is described in more detail in SAP Note 0543164.

Monitoring and Troubleshooting

An SAP system contains some tools for monitoring the execution of RFC calls and consequently informing you of errors. You can use Transaction ST22 to list and analyze *ABAP short dumps* that were triggered by RFC function modules. An ABAP short dump contains information on an error that has occurred and the part of the program where it happened. It also provides details on system variable contents, the call stack, and other useful information.

You can use the *Gateway Monitor* (Transaction SMGW) to display a gateway trace. To do this, you select the GOTO • TRACE • GATEWAY • DISPLAY FILE menu options.

RFC tracing — You can activate *RFC tracing* for a user in Transaction ST05. Until this setting is deactivated, an RFC trace will also be recorded for this user and can then be analyzed in Transaction ST05. RFC traces can also be recorded based on a destination. The TRACE flag is set for this when you maintain the destination in Transaction SM59. You can subsequently display this trace by selecting the RFC • DISPLAY TRACE menu options.

1.4.3 BAPIs

Business objects provide an object-oriented view of a major part of business data and transactions for an SAP system. You maintain object types of business objects in the *Business Object Repository* (BOR) using Transactions SWO1 and SWO. The components of such an object type are

- **Basic data**
  The technical data about the object type, such as the internal name, the release, or transport data.

- **Interfaces**
  The interfaces implemented by the object type.

- **Key fields**
  Fields whose contents uniquely identify an object type instance. They are often fields of database tables where the objects are stored persistently.

- **Attributes**
  The object type properties, either references to database fields or to other business objects.

- **Methods**
  Used to call transactions or function modules.

- **Events**
  Used in workflow definitions. Events are triggered through messages or status changes.

Business object methods — Some object type methods can be identified as Business Application Programming Interfaces (BAPIs). You always implement BAPIs as RFC function modules and can therefore use them like other RFC function modules. BAPIs also have other properties:

- **BAPIs have a stable interface.**
  SAP guarantees that a published BAPI interface is not changed incom-

patibly in a higher release. This means that optional parameters at most will be added in a higher release. But the BAPI normally remains untouched in higher releases. If there are function changes or enhancements, SAP provides a new BAPI with a new name. For example, the `BAPI_SALESORDER_CREATEFROMDATA` and `BAPI_SALESORDER_CREATE_FROMDAT1` BAPIs were provided for creating sales orders. BAPIs that have become obsolete are kept for two more releases at least, so that old clients can also work with the new release.

- **BAPIs do not have a presentation layer.**
  BAPIs do not call dynpros using `CALL SCREEN`. They only communicate through the interface of their implementing function module. If BAPI results are to be displayed, the caller will be responsible for this. BAPIs can therefore also be used in programs where two hosts are to communicate between each other without user intervention.

- **BAPIs do not trigger exceptions.**
  BAPIs use the `RETURN` export parameter for success, warning, and error confirmations. Depending on the BAPI, this parameter is a `BAPIRETURN`, `BAPIRETURN1`, `BAPIRET1`, or `BAPIRET2` type structure or an internal table with these line types. All these structures have the following two important fields in common:
  - `TYPE`
    This field can include the values S (for Success), E (for Error), W (for Warning), or I (for Information). This field may also contain a space instead of the value S.
  - `MESSAGE`
    This field contains a message text with information about an error.

- **Databases are updated in the update task.** *Transaction concept for BAPIs*
  BAPIs always perform database updates by calling an update module using `CALL FUNCTION IN BACKGROUND TASK`. A `COMMIT WORK` or `ROLLBACK WORK` is not programmed within the BAPI. The following two BAPIs are available to actually perform or reject the database update:
  - `BAPI_TRANSACTION_COMMIT`
    Performs all allocated update tasks. You can specify in an import parameter for this BAPI whether you want the database to be updated synchronously or asynchronously.

1 Basic Principles of SAP Interface Programming

▶ BAPI_TRANSACTION_ROLLBACK
Rejects the allocated database updates.

Standard BAPIs Most business objects provide the following standard BAPIs:

▶ GetList
Search criteria can generally be transferred to this BAPI. A table containing all object keys corresponding to this search criteria is returned as the result.

▶ GetDetail
This BAPI requires an object key as an import parameter. It returns the other attributes for the object.

▶ Change
With this BAPI, by specifying an object key and the new attributes, you can change the previous object attributes.

▶ CreateFromData
With this BAPI, you can specify the attributes of a new object to be created. The key of the new object to be created is returned.

Transaction BAPI You can use Transaction BAPI to display a list of all business objects and their BAPIs. The display is either arranged by application area or alphabetically by business object. Transaction BAPI provides detailed documentation for every business object, its BAPIs, and their parameters. From this transaction, you can also call the tools used to test and manage BAPIs.

Transaction BAPI differentiates between instance-dependent and instance-independent BAPIs. To call *instance-dependent BAPIs*, you must specify a business object key. The standard GetDetail and Change BAPIs are examples of instance-dependent BAPIs. *Instance-independent BAPIs* in contrast do not need a key specified for them. They work independently of an object instance. Examples are the standard GetList and CreateFromData BAPIs.

1.4.4 Application Link Enabling

Application Link Enabling (ALE) provides services and tools within SAP systems to exchange messages between applications in different systems. The messages are normally exchanged by sending and receiving electronic documents known as *Intermediate Documents* (IDocs). The purpose of sending these messages is to implement shared business processes. ALE enables customizing data, master data, and application data to be shared on different systems.

One example is the delivery of sales orders in SAP ERP. As soon as it has been established when certain goods will be delivered to certain customers, the SAP system sends a delivery order to an external warehouse. The goods are loaded onto pallets and trucks there. As soon as the truck moves off with the delivery, an order confirmation is sent back to the SAP system. Apart from delivery orders and order confirmations, customer and material master data must also be exchanged in this scenario.

A diagram of the ALE architecture is illustrated in Figure 1.21. The sending application is responsible for setting up the IDoc, possibly determining the receivers and transferring the IDoc to the ALE layer.

ALE architecture

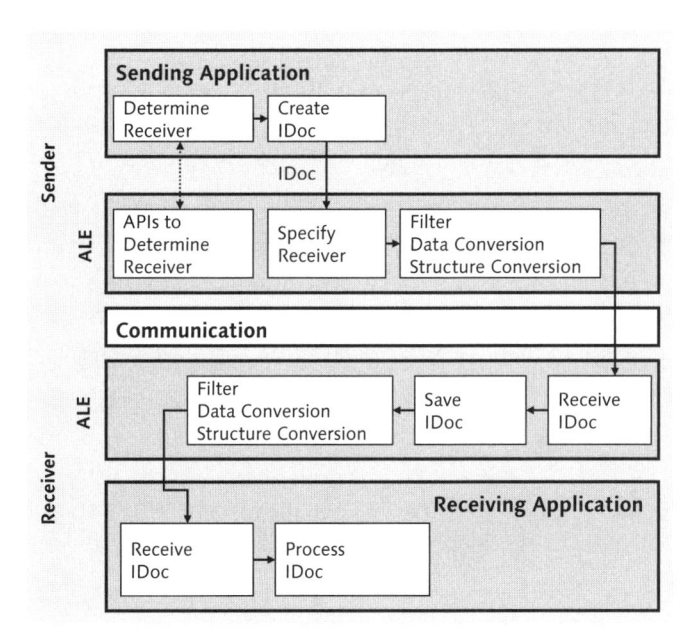

Figure 1.21 ALE Architecture

After the IDoc is received, the ALE layer determines the receivers, if this has not already been done by the sending application. The IDoc is then processed further according to configurable rules: Individual fields or segments can be filtered, data converted, or the IDoc structure adapted to the structure of older releases. An IDoc is created for every receiver in this case and transferred to the communication layer for transporting further.

The communication layer forwards the IDoc to the target system. The IDOC_INBOUND_ASYNCHRONOUS function module is normally called for this in the target system through tRFC. But you can also configure other transport mechanisms such as the transfer of data through the file system.

After it is received, the IDoc is stored in the target system and forwarded to the ALE layer. Like in the sender, in the ALE layer, the received IDoc can go through some more processing steps before it is forwarded to a function module of the receiving application.

Logical systems Senders and receivers in the ALE context are referred to as *logical systems*. Logical systems are identified by names that are 10 characters long. You maintain logical system names in Transaction SALE as part of ALE Customizing. A short description of the logical system is also stored there in addition to a name. Every client in an SAP system gets a logical name. It generally consists of the system ID and client, for example, UL0CLNT800 for the logical system, which corresponds to client 800 in the UL0 system.

Messages Messages are exchanged between logical systems with ALE. You maintain the names of possible messages together with a short description in Transaction WE81. For instance, the MATMAS message (material master) stands for an exchange of material master data, and the DELVRY message (delivery) describes an exchange of delivery orders.

Intermediate Documents

Messages between two logical systems are sent in the form of intermediate documents (IDocs). These documents contain data to be exchanged.

IDoc segments An IDoc is made up of data records also known as *segments*. Each segment begins with a header 63 bytes long, followed by the actual data up to 1,000 characters in length. The header in every segment has the same structure and the entire IDoc follows a hierarchical structure: Each segment can point to a parent segment located above the corresponding segment in the hierarchy (Table 1.6).

You define IDoc segments in Transaction WE31. You give the segments a name and short description there. But above all, you give the SDATA field structure a more detailed description.

Field	Length	Description
SEGNAM	30	Type name of segment. This defines the SDATA data field structure.
MANDT	3	SAP client number.
DOCNUM	16	Unique IDoc number to which this segment belongs.
SEGNUM	6	Sequential segment number within the IDoc.
PSGNUM	6	Sequential number of parent segment.
HLEVEL	2	Hierarchy level of this segment.
SDATA	1,000	Actual application data.

Table 1.6 IDoc Segment Structure

An IDoc segment can be found in several *IDoc types*. You define IDoc types in Transaction WE30. In doing so, you determine which segments are found in the IDoc type, whether the segment in question is optional, how many segments of this type maximum can be found, and which are the child segments of the segment in this IDoc type.

An IDoc type is assigned to one or more *message types*. For example, you can use the ORDERS04 IDoc to transport ORDER (purchase order) or ORDRSP (order confirmation) messages. You assign messages to IDoc types in Transaction WE82. The SAP NetWeaver AS ABAP release and message name determine the IDoc type uniquely in this case. IDoc types used, for instance, are ORDERS01 as of Release 3.0, ORDERS02 as of Release 3.0D, ORDERS03 as of Release 4.0A, and ORDERS04 as of Release 4.5A.

Message types

ALE Distribution Model

Which messages will be sent to which receivers by a sender is defined in a *distribution model* as part of ALE Customizing. The distribution model has a hierarchical structure with the sender system as its root. Under the sender system is the list of receiving systems, under that the messages, and under that the filters to be used on the messages.

1 | Basic Principles of SAP Interface Programming

ALE configuration
You maintain the settings in the ALE system in Transaction SALE. This transaction is a subset of the *SAP Implementation Guide,* which you can access in project management (Transaction SPRO) by selecting the SAP Reference Implementation Guide button. The steps required to set the ALE system are listed in this transaction. In the simplest case, they are the following steps:

1. Name the logical systems.
2. Assign a logical system to each SAP client.
3. Use Transaction SM59 to create tRFC destinations for the logical systems. To enable other definitions to be generated automatically in a later step, you should name the destination for a logical system exactly like the logical system itself.
4. Maintain the distribution model by defining which messages will be sent to specific receivers and the filters that will be used to do this. You can generate partner profiles from maintaining the distribution model. Partner profiles control the processing of inbound and outbound IDocs.

Partner profiles
5. Check the automatically generated partner profiles. Important distribution profile parameters are

   - **Outbound port**
     The outbound port defines how a partner can be reached. When the partner profiles are generated, the ports are created automatically if the logical systems and tRFC destinations created for them have the same name.

   - **Sending and processing mode**
     IDocs can either be sent and processed immediately or accumulated until a package containing a defined number of IDocs has been produced. The IDocs in this package are then sent and processed together.

   - **Package size**
     You can specify the size of the packages to be sent and processed.

Transaction SALE also provides access to many other functions for configuring IDoc processing and monitoring.

BAPIs and ALE

Calling BAPIs asynchronously
Since SAP R/3 Release 4.0, BAPIs can also be called asynchronously through ALE. In fact, all new asynchronous interfaces (IDocs) since this

release are based on BAPIs. You can generate the necessary definitions for a given BAPI in Transaction BDBG:

- **Message type**
  A message type is generated for a BAPI.

- **IDoc type**
  Segments are generated for the BAPI export parameters, as is an IDoc type that can be used to transport these parameters. The IDoc type is assigned to the generated message type.

- **Outbound function module**
  This function module has the same import parameters as the BAPI and is called by the sending application instead of the BAPI. It creates an IDoc from the transfer parameters and transfers it to the ALE services for further processing.

- **Inbound function module**
  The ALE services use this function module to process the inbound IDoc. The function module extracts the data from the IDoc and calls the corresponding BAPI in the receiving system.

The generated message type can then be used like every other message type when an ALE distribution model is being created. If an application wants to call BAPIs in external systems, it proceeds as follows:

1. **Querying filters**
   The `ALE_BAPI_GET_FILTEROBJECTS` function module is called to determine filter objects for a specific BAPI that were created when the distribution model was being maintained.

   Using the ALE BAPI interface

2. **Querying receivers**
   The `ALE_ASYNC_BAPI_GET_RECEIVER` function module is called to get a list of logical receiving systems from the distribution models. The calling application must transfer the table of filter objects for this purpose.

3. **Calling the BAPI asynchronously**
   The generated outbound function module for which (apart from the BAPI import parameters) the list of receiving systems is also specified is now called.

4. **COMMIT WORK**
   Finally, the application must ensure it forwards the generated IDoc to the ALE layer using the `COMMIT WORK` ABAP command.

1 | Basic Principles of SAP Interface Programming

This procedure means BAPI calls can be sent from one application to another as IDocs.

1.4.5 SOAP

Since Release 6.20, SOAP (*Service-Oriented Architecture Protocol*) services and clients can also be implemented using SAP NetWeaver AS ABAP. SOAP over HTTP involves the SOAP client sending a request in the form of an XML SOAP document to a SOAP server that replies with an XML SOAP document.

Internet Connection Manager

SAP NetWeaver AS ABAP calls a SOAP web service over HTTP POST. The call is first received by the *Internet Connection Manager* (ICM). You can use Transaction SMICM to view and change the ICM configuration. By selecting the GOTO • SERVICES menu options, you can see the TCP port on which the ICM receives HTTP requests. You can view the configured J2EE server ports (for a double-stack system) and a table of URL prefixes by choosing the GOTO • HTTP SERVER • DISPLAY DATA menu options. If an HTTP client requests a URL that begins with one of these prefixes, the ICM forwards the request to the *Internet Connection Framework* (ICF) on the ABAP stack; otherwise, it forwards it to the configured J2EE server.

Internet Connection Framework

You view the configured services in the ICF in Transaction SICF. Choose Service as the Hierarchy Type on the selection screen that appears when you start the transaction. A list of all HTTP services configured in the ICF is subsequently displayed. SOAP web services are implemented by SAP NetWeaver AS ABAP 7.0 through the services under the /sap/bc/srt node. You will see the IDoc (SOAP entry for IDoc), rfc (SOAP runtime for RFC), and xip (SOAP runtime for XI message interface) nodes directly under this node.

If you double-click the srt entry, you will see on the Handler List tab that the CL_SOAP_HTTP_EXTENSION ABAP class is entered as the handler for requests whose URL path begins with */sap/bc/srt/rfc*. The ICF analyzes the URL path of the request and forwards it to the corresponding handler class.

Web service

In Chapter 6, Service-Oriented Architecture Protocol, we will show you how to create a web service in the Object Navigator. After you create it, you will have to release a web service for the SOAP runtime environment in Transaction WSCONFIG. You can use Transaction WSADMIN to change trace and log settings for web services, call the WSDL file (*Web Service Description Language*) for a web service, and test a web service. SAP provides the `wsnavigator` application on every SAP NetWeaver AS Java for this test. A URL on the web service WSDL can be transferred to this application. From the WSDL, it then creates a graphical user interface through which the web service can be tested.

To ensure you can test a web service from Transaction WSADMIN, select the GOTO • SETTINGS • ADMINISTRATION menu path to enter the URL for SAP NetWeaver AS Java in the form of *http://<javaserver>:<httport>*. As soon as you have configured SAP NetWeaver AS Java, you can click the Web Service Homepage button ($\boxed{\text{Ctrl}}$ + $\boxed{\text{F8}}$) to start a browser that will navigate to the `wsnavigator` application on the configured SAP NetWeaver AS Java. From there you can test the web service. Figure 1.22 shows the test screen for the SRT_TESTS_FB_ADD_WS web service.

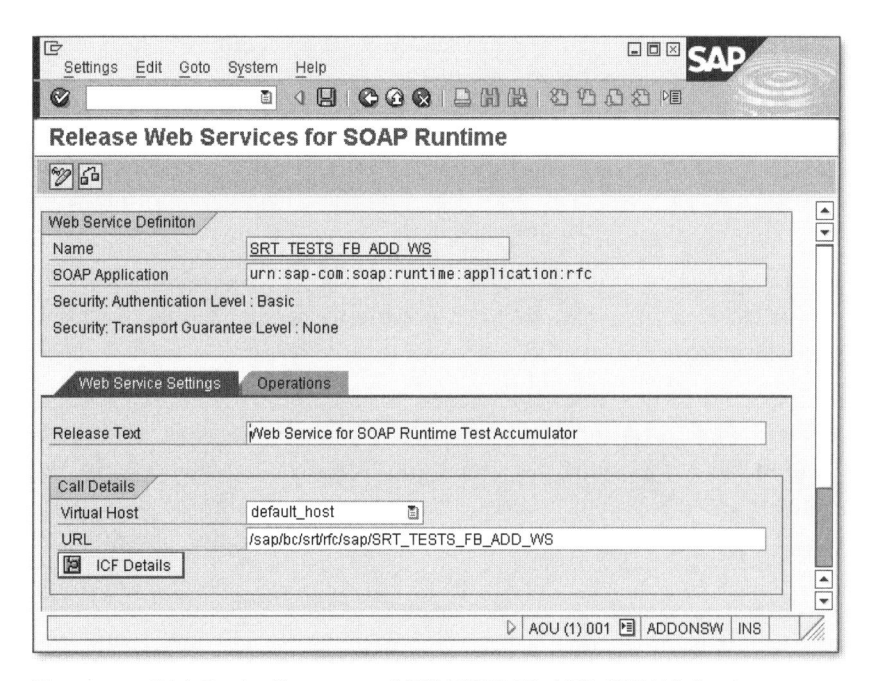

Figure 1.22 Web Service Homepage of SRT_TESTS_FB_ADD_WS Web Service

1 | Basic Principles of SAP Interface Programming

1.4.6 XI SOAP

SAP NetWeaver PI and XI

With *SAP NetWeaver Process Integration* (SAP NetWeaver PI, formerly *SAP Exchange Infrastructure*, SAP NetWeaver XI), SAP provides a central platform for distributing application messages. The central *integration engine* within an SAP NetWeaver PI system communicates in this case with an SAP-specific version of SOAP over HTTP. This protocol is generally referred to as *XI SOAP*.

With this SOAP version, the HTTP body contains a MIME document (*Multipurpose Internet Mail Extensions*) consisting of a SOAP document and the actual message as an attachment. This means that — unlike standard SOAP — any number of binary files can be sent without the need to convert code. The SOAP header of an XI SOAP message contains SAP-specific information about the sender, message interface used, and required *quality of service*. The quality of service can take one of the following three values:

- **Best Effort (BE)**
  Communication occurs synchronously. If a communication error occurs, the client must repeat the call.

- **Exactly Once (EO)**
  Communication occurs asynchronously. If a communication error occurs, the message can be resent from the technical monitors. This value makes sure the message is only processed once.

- **Exactly Once In Order (EOIO)**
  Communication occurs like EO, but the processing sequence of several messages is also adhered to.

Transaction SPROXY

As we will show you in Chapter 7, SAP NetWeaver Process Integration, it is very easy on SAP NetWeaver AS ABAP to create client and server applications that use XI SOAP for communicating. First we will describe the outbound and inbound message interfaces in the *Integration Repository* of the SAP NetWeaver PI system. Then we will use Transaction SPROXY on SAP NetWeaver AS ABAP to create proxy classes that an application can use to send or receive messages with XI SOAP. Figure 1.23 shows Transaction SPROXY for the `Booking_Order_Confirmation_In` inbound message interface.

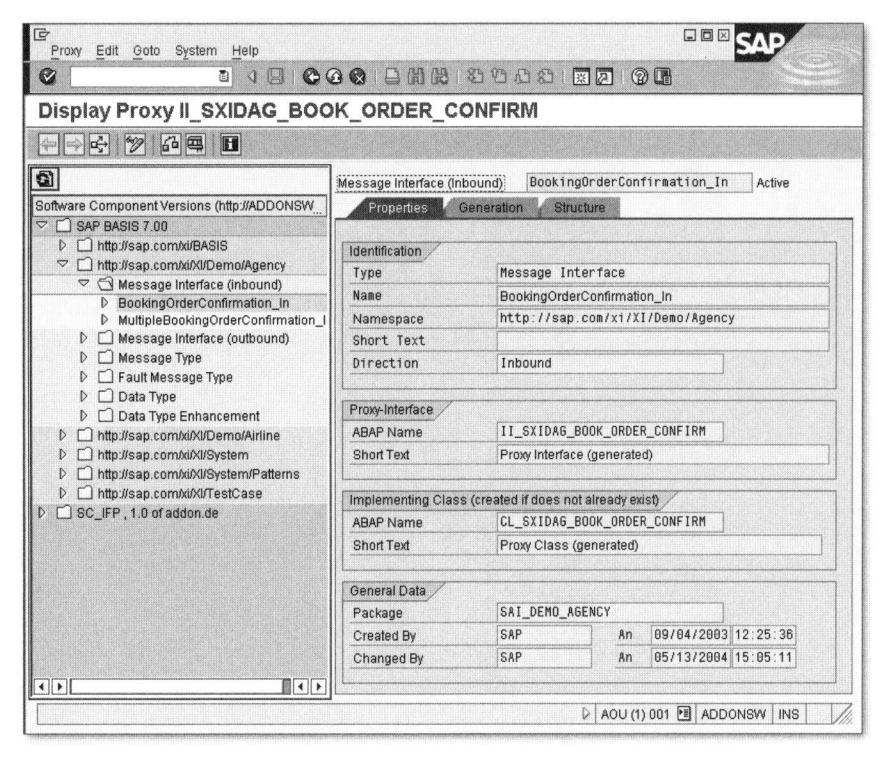

Figure 1.23 Transaction SPROXY for an Inbound Message Interface

This chapter details the interface programming process in ABAP using RFC and BAPIs. You learn how to develop RFC function modules for reading, writing, and changing data records and how to use these function modules for developing a business object and its BAPIs.

2 Remote Function Call with ABAP

Remote Function Call (RFC) is the SAP interface technology that enables you to call function modules in another system. This chapter describes the forms of RFCs and explains business objects and their BAPIs (Business Application Programming Interfaces) as specific RFC function modules. The example, which was introduced in Chapter 1, Section 1.3, Programming SAP NetWeaver AS ABAP, is used to show you how to program RFC clients and RFC servers using the programming language, ABAP.

2.1 RFC Function Modules in ABAP

In this section, you develop some function modules that enable you to create, change, and delete customer purchase orders. These function modules are intended to be available for use by external systems; that is, they are RFC-enabled. These function modules are to be created in the ZIFP function group.

2.1.1 Function Modules for Reading

First, we will create function modules for reading customer purchase orders and vendor purchase orders. Every purchase order is clearly defined by its ORDERID. These ORDERIDs, however, are usually not known to the orderer because they are created when the sales order is created on the vendor side. Therefore, you first need a function module that provides a table of all ORDERIDs in case of a given purchase order category and an optional REFID. If you only specify the purchase order category,

Reading customer purchase orders and vendor purchase orders

the function module returns all order IDs of this category. If you specify the REFID (the customer purchase order ID), the function module returns the vendor purchase order ID for a customer purchase order ID. Listing 2.1 shows the source code of the Z_IFP_ORER_GETLIST function module, which performs this task.

```
FUNCTION z_ifp_order_getlist.
*"----------------------------------------------------------
*"*"Local interface:
*"  IMPORTING
*"     VALUE(IM_ORDERTYPE) TYPE  ZIFPORDERTYPE DEFAULT 'SO'
*"     VALUE(IM_REFID)     TYPE  ZIFPREFID OPTIONAL
*"  TABLES
*"      TA_ORDERS STRUCTURE  ZIFPORDER
*"  EXCEPTIONS
*"     NOT_AUTHORIZED
*"     NO_DATA
*"----------------------------------------------------------
  AUTHORITY-CHECK OBJECT 'ZIFPORDER' ID 'ACTVT' FIELD '03'.
  IF sy-subrc NE 0.
    RAISE not_authorized.
  ENDIF.
  IF NOT im_refid IS INITIAL.
    SELECT * FROM zifporder INTO TABLE ta_orders WHERE
      type  = im_ordertype AND
      refid = im_refid.
  ELSE.
    SELECT * FROM zifporder INTO TABLE ta_orders WHERE
      type  = im_ordertype.
  ENDIF.
  IF sy-subrc NE 0.
    RAISE no_data.
  ENDIF.
ENDFUNCTION.
```

Listing 2.1 "Z_IFP_ORDER_GETLIST" Function Module

This function module defines the two optional import parameters, IM_ORDERTYPE and IM_REFID, in its interface. IM_ORDERTYPE is provided with the 'SO' default value so that the function module searches for sales orders if the 'PO' value isn't explicitly assigned to IM_ORDERTYPE. The function module then writes the found purchase orders into the TA_ORDERS table parameter.

The function module first checks whether the calling program is authorized to read purchase orders. If the calling program isn't authorized to read purchase orders, the function module raises the NOT_AUTHORIZED exception. Then, the function module uses a SELECT command to read purchase orders from the database and considers the import parameters in the WHERE condition. If it cannot find any data, it raises the NO_DATA exception.

Authorization check

The next function module, Z_IFP_ORDER_GETDETAIL, provides details on a purchase order if the ORDERID is known. Listing 2.2 shows the source code of this function module. The interface defines an import parameter for the ORDERID, an export parameter for the header of the purchase order, a table parameter for the purchase order item, and the NOT_AUTHORIZED and NO_DATA exceptions.

```
FUNCTION z_ifp_order_getdetail.
*"----------------------------------------------------------
*"*"Local interface:
*"  IMPORTING
*"     VALUE(IM_ORDERID)   TYPE   ZIFPORDERID
*"  EXPORTING
*"     VALUE(EX_ORDERHEAD) TYPE   ZIFPORDER
*"  TABLES
*"     TA_ORDERPOS STRUCTURE   ZIFPORDERPOS
*"  EXCEPTIONS
*"     NOT_AUTHORIZED
*"     NO_DATA
*"----------------------------------------------------------
  AUTHORITY-CHECK OBJECT 'ZIFPORDER' ID 'ACTVT' FIELD '03'.
  IF sy-subrc NE 0.
    RAISE not_authorized.
  ENDIF.
  SELECT SINGLE * FROM zifporder INTO ex_orderhead WHERE
      orderid = im_orderid.
  IF sy-subrc NE 0.
    RAISE no_data.
  ELSE.
    SELECT * FROM zifporderpos INTO TABLE ta_orderpos WHERE
      orderid = im_orderid.
  ENDIF.
ENDFUNCTION.
```

Listing 2.2 "Z_IFP_ORDER_GETDETAIL" Function Module

Scalar and structured parameters

The `IM_ORDERID` import parameter must contain the `ORDERID` of the required purchase order when called. The import parameter is of the `ZIFPORDERID` category; that is, it directly refers to a data element. Consequently, it is a *scalar parameter*. After the call, the `EX_ORDERHEAD` export parameter contains the header data of the purchase order, while the `TA_ORDERPOS` table parameter contains the purchase order items.

If you specify a non-existing `ORDERID` in the `IM_ORDERID` import parameter, the function module raises the `NO_DATA` exception, and the export and table parameters remain initial. This means that they keep their type-specific initial values (zero for numeric, spaces for character-like variables). The export parameter is of the `ZIFPORDER` category; that is, it refers to a transparent table in the data dictionary. This parameter is a *structured parameter*.

Pass by value

Both import and export parameters of an RFC-enabled function module need to be passed by values. You cannot use the pass by reference method here. Ensure that the Remote radio button is selected in the properties of the function modules.

2.1.2 Call via sRFC

Listing 2.3 shows the source code of a report that calls the two function modules via sRFC (synchronous RFC). This is done using the `CALL FUNCTION ... DESTINATION p_dest ...` ABAP statement. The `p_dest` variable has been declared with the `PARAMETERS` statement and is of the `RFCDEST` category. The `PARAMETERS` statement ensures that the system generates a selection screen that is displayed during the start. The selection screen contains an input field in which the user can enter a value for the `p_dest` variable. The value must be the name of a valid RFC destination that has been maintained using Transaction SM59.

```
*&---------------------------------------------------------------
*& Report  ZIFP_ORDERS_READ
*&---------------------------------------------------------------
REPORT  zifp_orders_read.
DATA:
  it_orderhead TYPE STANDARD TABLE OF zifporder,
  wa_orderhead TYPE zifporder,
  it_orderpos  TYPE STANDARD TABLE OF zifporderpos,
  wa_orderpos  TYPE zifporderpos,
  msg_text(80) TYPE c.
```

```abap
PARAMETERS:
  p_dest TYPE rfcdest.
START-OF-SELECTION.
*Get list of the ORDERIDs
  CALL FUNCTION 'Z_IFP_ORDER_GETLIST'
    DESTINATION p_dest
    TABLES
      ta_orders             = it_orderhead
    EXCEPTIONS
      not_authorized        = 1
      no_data               = 2
      system_failure        = 3  MESSAGE msg_text
      communication_failure = 4  MESSAGE msg_text
      OTHERS                = 5.
  IF sy-subrc <> 0.
    WRITE:/ msg_text.
  ENDIF.
* Output all purchase orders
  LOOP AT it_orderhead INTO wa_orderhead.
    WRITE:/
      wa_orderhead-orderid COLOR COL_KEY,
      wa_orderhead-type,
      wa_orderhead-refid,
      wa_orderhead-buyer,
      wa_orderhead-seller,
      wa_orderhead-orderdate.
* Get purchase order details
    CALL FUNCTION 'Z_IFP_ORDER_GETDETAIL'
      DESTINATION p_dest
      EXPORTING
        im_orderid            = wa_orderhead-orderid
*     IMPORTING
*       EX_ORDERHEAD          =
      TABLES
        ta_orderpos           = it_orderpos
      EXCEPTIONS
        not_authorized        = 1
        no_data               = 2
        system_failure        = 3  MESSAGE msg_text
        communication_failure = 4  MESSAGE msg_text
        OTHERS                = 5.
    IF sy-subrc <> 0.
      WRITE:/ msg_text.
    ENDIF.
```

```
* Output purchase order details
    LOOP AT it_orderpos INTO wa_orderpos.
      WRITE:/
        wa_orderpos-orderid COLOR COL_KEY,
        wa_orderpos-orderpos COLOR COL_KEY,
        wa_orderpos-matid,
        wa_orderpos-mattext,
        wa_orderpos-ordercount,
        wa_orderpos-price,
        wa_orderpos-currency.
    ENDLOOP.
    ULINE.
  ENDLOOP.
```

Listing 2.3 "ZIFP_ORDERS_READ" Report

System exceptions | As the source code illustrates, the calling program should respond not only to exceptions that are defined in the function modules' interfaces but also to the two system exceptions, system_failure and communication_failure. The system_failure exception is raised for system errors, for example, if the called function module doesn't exist in the target system. The communication_failure exception is raised for communication errors, for example, if the target system isn't available or the defined destination hasn't been maintained. For both errors, the MESSAGE addition enables you to store the system message in a variable of the C category to display the system information on the error.

In addition to the destinations that are maintained using Transaction SM59, there are also three *standard destinations*: SPACE, 'NONE', and 'BACK'. If p_dest is initial or the SPACE constant is used instead, the function module is called locally. If p_dest contains the 'NONE' value, the function module is also called locally. The call, however, is directed to the gateway of the current SAP instance and treated as an external call. If only one system is available, you can use this destination for an RFC test. If you want to call a function module from an RFC module in the calling system, you can use the 'BACK' destination. It serves to recall the calling program.

Implicit database commit | After each CALL FUNCTION, a commit is implicitly executed on the database in the calling system. Changes to the database that were made prior to the function call with INSERT, UPDATE, MODIFY, or DELETE can then no longer be undone. In the called system, an implicit commit is also executed in the database; that is, every RFC function call corresponds to a dialog step. The sRFC in this form is therefore only suited for reading, not implementing, cross-system transactions.

2.1.3 Function Modules for Deleting and Changing

Listing 2.4 shows the source code of the Z_IFP_ORDER_CHANGE function module, which enables you to change the data of a purchase order.

Changing purchase order data

```
FUNCTION z_ifp_order_change.
*"----------------------------------------------------------
*"*"Local interface:
*"  IMPORTING
*"     VALUE(IM_ORDERHEADER)  TYPE   ZIFPORDER
*"     VALUE(IM_ORDERHEADERX) TYPE   ZIFPORDERX
*"     VALUE(IM_TESTRUN)      TYPE   CHAR1 DEFAULT SPACE
*"     VALUE(IM_COMMIT)       TYPE   CHAR1 DEFAULT SPACE
*"  TABLES
*"     TA_ORDERPOS   STRUCTURE  ZIFPORDERPOS
*"     TA_ORDERPOSX STRUCTURE  ZIFPORDERPOSX
*"  EXCEPTIONS
*"     NOT_AUTHORIZED
*"     NO_DATA
*"     NO_LOCK
*"----------------------------------------------------------
  DATA:
    orderheader_old TYPE zifporder,
    orderpos_old    TYPE zifporderpos,
    orderpos_new    TYPE zifporderpos,
    orderposx       TYPE zifporderposx.
  AUTHORITY-CHECK OBJECT 'ZIFPORDER' ID 'ACTVT' FIELD '02'.
  IF sy-subrc NE 0.
    RAISE not_authorized.
  ENDIF.
  CALL FUNCTION 'ENQUEUE_EZIFPORDER'
    EXPORTING
      orderid = im_orderheader-orderid
    EXCEPTIONS
      OTHERS  = 1.
  IF sy-subrc <> 0.
    RAISE no_lock.
  ENDIF.
  SELECT SINGLE * FROM zifporder
    INTO orderheader_old
```

```abap
          WHERE orderid = im_orderheader-orderid.
  IF sy-subrc <> 0.
    CALL FUNCTION 'DEQUEUE_EZIFPORDER'
      EXPORTING
        orderid = im_orderheader-orderid.
    RAISE no_data.
  ELSE.
    IF im_testrun IS INITIAL.
      IF NOT im_orderheaderx-type IS INITIAL.
        orderheader_old-type     = im_orderheader-type.
      ENDIF.
      IF NOT im_orderheaderx-refid IS INITIAL.
        orderheader_old-refid    = im_orderheader-refid.
      ENDIF.
      IF NOT im_orderheaderx-buyer IS INITIAL.
        orderheader_old-buyer    = im_orderheader-buyer.
      ENDIF.
      IF NOT im_orderheaderx-seller IS INITIAL.
        orderheader_old-seller   = im_orderheader-seller.
      ENDIF.
      IF NOT im_orderheaderx-orderdate IS INITIAL.
        orderheader_old-orderdate =
          im_orderheader-orderdate.
      ENDIF.
      CALL FUNCTION 'Z_IFP_V_UPDATE_ORDER'
        IN UPDATE TASK
        EXPORTING
          im_orderheader = orderheader_old.
    ENDIF.
  ENDIF.
  LOOP AT ta_orderpos INTO orderpos_new.
    READ TABLE ta_orderposx INTO orderposx INDEX sy-index.
    SELECT SINGLE * FROM zifporderpos
      INTO orderpos_old
      WHERE
      orderid  = orderpos_new-orderid AND
      orderpos = orderpos_new-orderpos.
    IF sy-subrc <> 0.
      CALL FUNCTION 'DEQUEUE_EZIFPORDER'
        EXPORTING
          orderid = im_orderheader-orderid.
      ROLLBACK WORK.
      RAISE no_data.
    ELSE.
```

```
      IF im_testrun IS INITIAL.
        IF NOT orderposx-matid IS INITIAL.
          orderpos_old-matid    = orderpos_new-matid.
        ENDIF.
        IF NOT orderposx-mattext IS INITIAL.
          orderpos_old-mattext  = orderpos_new-mattext.
        ENDIF.
        IF NOT orderposx-ordercount IS INITIAL.
          orderpos_old-ordercount = orderpos_new-ordercount.
        ENDIF.
        IF NOT orderposx-price IS INITIAL.
          orderpos_old-price    = orderpos_new-price.
        ENDIF.
        IF NOT orderposx-currency IS INITIAL.
          orderpos_old-currency = orderpos_new-currency.
        ENDIF.
        CALL FUNCTION 'Z_IFP_V_UPDATE_ORDERPOS'
          IN UPDATE TASK
          EXPORTING
            im_orderpos = orderpos_old.
      ENDIF.
    ENDIF.
  ENDLOOP.
  IF im_commit = 'X'.
    COMMIT WORK.
    CALL FUNCTION 'DEQUEUE_ALL'.
  ENDIF.
ENDFUNCTION.
```

Listing 2.4 "Z_IFP_ORDER_CHANGE" Function Module

The function module contains the structured import parameter, IM_ORDER_HEADER, for the header data and the TA_ORDERPOS table parameter for the item data of the purchase order. The IM_ORDER_HEADER-ORDERID field clearly identifies the purchase order. The function module doesn't implement the database changes directly but calls the update modules from Section 1.3.5, Update Modules, using the IN UPDATE TASK addition. The optional import parameter, IM_COMMIT, controls whether the function module itself triggers a COMMIT WORK.

The function module contains a second import parameter for every import parameter with the data that needs to be changed. In this second parameter, the calling program can define which of the transferred data

X parameter with change indicators

is actually supposed to be changed in the first parameter. This is necessary because you cannot transfer NULL values in parameters to an RFC function module. If an import parameter is initial (i.e., has its type-specific initial value), the function module cannot decide whether the calling program wants to change the corresponding value in the database to the initial value or whether the data isn't supposed to be changed at all.

The function module therefore contains the two additional parameters, IM_ORDERHEADERX and TA_ORDERPOSX. The IM_ORDERHEADERX import parameter is of the ZIFPORDERX category. Except for MANDT and ORDERID, this category has the same components as the transparent table, ZIFPORDER. All components, however, are of the CHAR1 category. 'X' is defined for a component of the IM_ORDERHEADERX parameter of the value if the corresponding component of the purchase order header is supposed to be replaced by the value in the IM_ORDERHEADER import parameter. The same applies to the TA_ORDERPOSX import parameter, which is of the ZIFPORDERPOSX line type.

Exclusive write lock

The function module first checks if the calling program is authorized to change purchase orders. If not, it raises the NOT_AUTHORIZED exception. If the calling program is authorized to change a purchase order, the function module sets an exclusive write lock for the purchase order and all of its items. If the process for setting the lock fails, the system raises the NO_LOCK exception, and no changes are implemented. If the system can set the lock successfully, the changes are implemented.

Before the update modules are called, the function module checks if the purchase order and purchase order items exist. If not, the lock is deleted, a ROLLBACK WORK is initiated, and the NO_DATA exception is raised.

Finally, the function module checks the IM_COMMIT import parameter. If 'X' is defined for this parameter, the function module triggers a COMMIT WORK and releases the set locks. This way, you can implement various changes in an LUW. Only the last function module in the change series needs to be provided with IM_COMMIT = 'X' then.

Deleting data

The Z_IFP_ORDER_DELETE and Z_IFP_ORDER_DELETEPOS function modules for deleting a purchase order and a purchase order item have the same structure. This time, however, the complete data is not transferred, only the ORDERID and ORDERPOS. They clearly identify the data records that are supposed to be deleted. Listing 2.5 shows the Z_IFP_ORDER_DELETE function module.

```
FUNCTION Z_IFP_ORDER_DELETE.
*"----------------------------------------------------------
*"*"Local interface:
*"  IMPORTING
*"     VALUE(IM_ORDERID) TYPE  ZIFPORDERID
*"     VALUE(IM_COMMIT)  TYPE  CHAR1 DEFAULT SPACE
*"  EXCEPTIONS
*"     NOT_AUTHORIZED
*"     NO_DATA
*"     NO_LOCK
*"----------------------------------------------------------
  AUTHORITY-CHECK OBJECT 'ZIFPORDER' ID 'ACTVT' FIELD '06'.
  IF sy-subrc NE 0.
    RAISE not_authorized.
  ENDIF.
  CALL FUNCTION 'ENQUEUE_EZIFPORDER'
    EXPORTING
      orderid = im_orderid
    exceptions
      others  = 1.
  IF sy-subrc <> 0.
    RAISE no_lock.
  ENDIF.
  SELECT SINGLE COUNT( * ) FROM zifporder WHERE
    orderid = im_orderid.
  IF sy-subrc <> 0.
    CALL FUNCTION 'DEQUEUE_EZIFPORDER'
      EXPORTING
        orderid = im_orderid.
    RAISE no_data.
  ELSE.
    CALL FUNCTION 'Z_IFP_V_DELETE_ORDER'
      IN UPDATE TASK
      EXPORTING
        im_orderid = im_orderid.
  ENDIF.
  IF im_commit = 'X'.
    COMMIT WORK.
    CALL FUNCTION 'DEQUEUE_ALL'.
  ENDIF.
ENDFUNCTION.
```

Listing 2.5 "Z_IFP_ORDER_DELETE" Function Module

Call via sRFC You can call these three function modules using the synchronous RFC. In case of the `communication_failure` exception, you can readily repeat the call at a later stage. Even if the function modules are executed on the target system despite the communication error, a repeated call doesn't change the state of the database in the target system. In the worst case, the data record will be unnecessarily changed again or the system will try to delete a data record that has already been deleted.

2.2 Transactional RFC

Call via tRFC However, it is easier to call function modules using a transactional RFC (tRFC). Here, the calling system stores the transferred parameters, and you can repeat the call using Transaction SM58.

You implement a tRFC call by using the IN BACKGROUND TASK addition for the call. This addition must precede the DESTINATION addition. When the call is implemented, the function module is not executed on the target system yet. Instead the call, including its parameters and transaction ID, is stored in the ARFCSSTATE and ARFCSDATA tables in the local system. The call in the target system is then implemented during the COMMIT WORK. If the call is successful, the entries in the ARFCSSTATE and ARFCSDATA indicator tables are deleted.

Behavior in case of an error If the target system isn't available, the system can automatically generate a job, which repeats the call with the same transaction ID. The number of the retries and the length of the interval between the repetitions are defined in the tRFC options using Transaction SM59 when the destination is maintained. However, it is more advisable to regularly monitor the tRFC status tables via Transaction SM58 and repeat the canceled calls from there manually after the communication problem has been resolved.

If the remote function module terminates the process with an error, the target system automatically executes the ROLLBACK WORK command. The calling system doesn't schedule a job for repeating the call. The error that occurred in the target system is logged in the tRFC status tables. The canceled calls can also be repeated from Transaction SM58 in this case.

If the COMMIT WORK command also triggers the local update, the target system only executes the LUW if the local updates have been completed without errors.

When using the IN BACKGROUND TASK addition for a call, you can neither use the EXPORTING addition nor test it for exceptions that are defined in the function module's interface because these two aspects aren't determined until the target system has executed the function module. This isn't done until the COMMIT WORK.

All function modules that are called via the IN BACKGROUND TASK addition form a *Logical Unit of Work* (LUW) in the target system. They are processed in the target system within a single database transaction. If the function module fails, the target system automatically executes a ROLLBACK. The LUW is identified by a transaction ID. You can determine this transaction ID in the calling system using the ID_OF_BACKGROUNDTASK function module, which needs to be called prior to the COMMIT WORK. The STATUS_OF_BACKGROUNDTASK function module enables you to determine the execution status of the LUW when specifying the transaction ID. This function module must be called in the local system after the COMMIT WORK.

Specific function modules

If the LUW isn't supposed to be executed immediately in the target system, you can define the date and time of the execution prior to COMMIT WORK using the START_OF_BACKGROUNDTASK function module.

The respective data record may be locked for our two function modules. In this case, the two function modules are terminated with a RAISE. As already described, you can use Transaction SM58 to have the system execute the LUW again. Alternatively, you can also call the RESTART_OF_BACKGROUNDTASK function module to reschedule the job in the calling system.

Listing 2.6 shows a function module that enables you to create purchase orders. The details of the purchase order that is supposed to be newly created are transferred as import parameters. As usual, the function module first checks if the calling program is authorized to create a purchase order. Then, it creates an order ID, which is returned in the EX_ORDERID export parameter.

Function modules for creating

```abap
FUNCTION z_ifp_order_create.
*"----------------------------------------------------------
*"*"Local interface:
*"  IMPORTING
*"     VALUE(IM_ORDERHEADER) TYPE  ZIFPORDER
*"     VALUE(IM_TESTRUN)     TYPE  CHAR1 DEFAULT SPACE
*"     VALUE(IM_COMMIT)      TYPE  CHAR1 DEFAULT SPACE
*"  EXPORTING
*"     VALUE(EX_ORDERID)     TYPE  ZIFPORDERID
*"  TABLES
*"     TA_ORDERPOS STRUCTURE  ZIFPORDERPOS
*"  EXCEPTIONS
*"     NOT_AUTHORIZED
*"     NO_NUMBER
*"     NO_LOCK
*"----------------------------------------------------------
  AUTHORITY-CHECK OBJECT 'ZIFPORDER' ID 'ACTVT' FIELD '01'.
  IF sy-subrc NE 0.
    RAISE not_authorized.
  ENDIF.
  CALL FUNCTION 'NUMBER_GET_NEXT'
    EXPORTING
      nr_range_nr = '01'
      object      = 'ZIFPORDER'
    IMPORTING
      number      = im_orderheader-orderid
    EXCEPTIONS
      OTHERS      = 1.
  IF sy-subrc <> 0.
    RAISE no_number.
  ENDIF.
  CALL FUNCTION 'ENQUEUE_EZIFPORDER'
    EXPORTING
      orderid    = im_orderheader-orderid
    EXCEPTIONS
      OTHERS     = 1.
  IF sy-subrc <> 0.
    RAISE no_lock.
  ENDIF.
  IF im_testrun IS INITIAL.
    CALL FUNCTION 'Z_IFP_V_CREATE_ORDER'
      IN UPDATE TASK
      EXPORTING
        im_orderheader = im_orderheader
```

```abap
    TABLES
      im_orderpos    = ta_orderpos.
    IF im_commit = 'X'.
      COMMIT WORK.
      CALL FUNCTION 'DEQUEUE_ALL'.
    ENDIF.
ENDIF.
  ex_orderid = im_orderheader-orderid.
ENDFUNCTION.
```

Listing 2.6 "Z_IFP_ORDER_CREATE" Function Module

Function modules for creating data records are normally called via a tRFC, as shown in Listing 2.7. The ZIFP_ORDER_CREATE report reads a vendor order from the local database to create a customer purchase order in the vendor system using this data. The call is transactional because in the case of communication_failure, the calling program doesn't know if the data record has already been created in the target. A repeated call would then create a second data record. However, if the function module is called transactionally, the calling system stores the transferred parameters, and in the case of communication_failure, you can repeat the call without any problems using Transaction SM58. This also means that, at any rate, the function module is executed only once in the target system.

Call via tRFC

```abap
*&---------------------------------------------------------------
*& Report  ZIFP_ORDER_CREATE
*&---------------------------------------------------------------
REPORT  zifp_order_create.
PARAMETERS:
  pa_id   TYPE zifporder-orderid,
  p_dest TYPE rfcdes-rfcdest value check.
DATA:
  orderheader   TYPE zifporder,
  it_orderpos   TYPE STANDARD TABLE OF zifporderpos,
  msg_text(80) TYPE c.
AT SELECTION-SCREEN.
  SELECT SINGLE * FROM zifporder
    INTO orderheader
    WHERE
      orderid  = pa_id AND
      type     = 'PO'.
  IF sy-subrc <> 0.
```

```
          Message e001(zifp).
        endif.
START-OF-SELECTION.
    orderheader-type  = 'SO'.
    orderheader-refid = orderheader-orderid.
    SELECT * FROM zifporderpos INTO TABLE it_orderpos
    WHERE
       orderid = pa_id.
    CALL FUNCTION 'Z_IFP_ORDER_CREATE'
       IN BACKGROUND TASK
       DESTINATION p_dest
       EXPORTING
          im_orderheader           = orderheader
          im_commit                = 'X'
       TABLES
          ta_orderpos              = it_orderpos
       EXCEPTIONS
          system_failure           = 1  MESSAGE msg_text
          communication_failure    = 2  MESSAGE msg_text
          OTHERS                   = 3.
    IF sy-subrc <> 0.
       WRITE:/ msg_text.
       ROLLBACK WORK.
    ENDIF.
    COMMIT WORK.
```

Listing 2.7 "ZIFP_ORDER_CREATE" Report

Export parameters cannot be accessed

If you call the function module via the tRFC, the system returns neither the export parameters nor an exception that may have been raised in the function module. Accordingly, you don't know which ORDERID the generated sales order obtained in the target system or if the order could be generated at all. The sales order is therefore provided with the ID of the original vendor purchase order in the REFID field. The Z_IFP_ORDER_GETLIST function module then enables you to search for sales orders using the REFID and then determine the ORDERID.

Transaction model for BAPIs

A different method is used for BAPIs, for example. Here, modifying or generating function modules are also called via sRFC. This way, the calling system is directly provided with the export parameters and exceptions. The RFC function module, however, doesn't directly implement the update but calls an update module with the IN UPDATE TASK addition. To trigger the update in the target system, the local system calls the

`BAPI_COMMIT_WORK` BAPI in the target system. This BAPI basically contains the `COMMIT WORK` code line and uses it to trigger the update in the target system. Our function module is designed so that it can be reused for a BAPI implementation.

2.3 Queued RFC

LUWs that have been created via tRFC are executed in the target system independently of each other. Particularly in the case of network problems, you cannot be sure that the call sequence of the function modules in the local system is the same as the processing sequence in the target system. To ensure this sequence, you can use a queued RFC (qRFC) as of Basis Release 4.5B.

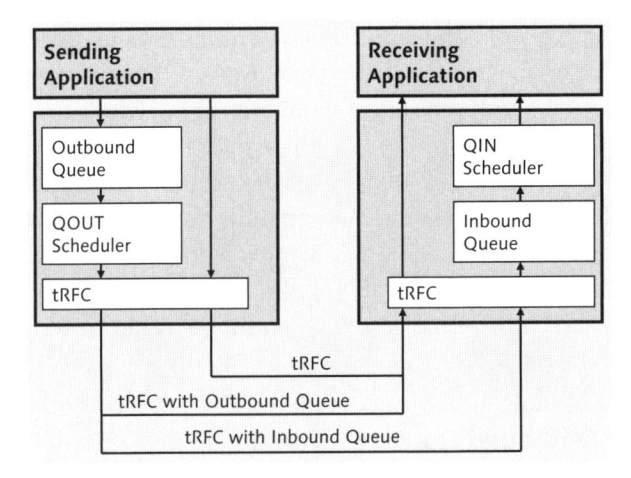

Figure 2.1 qRFC Communication Scenarios

qRFC is an enhancement of tRFC. This enhancement consists of an additional layer between the sending or receiving application and the tRFC layer. The qRFC communication model distinguishes between three scenarios, which are mapped in Figure 2.1:

- **tRFC**

  You can use this scenario if the pieces of data of function modules that are executed in sequence are not linked with each other. The calling application in the client system uses tRFC to ensure that the data in

qRFC architecture

the server system is processed only once. The sequence in which the called function modules are processed cannot be ensured. If transmission errors occur, it is possible that tRFCs that were triggered at a later stage are processed earlier in the receiving system.

- **qRFC with outbound queue**
  In this scenario, the sending system uses an *outbound queue* to ensure the serialization of the data. The called function modules are stored in the outbound queue of the sending system, which ensures that they are processed exactly once and in exactly this call sequence in the receiving system. The receiving system here doesn't know that an outbound queue exists in the sending system. Consequently, this scenario can also be used with external tRFC servers. You don't have to change the code in the external tRFC server for this purpose.

- **qRFC with outbound and inbound queue**
  Here, in addition to the outbound queue in the sending system, there is also an *inbound queue* in the receiving system. Even if the receiving system provides an inbound queue, the sending system always contains an outbound queue because it serves to serialize the calls. The inbound queue in the receiving system, however, separates the transfer of the calls from their processing. The inbound queue stores the transferred calls until the application or a standard process, the *QIN Scheduler*, triggers the processing. The RFC library provides functions that enable you to assign external clients to an inbound queue of a receiving SAP system via tRFCs.

2.3.1 qRFC with Outbound Queue

To assign a qRFC LUW to an outbound queue, you must specify the name of the outbound queue before the qRFC call by calling the TRFC_SET_QUEUE_NAME function module locally. You then use COMMIT WORK to complete the LUW. Listing 2.8 shows an example that assigns a qRFC LUW to a queue that is called ZIFPQUEUE. The LUW consists of several calls of the Z_IFP_ORDER_CREATE function module.

```
*&---------------------------------------------------------------------*
*& Report  ZIFP_QRFC
*&---------------------------------------------------------------------*
REPORT zifp_qrfc.
DATA:
```

```abap
    orderheader      TYPE zifporder,
    it_orderheader TYPE STANDARD TABLE OF zifporder,
    it_orderpos    TYPE STANDARD TABLE OF zifporderpos.
SELECT-OPTIONS:
  so_id FOR orderheader-orderid.
PARAMETERS:
  p_dest TYPE rfcdes-rfcdest VALUE CHECK.
AT SELECTION-SCREEN.
  SELECT * FROM zifporder
  INTO TABLE it_orderheader
  WHERE
    orderid IN so_id AND
    type    = 'PO'.
  IF sy-subrc <> 0.
    MESSAGE e001(zifp).
  ENDIF.
START-OF-SELECTION.
  CALL FUNCTION 'TRFC_QUEUE_INITIALIZE'.
  CALL FUNCTION 'TRFC_SET_QUEUE_NAME'
    EXPORTING
      qname             = 'ZIFPQUEUE'
    EXCEPTIONS
      invalid_queue_name = 1
      OTHERS            = 2.
  CHECK sy-subrc EQ 0.
  LOOP AT it_orderheader INTO orderheader.
    orderheader-type  = 'SO'.
    orderheader-refid = orderheader-orderid.
    SELECT * FROM zifporderpos INTO TABLE it_orderpos
    WHERE
      orderid = orderheader-orderid.
    CALL FUNCTION 'Z_IFP_ORDER_CREATE'
      IN BACKGROUND TASK
      DESTINATION p_dest
      EXPORTING
        im_orderheader      = orderheader
        im_commit           = 'X'
      TABLES
        ta_orderpos         = it_orderpos.
  ENDLOOP.
  COMMIT WORK.
```

Listing 2.8 qRFC with Outbound Queue

QOUT Scheduler The *QOUT Scheduler* initiates the processing of the outbound queues. You can monitor the scheduler via Transaction SMQS. When an LUW is completed in the sending system, two steps are carried out:

1. The target destination is registered in the QOUT Scheduler.
2. The QOUT Scheduler is activated and processes the queues for this target destination.

> **Monitoring the Outbound Queue**
>
> To actually see something in monitoring Transaction SMQ1, which monitors the outbound queues, you must use a little trick: In Transaction SMQS for the QOUT Scheduler, click on the Deregistration button to deregister your target destination with the QOUT Scheduler. If you then execute the ZIFP_QRFC report in Listing 2.8, Transaction SMQ1 — the qRFC monitor for outbound queues — displays the ZIFPQUEUE outbound queue. Select this outbound queue in Transaction SMQ, and have the system display the details.

LUWs of an outbound queue If you use the trick described in the gray box, the system displays all LUWs of an outbound queue. If you select an LUW and again have the system display the details, the function modules in this LUW (Figure 2.2) are displayed. From this screen, you can then send the outbound queue manually to the target system.

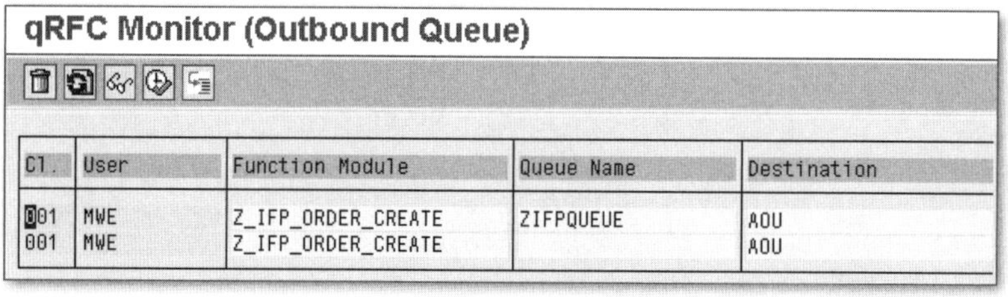

Figure 2.2 Function Modules in an Outbound Queue

Registering the target destination Normally, however, you register the target destination manually or automatically with the QOUT Scheduler. The QOUT Scheduler then immediately processes the outbound queue as soon as the LUW is completed with a COMMIT WORK.

2.3.2 qRFC with Outbound and Inbound Queue

To assign a tRFC LUW in a receiving system to an inbound queue first, you must specify the name of the inbound queue before each tRFC call in the sending system by calling the TRFC_SET_QIN_PROPERTIES function module locally. Optionally, you can also specify the name of the outbound queue using this parameter. Otherwise, this name is identical to the name of the inbound queue. Listing 2.9 shows an example:

```
*&---------------------------------------------------------------*
*& Report ZIFP_QRFC_IN
*&---------------------------------------------------------------
REPORT zifp_qrfc_in.
DATA:
  orderheader    TYPE zifporder,
  it_orderheader TYPE STANDARD TABLE OF zifporder,
  it_orderpos    TYPE STANDARD TABLE OF zifporderpos.
SELECT-OPTIONS:
  so_id FOR orderheader-orderid.
PARAMETERS:
  p_dest TYPE rfcdes-rfcdest VALUE CHECK.
AT SELECTION-SCREEN.
  SELECT * FROM zifporder
  INTO TABLE it_orderheader
  WHERE
    orderid IN so_id AND
    type    = 'PO'.
  IF sy-subrc <> 0.
    MESSAGE e001(zifp).
  ENDIF.
START-OF-SELECTION.
  CALL FUNCTION 'TRFC_QUEUE_INITIALIZE'.
  LOOP AT it_orderheader INTO orderheader.
    orderheader-type  = 'SO'.
    orderheader-refid = orderheader-orderid.
    SELECT * FROM zifporderpos INTO TABLE it_orderpos
    WHERE
      orderid = orderheader-orderid.
    CALL FUNCTION 'TRFC_SET_QIN_PROPERTIES'
      EXPORTING
        qout_name          = 'ZIFPQUEUE'
        qin_name           = 'ZIFPQUEUE'
      EXCEPTIONS
        invalid_queue_name = 1
```

```
            OTHERS                        = 2.
      CHECK sy-subrc EQ 0.
      CALL FUNCTION 'Z_IFP_ORDER_CREATE'
        IN BACKGROUND TASK
        DESTINATION p_dest
        EXPORTING
          im_orderheader          = orderheader
          im_commit               = 'X'
        TABLES
          ta_orderpos             = it_orderpos.
    ENDLOOP.
    COMMIT WORK.
```

Listing 2.9 qRFC with Inbound Queue

The system assigns a tRFC LUW to the outbound queue named ZIFPQUEUE. The receiving system doesn't directly process this LUW but assigns it to an outbound queue called ZIFPQUEUE. The LUW, in turn, consists of several calls of the Z_ORDER_CREATE function module. Prior to each call, the name of the inbound queue is specified with TRFC_SET_QIN_PROPERTIES.

Monitoring The system doesn't automatically process the inbound queue. Transaction SMQ2 — the qRFC monitor for inbound queues — therefore displays an entry for ZIFPQUEUE in the target system after you have executed the ZIFP_QRFC_IN report from Listing 2.9 in the sending system. Select this inbound queue in Transaction SMQ2, and have the system display the details. This inbound queue then lists all LUWs. If you select an LUW and again have the system display the details, the function modules in this LUW are displayed as illustrated in Figure 2.3. You can then initiate the processing of the inbound queue in the target system from this or the previous screen.

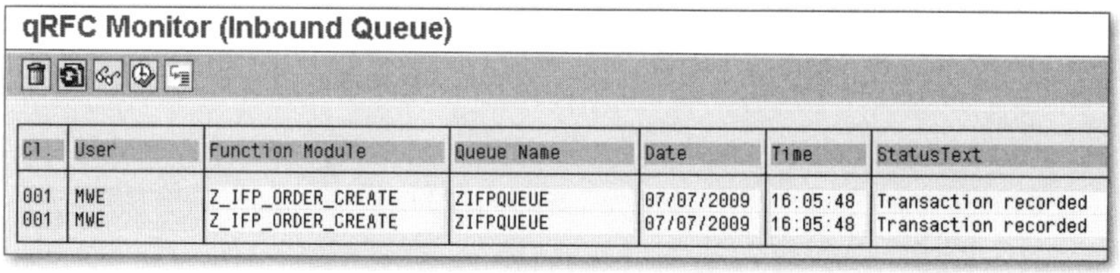

Cl.	User	Function Module	Queue Name	Date	Time	StatusText
001	MWE	Z_IFP_ORDER_CREATE	ZIFPQUEUE	07/07/2009	16:05:48	Transaction recorded
001	MWE	Z_IFP_ORDER_CREATE	ZIFPQUEUE	07/07/2009	16:05:48	Transaction recorded

Figure 2.3 Function Modules in an Inbound Queue

The processing of the function modules in the inbound queue is not carried out automatically but can be triggered by the application itself by calling the TRFC_QIN_RESTART function module. This function module can either be called from a batch program in the receiving system or via RFC from the sending system. The queue name must be transferred to this function module.

Processing using TRFC_QIN_RESTART

To prevent every qRFC application from having to write its own scheduler for triggering the queue processing, you are provided with the QIN Scheduler that processes the registered queues automatically. Here, the registration of an inbound queue is either program-driven via the QIWK_REGISTER function module or manual using the qRFC monitor for the SMQR QIN Scheduler. Figure 2.4 shows this transaction after the registration of the ZIFPQUEUE inbound queue

QIN Scheduler

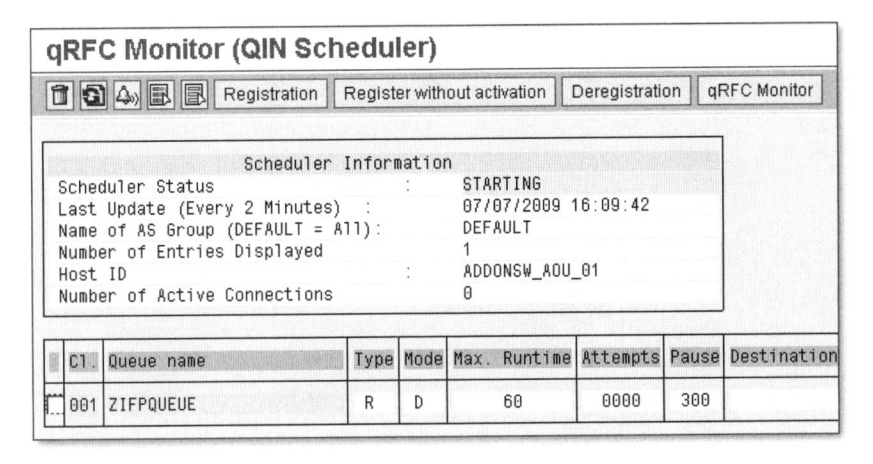

Figure 2.4 Registering an Inbound Queue

You use the asynchronous RFC (aRFC) to distribute tasks across multiple SAP systems. The STARTING NEW TASK t addition enables you to start a function module asynchronously on another system. Here, too, no export parameters and exceptions can be received during the call. Because aRFC isn't available for external systems, it is not critical for interface programming.

Parallelization using aRFC

2.4 Business Objects and BAPIs

Business Application Programming Interfaces (BAPIs) are methods of business objects. Examples for business objects in SAP ERP include *customer*, *employee*, or *material*. Usually, SAP customers don't develop their own business objects but use or enhance the BAPIs of SAP business objects. For custom-developed applications, however, it can be interesting to define your own business objects.

2.4.1 Developing Business Objects

You define business object types using Transaction SWO1 (*Business Object Builder*). For this purpose, start Transaction SWO1, and enter the name "Z_BUS4500" into the Object type/Interface type field. Choose Create (F5). Enter the information from Table 2.1 into the Create Object Type dialog box.

Screen Field	Input	Remark
Object name	Order	This is a descriptive name that is displayed for the business object in the Business Object Repository (BOR).
Name	Order (IFP example)	This description should be meaningful enough to use to select the object type.
Short Description	Sample purchase order for IFP	–
Program	Z_BUS4500	System proposal.
Application	Z	Customer programs.

Table 2.1 Creating a Business Object

Attributes of business objects

The newly created business object consists of five components (interfaces, key fields, attributes, methods, and events), which were already introduced in Chapter 1, Section 1.4.3, BAPIs.

Values of the key fields

After having created the business object, select the Key Fields entry and then Create (F5). Choose YES for the question Create with ABAP/4 Dictionary Field Specifications?, and select the ORDERID field from the

ZIFPORDER table. Use this selection to create the orderid key field of the object type. Your object type should now look like Figure 2.5.

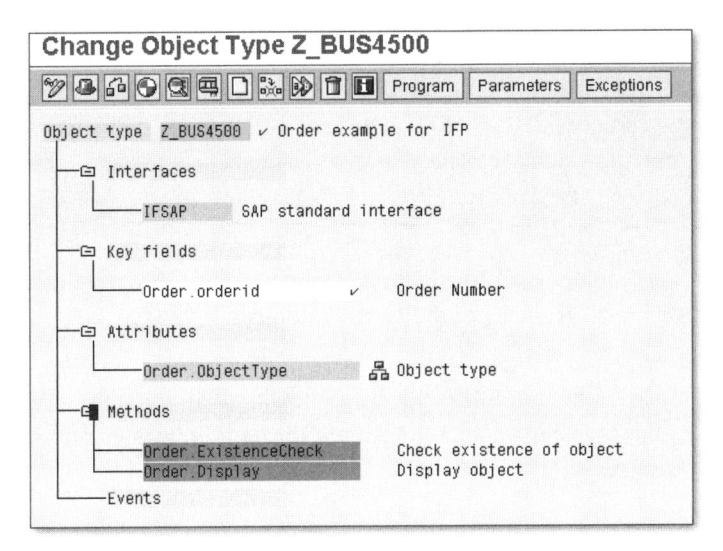

```
Change Object Type Z_BUS4500
                                    Program   Parameters   Exceptions
Object type  Z_BUS4500  ✓ Order example for IFP
    ─ Interfaces
        └─ IFSAP        SAP standard interface
    ─ Key fields
        └─ Order.orderid         ✓   Order Number
    ─ Attributes
        └─ Order.ObjectType         Object type
    ─ Methods
        ├─ Order.ExistenceCheck    Check existence of object
        └─ Order.Display           Display object
    ─ Events
```

Figure 2.5 "Order" Business Object

Select the EDIT • CHANGE RELEASE STATUS • OBJECT TYPE • TO IMPLEMENTED menu entry, and generate the object type via Generate ([Ctrl] + [F3]).

2.4.2 Developing BAPIs

In the next step, you develop the BAPIs and assign them to the object type. To do so, you first define the required domains, data elements, and structures for the BAPI parameters in the ABAP Dictionary. Then, you implement the RFC function module for the BAPI using the Function Builder. You assign this function module as an API method to the business object in the Object Builder.

BAPIs must meet some conventions:

Conventions for BAPIs

- For standard BAPIs, you should use generic names:
  - `Create` and `CreateFromData`
    These BAPIs generate new business object instances. They are instance-independent.

- **Change**
  This instance-dependent BAPI changes the status of an existing instance of a business object. The instance is identified through the values of the key fields here.

- **Delete**
  This instance-dependent BAPI deletes an instance of a business object from the database. The instance is identified through the values of the key fields here.

- **GetList**
  This instance-independent BAPI provides a table of the key values that identify the instances of the business object.

- **GetDetail**
  This instance-independent BAPI returns details of an instance of a business object. The instance is identified through the values of the key fields here.

- According to the SAP-defined convention for BAPIs, you should use English methods names, which should contain a maximum of 30 characters.

- Underscores are not permitted in BAPI names.

Conventions for parameters

Parameters must also meet some conventions:

- If you use standardized parameters, you should also use the names provided for this purpose.

  - **RETURN**
    Every BAPI must have a parameter called RETURN, which returns messages to the calling program. This parameter can be an export parameter or a table parameter. It is usually of the BAPIRET2 type.

  - **TestRun**
    This import parameter is used in write BAPIs to execute test calls. If this parameter isn't initial, the BAPI only executes the designated checks but doesn't implement changes for the database.

  - **ExtensionIn** and **ExtensionOut**
    To extend the BAPI without modifications, it should have the ExtensionIn and ExtensionOut parameters of the BAPIPAREX type. To enable customer extensions to read the ExtensionIn parameter, a BAdI (*Business Add-In*) should be defined and called at the begin-

ning of the BAPI. The system then transfers this parameter to the BAdI. At the end of the BAPI, a second BAdI should be defined and called, which enables customer extensions to populate the `ExtensionOut` parameter.

- The parameter names should be as meaningful as possible.
- The parameter names must be in English and should contain a maximum of 30 characters.
- The parts of the parameter names in the BOR start with a capital letter, such as in `TestRun` or `ExtensionIn`.
- Values that belong together semantically should be transferred within a structure and not in multiple scalars.
- For every field that contains an amount or a currency value, a corresponding field with the unit of measure or currency should be provided.
- For fields for country, language, unit of measure, or currency, a field that contains the respective ISO code should be available.

In this section, we will program BAPIs for creating, changing, deleting, and reading customer purchase orders. For this purpose, you must first create the necessary structures in the ABAP Dictionary. Then, you need to write the RFC function modules and assign them as BAPIs to the business object.

BAPIs for the purchase order application

You need to create an instance of the `Book` business object type using the `CreateFromData` BAPI. The interface of this BAPI must meet some conventions:

"CreateFromData" BAPI

- The import parameters of the BAPI provide the data that is required for generating the instance. In the case of the `Order` business object, this is the header and item data of the purchase order.
- The BAPI must have a parameter called `TestRun`. If this parameter contains the value '`X`', the BAPI is executed as usual but doesn't write data to the update task. This means that the data isn't written to the database after `BapiService.TransactionCommit` has been called.
- To extend the import parameters of the BAPIs without modifications, the interface must provide the `ExtensionIn` import parameter.

- The system must return the key fields of the newly generated object as export parameters.
- To return warnings and error messages to the calling program, an export parameter named RETURN must be returned. When populating this parameter, you must adhere to some rules, which are described in the following two sections.

After the new instance has been created successfully, the system must return a standard message from the T100 table (see Table 2.2).

Field	Content
TYPE	S
ID	BAPI
NUMBER	000
MESSAGE_V1	<object name>
MESSAGE_V2	<object ID>
MESSAGE_V3	<object ID>
MESSAGE_V4	<reference ID>
SYSTEM	<system>

Table 2.2 Fields of the "RETURN" Parameter in Case of Success

The MESSAGE_V1 field contains the name of the business object type, Order, in this case. The key of the newly generated object is specified in MESSAGE_V2. If there are several key fields, the fields must be listed one after the other. If the 50 characters of MESSAGE_V2 aren't sufficient, the system additionally uses the MESSAGE_V3 field. The MESSAGE_V4 field returns a reference key (e.g., from an external system).

Error messages If the system cannot create the object, it outputs a standardized message (see Table 2.3).

Asynchronous update When implementing the BAPI, you must also consider some aspects: Of course, the BAPI must be an RFC function module. It mustn't generate the data records directly but needs to call an update module, IN UPDATE TASK, for this task. This update module should store the data transferred to it in an internal table within the function group and then use the ON COMMIT statement to call a subroutine that will perform the actual update with array insert technologies. This enables you to generate multiple objects within one transaction with a high performance. The subroutine that performs the actual update is only executed once and saves all data records in a single database access. This is important if the BAPI will import mass data.

Field	Content
TYPE	E
ID	BAPI
NUMBER	001
MESSAGE_V1	<object name>
MESSAGE_V2	–
MESSAGE_V3	–
MESSAGE_V4	<reference ID>
SYSTEM	<system>

Table 2.3 Fields of the "RETURN" Parameter in Case of Error

The update module was already programmed in Listing 1.5 from Chapter 1, Section 1.3.5, Update Modules. Listing 2.10 now shows the actual BAPI. It receives the data for the customer purchase order, which is supposed to be newly generated, in its import parameters. Error and success messages are output in the RETURN table whose lines have the BAPIRET2 structure.

```
FUNCTION z_bapi_order_createfromdata.
*"----------------------------------------*"*"Local interface:
*"  IMPORTING
*"     VALUE(IM_ORDERHEADER) TYPE  ZIFPORDER
*"     VALUE(TESTRUN)        TYPE  BAPISFLAUX-TESTRUN
*"        DEFAULT SPACE
*"  EXPORTING
*"     VALUE(ORDERID)        TYPE  ZIFPORDERID
*"  TABLES
*"     RETURN STRUCTURE  BAPIRET2
*"     TA_ORDERPOS STRUCTURE  ZIFPORDERPOS
*"----------------------------------------
DATA:
  l_orderid TYPE zifporderid,
  msg_hlp_extkey LIKE sy-msgv1,
  msg1_hlp LIKE sy-msgv1.
```

```abap
* Initialize return parameter
  REFRESH: return.
  CLEAR:   orderid.
  CALL FUNCTION 'Z_IFP_ORDER_CREATE'
    EXPORTING
      im_orderheader = im_orderheader
      im_testrun     = testrun
      im_commit      = ' '
    IMPORTING
      ex_orderid     = l_orderid
    TABLES
      ta_orderpos    = ta_orderpos
    EXCEPTIONS
      not_authorized = 1
      no_number      = 2
      no_lock        = 3
      OTHERS         = 4.
  CASE sy-subrc.
    WHEN 1.
      "No authorization
      CALL FUNCTION 'BALW_BAPIRETURN_GET2'
          EXPORTING
              type      = 'E'
              cl        = 'ZIFP'
              number    = 101
              parameter = ''
              field     = ''
          IMPORTING
              return    = return.
      APPEND return.
    WHEN 2.
      "No purchase order ID
      CALL FUNCTION 'BALW_BAPIRETURN_GET2'
          EXPORTING
              type      = 'E'
              cl        = 'ZIFP'
              number    = 103
              parameter = ''
              field     = ''
          IMPORTING
              return    = return.
      APPEND return.
    WHEN 3.
      "No lock
```

```
        CALL FUNCTION 'BALW_BAPIRETURN_GET2'
          EXPORTING
            type      = 'E'
            cl        = 'ZIFP'
            number    = 104
            parameter = ''
            field     = ''
          IMPORTING
            return    = return.
        APPEND return.
    ENDCASE.
*   Termination in case of error
    IF return-type = 'E'.
      PERFORM final_return_message_create    "BAPI failed
        USING     'E' '' msg_hlp_extkey
        CHANGING  return[].
      RETURN.
    ELSE.
      CLEAR sy-subrc.
    ENDIF.
*   Generate information message in test run
    IF testrun IS NOT INITIAL.
      CALL FUNCTION 'BALW_BAPIRETURN_GET2'    "TestRun
        EXPORTING
          type   = 'I'
          cl     = 'ZIFP'
          number = 105
        IMPORTING
          return = return.
    ENDIF.
*   Generate success message
    WRITE: l_orderid TO msg1_hlp.
    PERFORM final_return_message_create     "BAPI successful
      USING     'S' msg1_hlp msg_hlp_extkey
      CHANGING  return[].
*   Populate return parameter
    orderid = l_orderid.
ENDFUNCTION.
```

Listing 2.10 "Z_BAPI_ORDER_CREATEFROMDATA" BAPI

After the purchase order has been created successfully, the ORDERID export parameter contains the key value with which the new customer purchase order can be identified.

The BAPI delegates the main tasks (checking and calling the update task) to the z_ifp_order_create function module from Listing 2.6 shown earlier in Section 2.2, Transactional RFC. If this function module returns an error, the system writes an error message to the internal table, RETURN.

Designing error messages To design the error message, the BAPI uses the BALW_BAPIRETURN_GET2 function module. This function module ensures that the RETURN message field is populated with a message from a message class. The message number and message class are passed to this function module in its number and cl import parameters. In addition, this function module populates the RETURN-PARAMETER, RETURN-ROW, RETURN-FIELD, and RETURN-MESSAGE_V1 to RETURN-MESSAGE_V4 fields from the PARAMETER, ROW, FIELD, and PAR1 to PAR4 import parameters.

If the checks have determined an error, the final_return_message_create subroutine (Listing 2.11) attaches an error message to the RETURN table and exits the BAPI.

If the checks have been successful, however, the program attaches a success message to the RETURN table and populates the export parameter before it exits the BAPI.

```
**** Subroutine for creating the final message
FORM final_return_message_create
    USING
        value(mess_type)   TYPE bapi_mtype
        value(mess_var2)   TYPE symsgv
        value(mess_var4)   TYPE symsgv
    CHANGING
        return TYPE return_type.
  DATA: return_item TYPE bapiret2.
  IF mess_type = 'S'.
    "Purchase order generated
    CALL FUNCTION 'BALW_BAPIRETURN_GET2'
        EXPORTING
            type    = 'S'
            cl      = 'BAPI'
            number  = 0
            par1    = 'Order'
            par2    = mess_var2
            par4    = mess_var4
        IMPORTING
            return = return_item.
    APPEND return_item TO return.
```

```
      ENDIF.
      IF mess_type = 'E'.
        "Purchase order not generated
        CALL FUNCTION 'BALW_BAPIRETURN_GET2'
            EXPORTING
                 type   = 'E'
                 cl     = 'BAPI'
                 number = 1
                 par1   = 'Order'
                 par4   = mess_var4
            IMPORTING
                 return = return_item.
         APPEND return_item TO return.
       ENDIF.
     ENDFORM.                    "final_return_message_create
```

Listing 2.11 "final_return_message_create" Subroutine

When you have tested the BAPI, you can release it in the Function Builder via the FUNCTION MODULE • RELEASE • RELEASE menu path. You can only select this menu path, however, if you are in change mode in the Function Builder and if you are in the Attributes tab.

Releasing and assigning the function module

Afterward, you can assign the function module as an API method to the Z_BUS4500 business object in Transaction SWO1. For this purpose, select the UTILITIES • API METHODS • ADD METHOD menu entry. In the next dialogs, select the function module, assign a name to the methods, and then define the parameter names for the method.

Release the business object first and the API method using the EDIT • CHANGE RELEASE STATUS menu. As a result, the business object now has a new BAPI and is displayed in Transaction BAPI.

Releasing the BAPI

The ZIFP_TEST_CREATE_BAPI report in Listing 2.12 enables you to test the CreateFromData BAPI. The report receives the ORDERID of a vendor purchase order from the user in a selection parameter. It then calls the BAPI and outputs an error message or a success message.

Testing the BAPI

```
*&---------------------------------------------------------------*
*& Report ZIFP_TEST_CREATE_BAPI.
*&---------------------------------------------------------------*
REPORT zifp_test_create_bapi.
PARAMETERS:
  pa_id   TYPE zifporder-orderid,
```

```abap
      p_dest TYPE rfcdes-rfcdest VALUE CHECK.
DATA:
  orderheader TYPE zifporder,
  it_orderpos TYPE STANDARD TABLE OF zifporderpos,
  ret         TYPE STANDARD TABLE OF bapiret2,
  waret       TYPE bapiret2,
  orderid     TYPE zifporderid.
AT SELECTION-SCREEN.
  SELECT SINGLE * FROM zifporder
  INTO orderheader
  WHERE
    orderid   = pa_id AND
    type      = 'PO'.
  IF sy-subrc <> 0.
    MESSAGE e001(zifp).
  ENDIF.
START-OF-SELECTION.
  orderheader-type  = 'SO'.
  orderheader-refid = orderheader-orderid.
  SELECT * FROM zifporderpos INTO TABLE it_orderpos
  WHERE
    orderid = pa_id.

  CALL FUNCTION 'Z_BAPI_ORDER_CREATEFROMDATA'
    DESTINATION p_dest
    EXPORTING
      im_orderheader = orderheader
      im_testrun     = space
    IMPORTING
      orderid        = orderid
    TABLES
      return         = ret
      ta_orderpos    = it_orderpos.
  READ TABLE ret WITH KEY type = 'E' TRANSPORTING NO FIELDS.
  IF sy-subrc = 0.
* Error output
    WRITE:/ 'Sales order could not be created.'.
    LOOP AT ret INTO waret.
      WRITE:/
        waret-type,
        waret-id,
        waret-number,
        waret-message.
    ENDLOOP.
```

```
    ELSE.
*   Success message
      CALL FUNCTION 'BAPI_TRANSACTION_COMMIT'
        DESTINATION p_dest.
      WRITE:/ 'New customer purchase order', orderid.
    ENDIF.
```
Listing 2.12 "ZIFP_TEST_CREATE_BAPI" Test Program

We will now develop the Change BAPI. It is an *instance-dependent* method because it changes a certain instance of a business object. The BAPI must consequently have the key fields of the business object as import parameters. These import parameters must have the same name and data type as the key fields of the business object.

"Change" BAPI

For every import parameter with the data that is supposed to be changed, the BAPI should provide a second import parameter in which the calling program can define which of the transferred data is actually supposed to be changed in the first parameter. Listing 2.4 in Section 2.1.3, Function Modules for Deleting and Changing, already introduced this technique.

X parameter with change indicators

After the instance has been changed successfully, the system must return a standard message from the T100 table (see Table 2.4).

Output in case of success

Field	Content
TYPE	S
ID	BAPI
NUMBER	002
MESSAGE_V1	<object name>
MESSAGE_V2	<object ID>
MESSAGE_V3	<object ID>
MESSAGE_V4	–
SYSTEM	<system>

Table 2.4 Fields of the "RETURN" Parameter in Case of Success

The MESSAGE_V1 field contains the name of the business object type, Order, in this case. The key of the changed object is specified in MESSAGE_V2. If there are several key fields, the fields must be listed one after the other. If the 50 characters of MESSAGE_V2 aren't sufficient, the system additionally uses `MESSAGE_V3`. In contrast to the creation of a new instance, no reference key has to be returned in the `MESSAGE_V4` field here because no new object ID is generated that needs to correlate with the reference key.

Output in case of error

If the system cannot change the object, it outputs a standardized message as shown in Table 2.5.

Field	Content
TYPE	E
ID	BAPI
NUMBER	003
MESSAGE_V1	<object name>
MESSAGE_V2	–
MESSAGE_V3	–
MESSAGE_V4	–
SYSTEM	<system>

Table 2.5 Fields of the "RETURN" Parameter in Case of Error

Other messages

In addition to these two standardized error messages, the BAPI can and is supposed to return further, more detailed messages, particularly if an error occurs. For this purpose, the BAPI can also use the `RETURN-PARAMETER`, `RETURN-ROW`, and `RETURN-FIELD` fields of the `RETURN` parameter to exactly identify where the error occurred.

This BAPI, too, which is shown in Listing 2.13, delegates the main tasks to the `z_ifp_order_change` function module from Listing 2.4. If this function module raises an exception, the BAPI populates the `RETURN` parameter and cancels further processing.

```
FUNCTION Z_BAPI_ORDER_CHANGE.
*"----------------------------------------------------------------------
*"*"Local interface:
*"  IMPORTING
*"     VALUE(ORDERID)         TYPE  ZIFPORDERID
*"     VALUE(IM_ORDERHEADER)  TYPE  ZIFPORDER
*"     VALUE(IM_ORDERHEADERX) TYPE  ZIFPORDERX
*"     VALUE(TESTRUN)         TYPE  BAPISFLAUX-TESTRUN
```

```abap
*"          DEFAULT SPACE
*"  TABLES
*"      RETURN          STRUCTURE   BAPIRET2
*"      TA_ORDERPOS     STRUCTURE   ZIFPORDERPOS
*"      TA_ORDERPOSX    STRUCTURE   ZIFPORDERPOSX
*"----------------------------------------------------------
  DATA:
    l_orderid TYPE zifporderid,
    msg1_hlp LIKE sy-msgv1.
* Initialize return parameter
  REFRESH: return.
  CALL FUNCTION 'Z_IFP_ORDER_CHANGE'
    EXPORTING
      im_orderheader  = im_orderheader
      im_orderheaderx = im_orderheaderx
      im_testrun      = testrun
      im_commit       = ' '
    TABLES
      ta_orderpos     = ta_orderpos
      ta_orderposx    = ta_orderposx
    EXCEPTIONS
      not_authorized  = 1
      no_data         = 2
      no_lock         = 3
      OTHERS          = 4.
  CASE sy-subrc.
    WHEN 1.
      "No authorization
      CALL FUNCTION 'BALW_BAPIRETURN_GET2'
          EXPORTING
              type      = 'E'
              cl        = 'ZIFP'
              number    = 101
              parameter = ' '
              field     = ' '
          IMPORTING
              return    = return.
      APPEND return.
    WHEN 2.
      CALL FUNCTION 'BALW_BAPIRETURN_GET2'      "no data
          EXPORTING
              type      = 'E'
              cl        = 'ZIFP'
              number    = 106
              parameter = ' '
```

```abap
                 field     = ''
          IMPORTING
                 return    = return.
      APPEND return.
    WHEN 3.
      CALL FUNCTION 'BALW_BAPIRETURN_GET2'       "no lock
          EXPORTING
                 type      = 'E'
                 cl        = 'ZIFP'
                 number    = 104
                 parameter = ''
                 field     = ''
          IMPORTING
                 return    = return.
      APPEND return.
  ENDCASE.
* Termination in case of error
  IF return-type = 'E'.
    PERFORM final_return_message_change      "BAPI failed
      USING     'E' ''
      CHANGING  return[].
    RETURN.
  ELSE.
    CLEAR sy-subrc.
  ENDIF.
* Generate information message in test run
  IF testrun IS NOT INITIAL.
    CALL FUNCTION 'BALW_BAPIRETURN_GET2'       "TestRun
        EXPORTING
               type   = 'I'
               cl     = 'ZIFP'
               number = 105
        IMPORTING
               return = return.
  ENDIF.
* Generate success message
  WRITE: orderid TO msg1_hlp NO-GAP.
  "BAPI successful
  PERFORM final_return_message_change
    USING    'S'  msg1_hlp
    CHANGING return[].
ENDFUNCTION.
```

Listing 2.13 "Z_BAPI_ORDER_CHANGE" Function

In the case of success as well as in the case of error, the BAPI adds a line to the RETURN parameter. To write the error messages to the RETURN table, the BAPI uses the `final_return_message_change` subroutine, which is shown in Listing 2.14.

Populating "RETURN"

```
**** Subroutine for creating the final message
*    (Change)
* Writes success or error messages
************************************************************
FORM final_return_message_change
    USING
        value(mess_type)   TYPE bapi_mtype
        value(mess_var2)   TYPE symsgv
    CHANGING
        return             TYPE return_type.
  DATA: return_item TYPE bapiret2.
  IF mess_type = 'S'.
    "Purchase order changed
    CALL FUNCTION 'BALW_BAPIRETURN_GET2'
        EXPORTING
            type    = 'S'
            cl      = 'BAPI'
            number  = 2
            par1    = 'Order'
            par2    = mess_var2
        IMPORTING
            return = return_item.
    APPEND return_item TO return.
  ENDIF.
  IF mess_type = 'E'.
     "Purchase order not changed
    CALL FUNCTION 'BALW_BAPIRETURN_GET2'
        EXPORTING
            type    = 'E'
            cl      = 'BAPI'
            number  = 3
            par1    = 'Order'
        IMPORTING
            return = return_item.
    APPEND return_item TO return.
  ENDIF.
ENDFORM.                      "final_return_message_change
```

Listing 2.14 "final_return_message_change" Subroutine

Testing the "Change" BAPI

The ZIFP_TEST_CHANGE_BAPI report in Listing 2.15 enables you to test the Change BAPI. The report receives the ORDERID of the purchase order that needs to be changed as well as the new values for buyer, seller, and currency of the user in selection parameters. If a selection parameter isn't initial, the respective change indicator is set in orderheaderx or ta_orderposx, and the content of the parameter is copied to im_orderheader or ta_orderpos. Then, the system calls the Z_BAPI_ORDER_CHANGE BAPI. If the RETURN table contains an error entry, the report outputs this table completely. In case of success, the report calls the BAPI_TRANSACTION_COMMIT BAPI and writes a message for the user.

```abap
*&---------------------------------------------------------------*
*& Report ZIFP_TEST_CHANGE_BAPI.
*&---------------------------------------------------------------*
REPORT zifp_test_change_bapi.
PARAMETERS:
  pa_id    TYPE zifporder-orderid,
  p_dest   TYPE rfcdes-rfcdest VALUE CHECK.
SELECTION-SCREEN BEGIN OF BLOCK new WITH FRAME
     TITLE text-new.
  PARAMETERS:
    seller   TYPE zifpseller LOWER CASE,
    buyer    TYPE zifpbuyer LOWER CASE,
    currency TYPE zifpcurrency.
SELECTION-SCREEN END OF BLOCK new.
DATA:
  orderheader   TYPE zifporder,
  orderheaderx  TYPE zifporderx,
  it_orderpos   TYPE STANDARD TABLE OF zifporderpos,
  it_orderposx  TYPE STANDARD TABLE OF zifporderposx,
  wa_orderpos   TYPE zifporderpos,
  wa_orderposx  TYPE zifporderposx,
  ret           TYPE STANDARD TABLE OF bapiret2,
  waret         TYPE bapiret2,
  orderid       TYPE zifporderid.
AT SELECTION-SCREEN.
  SELECT SINGLE * FROM zifporder
  INTO orderheader
  WHERE
     orderid  = pa_id AND
     type     = 'SO'.
  IF sy-subrc <> 0.
```

```abap
      MESSAGE e001(zifp).
    ENDIF.
START-OF-SELECTION.
  IF seller IS NOT INITIAL.
    orderheaderx-seller = 'X'.
    orderheader-seller  = seller.
  ENDIF.
  IF buyer IS NOT INITIAL.
    orderheaderx-buyer = 'X'.
    orderheader-buyer  = buyer.
  ENDIF.
  IF currency IS NOT INITIAL.
    SELECT * FROM zifporderpos INTO TABLE it_orderpos
    WHERE
      orderid = pa_id.
    LOOP AT it_orderpos INTO wa_orderpos.
      wa_orderposx-currency = 'X'.
      APPEND wa_orderposx TO it_orderposx.
      wa_orderpos-currency  = currency.
      MODIFY it_orderpos FROM wa_orderpos.
    ENDLOOP.
  ENDIF.
  CALL FUNCTION 'Z_BAPI_ORDER_CHANGE'
    DESTINATION p_dest
    EXPORTING
      orderid          = pa_id
      im_orderheader   = orderheader
      im_orderheaderx  = orderheaderx
      im_testrun       = space
    TABLES
      return           = ret
      ta_orderpos      = it_orderpos
      ta_orderposx     = it_orderposx.
  READ TABLE ret WITH KEY type = 'E' TRANSPORTING NO FIELDS.
  IF sy-subrc = 0.
* Error output
    WRITE:/ 'Purchase order could not be changed.'.
    LOOP AT ret INTO waret.
      WRITE:/
        waret-type,
        waret-id,
        waret-number,
        waret-message.
    ENDLOOP.
```

```abap
    ELSE.
*   Success message
      CALL FUNCTION 'BAPI_TRANSACTION_COMMIT'
        DESTINATION p_dest.
      WRITE:/ 'Purchase order changed'.
    ENDIF.
```

Listing 2.15 "ZIFP_TEST_CHANGE_BAPI" Test Program

"GetList" Compared to the change BAPIs, the read BAPIs have a rather simple structure. Listing 2.16 shows the GetList BAPI for the Order business object. The GetList BAPIs are instance-independent and provide a list of key values for their business objects that correspond to the selection criteria transferred during the call. The Z_BAPI_ORDER_GETLIST BAPI receives a reference ID and provides a list of customer purchase orders with this reference ID in the TA_ORDERS table. If the reference ID is initial, it returns a list of all purchase orders. In case of success as well as in case of error, the system populates the RETURN parameter of the BAPIRET2 type.

```abap
FUNCTION z_bapi_order_getlist.
*"----------------------------------------------------------
*"*"Local interface:
*"  IMPORTING
*"     VALUE(IM_REFID) LIKE ZIFPORDER-REFID OPTIONAL
*"  EXPORTING
*"     VALUE(RETURN) TYPE  BAPIRET2
*"  TABLES
*"     TA_ORDERS STRUCTURE  ZIFPORDER
*"----------------------------------------------------------
* Initialize return parameter
  REFRESH ta_orders.
  CLEAR   return.
  CALL FUNCTION 'Z_IFP_ORDER_GETLIST'
    EXPORTING
      im_ordertype = 'SO'
      im_refid     = im_refid
    TABLES
      ta_orders    = ta_orders
```

```abap
      EXCEPTIONS
        not_authorized = 1
        no_data        = 2
        OTHERS         = 3.
    CASE sy-subrc.
      WHEN 0.
        return-type     = 'S'.
      WHEN 1.
        "No authorization
        CALL FUNCTION 'BALW_BAPIRETURN_GET2'
            EXPORTING
                type      = 'E'
                cl        = 'ZIFP'
                number    = 101
                parameter = ''
                field     = ''
            IMPORTING
                return    = return.
      WHEN 2.
        CALL FUNCTION 'BALW_BAPIRETURN_GET2'      "No data
            EXPORTING
                type      = 'E'
                cl        = 'ZIFP'
                number    = 106
                parameter = ''
                field     = ''
            IMPORTING
                return    = return.
    ENDCASE.
ENDFUNCTION.
```

Listing 2.16 "GetList" BAPI

In real life, `GetList` BAPIs are often more complex than this simple example. They usually allow for a transfer of a selection table with the SIGN, OPTION, HIGH, and LOW columns for selected attributes of the business object. This enables the user of the BAPI to transfer complex selection criteria, which is also possible for ABAP reports if you use the SELECT-OPTIONS keyword. Frequently, `GetList` BAPIs also have the `MaxRows` import parameter. If this parameter isn't initial for the call, the BAPI only returns as many lines with key values as specified in `MaxRows`.

Selection table

2 | Remote Function Call with ABAP

"GetDetail" BAPI   The instance-dependent `GetDetail` BAPI in Listing 2.17 expects a purchase order number as the transfer parameter. It selects the corresponding data from the `ZIFPORDER` and `ZIFPORDERPOS` database tables. If it cannot find any data there, it writes an error message to the `RETURN` parameter. If it finds the required data record, the BAPI writes a success message to the `RETURN` parameter and copies the found data to the `EX_ORDERHEADER` and `TA_ORDERPOS` return parameters.

```
FUNCTION z_bapi_order_getdetail.
*"----------------------------------------------------------------
*"*"Local interface:
*"  IMPORTING
*"     VALUE(ORDERID)      TYPE   ZIFPORDERID
*"  EXPORTING
*"     VALUE(EX_ORDERHEAD) TYPE   ZIFPORDER
*"     VALUE(RETURN)       TYPE   BAPIRET2
*"  TABLES
*"     TA_ORDERPOS STRUCTURE  ZIFPORDERPOS
*"----------------------------------------------------------------
* Initialize return parameter
  CLEAR:
    return,
    ex_orderhead.
  REFRESH ta_orderpos.
  CALL FUNCTION 'Z_IFP_ORDER_GETDETAIL'
    EXPORTING
      im_orderid    = orderid
    IMPORTING
      ex_orderhead  = ex_orderhead
    TABLES
      ta_orderpos   = ta_orderpos
    EXCEPTIONS
      not_authorized = 1
      no_data        = 2
      OTHERS         = 3.
  CASE  sy-subrc.
    WHEN 0.
      return-type   = 'S'.
    WHEN 1.
      "No authorization
      CALL FUNCTION 'BALW_BAPIRETURN_GET2'
        EXPORTING
```

```
                    type      = 'E'
                    cl        = 'ZIFP'
                    number    = 101
                    parameter = ''
                    field     = ''
                 IMPORTING
                    return    = return.
        WHEN 2.
          CALL FUNCTION 'BALW_BAPIRETURN_GET2'       "No data
                 EXPORTING
                    type      = 'E'
                    cl        = 'ZIFP'
                    number    = 106
                    parameter = ''
                    field     = ''
                 IMPORTING
                    return    = return.
      ENDCASE.
ENDFUNCTION.
```

Listing 2.17 "GetDetail" BAPI

The `ZIFP_TEST_READ_BAPIS` report in Listing 2.18 enables you to test the `GetList` and `GetDetail` BAPI. The report queries a reference ID from the user and uses it to call the `Z_BAPI_ORDER_GETLIST` BAPI. If the operation is successful, it makes a loop through all lines of the `it_orderhead` table, which contains the key values of the purchase orders. Within the loop, the report calls the `Z_BAPI_ORDER_GETDETAIL` BAPI for each purchase order. In case of success, these details are provided in the output list, in case of error, the system writes the corresponding message.

Testing the reading BAPIs

```
REPORT   zifp_test_read_bapis.
DATA:
  it_orderhead   TYPE STANDARD TABLE OF zifporder,
  wa_orderhead   TYPE zifporder,
  it_orderpos    TYPE STANDARD TABLE OF zifporderpos,
  wa_orderpos    TYPE zifporderpos,
  msg_text(80)   TYPE c,
  return         TYPE bapiret2.
PARAMETERS:
  p_dest TYPE rfcdest.
START-OF-SELECTION.
*Get list of the ORDERIDs
  CALL FUNCTION 'Z_BAPI_ORDER_GETLIST'
    DESTINATION p_dest
```

```
      IMPORTING
        return   = return
      TABLES
        ta_orders = it_orderhead.
  IF return-type = 'E'.
    WRITE:/ return-message.
  ELSE.
* Output all purchase orders
    LOOP AT it_orderhead INTO wa_orderhead.
      WRITE:/
        wa_orderhead-orderid COLOR COL_KEY,
        wa_orderhead-type,
        wa_orderhead-refid,
        wa_orderhead-buyer,
        wa_orderhead-seller,
        wa_orderhead-orderdate.
* Get purchase order details
      CALL FUNCTION 'Z_BAPI_ORDER_GETDETAIL'
        DESTINATION p_dest
        EXPORTING
          orderid    = wa_orderhead-orderid
        IMPORTING
          return     = return
        TABLES
          ta_orderpos = it_orderpos.
      IF return-type = 'E'.
        WRITE:/ return-message.
      ELSE.
* Output purchase order details
        LOOP AT it_orderpos INTO wa_orderpos.
          WRITE:/
            wa_orderpos-orderid COLOR COL_KEY,
            wa_orderpos-orderpos COLOR COL_KEY,
            wa_orderpos-matid,
            wa_orderpos-mattext,
            wa_orderpos-ordercount,
            wa_orderpos-price,
            wa_orderpos-currency.
        ENDLOOP.
        ULINE.
      ENDIF.
    ENDLOOP.
  ENDIF.
```

Listing 2.18 "ZIFP_TEST_READ_BAPIS" Test Program

2.4.3 "Helpvalues" Business Object

The `Helpvalues` business object provides two BAPIs that enable you to search for valid values for fields of BAPI parameters of other business objects. These BAPIs are useful if an external program wants to provide input helps that are similar to the SAP value help (F4 help). These two BAPIs expect the name or object type of the business object, the name of a BAPI of the business object, the name of a parameter in this BAPI, and the name of a field in this parameter as the import parameters.

BAPIs for input helps

With this information, the `GetSearchhelp` BAPI delivers a list of the search helps for the respective field. The `GetList` BAPI delivers a hit list with this information and the output of a search help.

Search helps and hit lists

By calling a function module, both BAPIs first check if the calling user is authorized to obtain this information. This function module must be stored in the `BAPIF4T` table. The data element of the requested field serves as a selection criterion for browsing this table for the `Helpvalue` BAPI.

Authorization check

That means if you want to use this mechanism for your `Order` business object, you must first implement a function module that carries out the authorization check and then enter this function module into the `BAPIF4T` table using Transaction SM30. As a template for this module, you can use any function module that already exists in this table. Listing 2.19 shows the complete function module.

```
FUNCTION z_orderid_f4_authority.
*"----------------------------------------------------------
*"*"Local interface:
*"  IMPORTING
*"     VALUE(OBJTYPE)  LIKE  BAPIF4F-OBJTYPE
*"     VALUE(METHOD)   LIKE  BAPIF4F-METHOD OPTIONAL
*"     VALUE(DTEL)     LIKE  BAPIF4F-DTEL OPTIONAL
*"     VALUE(SHLPNAME) LIKE  BAPIF4F-SHLPNAME OPTIONAL
*"     VALUE(TABNAME)  LIKE  BAPIF4F-TABNAME OPTIONAL
*"  EXPORTING
*"     VALUE(RETURN) LIKE   BAPIF4F-RETURN
*"----------------------------------------------------------
  AUTHORITY-CHECK OBJECT 'ZIFPORDER' ID 'ACTVT' FIELD '03'.
  IF sy-subrc = 0.
    MOVE ' ' TO return.
  ELSE.
```

```
         MOVE 'X' TO return.
      ENDIF.
ENDFUNCTION.
```
Listing 2.19 "Z_ORDERID_F4_AUTHORITY" Check Module

If the authorization check is successful, that is, if the user is authorized to display the requested data, you must initialize the RETURN export parameter. In the contrary case, 'X' must be assigned to it.

Registering a check module

Figure 2.6 illustrates the registration of this function module for the ZIFPORDERID data element. After the registration has been carried out, you can use the two Helpvalues BAPIs, which will be explained in the following sections.

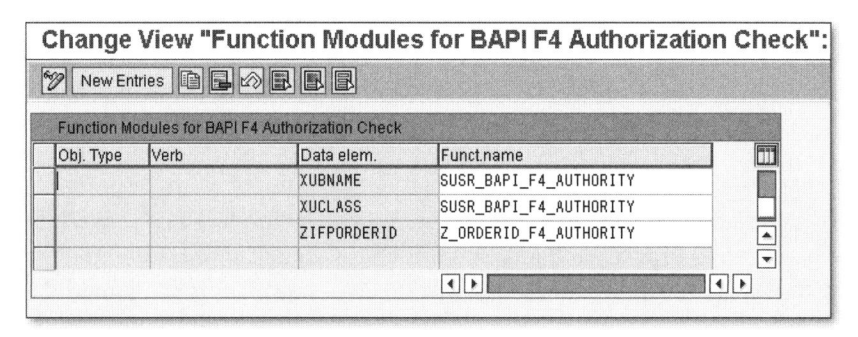

Obj. Type	Verb	Data elem.	Funct.name
		XUBNAME	SUSR_BAPI_F4_AUTHORITY
		XUCLASS	SUSR_BAPI_F4_AUTHORITY
		ZIFPORDERID	Z_ORDERID_F4_AUTHORITY

Figure 2.6 Registering the Check Modules

"GetSearchhelp" BAPI

Figure 2.7 shows the result of a call of the Helpvalues BAPI, GetSearchhelp. The OBJNAME, METHOD, PARAMETER, and FIELD parameters transfer the Order object name, the GetDetail BAPI name, the ExOrderhead parameter name, and the ORDERID field name. In the SHLP_FOR_HELPVALUES_GET table parameter, the BAPI returns the names, the type (SH in this case), and the title of the two simple search helps, ZIFPORDERA and ZIFPORDERB. The DESCRIPTION_FOR_HELPVALUES table parameter provides information on the search help parameters. You can then use this information, for example, to have the user choose one of the existing search helps.

```
Test Function Module: Result Screen

Test for function group      BFHV
Function module              BAPI_HELPVALUES_GET_SEARCHHELP
Uppercase/Lowercase   ☑

Runtime:        5,461 Microseconds

RFC target sys:
```

Import parameters	Value
OBJTYPE	
OBJNAME	Order
METHOD	GetDetail
PARAMETER	ExOrderhead
FIELD	ORDERID

Export parameters	Value
RETURN	

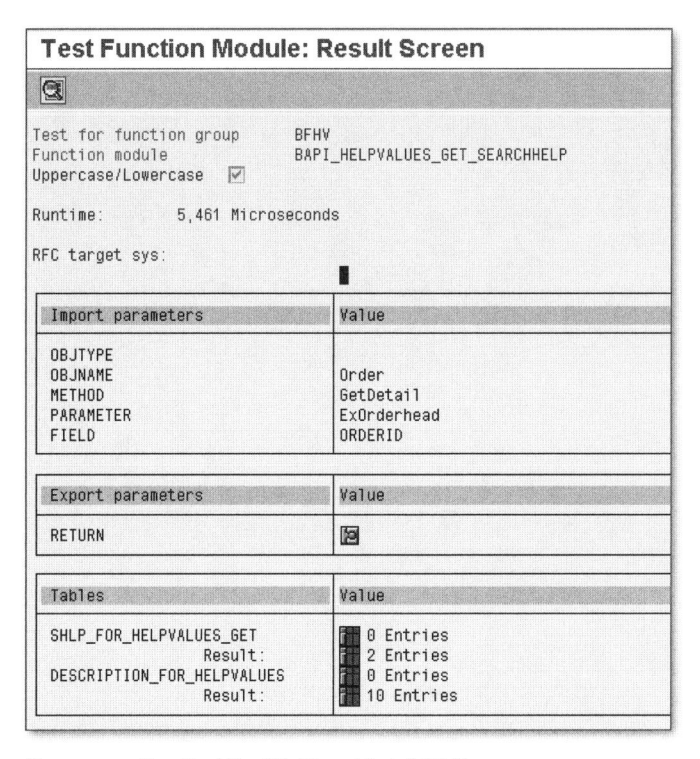

Tables	Value
SHLP_FOR_HELPVALUES_GET	0 Entries
Result:	2 Entries
DESCRIPTION_FOR_HELPVALUES	0 Entries
Result:	10 Entries

Figure 2.7 Result of the "GetSearchhelp" BAPI

Figure 2.8 shows the result of a call of the Helpvalues BAPI, GetList. As before, the OBJNAME, METHOD, PARAMETER, and FIELD parameters transfer the Order object name, the GetDetail BAPI name, the ExOrderhead parameter name, and the ORDERID field name. In addition, the structured import parameter, EXPLICIT_SHLP, passes the name and type of a previously found search help.

"Helpvalues" BAPI

The GetList BAPI is called twice. When it is called first, 'X' is defined for the DESCRIPTIONONLY import parameter. In this case, only the DESCRIPTION_FOR_HELPVALUES table is evaluated. This table contains the parameter names of the search help and their descriptions. This information can then be used to map a selection screen for the user.

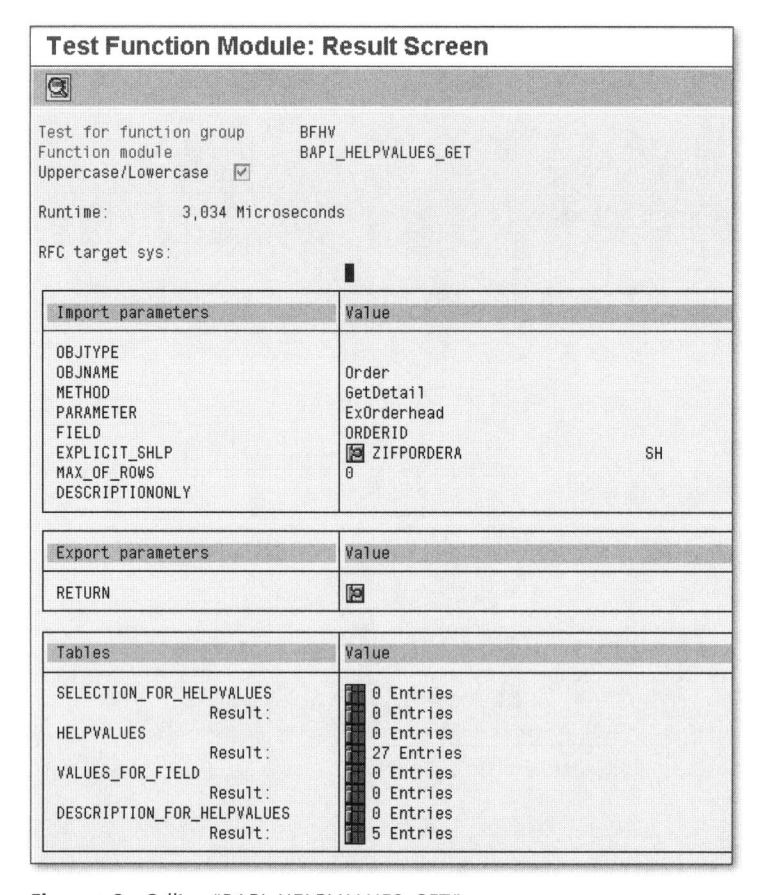

```
Test Function Module: Result Screen

Test for function group    BFHV
Function module            BAPI_HELPVALUES_GET
Uppercase/Lowercase   ☑

Runtime:       3,034 Microseconds

RFC target sys:            ▮

| Import parameters | Value |
|---|---|
| OBJTYPE | |
| OBJNAME | Order |
| METHOD | GetDetail |
| PARAMETER | ExOrderhead |
| FIELD | ORDERID |
| EXPLICIT_SHLP | ZIFPORDERA         SH |
| MAX_OF_ROWS | 0 |
| DESCRIPTIONONLY | |

| Export parameters | Value |
|---|---|
| RETURN | |

| Tables | Value |
|---|---|
| SELECTION_FOR_HELPVALUES | 0 Entries |
| Result: | 0 Entries |
| HELPVALUES | 0 Entries |
| Result: | 27 Entries |
| VALUES_FOR_FIELD | 0 Entries |
| Result: | 0 Entries |
| DESCRIPTION_FOR_HELPVALUES | 0 Entries |
| Result: | 5 Entries |
```

Figure 2.8 Calling "BAPI_HELPVALUES_GET"

Two calls   In a second call, ' ' is specified for the DESCRIPTIONONLY import parameter, and the selection criteria entered by the user are transferred to the SELECTION_FOR_HELPVALUES table. This table has the common structure of a selection table with the SELECT_FLD column for the name of the selection field as well as the SIGN, OPTION, LOW, and HIGH columns. SIGN can adopt the values I (for include) or E (for exclude). OPTION includes a Boolean operator (EQ for equal, LT for less than, BT for between, CP for contains pattern, etc.). LOW uses the comparison value specified by the user. If OPTION = BT, LOW includes the lower interval limit and HIGH the upper interval limit. The HELPVALUES table then contains the list of the found values. Here, the column contents of the hit list are simply listed one after the other. The DESCRIPTION_FOR_HELPVALUES table contains the information on the position, offset, and length of a column.

This chapter introduces you to the C RFC library, which forms the basis of RFC programming in external systems. This library is available for the most essential operating systems and is the technical basis for Java RFC libraries.

3 Remote Function Call with C

In this chapter, you learn how to write RFC and BAPI clients and servers with the programming language C. With C, you can directly access the SAP RFC library. This is particularly important if you don't have a Java or a .NET environment available on your platform or if your interface requires the maximum execution speed.

To use the programming language C for writing interface programs for SAP, you need a C compiler and the SAP RFC library for your platform.

3.1 C RFC Library

The SAP *RFC library* is also written in C and is available for all platforms on which SAP systems run. Among others, these include Intel systems with Windows 9x, NT, XP, 2000, 2003, or Linux as the operating system; AS400; and several UNIX systems, such as HP-UX, Sun Solaris, and others. Using the RFC library, you can call RFC function modules from an external program and receive function calls from an SAP program.

The RFC library is made up of three parts:

Parts of the RFC library

- **"saprfc.h" header file**
  This header file contains definitions of data types and structures as well as declarations (prototypes) of functions that form the RFC-API.

- **"sapitab.h" header file**
  This header file defines the necessary APIs for processing internal tables.

▶ **Library**
The *librfc.a* or *librfc32.dll* and *librfc32.lib* libraries contain the compiled functions of the RFC-API.

3.1.1 RFC Software Development Kit

In addition to the RFC library, the *RFC Software Development Kit* (RFC SDK) is also helpful. It includes the documentation, several sample programs that are useful for getting started, and initial tests.

The RFC SDK can be found in the *rfcsdk* subdirectory on the SAP GUI CD. You can have it installed either together with the SAP GUI or have it copied to your development computer later on. The RFC SDK comprises four subdirectories with the following content:

Subdirectories

▶ **bin**
This directory contains compiled test and sample programs:

 ▶ sapinfo(.exe)
 Call system information from an SAP system.

 ▶ rfcping(.exe)
 Executes connection tests.

 ▶ startrfc(.exe)
 Starts any function module via RFC.

 ▶ rfcexec(.exe)
 RFC server program that can be started from an SAP system to access the files and pipes.

 ▶ srfctest(.exe)
 RFC client program for connection and performance tests.

 ▶ srfcserv(.exe)
 RFC server program for connection and performance tests.

 ▶ trfctest(.exe)
 RFC client program as an example of the transactional RFC (tRFC).

 ▶ trfcserv(.exe)
 RFC server program as an example of the tRFC.

 ▶ rfchcli(.exe)
 RFC client program as an example and test for the multithreaded RFC library on 32-bit Windows.

- rfchserv(.exe)
  RFC server program as an example and test for the multithreaded RFC library on 32-bit Windows.
- genh(.exe)
  Generates C header files for structures that are defined in the data dictionary of an SAP system.
- rfcnpass(.exe)
  Changes the password of a user via RFC.

- **include**
  This directory contains the header files of the RFC library and some sample programs:
  - *saprfc.h*
    Header file for general RFC functions.
  - *sapitab.h*
    Header file for the use of internal tables.
  - *rfcsi.h*
    Header file for the *sapinfo.c* program.
  - *srfctest.h*
    Header file for the *srfctest.c* program.
  - *srfcserv.h*
    Header file for the *srvcserv.c* program.
  - *trfctest.h*
    Header file for the *trfctest.c* program.
  - *trfcserv.h*
    Header file for the *trfserv.c* program.

Sample programs

- **lib**
  This directory contains the RFC library:
  - *librfc.a*
    RFC library for supported UNIX platforms.
  - *librfc32.dll* and *librfc32.lib*
    RFC library and import library for 32-bit Windows.

RFC library

- **text**
  This directory contains the documentation of the RFC library and the C source files of the sample programs:

3 | Remote Function Call with C

Sample programs
- `saprfc.hlp`
  Help for the use of the RFC library.
- `saprfc.ini`
  Example of the *saprfc.ini* file in which the technical connection information is stored.
- `sapinfo.c`
  Call system information from an SAP system.
- `rfcping.c`
  Implement connection tests.
- `sartrfc.c`
  Call any function module via RFC.
- `rfcexec.c`
  RFC server program that can be started from an SAP system to access the files and pipes.
- `srfctest.c`
  RFC client program for connection and performance tests.
- `srfcserv.c`
  RFC server program for connection and performance tests.
- `trfctest.c`
  RFC client program as an example of the tRFC.
- `trfcserv.c`
  RFC server program as an example of the tRFC.
- `rfchcli.c`
  RFC client program as an example and test for the multithreaded RFC library on 32-bit Windows.
- `rfchsrv.c`
  RFC server program as an example and test for the multithreaded RFC library on 32-bit Windows.

It is recommended that you become familiar particularly with the documentation in the *saprfc.hlp* file in the *text* subdirectory.

3.1.2 Connection Tests

"sapinfo" and "rfcping" programs

After you've installed the RFC library, it is useful to first implement connection tests using the programs, `sapinfo` or `rfcping`. For the connection tests, you must specify with which SAP system you want to communicate. You can make this specification either in the command line or in a file called *saprfc.ini*. But first, let's discuss how to specify the connection parameter in the command line.

Basically, there are two options to open a session with an SAP system:

- **Without load balancing**
  In this case, you connect with a specific SAP NetWeaver Application Server (SAP NetWeaver AS) of an SAP system. For this purpose, you must enter the host name or the IP address as well as the system number of the application server. In this case, the call of *sapinfo* is *sapinfo ashost=<host> sysnr=<sysnr>*. Here, you must replace *<host>* with the host name or the IP address of the SAP instance, and replace *<sysnr>* with the system number of the SAP NetWeaver AS.

- **With load balancing**
  In this case, you let the message server of the SAP system decide with which application server your session is supposed to be started. For this purpose, you must enter the host name or the IP address of the message server and the System ID (SID) of the SAP system. Optionally, you can also specify a logon group. For the variant with load balancing, it is important that the services file contains an entry for the message service of the SAP system. The name of the TCP service is `sapms<SID>`, whereas `<SID>` is the system ID of your SAP system. The port number for this TCP service is freely assigned by the administrator of the SAP system. In this case, the call of *sapinfo* is *sapinfo mshost=<host> r3name=<SID> group=<group>*. Here, you must replace *<host>* with the host name or the IP address of the message server of your SAP system, replace *<r3Name>* with the system ID, and replace *<group>* with the desired logon group.

In addition to these parameters, you can also specify via which SAP gateway the communication is supposed to take place. For this purpose, you transfer the host name or the IP address of the gateway host in the `gwhost` command-line parameter and the name of the gateway service in the `gwserv` command-line parameter. The name of the gateway service is *sapgw<sysnr>*, whereas *<sysnr>* is the two-digit system number of the SAP NetWeaver AS on which the gateway runs.

If one or multiple SAP routers are between your development machine and the SAP system, you must consider them in the specification of the

Connection test using the SAP router

host names in the `ashost`, `mshost`, and `gwhost` command-line parameters. The host names and the port numbers of the SAP routers are prefixed to the host name in the following form:

sapinfo ashost=/H/<sapgate1>/S/<port1>/.../H/<host>

Here, you must replace *<sapgate1>* with the host name or the IP address of the SAP router with which your development system is supposed to communicate initially, and *<port1>* with the TCP port on which this SAP router accepts queries. Repeat the */H/<sapgate> /S/<port>* sequence for each router that is on the way from your development system to the SAP system with which you want to communicate.

Transfer of logon information

The *sapinfo* and *rfcping* programs can also receive logon information. For this purpose, you transfer the user name, password, client, and logon language in the command-line parameters, `user`, `passwd`, `client`, and `lang`. However, the two programs also work without these specifications.

Debugging and tracing

Additionally, there are three special command-line parameters that are critical for debugging and tracing:

- `trace`
  This parameter can adopt the values "0" or "1." If it has the value "1," an RFC trace is written to the *dev_rfc.trc* file, which is only stored in case of error. The RFC communication between the C client and the SAP server is logged in detail in this file.

- `abap_debug`
  This parameter can also adopt the values "0" or "1." If it has the value "1," it is started for the RFC call of the ABAP Debuggers. The execution of the function module is canceled directly after the parameter transfer. This is useful to determine which parameter values are actually transferred to the function module via RFC.

- `use_sapgui`
  This parameter can adopt the values "0," "1," or "2." If the value is "1," the SAP GUI is used for the RFC call, but it remains invisible. If the value is "2," it is visible. If the default value "0" is used, the SAP GUI is not used.

"saprfc.ini" file

Instead of transferring these options of the *sapinfo* and *rfcping* programs on the command line, they can also be read from the *saprfc.ini* file. For this purpose, the *saprfc.ini* file must be in the same directory as the external RFC program. Alternatively, you have the option to store the complete path of this file in the `RFC_INI` environment variable.

The *saprfc.ini* file assumes the role of Transaction SM59 for external RFC programs. It stores information about the RFC destinations. The file can store information about multiple RFC destinations. Each entry starts with `DEST=<DESTNAME>`, whereas `<DESTNAME>` is the freely selectable name of the destination. In the `DEST` command-line parameter (`SAPINFO DEST=<DEST>`), you specify which destination from the *saprfc.ini* file the `sapinfo` or `rfcping` programs are supposed to use.

For each destination in the *saprfc.ini* file, the `TYPE=<T>` line follows after the `DEST=<DESTNAME>` entry. Here, `<T>` has the value A if you want to connect to a specific SAP NetWeaver AS. If you want to use load balancing, use the value B for `<T>`.

Listing 3.1 shows an example of the *saprfc.ini* file. Load balancing is used in the first entry with `DEST=BSP`. For this purpose, you must specify the SAP SID, the message server, and optionally the logon group. These specifications are made in the entries, `R3NAME`, `MSHOST`, and `GROUP`. The second entry with `DEST=BSP_H001` stores the connection information for a specific application server. For this purpose, you must give details on the host and the system number of the server in the `ASHOST` and `SYSNR` entries.

```
/*********************************************************/
/*                      SAPRFC.INI                         */
/*********************************************************/
DEST=BSP
TYPE=B
R3NAME=BSP
MSHOST=miniwas
GROUP=PUBLIC
RFC_TRACE=0
ABAP_DEBUG=0
USE_SAP GUI=0
DEST=BSP_H001
TYPE=A
ASHOST=h001
SYSNR=00
RFC_TRACE=0
ABAP_DEBUG=0
USE_SAP GUI=0
```

Listing 3.1 "saprfc.ini" File

3.1.3 Compiling and Linking

The most difficult step in the development of C RFC programs is certainly the setup of the switches for the *compiler* and the *linker*. The general rule applies that you must set the include search path to the *rfcsdk/include* directory and the library search path to the *rfcsdk/lib* directory. Of course, you must also link the C RFC library to the program.

Microsoft Visual Studio
This section details how you can compile the `sapinfo.c` program using Microsoft Visual Studio .NET 2003. First, copy the *sapinfo.c* and *rfcsi.h* files from the *rfcsdk/text* or *rfcsdk/include* directories to a current directory. Then start Microsoft Visual Studio .NET 2003, and create a new Visual C++ project. Select Win32 Console Project as the template and your current directory as the storage location (see Figure 3.1).

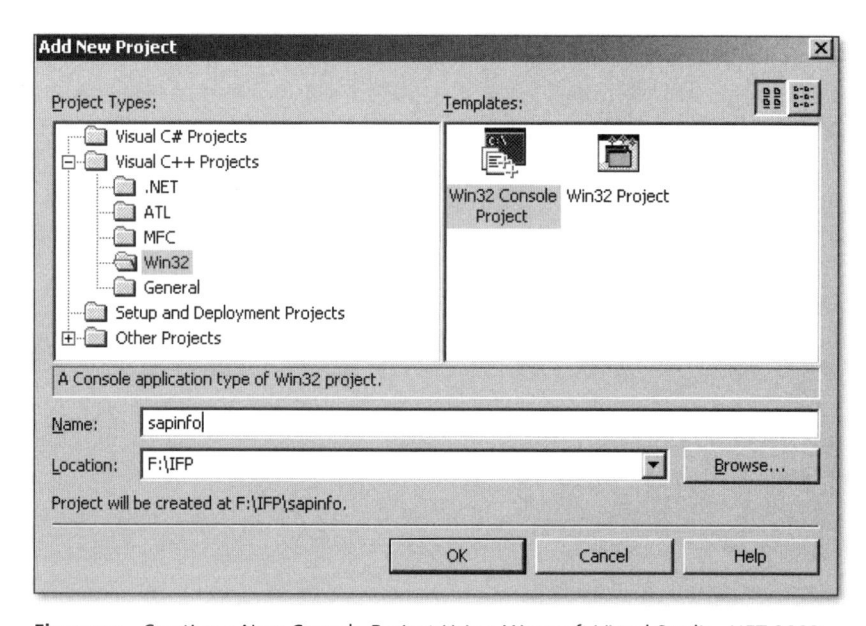

Figure 3.1 Creating a New Console Project Using Microsoft Visual Studio .NET 2003

Remove the generated files, *stdafx.h*, *stdafx.cpp*, and *sapinfo.cpp*, from your project and add *sapinfo.c* as the source file and *rfcsi.h* as the header file to your project instead.

Switches for compiler and linker
Now, you must set the switches for the compiler and the linker. For this purpose, right-click your project in the Solution Explorer, and select

Properties from the context menu displayed. The system displays a dialog in which you can change the configuration properties of your project.

You need to implement five changes:

Configure project

- **C/C++/General**
  Under Additional Include Directories, specify the *rfcsdk/include* path. This way, the compiler finds the required includes, *saprfc.h* and *sapitab.h*.

- **C/C++/Preprocessor**
  Under Preprocessor Definitions, enter "SAPwithUNICODE" if you want to use the Unicode version of the RFC library. If you don't want to use Unicode, omit this preprocessor definition.

- **C/C++/Precompiled Headers**
  Under Create/Use Precompiled Header, select the Not Using Precompiled Headers entry.

- **Linker/General**
  Under Additional Library Directories, specify the *rfcsdk/lib* path. This way, the linker finds the libraries, *librfc32.lib* or *librfc32u.lib*, and *libsapucum.lib*.

- **Linker/Input**
  Under Additional Dependencies, specify the *librfc32u.lib* and *libsapucum.lib* libraries in the Unicode case, or the *librfc32.lib* library in the non-Unicode case. This way, you link these libraries with your program.

Make sure that you make these settings for all configurations (debug, release, etc.). Subsequently, you can compile and link your project via the Build menu.

Of course, this procedure is different for other development environments. The *saprfc.hlp* file describes the command-line arguments of different platforms that you require for compiling and linking.

Other development environments

3.2 Simple RFC Clients and RFC Parameters

In this section, we will consider the basic structure of the RFC client based on simple RFC client programs. We will also learn how to handle simple, structured, and table parameters.

153

3.2.1 Structure of an RFC Client Program

Listing 3.2 shows the basic structure of an RFC client. This client calls only three functions from the RFC-API. It first opens a connection to an SAP system using the `RfcOpenEx` function. It then calls the `RFC_PING` function module via the RFC-API function, `RfcCallReceiveEx`. Finally, it closes the connection again by calling the `RfcClose` function. In case of error, the program returns code 1; in case of success, it returns code 0.

```
#include "saprfc.h"
RFC_ERROR_INFO_EX   error_info;
int mainU (int argc, rfc_char_t ** argv)
{
    RFC_HANDLE          handle = RFC_HANDLE_NULL;
    RFC_RC              rfc_rc = RFC_OK;
    RFC_PARAMETER       exporting[1];
    RFC_PARAMETER       importing[1];
    RFC_PARAMETER       changing[1];
    RFC_TABLE           tables[1];
    rfc_char_t          exception[64];
    rfc_char_t        * exception_ptr = exception;
    rfc_char_t          connect_param[1024];
    /* Fill connection parameter                           */
    sprintfU (connect_param,
       cU("ASHOST=%s SYSNR=%s ")
       cU("CLIENT=%s USER=%s PASSWD=%s LANG=%s"),
       cU("127.0.0.1"),  /* Host name or IP address       */
       cU("01"),         /* System number                 */
       cU("001"),        /* Client                        */
       cU("mwe"),        /* User                          */
       cU("secret"),     /* Password                      */
       iU("de")          /* Language                      */
    );
    /* Open connection                                     */
    handle = RfcOpenEx (connect_param, &error_info);
    if (handle == RFC_HANDLE_NULL)
        exit(1);
    /* Initialize parameter                                */
    importing[0].name = NULL;
    exporting[0].name = NULL;
    changing[0].name  = NULL;
    tables[0].name    = NULL;
    /* Call RFC function                                   */
    rfc_rc = RfcCallReceiveEx (
```

```
        handle, cU("RFC_PING"),
        exporting,
        importing,
        changing,
        tables,
        &exception_ptr);
    if (rfc_rc != RFC_OK)
        exit(1);
    /* Close connection                                      */
    RfcClose( handle );
    return 0;
}
```

Listing 3.2 Simple RFC Client "rfcclient.c"

Now let's discuss the program in detail. Initially, it includes the header file, *saprfc.h*. This file contains the definitions of the types and constants as well as the declarations (prototypes) of the functions in the C RFC-API. Then, the global variable, `error_info` (RFC_ERROR_INFO_EX type), is defined. The address of this variable is transferred to the `RfcOpenEx` function later on. In case of error, it contains more detailed information on the error that occurred.

The `RFC_ERROR_INFO_EX` structure is defined in the *saprfc.h* file and is shown in Listing 3.3.

"RFC_ERROR_INFO_EX" structure

```
typedef struct {
    RFC_ERROR_GROUP    group;
    RFC_CHAR           key[33];
    RFC_CHAR           message[513];
} RFC_ERROR_INFO_EX;
```

Listing 3.3 "RFC_ERROR_INFO_EX" Structure

The components of the structure are:

Structure components

- **group**
  Error group of the `RFC_ERROR_GROUP` type. This type is an enumeration of the possible errors.

- **key**
  An error code to identify the error. Error group and error code have exactly the same meaning. Therefore, it is easier for a program to use the error group for error handling because it can then work with symbolic constants instead of character strings.

▶ message

An error text that describes the error.

Listing 3.4 shows the elements of the RFC_ERROR_GROUP enumeration type.

```
enum RFC_ERROR_GROUP {
  RFC_ERROR_PROGRAM,
  /* Error in RFC program              */
  RFC_ERROR_COMMUNICATION,
  /* Network & communication error */
  RFC_ERROR_LOGON_FAILURE,
  /* SAP logon error                   */
  RFC_ERROR_SYSTEM_FAILURE,
  /* SAP system exception occurred */
  RFC_ERROR_APPLICATION_EXCEPTION,
  /* Exception in called FB            */
  RFC_ERROR_RESOURCE,
  /* Resource not available            */
  RFC_ERROR_PROTOCOL,
  /* RFC protocol error                */
  RFC_ERROR_INTERNAL,
  /* Internal RFC error                */
  RFC_ERROR_CANCELLED,
  /* RFC server was canceled           */
  RFC_ERROR_BUSY
  /* System is busy                    */
};
```

Listing 3.4 "RFC_ERROR_GROUP" Enumeration

ABAP data types

The *saprfc.h* header file defines corresponding C data types for the elementary ABAP data types. For example, one of these, RFC_CHAR, is used for the key and message components of the RFC_ERROR_INFO_EX structure. Listing 3.5 shows the definitions for the ABAP data types.

```
RFC_CHAR    /* ABAP type C, character                          */
RFC_NUM     /* ABAP type N, numbers                            */
RFC_INT     /* ABAP type I, 32-bit integer                     */
RFC_BYTE    /* ABAP type X, Hexadecimal data                   */
RFC_BCD     /* ABAP type P, Binary coded decimals              */
RFC_DATE    /* ABAP type D, Date                               */
RFC_TIME    /* ABAP type T, Time                               */
RFC_
FLOAT      /* ABAP type F, 64-bit IEEE floating point number */
```

```
RFC_WCHAR     /* ABAP type W, wide character          */
RFC_IUNKNOWN  /* COM object. No ABAP type             */
RFC_WSTRING   /* Null-terminated wide character string */
```

Listing 3.5 ABAP Data Types in the C RFC Library

The `main()` function starts in the third line of the *rfcclient.c* program. Instead of `main`, the system uses the `mainU` macro that is defined in the *sapuc.h* header file. Functions are declared in this header file that are supposed to replace the corresponding system functions that work with `char` data types.

This replacement is necessary so that the RFC programs with identical source code can be compiled both for the Unicode and for the non-Unicode library. In these functions, `rfc_char_t` is used instead of `char`. To convert string literals into these types, you can use the `cU` function.

Unicode

At the beginning of the `mainU` function, some local variables are declared:

Local variables

▶ `handle`
   A handle of the `RFC_HANDLE` type that identifies the connection to the SAP system. A handle simply is an integer that you can use to identify a complex resource. In the definition, the `handle` variable is initialized to the `RFC_HANDLE_NULL` value because the connection is not opened yet.

▶ `rfc_rc`

Local variables

   The RFC return code of the `RFC_RC` type. This type is an enumeration, which is shown in Listing 3.6. In the definition, the `rfc_rc` variable is initialized to the `RFC_OK` value.

```
enum RFC_RC {
   RFC_OK,            /* Okay                                    */
   RFC_FAILURE,       /* Error occurred                          */
   RFC_EXCEPTION,     /* Exception triggered                     */
   RFC_SYS_EXCEPTION,
   /* System exception triggered, connection closed              */
   RFC_CALL,          /* Call received                           */
   RFC_INTERNAL_COM,  /* Internal communication                  */
   RFC_CLOSED,        /* Connection closed by partner            */
   RFC_RETRY,         /* No data available yet                   */
   RFC_NO_TID,        /* No transaction ID available             */
   RFC_EXECUTED,      /* Function already executed               */
```

3 | Remote Function Call with C

```
        RFC_SYNCHRONIZE,       /* Synchronous call is executed   */
        RFC_MEMORY_INSUFFICIENT, /* Insufficient memory          */
        RFC_VERSION_MISMATCH,  /* Wrong version                  */
        RFC_NOT_FOUND,         /* Function not found             */
        RFC_CALL_NOT_SUPPORTED,/* Call not supported             */
        RFC_NOT_OWNER,         /* Caller does not own handle     */
        RFC_NOT_INITIALIZED,   /* RFC not yet initialized        */
        RFC_SYSTEM_CALLED,     /* System call is executed        */
        RFC_INVALID_HANDLE,    /* Invalid handle                 */
        RFC_INVALID_PARAMETER, /* Invalid parameter              */
        RFC_CANCELED,          /* RFC canceled by user           */
        RFC_CONVERSION,        /* Error during data conversion   */
        RFC_INVALID_PROTOCOL   /* Not supported format           */
};
```

Listing 3.6 RFC Return Codes

▶ exporting

An array with the export parameters that are transferred to the function module. These parameters are of the RFC_PARAMETER type, which is illustrated in Listing 3.7. The array contains an entry for every export parameter. After the last parameter, there is an additional entry for which the name component is set to NULL.

```
typedef struct {
   void           *name;    /* Parameter name               */
   unsigned       nlen;     /* Length of name               */
   RFC_TYPEHANDLE type;     /* Data type of the parameter   */
   void           * addr;   /* Address of the data          */
} RFC_PARAMETER;
```

Listing 3.7 "RFC_PARAMETER" Type

Local variables

▶ importing

An array with the import parameters that are received by the caller of the function module. These parameters are also of the RFC_PARAMETER type. The array contains an entry for every import parameter. After the last parameter, there is an additional entry for which the name component is set to NULL.

▶ changing

An array with the changing parameters that are transferred to the function module, changed by it, and received by the caller after the call. These parameters are also of the RFC_PARAMETER type. The array contains an entry for every changing parameter. After the last parameter, there is an additional entry for which the `name` component is set to `NULL`.

▶ `tables`
An array with the table parameters that are transferred to the function module, changed by it, and received by the caller after the call. These parameters are of the `RFC_TABLE` type, which is illustrated in Listing 3.8. The array contains an entry for every table parameter. After the last parameter, there is an additional entry for which the `name` component is set to `NULL`.

```
typedef struct {
   void           *name;     /* Parameter name              */
   unsigned       nlen;      /* Length of name              */
   RFC_TYPEHANDLE type;      /* Data type of a table line   */
   unsigned       leng;      /* Length of line in byte      */
   ITAB_H         ithandle;  /* Handle of the internal table */
   RFC_ITMODE     itmode;    /* Always RFC_ITMODE_BYREFERENCE */
   int            newitab;   /* For internal use            */
} RFC_TABLE;
```

Listing 3.8 "RFC_TABLE" Type

▶ `exception`
This character array accepts the name of the exception that is possibly triggered by the function module or the system.

▶ `exception_ptr`
This is a pointer to the first character in the `exception` array.

▶ `connect_param`
This character string is populated with the connection parameters and transferred to the `RfcOpenEx` function.

After the definition of the variables, you enter the connection parameters into the `connect_param` array using the `sprintfU` function. The host name and the system number of an SAP NetWeaver AS as well as the client, user name, password, and logon language for the logon to the SAP system are the connection parameters.

In the next step, the program transfers this information to the `RfcOpenEx` function to obtain a handle for an RFC connection in the `handle` variable. In case of error, the `RfcOpenEx` function writes further information

Local variables

"RfcOpenEx" function

into the `error_info` structure whose address is also transferred during the call. If `handle` still has the `RFC_HANDLE_NULL` value after the call, the `RfcOpenEx` function was not able to establish a connection, and the program cancels with the exit code 1.

If the call of the `RfcOpenEx` function was successful, the program initializes the transfer parameters for the function module in the next step. Because the function module to be called, `RFC_PING`, has no parameters, only one entry is written to the `importing`, `exporting`, `changing`, and `tables` arrays whose `name` component is set to `NULL`.

"RfcCallReceiveEx" function

Finally, the program calls the `RFC_PING` function module using the `RfcCallReceiveEx` function. This function receives the RFC handle, the name of the function module, the parameters, and the address of `exception_ptr`. If an error occurred during the call, the `rfc_rc` return code is not equal to `RFC_OK`, and the name of a possibly occurred exception is available in the `exception` variable.

The program now checks the return code `rfc_rc`. In case of error, it cancels with the exit code 1. In case of success, the program uses the `RfcClose` function to close the SAP connection, which is identified by the `handle` variable, and returns 0 as the return code.

"RfcCallEx" and "RfcReceiveEx" functions

This simple RFC client uses the `RfcCallReceiveEx` function to call the function module. Here, the export, changing, and table parameters are transferred to the RFC library and transported to the server via TCP/IP from there. `RfcCallReceiveEx` waits until a response is returned. To enable the client to do something else in the meantime or cancel the waiting in case of timeout, you can also use the function pair, `RfcCallEx` and `RfcReceiveEx`, instead of `RfcCallReceiveEx`.

```
RFC_RC rc;
...
/* Trigger call                                          */
rc = RfcCallEx( handle, cU("RFC_PING"),
   exporting, changing, tables );
do
{
  rc = RfcListen( handle );
  if( rc == RFC_RETRY )
  {
     /* no  RFC response yet—do something else      */
     ...
```

```
    }
} while ( rc == RFC_RETRY );
/* Receive response                                     */
if( rc == RFC_OK )
  rc = RfcReceiveEx( handle,
     importing, changing, tables, &exception_ptr );
...
```

Listing 3.9 Use of "RfcCallEx," "RfcListen," and "RfcReceiveEx"

Listing 3.9 shows the use of the function pair, `RfcCallEx` and `RfcReceiveEx`. Using the `RfcCallEx` function, the client transfers only the export, changing, and table parameters initially. This call doesn't wait for a response but returns immediately. Then, the client uses the `RfcListen` function to check whether the server has returned a response. This function returns with a return code immediately. As long as this return code equals `RFC_RETRY`, the server has not yet returned a response, and the client can do something else in a loop and can then retry using `RfcListen`. As soon as a response is returned by the server, the return code equals `RFC_OK` (or `RFC_FAILURE` in case of error). Then, the client receives the changing, export, and table parameters by calling `RfcReceiveEx`.

"RfcListen" function

The client uses the `RfcOpenEx` function to open a connection. This function receives call connection parameters in the `connect_param` argument. The transfer of the parameter names and the parameter values is done in the form `<ID>=<value>`. Table 3.1 lists the most important parameter IDs and their meaning.

"RfcOpenEx" function

ID	Description
CLIENT	SAP logon client
USER	SAP user
PASSWD	SAP logon password
LANG	SAP logon language
LCHECK	Logon check during opening (0/1 without/with check; default value = 1)
TRACE	RFC trace (0/1 without/with trace; default value = 1)
DEST	Destination in *saprfc.ini*
GWHOST	Host name of the RFC gateway

Table 3.1 Important Connection Parameters in the "RfcOpenEx" Function

ID	Description
GWSERV	Service name of the RFC gateway
MSHOST	Host name of the message server
MSSERV	Service name of the message server
R3NAME	Name of the SAP system
GROUP	Logon group
ASHOST	Host name of the SAP application server
SYSNR	System number of the SAP application server
USE_SAP GUI	RFC with SAP GUI (0/1/2 without/with/invisible SAP GUI between RFC functions; default value = 0)
ABAP_DEBUG	RFC with ABAP Debugger (0/1 without/with ABAP Debugger; default value = 0)

Table 3.1 Important Connection Parameters in the "RfcOpenEx" Function (Cont.)

Error handling

The simple RFC client from Listing 3.2 shown earlier only uses a rudimentary error handling. Listing 3.10 shows how this error handling can be improved slightly. For this purpose, the client defines the rfc_error function that can receive a string with an error description. This string displays the function in the console. Moreover, it queries the error that occurred last from the RFC library by calling RfcLastErrorEx. This error is stored in a structure of the RFC_ERROR_INFO_EX type. This structure has already been shown in Listing 3.3. The rfc_error function displays the components, group, key, and message.

```
/* Define error handler                                       */
void DLL_CALL_BACK_FUNCTION rfc_error (
  rfc_char_t * operation)
{
    printfU (cU("RFC error: %s\n"), operation );
    RfcLastErrorEx(&error_info);
    printfU (cU("\nGroup       %d"), error_info.group);
    printfU (cU("\nKey         %s"), error_info.key);
    printfU (cU("\nMessage     %s\n"), error_info.message);
    exit(1);
} /* rfc_error */
int mainU (int argc, rfc_char_t ** argv)
{
    RFC_ENV            new_env;
    RFC_RC             rfc_rc = RFC_OK;
```

```
        rfc_char_t          exception[64];
        rfc_char_t         * exception_ptr = exception;
        ...
        /* Install error handler                          */
        new_env.allocate = NULL;
        new_env.errorhandler = rfc_error;
        RfcEnvironment (&new_env);
        ...
        rfc_rc = RfcCall(handle,...);
        if(rfc_rc != RFC_OK)
          rfc_error( (cU("RfcCall") );
        ...
        rfc_rc = RfcReceive (handle, ..., &exception_ptr);
        if (rfc_rc != RFC_OK)
        {
            if ((rfc_rc == RFC_EXCEPTION) ||
                (rfc_rc == RFC_SYS_EXCEPTION))
            {
                rfc_error (exception_ptr);
            }
            else
            {
                rfc_error (cU("RfcReceive"));
            }
        }
        ...
}
```

Listing 3.10 Error Handling Using "RfcLastErrorEx"

At the beginning of the program, the client transfers a pointer to the error handling function, rfc_error, to the RFC library by calling RfcEnvironment. This function then transfers a pointer to a structure of the RFC_ENV type, which is defined in Listing 3.11 in the *saprrf.h* file.

"RfcEnvironment" function

```
typedef struct
{
   RFC_ERROR_HANDLER errorhandler;
   RFC_ALLOCATE      allocate;
}
RFC_ENV;
```

Listing 3.11 "RFC_ENV" Structure

The `errorhandler` component of this structure points to the `rfc_error` function.

"RfcLastErrorEx" function

Whenever the client calls a function that returns an RFC return code, this return code is checked. If the RFC return code doesn't equal `RFC_OK`, an error occurred. In this case, the client calls the `rfc_error` function. This function retrieves detailed information on the occurred error by calling the `RfcLastErrorEx` function and displays this information. After the call of API functions that receive a pointer to a structure of the `RFC_ERROR_INFO_EX` type themselves, `RfcLastErrorEx` and consequently `rfc_error` must not be called. In case of error, the populated structure doesn't need to be evaluated directly. This is the case, for example, when `RfcOpenEx` is called if an invalid RFC handle (`RFC_HANDLE_NULL`) is returned.

3.2.2 Simple Parameters

The `RFC_PING` function module defines no parameters in its interface at all. It is only intended for a pure connection test. The next more difficult case is to call a function module whose interface only has simple (unstructured) parameters. These can be import, changing, or export parameters of the function module.

"RFC_PARAMETER" type

These parameters are transferred to all arrays of the `RFC_PARAMETER` type, which is illustrated in Listing 3.7 earlier in this chapter. The `name` component of this structure points to a string that contains the name of the parameter. The `nlen` component indicates the length of this string.

The `type` component is of the `RFC_TYPEHANDLE` type, which is only an alias for the `unsigned` type. So each parameter type is uniquely identified by an unsigned integer. For the elementary ABAP data types in shown previously Listing 3.5, you can use the members of the `RFCTYPE` enumeration as the values of the `type` component. Table 3.2 lists the most important members of `RFCTYPE` and specifies how the contents of the parameters must be formatted.

The `addr` component finally contains a pointer to the actual parameter content. The type of the variables with the parameter content must correspond to the type specification in `type`. For this purpose, the *saprfc.h* file defines C types that have already been shown in Listing 3.5.

Member	Usage
RFCTYPE_CHAR	Single-byte or multibyte character string filled with blanks at the end
RFCTYPE_DATE	Date in the format YYYYMMDD
RFCTYPE_BCD	Packed *binary coded decimal*, length between 1 and 16 bytes
RFCTYPE_TIME	Time in the format HHMMSS
RFCTYPE_BYTE	Binary raw data filled with zeros at the beginning
RFCTYPE_ITAB	Internal table
RFCTYPE_NUM	Number sequence filled with zeros at the beginning
RFCTYPE_FLOAT	Floating point number double
RFCTYPE_INT	4-byte integer
RFCTYPE_IUNKNOWN	An IUnknown object for the use of COM
RFCTYPE_WSTRING	Null-terminated wide character string
RFCTYPE_XMLDATA	Null-terminated string with XML data
RFCTYPE_STRING	Null-terminated string
RFCTYPE_XSTRING	Raw data with length field in bytes
RFCTYPE_WCHAR	Wide character strings filled with blanks at the end

Table 3.2 Some Members of the "RFCTYPE" Enumeration

As an example of the use of simple parameters, Listing 3.12 shows excerpts of an RFC client program that calls the `DDIF_FIELDLABEL_GET` function module. This function module returns a field label for a table field or a data element in the ABAP Dictionary.

Use of simple parameters

```
#define ERROR_OK       0 /* Okay             */
#define ERROR_CONNECT  1 /* Connection error */
#define ERROR_FAILURE  2 /* Other error      */
int mainU (int argc, rfc_char_t ** argv)
{
    ...
```

3 | Remote Function Call with C

```
RFC_PARAMETER          exporting[2];
RFC_PARAMETER          importing[2];
RFC_PARAMETER          changing[1];
RFC_TABLE              tables[1];
SAP_CHAR               tabname [30];
RFC_STRING             label;
...
/* Initialize parameter  */
memsetU(tabname,cU(' '),30);
memcpyU(tabname,cU("ZIFPORDERID"),11);
exporting[0].name = cU("TABNAME");
exporting[0].nlen = 7;
exporting[0].type = RFCTYPE_CHAR;
exporting[0].leng = sizeofR(tabname);
exporting[0].addr = &tabname;
exporting[1].name = NULL;
importing[0].name = cU("LABEL");
importing[0].nlen = 5;
importing[0].type = RFCTYPE_CHAR;
importing[0].leng = sizeofR(label);
importing[0].addr = &label;
importing[1].name = NULL;
...
/* Call RFC function                                    */
rfc_rc = RfcCallReceiveEx (handle,
         cU("DDIF_FIELDLABEL_GET"),
         exporting, importing, changing, tables,
         &exception_ptr);
if (rfc_rc != RFC_OK)
    rfc_error(cU("RfcCallReceiveEx"));
/* Display import parameter                             */
printf("label=%s",label);
...
}
```

Listing 3.12 RFC Client with Simple Parameters

Import and export from the client's perspective

The program uses the TABNAME import parameter and the LABEL export parameter of the function module. From the program's perspective, however, it exports the TABNAME parameter and imports the LABEL parameter. For these two parameters, the tabname field of the RFC_CHAR type and the label pointer of the RFC_String type are defined at the beginning of the program.

The result of the interface definition of the function module is that the TABNAME import parameter is of the DDOBJNAME type. The ABAP Dictionary determines that this type comprises 30 characters. Therefore, the tabname array has exactly 30 characters.

The LABEL parameter is of the STRING type. Consequently, label must be of the RFC_STRING type. An RFC_STRING is a null-terminated character string that is automatically managed by the RFC library.

Next, the program fills the tabname variable with the name of the data element for which a field label is supposed to be determined. For this purpose, memsetU is used to fill the variable with blanks whereupon the ZIFPORDERID string is copied into the variable with left justification. This filling with blanks is important because otherwise the data element cannot be found.

Fill character strings with blanks

Then the program describes the parameter to be exported in the components of the exporting[0] array element. For this purpose, the program assigns the name component with TABNAME. This name has a length of seven characters, which is described in the nlen component. The parameter is a character string, which is why the type component is assigned with RFCTYPE_CHAR. The leng component includes the length of the tabname variable; the addr component contains its address.

The same procedure applies to the parameter to be imported, LABEL, in the components of importing[0]. To indicate to the RFC library that no further parameters follow, the exporting[1].name and importing[1].name components are assigned with NULL. Finally, the program displays the field label using the printfU function.

3.2.3 Structured Parameters

You can also transfer structured parameters in the importing, exporting, and changing arrays. For this purpose, you must define a corresponding C structure and describe this structure for the RFC library.

To simplify this task, the RFC SDK provides the genh program. This program extracts the structure information from the ABAP Dictionary and generates the corresponding C structures.

We want to illustrate this based on a client that calls the RFC_SYSTEM_INFO function module. This function module has the structured export parameter, `RFCSI_EXPORT`, of the `RFCSI` type. To generate the *rfcsi.h* header file with the definitions for the `RFCSI` structure, call the `genh` program as follows:

genh dest=bsp user=<user> passwd=<passwd> client=<client>
　rfcsi > rfcsi.h

Macros for structure parameters

Listing 3.13 shows excerpts of the generated file. First, you define the `RFCSI` structure with the components, `Rfcproto`, `Rfcchartyp`, `Rfcinttyp`, `Rfcflotyp`, `Rfcdest`, `Rfchost`, and so on. Additionally, macros for the length, the number of characters, and the type of the component are defined for each component.

```
#ifndef RFCSI_H
#define RFCSI_H
typedef struct RFCSI
{
    SAP_CHAR    Rfcproto [3];
#define RFCSI_RFCPROTO_LN   CCQ_CAST(intR)(3*sizeofR(SAP_CHAR))
#define RFCSI_RFCPROTO_CCNT CCQ_CAST(intU)3
#define RFCSI_RFCPROTO_TYP  RFCTYPE_CHAR
    SAP_CHAR    Rfcchartyp [4];
#define RFCSI_RFCCHARTYP_LN
CCQ_CAST(intR)(4 * sizeofR(SAP_CHAR))
#define RFCSI_RFCCHARTYP_CCNT   CCQ_CAST(intU)4
#define RFCSI_RFCCHARTYP_TYP    RFCTYPE_CHAR
    SAP_CHAR    Rfcinttyp [3];
#define RFCSI_RFCINTTYP_LN
CCQ_CAST(intR)(3 * sizeofR(SAP_CHAR))
#define RFCSI_RFCINTTYP_CCNT CCQ_CAST(intU)3
#define RFCSI_RFCINTTYP_TYP  RFCTYPE_CHAR
...}
RFCSI;
#define RFCSI_LN sizeofR( RFCSI )
#ifdef RFC_DEFINE_U_STRUCTURE
static RFC_UNICODE_TYPE_ELEMENT Description_U_RFCSI[] =
{
{ cU("Rfcproto"),    RFCSI_RFCPROTO_TYP,   0,3,0,6, 0,12, 0},
{ cU("Rfcchartyp"),  RFCSI_RFCCHARTYP_TYP,0,4,3,8, 6,16,12},
{ cU("Rfcinttyp"),   RFCSI_RFCINTTYP_TYP,  0,3,7,6,14,12,28},
...
};
#define ENTRIES_OF_U_RFCSI
(sizeofR(Description_U_RFCSI)/
sizeofR((Description_U_RFCSI)[0]))
```

Listing 3.13 Header File Generated Using the "genh" Program

Then, the header defines the `Description_U_RFCSI` array that contains the description of the structure for the C RFC library. Each entry of the array contains the description of a component of the `RFCSI` structure. The entries are of the `RFC_UNICODE_TYPE_ELEMENT` type. This type is shown in Listing 3.14. The `ENTRIES_OF_U_RFCSI` macro specifies the number of entries in the `Description_U_RFCSI` array.

Structure descriptions

```
typedef struct {
  rfc_char_t       *name;      /* Name of component               */
  RFC_TYPE_HANDLE  type;       /* Type of component               */
  unsigned         decimals;
  /* Number of decimals for type BCD                              */
  unsigned         c1_length;
  /* Length in byte in systems with 1 byte per SAP_CHAR           */
  unsigned         c1_offset;
  /* Offset in byte in systems with 1 byte per SAP_CHAR           */
  unsigned         c2_length;
  /* Length in byte in systems with 2 bytes per SAP_CHAR          */
  unsigned         c2_offset;
  /* Offset in byte in systems with 2 bytes per SAP_CHAR          */
  unsigned         c4_length;
  /* Length in byte in systems with 4 bytes per SAP_CHAR          */
  unsigned         c4_offset;
  /* Offset in byte in systems with 4 bytes per SAP_CHAR          */
} RFC_UNICODE_TYPE_ELEMENT;
```

Listing 3.14 "RFC_UNICODE_TYPE_ELEMENT" Type

Listing 3.15 shows excerpts from an RFC client that calls the `RFC_SYSTEM_INFO` function module. The client initially defines the `RFC_DEFINE_U_STRUCTURE` symbol before it includes the generated header, *rfcsi.h*. This is necessary so that the description of the structure is available later on.

RFC client with structure parameters

```
#define RFC_DEFINE_U_STRUCTURE
#include "saprfc.h"
#include "rfcsi.h"
#define OUTC(text, value) \
  printfU (cU("%-15s %-.*s\n"), text, \
    (int) sizeofU (rfcsi_export.value), rfcsi_export.value )
int mainU (int argc, rfc_char_t ** argv)
{
    RFC_TYPEHANDLE      typeHandleRFCSI;
    RFCSI               rfcsi_export;
    ...
```

```
                    /* Install structure                          */
                    rfc_rc = RfcInstallUnicodeStructure(
                       cU("RFCSI"), Description_U_RFCSI, ENTRIES_OF_U_RFCSI,
                         0, NULL, &typeHandleRFCSI);
                    if (rfc_rc != RFC_OK)
                       rfc_error(cU("RfcInstallUnicodeStructure"));
                    ...
                    /* Initialize parameter                        */
                    importing[0].name = cU("RFCSI_EXPORT");
                    importing[0].nlen = 12;
                    importing[0].type = typeHandleRFCSI;
                    importing[0].leng = RFCSI_LN;
                    importing[0].addr = &rfcsi_export;
                    importing[1].name = NULL;
                    exporting[0].name = NULL;
                    changing[0].name  = NULL;
                    tables[0].name    = NULL;
                    /* Call RFC function                           */
                    rfc_rc = RfcCallReceiveEx (handle, U("RFC_SYSTEM_INFO"),
                           exporting, importing, changing, tables,
                           &exception_ptr);
                    if (rfc_rc != RFC_OK)
                       rfc_error("RfcCallReceiveEx");
                    /* Display import parameter                    */
                    OUTC(cU("Name of SAP system"),    Rfcsysid);
                    OUTC(cU("Database host name "),   Rfcdbhost);
                    OUTC(cU("SAP release       "),    Rfcsaprl);
                    }
```

Listing 3.15 RFC Client with Structure Parameters

Type handle identifies structures

In the `main` function, the client defines variables for the import and export parameters as always. In addition to the `rfcsi_export` structure, it also defines the `typeHandleRFCSI` variable of the `RFC_TYPEHANDLE` type. This variable accepts a type handle for the `RFCSI` structure. The handle is generated by the C RFC library and uniquely identifies the structure. The client receives the handle by calling the `RfcInstallUnicodeStructure` function. The client transfers the name of the structure, the `Description_U_RFCSI` array with the structure description, the number of entries in this array, and the address of `typeHandleRFCSI` to this function. Instead of a member of the `RFCTYPE` enumeration, the client enters the received type handle, `typeHandleRFCSI`, into the `type` component for the description of the `RFCSI_EXPORT` import parameter.

To output the individual components of the `RFCSI_EXPORT` return parameter, the client defines the `OUTC` macro. A text and the component name are transferred to this macro. The macro outputs the text and the value of the specified component of `rfcsi_export`. Because the RFC character strings are not `NULL`-terminated, the macro ensures that the correct number of characters is output, respectively.

3.2.4 Table Parameters

Finally, let's have a look at how table parameters are used. In a C RFC program, internal tables are manipulated by functions with the `It` prefix. These functions are declared in the *sapitab.h* header file.

Table 3.3 lists the functions for processing internal tables. An RFC program generates internal tables by calling the `ItCreate` function. Here, the program specifies how long a line of the internal table is supposed to be. The function returns a handle to the calling program that uniquely identifies the internal table. This handle is transferred to the other `It` functions as the first parameter, respectively.

Generate tables using "ItCreate"

Function	Usage
ItCreate	Creates a new internal table and returns a handle for it.
ItFree	Removes all of the lines of an internal table. This table can still be used.
ItDelete	Deletes an internal table and release the memory space occupied by it.
ItAppLine	Appends a new empty line to the internal table and returns a pointer to it.
ItPutLine	Copies a structure to a specific line of an internal table.
ItCpyLine	Copies a specific line of an internal table into a structure.
ItDelLine	Deletes a specific line of an internal table.
ItGetLine	Returns the pointer to a specific line. The pointer must only be used for reading.
ItGupLine	Returns the pointer to a specific line. The pointer must only be used for changing.
ItLengLine	Returns the size of a line of an internal table.
ItFill	Returns the number of lines of an internal table.

Table 3.3 Functions for Manipulating Internal Tables

| Append line using "ItAppLine" | To populate the internal table, an RFC program calls the ItAppLine function. This function allocates memory space for a new line and returns a pointer to this line. The program converts this pointer into a pointer to the desired line type and then fills the individual components of the line. |

| Determine the number of lines | To read an internal table, an RFC program determines the number of lines by calling ItFill. In a loop, the ItGetLine function is then called for each line; this function returns a pointer to a specific line of the internal table. The program converts this pointer to the desired line type and then reads the individual components of the line. In this process, the loop runs from index 1 up until ItFill because the lines of an internal table are numbered starting with 1. |

In the functions, RfcCallReceiveEx, RfcCallEx, and RfcReceiveEx, the table parameters are transferred in an array whose elements have the RFC_TABLE type (refer to Listing 3.8). Its structure is similar to the RFC_PARAMETER type shown earlier in Listing 3.7. Instead of the address of the data, RFC_TABLE contains the handle of the internal table and additionally information on the length of the table line.

| RFC client with table parameters | Listing 3.16 shows excerpts of an RFC client that calls the Z_IFP_ORDER_GETLIST function module. This function module has the TA_ORDERS table parameter whose lines are of the ZIFPORDER type. Using the genh program, you generate the description of this structure and save it in the *zifporder.h* header file. The RFC client includes this header together with *saprfc.h* and *sapitab.h*. Then, the client defines the OUTC macro to be able to conveniently output the components of this structure. |

```
...
#include "sapitab.h"
#include "zifporder.h"
#define OUTC(text, value) \
  printfU (cU("%-15s %-.*s\n"), text, \
    (int) sizeofU (order->value), order->value )
int mainU (int argc, rfc_char_t ** argv)
{
    ...
    RFC_TYPEHANDLE      typeHandleZifporder;
    ZIFPORDER         * order;
    ITAB_H              ta_orders = ITAB_NULL;
    unsigned            i;
    ...
```

```
    /* Install structure                          */
    rfc_rc = RfcInstallUnicodeStructure(
      cU("RFCSI"), Description_U_ZIFPORDER,
      ENTRIES_OF_U_ZIFPORDER, 0, NULL,
      &typeHandleZifporder);
    if (rfc_rc != RFC_OK)
      rfc_error(cU("RfcInstallUnicodeStructure"));
    /* Create internal table                      */
    ta_orders = ItCreate(cU("ORDERS"), ZIFPORDER_LN, 0, 0);
    if (ta_orders == ITAB_NULL)
        rfc_error(cU("ItCreate"));
    /* Fill internal table (for demo, not required) */
    order = (ZIFPORDER*) ItAppLine(ta_orders);
    memcpyU(order->Orderid, cU("0000000001"),10);
    /* Initialize parameter                       */
    importing[0].name  = NULL;
    exporting[0].name  = NULL;
    changing[0].name   = NULL;
    tables[0].name     = cU("TA_ORDERS");
    tables[0].nlen     = 9;
    tables[0].type     = typeHandleZifporder;
    tables[0].leng     = ZIFPORDER_LN;
    tables[0].ithandle = ta_orders;
    tables[0].itmode   = RFC_ITMODE_BYREFERENCE;
    tables[0].newitab  = 0;
    tables[1].name     = NULL;
    /* Call RFC function                          */
    rfc_rc = RfcCallReceiveEx (handle,
        cU("Z_IFP_ORDER_GETLIST"),
        exporting, importing, changing, tables,
        exception_ptr);
    if (rfc_rc != RFC_OK)
        rfc_error("RfcCallReceiveEx");
    /* Output table parameter                     */
    for(i=1;i<=ItFill(ta_orders);i++)
    {
        order = (ZIFPORDER*) ItGetLine(ta_orders, i);
        OUTC(cU("ORDERID"), Orderid);
    }
    ...
}
```

Listing 3.16 RFC Client with Table Parameters

3 | Remote Function Call with C

In the `main` function, the client defines the `typeHandleZifporder` variable that should include a type handle for the `ZIFPORDER` structure. The `ta_orders` variable should include a handle for the internal table, `TA_ORDERS`. The client uses the `order` pointer of the `ZIFPORDER*` type to point to individual lines of this table.

Write internal tables

By calling the `RfcInstallUnicodeStructure` function, the RFC client publishes the `ZIFPORDER` structure to the RFC library. Then it uses the `ItCreate` function to create a new internal table. For demonstration purposes, this table is filled with a line. To do that, the client calls the `ItAppLine` function that returns a `void*` pointer to a new empty line. The client converts this pointer into the `ZORDER*` type to be able to access the individual components of this structure.

Read internal table

Then the client calls the function module and returns the lines of the internal table. For this purpose, the client determines the number of lines by calling the `ItFill` function and accesses the individual lines in a loop using the `ItGetLine` function. Here as well, the type of the line pointer is converted from `void*` to `ZORDER*` to be able to access the individual components.

3.3 More Complex RFC Clients

This section introduces you to the more complex RFC clients. You will learn how you can call BAPIs and implement tRFC and qRFC clients.

3.3.1 Calling BAPIs

You can also use the previously described techniques to call BAPIs because they are implemented as RFC function modules. The specific features only result from the special implementation rules for BAPIs.

Transaction model for BAPIs

One of these implementation rules is the *transaction model* for BAPIs that accesses the database with write access. Write BAPIs call an update module with the `IN UPDATE TASK` addition for database changes. To ensure that this update task is executed, the client must explicitly call `BAPI_TRANSACTION_COMMIT`.

Listing 3.17 shows excerpts from the source code of an RFC client that calls the `Order.CreateFromData` BAPI. The client populates the export

3.3 More Complex RFC Clients

parameter with order data for calling the Z_BAPI_ORDER_CREATEFROMDATA function module. After the call, the client checks the RETURN import parameter. If no error has occurred, it calls the BAPI_TRANSACTION_COMMIT function module.

```
int mainU (int argc, rfc_char_t ** argv)
{
  ...
  RFC_TYPEHANDLE     typeHandleZifporder;
  ZIFPORDER          order;
  RFC_NUM            orderid[10];
  RFC_TYPEHANDLE     typeHandleZifporderpos;
  ZIFPORDERPOS     * orderpos;
  RFC_TYPEHANDLE     typeHandleBapiret2;
  BAPIRET2         * bapiret2;
  ITAB_H             ta_orderpos = ITAB_NULL;
  ITAB_H             ta_bapiret2 = ITAB_NULL;
  ...
  /* Install structures                              */
  ...
  /* Create internal tables                          */
  ...
  /* Fill order header                               */
  memcpyU(order.Mandt, cU("000"),3);
  memcpyU(order.Orderid, cU("0000000001"),10);
  memcpyU(order.Type, cU("SO"),2);
  memcpyU(order.Refid, cU("0000000001"), 10);
  memsetU(order.Buyer,cU(' '),50);
  memcpyU(order.Buyer, cU("Distributor Wegelin"),19);
  memsetU(order.Seller,cU(' '),50);
  memcpyU(order.Seller, cU("Publisher Hiller"),18);
  memcpyU(order.Orderdate, cU("20090131"),8);
  /* Fill purchase order items                       */
  orderpos = (ZIFPORDERPOS*) ItAppLine(ta_orderpos);
  memcpyU(orderpos->Mandt, cU("000"), 3);
  memcpyU(orderpos->Orderid, cU("0000000001"),10);
  memcpyU(orderpos->Orderpos, cU("00001"),5);
  memsetU(orderpos->Matid,cU(' '),20);
  memsetU(orderpos->Mattext,cU(' '),40);
  memcpyU(orderpos->Mattext, cU("ABAP for Beginners"),17);
  orderpos->Ordercount = 2;
  /* - 2649,7835 as packed decimal */
  orderpos->Price[0] = 0*16 +  2;   // 0*10000 + 2*1000
  orderpos->Price[1] = 6*16 +  4;   // 6*100   + 4*10
```

```
orderpos->Price[2] = 9*16 +  7;  // 9*1    + 7*0,1
orderpos->Price[3] = 8*16 +  3;  // 8*0,01 + 3*0,001
orderpos->Price[4] = 5*16 + 13;  // 5*0,0001, minus sign
memsetU(orderpos->Currency,cU(' '),5);
memcpyU(orderpos->Currency, cU("EUR"),3);
/* Initialize parameter                                  */
...
/* Call RFC function                                     */
rfc_rc = RfcCallReceiveEx (handle,
         cU("Z_BAPI_ORDER_CREATEFROMDATA"),
         exporting, importing, changing, tables,
         &exception_ptr);
if (rfc_rc != RFC_OK)
  rfc_error("RfcCallReceiveEx");
/* Output table parameter RETURN                         */
for(i=1;i<=ItFill(ta_bapiret2);i++)
{
  bapiret2 = (BAPIRET2*) ItGetLine(ta_bapiret2, i);
  OUTC(cU("TYPE"), Type);
  OUTC(cU("MESSAGE"), Message);
}
/* Output order number                                   */
printfU (cU("Orderid %-.*s\n"), \
    (int) sizeofU (orderid), orderid );
importing[0].name = NULL;
exporting[0].name = NULL;
tables[0].name    = NULL;
/* Call BAPI_TRANSACTION_COMMIT                          */
rfc_rc = RfcCallReceiveEx (handle,
         cU("BAPI_TRANSACTION_COMMIT"),
         exporting, importing, changing, tables,
         exception_ptr);
if (rfc_rc != RFC_OK)
  rfc_error(cU("RfcCallReceiveEx"));
...
}
```

Listing 3.17 BAPI Client

Evaluation of the "RETURN" parameter

The RETURN import parameter is an internal table of the BAPIRET2 line type. For this line type, the genh program is used to create a structure description from the ABAP Dictionary. The RFC client installs this structure using RfcInstallUnicodeStructure and creates an internal table with this line type using `ItCreate`. This has already been discussed in the previous section.

3.3.2 Transactional RFC

You should not use the synchronous RFC (sRFC) discussed so far to call function modules that create data in an SAP system because if a call fails with a communication error, the developer doesn't know whether the data has been created in the SAP system and whether the error has only occurred during the confirmation to the client. To ensure that a function module is called exactly once with the data transferred even in case of error, the developer should preferably use a *transactional RFC* (tRFC).

In the tRFC, the export and table parameters are transferred to the RFC library together with the *Transaction ID* (TID) when they are called. The SAP system calls the function module only if the data with the transferred TID has not been processed so far. When the TID is transferred for the first time, the function module is executed; if the TID has already been used, the function module is not executed.

<small>Transaction ID</small>

In case of error, the client can then repeat the call with the same data and the same TID any number of times. Due to the described mechanism, the client can be sure that the data is processed exactly once.

<small>Repetition in case of error</small>

The client retrieves the TID, which it transfers together with the data for the function module by calling the `RfcCreateTransID` function. The TID is then transferred to the function module together with the export and table parameters by calling the `RfcIndirectCallEx` function.

If the call was successful, the client should call the `RfcConfirmTransID` function to initiate the deletion of the used TID from the database tables of the SAP system.

In the following, we describe a tRFC client that writes a purchase order to an SAP system via calls of the `Z_IFP_ORDER_CREATE` function module. In the command line, the program expects the name of a file that contains the data of a purchase order. Before the client obtains a TID and transfers the data to the SAP system via tRFC, it checks the *order.tid* file whether the concerned file with the order data has been transferred already.

<small>tRFC client</small>

TID file The *order.tid* file saves the transfer time, the result of the transfer, and the name of the file with the purchase order. There are three options for the result of the transfer:

- **CREATED**

  A TID was created in a previous transfer attempt, but the `RfcIndirectCallEx` function failed. In this case, the client retransfers the data with the same TID and then confirms this TID.

- **EXECUTED**

  A TID was created in a previous transfer attempt, and `RfcIndirectCallEx` was executed successfully, but `RfcConfirmTransID` has not been called yet. In this case, the client only calls `RfcConfirmTransID` with the TID from *order.tid* and doesn't transfer the data again.

- **CONFIRMED**

  A previous transfer attempt was completed successfully. In this case, the client doesn't do anything.

Listing 3.18 shows an example for the *order.tid* file with three TIDs for the *order1.dat*, *order2.dat*, and *order3.dat* files.

```
*** tRFC TID management file ***
... C0A89F810CC849AAE89C006A  CONFIRMED  order1.dat
... C0A89F810CC849AAE9B4007E  CREATED    order2.dat
... C0A89F810CC849AAEE0A007F  EXECUTED   order3.dat
```

Listing 3.18 "order.tid" File for the TID Management

TID states The first transaction has been implemented successfully, and the TID has been confirmed. A TID has been created for the second transaction, but `RfcindirectCallEx` has not been executed at all or with errors. If the tRFC client is called again with `order2` as the command-line argument, it retransfers the data with the same TID and then confirms the TID. The third transaction has been implemented successfully, but the TID has not been confirmed yet. If the tRFC client is called again with `order3` as the command-line argument, it doesn't retransfer the data, it only confirms the TID.

TID management The client must define some functions for the *TID management*. Listing 3.19 shows the header file of the client, where the enumerations, `TID_RC` and `TID_STATE`, are defined. `TID_RC` defines the return values of the two TID management functions, `update_TID` and `search_TID`.

3.3 More Complex RFC Clients

```
#define RFC_DEFINE_U_STRUCTURE
#include <time.h>
#include "saprfc.h"
#define ERROR_OK        0 /* Okay                 */
#define ERROR_CONNECT   1 /* Connection error     */
#define ERROR_FAILURE   2 /* Other error          */
/* Return values from TID management              */
typedef enum
{
  TID_OK,              /* Okay                          */
  TID_CREATED_FOUND,   /* TID found in CREATED state    */
  TID_EXECUTED_FOUND,  /* TID found in EXECUTED state   */
  TID_CONFIRMED_FOUND, /* TID found in CONFIRMED state  */
  TID_ERROR_UPDATE
  /* TID state could not be changed */
}
TID_RC;
/* TID state in TID management                   */
typedef enum
{
  CREATED,              /* TID created              */
  EXECUTED,             /* Transaction executed     */
  CONFIRMED,            /* TID confirmed            */
  ROLLBACK              /* Transaction rolled back  */
}
TID_STATE;
```

Listing 3.19 Header File of the tRFC Client

The `search_TID` TID management function uses the tRFC client to search for a TID for the transferred file in the *author.tid* file. Depending on the result, it then executes the necessary action and changes the state of the TID using the `update_TID` function. The client transfers the new state, which is a member of the `TID_STATE` enumeration, to this function.

Listing 3.20 shows the `search_TID` TID management function. This function opens the TID file whose name is transferred as the third parameter. If the TID file does not exist, it is created by `search_TID`. Then the function searches for an entry for the transferred file in a `while` loop. The file name is transferred to the function as the second parameter. If no entry is found, the function returns the `TID_OK` message. If an entry is found, the function copies the found TID to the first transfer parameter and determines the state of the TID in the TID file. This state is then returned.

"search_TID" function

```
/* Search for existing TID for the data file       */
extern TID_RC search_TID(RFC_TID tid, rfc_char_t *datafile,
                         rfc_char_t *tid_file)
{
  rfc_char_t   *ptr, tbuf[MAXBUFF+1];
  TID_RC       tidrc;
  FILE         *fp;
  memsetU (tid, cU('\0'), RFC_TID_LN);
  /* Open file for search    */
  fp = fopenU (tid_file, cU("rb"));
  if (fp == NULL)
  {
    /* Create TID file     */
    fp = fopenU (tid_file, cU("ab"));
    if (fp == NULL)
      return TID_ERROR_UPDATE;
    strcpyU (tbuf,
        cU("*** tRFC TID management file ***\n"));
    if (fputsU (tbuf, fp) < 0)
      tidrc = TID_ERROR_UPDATE;
    else
      tidrc = TID_OK;
    fclose(fp);
    return tidrc;
  }
}
```

Listing 3.20 "search_TID" TID Management Function

"update_TID" function

Listing 3.21 shows the update_TID TID management function. The function expects the TID as a parameter, the new state, as well as the name of the data file and the TID file. If the state is CREATED, it writes the new TID at the end of the TID file. For this purpose, it opens the TID file and calls the write_TID function. In case the TID has other states, the function must open the TID file for changes and search the entry in a while loop. If the entry is found, the fp file pointer is positioned at the corresponding position, and the new state is written using write_TID.

```
/* Change TID state in TID file                             */
extern TID_RC update_TID(RFC_TID tid, TID_STATE tid_state,
    rfc_char_t *datafile, rfc_char_t * tid_file)
{
```

```
    rfc_char_t    *ptr, tbuf[MAXBUFF+1];
    TID_RC        tidrc;
    long          offset = 0;
    FILE          *fp;
    memsetU (tbuf, cU('\0'), LINE_SIZE/sizeofR(SAP_UC));
    if (tid_state == CREATED)
    {
      /* New TID: write to end        */
      fp = fopenU (tid_file, cU("ab"));
      if (fp == NULL)
        return TID_ERROR_UPDATE;
      else
      {
        if (write_TID(fp, tid, tid_state, datafile))
          tidrc = TID_ERROR_UPDATE;
        else
          tidrc = TID_OK;
        fclose(fp);
        return tidrc;
      }
    }
    /* Open file for update   */
    fp = fopenU (tid_file, cU("rb+"));
    if (fp == NULL)
      return TID_ERROR_UPDATE;
    /* Search TID                                          */
    while ((ptr = fgetsU (tbuf, LINE_SIZE+1, fp)) != NULL)
    {
      if (memcmpU (tbuf+26, tid, RFC_TID_LN) == 0)
        break;
      offset = offset + strlenU (tbuf)*sizeofR(SAP_UC);
    }
    /* Write new TID state                     */
    if ((ptr != NULL) && (fseek (fp, offset, SEEK_SET) == 0) &
        (write_TID (fp, tid, tid_state, datafile) == 0))
      tidrc = TID_OK;
    else
      tidrc = TID_ERROR_UPDATE;
    fclose(fp);
    return tidrc;
} /* update_tid */
```

Listing 3.21 "update_TID" TID Management Function

"write_TID" function

Listing 3.22 shows the write_TID TID management function. This function determines the current time and then writes the time, the transferred TID, the transferred state, and the transferred file name to the TID file. Before, the TID file was opened by the calling function (update_TID) and positioned at the correct location. The write_TID function receives the file pointer as the first parameter.

```
/* Write TID and data file in the TID file          */
static int write_TID(FILE *fp, RFC_TID tid,
   TID_STATE tid_state, rfc_char_t *datafile)
{
  struct tm     *time_ptr;
  time_t        actutime;
  rfc_char_t    datetime[25],
                tbuf[MAXBUFF+1];
  memsetU (tbuf, cU('\0'), LINE_SIZE/sizeofR(SAP_UC));
  actutime = time(NULL);
  time_ptr = localtime(&actutime);
  memcpyU (datetime, asctimeU(time_ptr), 24);
  switch(tid_state)
  {
    case CREATED:
      sprintfU (tbuf, cU("%.*s  %.*s   CREATED     %s\n"),
          24, datetime, RFC_TID_LN, tid, datafile);
      break;
    case EXECUTED:
      sprintfU (tbuf, cU("%.*s  %.*s   EXECUTED    %s\n"),
              24, datetime, RFC_TID_LN, tid, datafile);
      break;
    case CONFIRMED:
      sprintfU (tbuf, cU("%.*s  %.*s   CONFIRMED   %s\n"),
              24, datetime, RFC_TID_LN, tid, datafile);
      break;
    case ROLLBACK:
      sprintfU (tbuf, cU("%.*s  %.*s   ROLLBACK    %s\n"),
              24, datetime, RFC_TID_LN, tid, datafile);
      break;
  }
  if (fputsU (tbuf, fp) < 0)
    return 1;
  else
    return 0;
} /* write_tid */
```

Listing 3.22 "write_TID" TID Management Function

Listing 3.23 shows excerpts of the source code of the tRFC client. Initially, the `mainU` function declares the necessary variables. Among other things, this includes the names for the TID file and the data file, the memory space for the TID, and a file pointer for the data file.

```
#include "trfc.h"
int mainU (int argc, rfc_char_t ** argv)
{
    rfc_char_t          data_file[64];
    rfc_char_t          tid_file[11] = iU("order.tid");
    ...
    RFC_TYPEHANDLE      typeHandleZifporder;
    ZIFPORDER           order;
    RFC_TYPEHANDLE      typeHandleZifporderpos;
    RFC_CHAR            commit;
    ITAB_H              ta_orderpos = ITAB_NULL;
    RFC_TID             tid;
    TID_RC              tid_rc, tid_search_rc;
    FILE               *data_fp;
    /* Check arguments                                      */
    if(argc!=2)
    {
        printfU (cU("\nUsage: trfc <file>\n"));
        exit(ERROR_FAILURE);
    }
    strcpyU(data_file,argv[1]);
    /* Open file                                            */
    data_fp = fopenU (data_file, cU("r"));
    if (data_fp == NULL)
    {
      printfU(
        cU("\nFile %s cannot be opened.\n"),
        data_file);
        exit(ERROR_FAILURE);
    }
    ...
    /* Initialize parameter                                 */
    importing[0].name   = NULL;
    exporting[0].name   = cU("IM_ORDERHEADER");
    exporting[0].nlen   = 14;
    exporting[0].type   = typeHandleZifporder;
    exporting[0].leng   = sizeofR(order);
    exporting[0].addr   = &order;
    exporting[1].name   = cU("IM_COMMIT");
    exporting[1].nlen   = 9;
```

```c
              exporting[1].type   = RFCTYPE_CHAR;
              exporting[1].leng   = sizeofR(commit);
              exporting[1].addr   = &commit;
              exporting[2].name   = NULL;
              changing[0].name    = NULL;
              tables[0].name      = cU("TA_ORDERPOS");
              tables[0].nlen      = 11;
              tables[0].type      = typeHandleZifporderpos;
              tables[0].leng      = ZIFPORDERPOS_LN;
              tables[0].ithandle  = ta_orderpos;
              tables[0].itmode    = RFC_ITMODE_BYREFERENCE;
              tables[0].newitab   = 0;
              tables[1].name      = NULL;
              /* Search previous failed TID               */
              tid_search_rc = search_TID(tid, data_file, tid_file);
              switch(tid_search_rc)
              {
                case TID_CREATED_FOUND:
                {
                  printfU(
                    cU("\n** Previous tRFC failed **"));
                  printfU (cU("\n   TransID    : %.*s"),
                    RFC_TID_LN, tid);
                  printfU (cU("\n   State:     : CREATED\n"));
                  break;
                }
                case TID_EXECUTED_FOUND:
                {
                  printfU(
                    cU("\n** Previous tRFC executed   **"));
                  printfU (cU("\n   TransID    : %.*s"),
                    RFC_TID_LN, tid);
                  printfU (cU("\n   State:     : EXECUTED\n"));
                  break;
                }
                case TID_CONFIRMED_FOUND:
                {
                  printf(
                    cU("\n** Previous tRFC confirmed      *"));
                  printfU (cU("\n   TransID   : %.*s"),
                    RFC_TID_LN, tid);
                  printfU (cU("\n   State:    : CONFIRMED\n"));
                  break;
                }
```

```
    default:
    {
      printfU(
        cU("\n** First call of transaction    **\n"));
      /* Obtain new TID                              */
      rfc_rc = RfcCreateTransID(handle, tid);
      if(rfc_rc!=RFC_OK)
        rfc_error(cU("RfcCreateTransID"));
      printfU (cU("      TID = '%.*s'\n"),
        RFC_TID_LN, tid);
      /* Save TID in file                            */
      tid_rc = update_TID(tid, CREATED,
                 data_file, tid_file);
    }
  }
  if (tid_search_rc == TID_OK ||
      tid_search_rc == TID_CREATED_FOUND)
  {
    /* Save header data from input file in order */
    rfc_rc = (RFC_RC) write_file_to_structure(
                      data_fp, &order);
    if (rfc_rc!=RFC_OK)
      rfc_error(cU("write_file_to_structure"));
    /* Item data from input file in ta_pos    */
    rfc_rc = (RFC_RC) write_file_to_table(
                      data_fp, ta_orderpos);
    if (rfc_rc!=RFC_OK)
      rfc_error(cU("write_file_to_table"));
      fclose(data_fp);
    /* tRFC-Aufruf                                   */
    rfc_rc = RfcIndirectCallEx (handle,
             cU("Z_IFP_ORDER_CREATE"),
             exporting, tables, tid);
    if(rfc_rc!=RFC_OK)
      rfc_error(cU("RfcIndirectCallEx"));
    /* Save TID state in file                        */
    tid_rc = update_TID(tid, EXECUTED,
                      data_file, tid_file);
  }
  if(tid_search_rc != TID_CONFIRMED_FOUND)
  {
    /* Confirm transaction                           */
    rfc_rc = RfcConfirmTransID(handle, tid);
    if(rfc_rc!=RFC_OK)
```

```
                    rfc_error(cU("RfcConfirmTransID"));
          /* Save TID state in file                              */
          tid_rc = update_TID(tid, CONFIRMED,
                              data_file, tid_file);
      }
      /* Close connection                                        */
      RfcClose( handle );
      return 0;
  }
```

Listing 3.23 tRFC Client

The client initially checks the number of arguments and copies the first argument to data_file. The client then tries to open this file. If everything works properly, it installs an RFC error handler, populates the parameters for the RFC connection, opens the connection, and installs the structures, ZIFPORDER and ZIFPORDERPOS. You've already seen this code as well as the initialization of the export and table parameters in the previous listings of this chapter.

Reuse or newly create TID

Then the client uses search_TID to search the *order.tid* TID file to determine whether the data has already been processed and displays a corresponding message. If the data has never been processed before, the RfcCreateTransID function is used to create a new TID. If the TID_OK and TID_CREATED_FOUND messages are displayed, the client reads the data from the data file and transfers it to the SAP system together with the TID using the RfcIndirectCallEx function. It then changes the TID state to EXECUTED in the TID file. Subsequently, the client confirms the TID by calling the RfcConfirmTransID function and changes the state of the TID to CONFIRMED.

Listing 3.24 shows the write_file_to_structure and write_file_to_table functions. These functions read the purchase order header and the purchase order items from the opened fp file into the strorder structures and the internal table it_pos.

```
/* Copy purchase order header to structure                       */
int write_file_to_structure(FILE *fp, ZIFPORDER *strorder)
{
  int          rc = 0;
  rfc_char_t   buf[136];
  if (fgetsU (buf, 136, fp) != NULL)
```

```
    memcpyU(strorder,buf,133);
  else
    rc = 1;
  return rc;
}
/* Copy purchase order items to table             */
int write_file_to_table(FILE *fp, ITAB_H it_pos)
{
  int           rc = 0;
  rfc_char_t    buf[102];
  rfc_char_t    number[11];
  ZIFPORDERPOS  *pos;
  while (fgetsU (buf, 102, fp) != NULL)
  {
    pos = (ZIFPORDERPOS*) ItAppLine(it_pos);
    memcpyU(pos->Mandt,buf,3);
    memcpyU(pos->Orderid,buf+3,10);
    memcpyU(pos->Orderpos,buf+13,5);
    memcpyU(pos->Matid,buf+18,20);
    memcpyU(pos->Mattext,buf+38,40);
    memcpyU(number,buf+78,10);
    number[10] = 0;
    pos->Ordercount = atoiU(number);
    number[1]=0;
    memcpyU(number,buf+88,1);   // 1000
    pos->Price[0] = atoiU(number);
    memcpyU(number,buf+89,1);   //  100
    pos->Price[1] = 16*atoiU(number);
    memcpyU(number,buf+90,1);   //   10
    pos->Price[1] = pos->Price[1] + atoiU(number);
    memcpyU(number,buf+91,1);   //    1
    pos->Price[2] = 16*atoiU(number);
    memcpyU(number,buf+93,1);   // 0,1
    pos->Price[2] = pos->Price[2] + atoiU(number);
    memcpyU(number,buf+94,1);   // 0,01
    pos->Price[3] = 16*atoiU(number);
    pos->Price[4] = 0;
    memcpyU(pos->Currency,buf+95,5);
  }
  return rc;
}
```

Listing 3.24 "write_file_to_structure" and "write_file_to_table" Functions

3.3.3 Queued RFC

The C RFC library enables the use of *queued RFC* (qRFC). Here, multiple tRFC calls are placed in an inbound queue in an SAP system. This ensures that the calls in the target system are processed in the same sequence as they have been triggered in the receiving system.

<small>Insert using "RfcQueueInsert"</small>

The use of qRFC is identical to tRFC. Instead of `RfcIndirectCallEx`, the client must use the `RfcQueueInsert` function to inform the receiving SAP system that the call is supposed to be queued in an inbound queue for subsequent processing. If the call of `RfcQueueInsert` was successful, the client must call the `RfcConfirmTransID` function. In case of an error, the client must repeat the call of `RfcQueueInsert` with the same TID as before. So a qRFC client must call the following RFC functions:

1. `RfcOpen`
   Opens the RFC connection to the target system.

2. `RfcCreateTransID`
   Requests a transaction ID. If the call fails, the client must reopen the connection and repeat the call.

3. `RfcQueueInsert`
   This call ensures that the data is transferred to the receiving system via tRFC together with the TID and the queue name. In case of an error, the client must reopen the connection and repeat the call with the same TID. It must not request a new TID. Otherwise, it is not ensured that the call is processed only once in the target system. If the call was successful, the LUW is saved completely in the inbound queue in the SAP system.

4. `RfcConfirmTransID`
   This function confirms the local transaction processing by the client. The server can delete the transaction ID.

Compared to `RfcIndirectCallEx`, the `RfcQueueInsert` function has two additional parameters: The `qname` parameter receives the queue name, and in the `qcount` parameter, the client transfers the position of the call in the queue. Usually, a qRFC client transfers the value "0" for this parameter for every call. Then, the function modules are processed in the sequence of their call in the receiving system.

The processing of the function modules in an inbound queue is not carried out automatically but is triggered by the call of the `TRFC_QIN_RESTART` function module. This function module can either be called from a program in the SAP system or via RFC from an external system. The queue name must be transferred to this function module.

Processing using "TRFC_QIN_RESTART"

To prevent that every qRFC application must write its own logic for triggering the queue processing, you are provided with the QIN Scheduler that processes the registered queues automatically. Here, the registration of an inbound queue is either program-driven via the `QIWK_REGISTER` function module or manual using the qRFC monitor for the `SMQR` QIN Scheduler.

QIN Scheduler

3.4 RFC Server

As a C programmer you also have the option to write *RFC servers*. These are programs that provide functions that can be called via RFC. Here, the caller can be both an SAP system and any external RFC program.

An RFC server is started either when the client calls the gateway, or it is started independent of the client call and registers in a gateway. Because the second case is the more frequent one, we will discuss it in the following examples.

Starting an RFC server

Listing 3.25 shows the schema of a typical RFC server. After the start of the program, the server transfers the command-line arguments to the RFC library function, `RfcAccept`. In the command line, this function searches for information about the gateway with which the RFC server is supposed to communicate. This information is either transferred in the command line directly, or the command line contains the specification of the destination in the *saprfc.ini* file in which this information is stored. The `RfcAccept` function connects the server with the gateway and returns a handle to an RFC connection in case of success.

Server schema

```
int main ( int argc, char ** argv )
{
  RFC_HANDLE handle;
  RFC_RC     rc;
  handle = RfcAccept( argv );
  if ( handle == RFC_HANDLE_NULL )
  {
```

```
      ... Error handling
      return 1;
   }
   rc = RfcInstallFunction( ..... );
   if( rc != RFC_OK )
   {
      ... Error handling
      return 1;
   }
   do
   {
      rc = RfcDispatch( handle );
   }
   while( rc == RFC_OK );
   RfcClose( handle );
   return 0;
}
```

Listing 3.25   Schema of an RFC Server

Then, the server uses the `RfcInstallFunction` function to install the functions provided. In doing so, the server informs the RFC library about the function name and the pointer to a C function.

The server then calls the `RfcDispatch` function in an endless loop. This function waits for inbound client requests. If a client request is received, the RFC library calls the function that was previously installed using `RfcInstallFunction`.

Example of an RFC server

In the following sections, we will implement this simple schema as a functioning example. Our RFC server in Listing 3.26 provides the two functions, Z_IFP_ORDER_GETLIST and Z_IFP_ORDER_GETDETAIL. It reads the actual data from the files, *orders.dat* with the purchase order headers and *orderpos.dat* with the purchase order items.

```
#include "rfcserv.h"
...
mainU (int argc, rfc_char_t **argv)
{
   RFC_RC            rfc_rc;
   RFC_HANDLE        rfc_handle;
   setbuf(stderr, NULL);
   if (argc == 1)
```

```
{
  help();
  return 0;
}
rfc_handle = RfcAccept(argv);
if (rfc_handle == RFC_HANDLE_NULL)
  rfc_error( cU("RfcAccept"));
rfc_rc = install(rfc_handle);
if( rfc_rc != RFC_OK )
  return 1;
/* Wait for RFC call                                        */
do
{
  rfc_rc = RfcDispatch(rfc_handle);
} while (rfc_rc == RFC_OK);
if (rfc_rc != RFC_CLOSED)
  rfc_error(cU("RfcDispatch"));
return 0;
}
```

Listing 3.26 Simple RFC Server

When the RFC server starts, the `mainU` function checks the number of transferred parameters. If no parameters have been transferred, it calls the `help` function. This function is shown in Listing 3.27. It outputs a help text for the use of the RFC server.

```
/* Display of help for the start of the program            */
void help(void)
{
  printfU ( NL                                         );
  printfU (cU("Syntax:")                          NL );
  printfU (cU("  ")                               NL );
  printfU (cU("   rfcserv [options]")             NL );
  printfU (cU("  ")                               NL );
  printfU (cU("  options =")                      NL );
  printfU (cU("    -D<destination of Type R>")    NL );
  printfU (cU("    -t           RFC trace on")    NL );
  printfU (cU("  or options =")                   NL );
  printfU (cU("    -a<program ID>")               NL );
  printfU (cU("    -g<SAP gateway host name>")    NL );
  printfU (cU("    -x<SAP gateway service>")      NL );
  printfU (cU("    -t           RFC trace on")    NL );
```

```
         printfU (cU(" ")                                    NL );
         return;
}
```

Listing 3.27 Output of Help Text for Starting the Server

Logon to gateway   By calling the `RfcAccept` function, the server logs on to the gateway and receives a handle that uniquely identifies the RFC connection. If the logon was successful, the server calls the `install` function.

This function installs the RFC functions implemented by the server and is shown in detail later in this chapter in Listing 3.29.

After the functions have been installed, the server enters the `do` loop in which the `RfcDispatch` function is called.

3.4.1 Logon to Gateway

In the command line, you can make the specifications for logging on to the gateway in two different ways:

- **Direct specification**
  The specifications about the gateway are made directly in the command line. Here, you can use the following command-line parameters:
  - `-a<program ID>`
    The server logs on to the gateway with the specified program ID. The program ID should consist of the host name of the server, a period and the program name of the server (e. g. SRV0.RFCMAPPING).
  - `-g<SAP gateway host>`
    The server logs on to the gateway on the specified host.
  - `-x<SAP gateway service>`
    The server logs on to the specified gateway service. The gateway service is always called *sapgw<sysnr>*, where *sysnr* is the system number of the SAP instance on which the gateway runs.
  - `-t`
    This option activates the RFC trace.

3.4 RFC Server

▸ **Use of the "saprfc.ini" file**
The specifications about the gateway are taken from the *saprfc.ini* file. Here, you use the following command-line parameters:

▸ `-D<Destination>`
`<Destination>` is a destination of the `R` type in the *saprfc.ini* file. Listing 3.28 shows an example for such an entry.

▸ `-t`
This option activates the RFC trace.

```
/*                    SAPRFC.INI                  */
DEST=CSERV
TYPE=R
PROGID=c.rfcserv
GWHOST=192.168.171.131
GWSERV=SAPGW00
```
Listing 3.28 Entry of the R Type in the "saprfc.ini" File

To enable the ABAP programs to call the functions of the RFC server, you must maintain a destination of the `R` type and of the *registration* subtype in Transaction SM59. Here, you must specify the program ID exactly as it was specified for the start of the RFC server. Case sensitivity is important here.

Destination of the R type

Moreover, you should specify the gateway for the gateway options by all means. Figure 3.2 shows a destination in Transaction SM59 that is in line with the specification in the *saprfc.ini* file in Listing 3.28.

After you've started the server and it successfully logged on to the gateway, you can implement a connection test from the destination maintenance. In Transaction SMGW, you can view the entry for the logged-on server by selecting the GOTO • LOGGED ON CLIENTS menu.

Transaction SMGW

To manage registered servers from an external program, the C RFC library offers two useful functions: With `RfcCheckRegisterServer`, you can check whether and how many programs are logged on to a specific gateway under a specific program ID. With `RfcCancelRegisterServer`, you can deregister registered servers again.

Managing registered servers

3 | Remote Function Call with C

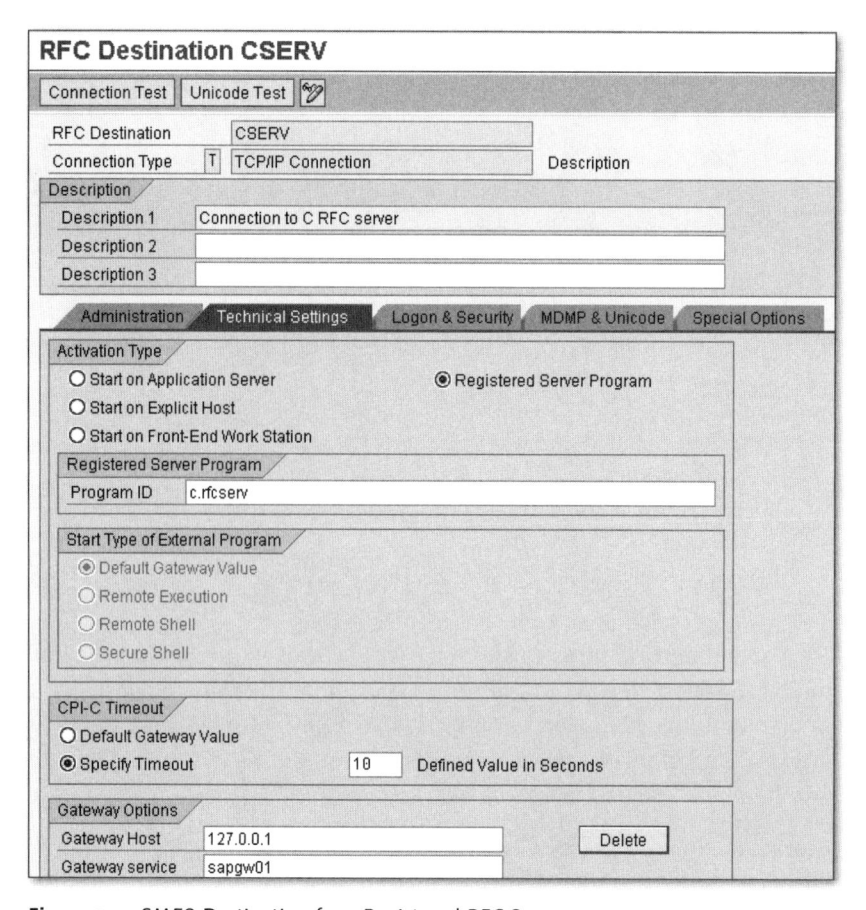

Figure 3.2 SM59 Destination for a Registered RFC Server

3.4.2 Installing and Executing Functions

After the `RfcAccept` function has been called, the server installs the RFC functions that it offers in the RFC library. Listing 3.29 shows the source code of the `install` function that the server uses for this purpose. Within `install`, the server uses the `RfcInstallFunction` function. This function transfers the name of the function to be installed, a pointer to the implementing C function, and a character string with the documentation for the function. In our case, this character string is provided by calling the functions, `z_ifp_order_getlist_docu` or `z_ifp_order_getdetail_docu`.

```
/* Z_IFP_ORDER_GETLIST                                         */
RFC_RC DLL_CALL_BACK_FUNCTION
                 z_ifp_order_getlist(RFC_HANDLE rfc_handle)
{
  RFC_RC           rfc_rc = 0;
  printfU(cU("Z_IFP_ORDER_GETLIST\n"));
  ...
  return rfc_rc;
}
/* Documentation of Z_IFP_ORDER_GETLIST                        */
static rfc_char_t *z_ifp_order_getlist_docu (void)
{
  static rfc_char_t docu[] =
  iU("Returns a list of purchase orders")       NL_AR
  iU("")                                        NL_AR
  iU("IMPORTING")                               NL_AR
  iU("   IM_ORDERTYPE     ZIFPORDERTYPE")       NL_AR
  iU("   IM_REFID         ZIFREFID")            NL_AR
  iU("TABLES")                                  NL_AR
  iU("   TA_ORDERS        ZIFPORDER")           NL_AR;
  return docu;
}
...
/* Installation of the RFC functions of the program            */
RFC_RC install(RFC_HANDLE rfc_handle)
{
  RFC_RC           rfc_rc;
  /* Install Z_IFP_ORDER_GETLIST */
  rfc_rc = RfcInstallFunction(cU("Z_IFP_ORDER_GETLIST"),
                   (RFC_ONCALL) z_ifp_order_getlist,
                   z_author_getlist_docu());
  if( rfc_rc != RFC_OK )
    function_abort(cU("Inst. von Z_IFP_ORDER_GETLIST"),
                rfc_handle);
  /* Install Z_IFP_ORDER_GETDETAIL */
  rfc_rc = RfcInstallFunction(cU("Z_IFP_ORDER_GETDETAIL"),
                    (RFC_ONCALL) z_ifp_order_getdetail,
                       z_author_getdetail_docu());
  if( rfc_rc != RFC_OK )
    function_abort(cU("Inst. von Z_IFP_ORDER_GETDETAIL"),
                rfc_handle);
  return RFC_OK;
} /* install */
```

Listing 3.29 Installation of Server Functions

3 | Remote Function Call with C

Implementation The implementing C functions receive a handle that identifies the RFC connection as the only parameter. Within this function, the RFC server must receive the import and table parameters using `RfcGetData`. This parameter then evaluates, calculates, or reads the requested information from a file or a database and populates the export and table parameter with this information. If an exception occurs, the server informs about this by calling the `RfcRaise` function or `RfcRaiseTables`. In case of success, it returns the export and table parameter using the `RfcSendData` function.

Let's have a look at the `z_ifp_order_getlist` function in Listing 3.30. It defines a type handle that identifies the `ZIFPORDER` structure, a handle for the internal table with the purchase order headers to be returned, the `parameters` array for the import and export parameters, as well as the `tables` array for the table parameters.

```
/* Z_IFP_ORDER_GETLIST                                          */
RFC_RC DLL_CALL_BACK_FUNCTION
                  z_ifp_order_getlist(RFC_HANDLE rfc_handle)
{
  RFC_RC            rfc_rc = RFC_OK;
  RFC_CHAR          ordertype[2];
  RFC_CHAR          refid[10];
  RFC_TYPEHANDLE    typeHandleZifporder;
  ITAB_H            itorders = ITAB_NULL;
  RFC_PARAMETER     parameters[3];
  RFC_TABLE         tables[2];
  parameters[0].name = cU("IM_ORDERTYPE");
  parameters[0].nlen = 12;
  parameters[0].type = RFCTYPE_CHAR;
  parameters[0].leng = sizeofR(ordertype);
  parameters[0].addr = &ordertype;
  parameters[1].name = cU("IM_REFID");
  parameters[1].nlen = 8;
  parameters[1].type = RFCTYPE_CHAR;
  parameters[1].leng = sizeofR(refid);
  parameters[1].addr = &refid;
  parameters[2].name = NULL;
  tables[0].name     = NULL;
```

```
  rfc_rc = RfcGetData (rfc_handle, parameters, tables);
  if (rfc_rc != RFC_OK)
    rfc_error (cU("RfcGetData"));
  /* Install structure                                    */
  rfc_rc = RfcInstallUnicodeStructure(
           cU("ZIFPORDER"), Description_U_ZIFPORDER,
             ENTRIES_OF_U_ZIFPORDER, 0, NULL,
                typeHandleZifporder );
  if (rfc_rc != RFC_OK)
    rfc_error(cU("RfcInstallUnicodeStructure"));
  /* Create internal table                                */
  itorders = ItCreate(cU("ORDERS"), ZIFPORDER_LN, 0, 0);
  if (itorders == ITAB_NULL)
    rfc_error(cU("ItCreate"));
  /* Initialize parameter                                 */
  tables[0].name     = cU("TA_ORDERS");
  tables[0].nlen     = 9;
  tables[0].type     = typeHandleZifporder;
  tables[0].leng     = ZIFPORDER_LN;
  tables[0].ithandle = itorders;
  tables[0].itmode   = RFC_ITMODE_BYREFERENCE;
  tables[0].newitab  = 0;
  tables[1].name     = NULL;
  /* Read data from file into internal table              */
  read_orders(ordertype,refid,itorders);
  rfc_rc = RfcSendData (rfc_handle, parameters, tables);
  if (rfc_rc != RFC_OK)
    rfc_error (cU("RfcSendData"));
  return rfc_rc;
}
```

Listing 3.30 "z_ifp_order_getlist" Function

These arrays are initialized respectively with the necessary information about the parameter name, type, and address before `RfcGetData` and `RfcSendData` are called.

Initialization of the parameters

After `RfcGetData` has been called, the function installs the `ZIFPORDER` structure for the internal table of the purchase order headers. As previously, the header file was generated with the necessary definitions using the *genh* RFC-SDK tool. After the installation of the structure, the internal table is created and the arrays are initialized for the return.

3 | Remote Function Call with C

"RfcSendData" Function

Before the `RfcSendData` function is called, the internal table is filled with the purchase order headers. For this purpose, the server defines the `read_orders` function from Listing 3.31. This function opens the *orders.dat* file and creates a line in the internal table for each line in this file. The server transfers a handle to this table to the `read_orders` function. The function copies the entire line in the file into the newly created table line. After the internal table has been populated, the server function returns it to the calling client using `RfcSendData`.

```
/* Read data from file into internal table              */
void read_orders(RFC_CHAR *type,RFC_CHAR *refid,ITAB_H itab)
{
  rfc_char_t    tbuf[MAXBUFF+1];
  ZIFPORDER     *zifporder;
  FILE          *fp;
  fp = fopenU (cU("orders.dat"), cU("rb"));
  if (memcmpU(type,cU("  "),2)==0)
    memcpyU(type,cU("SO"),2);
  while(fp && (fgetsU(tbuf, LINE_SIZE_ORDER+3, fp) != NULL))
  {
    if (((memcmpU(tbuf+15,refid,10)==0) ||
         (memcmpU(refid,cU("0000000000"),10)==0)) &&
        ((memcmpU(tbuf+13,type,2)==0)))
    {
       zifporder = (ZIFPORDER*) ItAppLine(itab);
       memcpyU(zifporder, tbuf, LINE_SIZE_ORDER);
    }
  }
  fclose(fp);
} /* read_orders */
```

Listing 3.31 "read_orders" Function

The `z_ifp_order_getdetail` function in Listing 3.32 defines the `orderid` variable for the purchase order number to be received, type handles for the `ZIFPORDER` and `ZIFPORDERPOS` structures, the `orderhead` and `itorderpos` variables for the detail data to be sent, the `parameters` array for the import and export parameters, and the `tables` array for the table parameters.

The `parameters` array is populated with information via the `orderid` import parameter. After the call of `RfcGetData`, the requested purchase order number is available in the `orderid` variable.

```
/* Z_IFP_ORDER_GETDETAIL                              */
RFC_RC DLL_CALL_BACK_FUNCTION
               z_ifp_order_getdetail(RFC_HANDLE rfc_handle)
{
  RFC_RC              rfc_rc = RFC_OK;
  RFC_CHAR            orderid[10];
  RFC_TYPEHANDLE      typeHandleZifporder;
  ZIFPORDER           orderhead;
  RFC_TYPEHANDLE      typeHandleZifporderpos;
  ITAB_H              itorderpos = ITAB_NULL;
  RFC_PARAMETER       parameters[2];
  RFC_TABLE           tables[2];
  parameters[0].name = cU("IM_ORDERID");
  parameters[0].nlen = 10;
  parameters[0].type = RFCTYPE_CHAR;
  parameters[0].leng = sizeofR(orderid);
  parameters[0].addr = &orderid;
  parameters[1].name = NULL;
  tables[0].name     = NULL;
  rfc_rc = RfcGetData (rfc_handle, parameters, tables);
  if (rfc_rc != RFC_OK)
    rfc_error (cU("RfcGetData"));
  /* Install structures                               */
  rfc_rc = RfcInstallUnicodeStructure(
     cU("ZIFPORDER"), Description_U_ZIFPORDER,
     ENTRIES_OF_U_ZIFPORDER,
     0, NULL, &typeHandleZifporder);
  if (rfc_rc != RFC_OK)
    rfc_error(cU("RfcInstallUnicodeStructure"));
  rfc_rc = RfcInstallUnicodeStructure(
     cU("ZIFPORDERPOS"), Description_U_ZIFPORDERPOS,
     ENTRIES_OF_U_ZIFPORDERPOS,
     0, NULL, &typeHandleZifporderpos);
  if (rfc_rc != RFC_OK)
    rfc_error(cU("RfcInstallUnicodeStructure"));
  /* Create internal table                            */
  itorderpos = ItCreate(
                  cU("ORDERPOS"), ZIFPORDERPOS_LN, 0, 0);
  if (itorderpos == ITAB_NULL)
    rfc_error(cU("ItCreate"));
  /* Initialize parameter                             */
  parameters[0].name = cU("EX_ORDERHEAD");
  parameters[0].nlen = 12;
  parameters[0].type = typeHandleZifporder;
```

```
            parameters[0].leng   = ZIFPORDER_LN;
            parameters[0].addr   = &orderhead;
            parameters[1].name   = NULL;
            tables[0].name       = cU("TA_ORDERPOS");
            tables[0].nlen       = 11;
            tables[0].type       = typeHandleZifporderpos;
            tables[0].leng       = ZIFPORDERPOS_LN;
            tables[0].ithandle   = itorderpos;
            tables[0].itmode     = RFC_ITMODE_BYREFERENCE;
            tables[0].newitab    = 0;
            tables[1].name       = NULL;
            /* Read data from file into structure                    */
            if(read_order(orderid, &orderhead, itorderpos)!=0)
            {
              rfc_rc = RfcRaise(rfc_handle, cU("NOT_FOUND"));
              if (rfc_rc != RFC_OK)
                rfc_error (cU("RfcSendData"));
            }
            else
            {
              rfc_rc = RfcSendData (rfc_handle, parameters, tables);
              if (rfc_rc != RFC_OK)
                rfc_error (cU("RfcSendData"));
            }
            return rfc_rc;
         }
```

Listing 3.32 "z_ifp_order_getdetail" Function

Subsequently, the server function installs the ZIFPORDER and ZIFPORDER-POS structures, creates the itorderpos internal table, and populates the parameters and tables arrays with the necessary information about the EX_ORDERHEAD export parameter and the TA_ORDERPOS table parameter.

"RfcRaise" function Before the function returns the details to the client using RfcSendData, it populates the orderheader structure and the itorderpos internal table by calling read_order in Listing 3.33. If this function does not find the requested purchase order, the server triggers a NOT_FOUND exception using RfcRaise. The read_order function opens the *orders.dat* file and reads each line from this file until it has found the requested purchase order number. After the purchase order number has been found, the function copies the entire line into the transferred structure of the ZIF-PORDER type. It then opens the *orderpos.dat* file, reads the associated purchase order items, and returns the value "0." If the function doesn't find the purchase order, it returns the value "1."

```c
/* Read data from file into structure               */
int read_order(
 RFC_CHAR *orderid, ZIFPORDER* orderhead, ITAB_H itorderpos)
{
  int           rc = 1;
  rfc_char_t    tbuf[MAXBUFF+1];
  ZIFPORDERPOS *pos;
  rfc_char_t    number[11];
  FILE          *fp;
  fp = fopenU (cU("orders.dat"), cU("rb"));
  while(fp && (fgetsU(tbuf, LINE_SIZE_ORDER+3, fp) != NULL))
  {
    if(memcmpU(tbuf+3,orderid,10)==0)
    {
      rc = 0;
      memcpyU(orderhead,tbuf,LINE_SIZE_ORDER);
      break;
    }
  }
  fclose(fp);
  fp = fopenU (cU("orderpos.dat"), cU("rb"));
  while(fp && (fgetsU(tbuf,LINE_SIZE_ORDERPOS+2,fp)!= NULL))
  {
    if(memcmpU(tbuf+3,orderid,10)==0)
    {
      pos = (ZIFPORDERPOS*) ItAppLine(itorderpos);
      memcpyU(pos->Mandt,tbuf,3);
      memcpyU(pos->Orderid,tbuf+3,10);
      memcpyU(pos->Orderpos,tbuf+13,5);
      memcpyU(pos->Matid,tbuf+18,20);
      memcpyU(pos->Mattext,tbuf+38,40);
      memcpyU(number,tbuf+78,10);
      number[10] = 0;
      pos->Ordercount = atoiU(number);
      number[1]=0;
      memcpyU(number,tbuf+88,1);   // 1000
      pos->Price[0] = atoiU(number);
      memcpyU(number,tbuf+89,1);   //  100
      pos->Price[1] = 16*atoiU(number);
      memcpyU(number,tbuf+90,1);   //   10
      pos->Price[1] = pos->Price[1] + atoiU(number);
      memcpyU(number,tbuf+91,1);   //    1
```

```
            pos->Price[2] = 16*atoiU(number);
            memcpyU(number,tbuf+93,1);    // 0,1
            pos->Price[2] = pos->Price[2] + atoiU(number);
            memcpyU(number,tbuf+94,1);    // 0,01
            pos->Price[3] = 16*atoiU(number);
            pos->Price[4] = 0;
            memcpyU(pos->Currency,tbuf+95,5);
        }
    }
    fclose(fp);
    return rc;
} /* read_order */
```

Listing 3.33 "read_order" Function

The RFC server is now complete. To test it, you can use the Z_IFP_ORDERS_READ ABAP program from Chapter 2, Listing 2.3 (Section 2.1.2, Call via sRFC). Here, you specify the destination that you previously created using Transaction SM59 in the selection screen (refer to Figure 3.2 in Section 3.4.1, Logon to Gateway).

3.4.3 Dispatching

The previously discussed server calls the RfcDispatch function to wait for an inbound RFC request. RfcDispatch blocks until a request is received. As soon as a request is received, RfcDispatch calls the C implementation of the desired function. Of course, the server must install it using RfcInstallFunction prior to the call of the RfcDispatch function.

To enable the RFC server to carry out a useful task during the wait time, it should call the RfcDispatch function only if a client request has actually been received. The server has two options to find out about it.

"RfcWaitFor Request" function

Listing 3.34 shows the first option. The server calls the RfcWaitForRequest function in a loop to wait for a client request for a specific period of time. The RfcWaitForRequest function returns after the time specified in the wtime parameter at the latest, even if no client request has been received.

```
    do
    {
        for (rfc_rc = RFC_RETRY; rfc_rc == RFC_RETRY;)
        {
```

3.4 RFC Server

```
      RFC_INT wtime = 60;      /* 60 sec. */
      rfc_rc = RfcWaitForRequest(rfc_handle, wtime);
      if (rfc_rc == RFC_RETRY)
      {
        /* Do something else */
      }
    }
    if (rfc_rc != RFC_OK)
    {
      if (rfc_rc != RFC_CLOSED)
        rfc_error(cU("RfcWaitForRequest"));
      else
        break;
    }
    rfc_rc = RfcDispatch(rfc_handle);
  } while (rfc_rc == RFC_OK);
```

Listing 3.34 Using the "RfcWaitForRequest" Function

If a client request is received during the wait time, `RfcWaitForRequest` returns the `RFC_OK` message immediately. In this case, the server leaves the `RfcWaitForRequest` loop and forwards the request to the corresponding C function by calling `RfcDispatch`.

If no client request is received during the wait time, `RfcWaitForRequest` returns the `RFC_RETRY` message immediately. In this case, the server can do something else before it enters the `RfcWaitForRequest` loop again.

The second option to find out whether a request has been received is shown in Listing 3.35. Here, the server uses the `RfcListen` function in a loop. This function returns immediately. If it returns the `RFC_RETRY` code, the server can do something else before it enters the `RfcListen` loop again. If `RfcListen` returns the `RFC_OK` code, the server leaves the `RfcListen` loop and calls the `RfcDispatch` function.

"RfcListen" function

```
  do
  {
    for (rfc_rc = RFC_RETRY; rfc_rc == RFC_RETRY;)
    {
      rfc_rc = RfcListen(rfc_handle);
      if (rfc_rc == RFC_RETRY)
      {
        /* Do something else */
      }
```

3 | Remote Function Call with C

```
        }
        if (rfc_rc != RFC_OK)
        {
          if (rfc_rc != RFC_CLOSED)
            rfc_error(cU("RfcListen"));
          else
            break;
        }
        rfc_rc = RfcDispatch(rfc_handle);
      } while (rfc_rc == RFC_OK);
```
Listing 3.35 Using the "RfcListen" Function

"RfcGetNameEx" function A completely different option is to omit the `RfcDispatch` function entirely and distribute the inbound client requests to the corresponding C functions yourself. Listing 3.36 shows this variant.

```
      for (;;)
      {
        rfc_rc = RfcGetNameEx(rfc_handle, function_name);
        if (rfc_rc == RFC_OK)
        {
          if(strcmpU(function_name,
              cU("Z_IFP_ORDER_GETLIST")) == 0)
            rfc_rc = z_ifp_order_getlist(rfc_handle);
          else if(strcmpU(function_name,
              cU("Z_IFP_ORDER_GETDETAIL")) == 0)
            rfc_rc = z_ifp_order_getdetail(rfc_handle);
          else
            function_abort(cU("Function not implemented"));
          if (rfc_rc != RFC_OK)
            break;
        }
        else
        {
          if (rfc_rc == RFC_SYSTEM_CALLED)
            continue;
          if (rfc_rc != RFC_CLOSED)
            rfc_error(cU("RfcGetNameEx"));
          break;
        }
      }
```
Listing 3.36 Using the "RfcGetNameEx" Function

The server calls the `RfcGetNameEx` function in an endless loop. This function blocks until a client request is received. In this case, it copies the name of the requested function to the transferred address. Due to the name, the server calls the corresponding C implementation.

3.4.4 Transactional RFC

The process in the RFC server for the tRFC is somewhat more complex than for the sRFC. First, the server must publish four functions for the *TID management* to the RFC library by calling `RfcInstallTransactionControl`. These four functions are called by the RFC library at specific points in time.

- `RFC_ON_CHECK_TID`

  This is the first function that the RFC library calls in the tRFC. This function must store the transferred TID permanently and return "0" if the TID has not been used so far. If the TID has already been used, the function must return a value not equal to "0."

- `RFC_ON_COMMIT`

  This function is called when the function module has been executed. Within this function, the RFC server can store its own database changes.

- `RFC_ON_ROLLBACK`

  This function is called when an error occurred in the tRFC processing. Within this function, the RFC server should undo its own database changes.

- `RFC_ON_CONFIRM_TID`

  This function is called when the entire tRFC processing has been completed. The server can delete the TID within this function.

Listing 3.37 shows the header file of a tRFC server that implements the `Z_IFP_ORDER_CREATE` function module. A tRFC client calls this function module to send a purchase order to the server. The server saves the data in a file. It selects *<TID>.dat* as the name of the file, where *<TID>* is the TID used for the tRFC transfer.

```
#define RFC_DEFINE_U_STRUCTURE
#define BLANK                    cU(' ')
#define MAXBUFF                  32000
#define LINE_SIZE                256
```

3 Remote Function Call with C

```
#define LINE_SIZE_ORDER         133
#define LINE_SIZE_ORDERPOS      102
#define NL_AR                   iU("\n")
#define NL                      cU("\n")
#include "saprfc.h"
#include "sapitab.h"
#include "zifporder.h"
#include "zifporderpos.h"
...
/* Return values of TID management                         */
typedef enum
{
  TID_OK,              /* Okay                             */
  TID_FOUND,           /* TID found                        */
  TID_ERROR_UPDATE     /* TID state changeable             */
}
TID_RC;
/* TID state in TID management                             */
typedef enum
{
  CREATED,             /* TID created                      */
  EXECUTED,            /* Transaction executed             */
  CONFIRMED,           /* TID confirmed                    */
  ROLLBACK             /* Transaction rolled back          */
}
TID_STATE;
rfc_char_t         tid_file[13] = iU("trfcserv.tid"),
                   data_file[65];
RFC_HANDLE         rfc_handle;
```

Listing 3.37 Header File of the tRFC Server

In the header, the server defines some preprocessor symbolic names, the `tid_file` and `data_file` global variables for the names of the TID management file and the data file, the `rfc_handle` global variable for the RFC connection, and the two enumeration types, `TID_RC` and `TID_STATE`.

TID management

The server uses the `TID_RC` enumeration type for the return codes of the TID management functions. `TID_STATE` lists the different states in which a TID can be stored in the TID management file. These are the same states as for the tRFC client.

Listing 3.38 shows the four functions that the tRFC server installs for the TID handling in the RFC library using the `RfcInstallTransactionControl` function. This installation is carried out when the program starts via the call in Listing 3.39.

Installation of the TID management

```
/* TID_check for TRFC                                         */
int DLL_CALL_BACK_FUNCTION TID_check(RFC_TID tid)
{
  TID_RC tid_rc;
  sprintfU(data_file,cU("%.*s.dat"),RFC_TID_LN,tid);
  tid_rc = check_TID(tid, tid_file, data_file);
  if (tid_rc == TID_OK)
    return 0;
  if (tid_rc == TID_FOUND)
    return 1;
  function_abort(cU("TID_check"),rfc_handle);
  return 1;
} /* TID_check */
/* TID_commit for TRFC                                        */
void DLL_CALL_BACK_FUNCTION TID_commit(RFC_TID tid)
{
  TID_RC         tid_rc;
  tid_rc = update_TID(tid, EXECUTED, tid_file, data_file);
  if (tid_rc == TID_OK)
    return;
  function_abort(cU("TID_commit"), rfc_handle);
  return;
} /* TID_commit */
/* TID_confirm for TRFC                                       */
void DLL_CALL_BACK_FUNCTION TID_confirm(RFC_TID tid)
{
  TID_RC    tid_rc;
  tid_rc = update_TID(tid, CONFIRMED, tid_file, data_file);
  if (tid_rc == TID_OK)
    return;
  function_abort(cU("TID_confirm"), rfc_handle);
  return;
} /* TID_confirm */
/* TID_rollback for TRFC                                      */
void DLL_CALL_BACK_FUNCTION TID_rollback(RFC_TID tid)
{
  TID_RC tid_rc;
  tid_rc = update_TID(tid, ROLLBACK, tid_file, data_file);
  if (tid_rc == TID_OK)
    return;
```

```
        function_abort(cU("TID_rollback"), rfc_handle);
        return;
      } /* TID_rollback */
```

Listing 3.38 Functions for the Transaction Handling of a tRFC Server

```
RfcInstallTransactionControl(
  (RFC_ON_CHECK_TID)   TID_check,
  (RFC_ON_COMMIT)      TID_commit,
  (RFC_ON_ROLLBACK)    TID_rollback,
  (RFC_ON_CONFIRM_TID) TID_confirm
);
```

Listing 3.39 Installation of the TID Management

The TID_check function calls the TID file management function, check_TID. This function opens the TID file and searches the transferred TID. If the TID is found (return code TID_FOUND), the data for this TID has already been processed by the server. In this case, the server must return a value not equal to "0." If the TID is not found (return code TID_OK), this TID has not yet been processed by the server and it returns "0."

Commit If the TID_check function returns the value "0," the RFC library calls the requested functions in the next step. If all called functions return the RFC_OK message, the RFC library calls TID_commit to conclude the transaction. In our implementation, TID_commit changes the state of the TID from CREATED to EXECUTED in the TID file. For this purpose, it calls the TID management function, update_TID.

Rollback If one of the implementing functions returns a return code that is not equal to RFC_OK, the RFC library calls TID_rollback. The server must roll back the local transaction that was started in TID_check, that is, undo all changes made. In our simple implementation, the server simply changes the state of the TID to ROLLBACK in the TID management file.

Finally, the RFC library calls the TID_confirm function. Within this function, the server can delete the temporarily stored TID and its state to release permanent memory. In our implementation, the server sets the state of the TID to CONFIRMED in the TID file.

Initialize TID file The server defines four functions for the management of a TID file. When it is started, it calls the init_TID function (Listing 3.40) to initialize the TID file. This function opens the TID file for the update. If the TID file does not exist, a new one is created. If the TID file exists, the function searches for TIDs in the CREATED state in the while loop. This state is replaced by the ROLLBACK state. This is important for the functioning of check_TID in Listing 3.41.

```
/* Initialize TID file                                  */
static void init_TID()
{
  FILE          *fp;
  rfc_char_t    *ptr, tbuf[MAXBUFF+1];
  RFC_TID       TransID;
  TID_RC        tid_rc;
  /* Open TID file for update     */
  fp = fopenU (tid_file, cU("rb+"));
  if (fp == NULL)
  {
    /* Create new TID file       */
    fp = fopenU (tid_file, cU("ab"));
    if (fp == NULL)
    {
      fprintfU(stderr, cU("init_TID\n")); exit(1);
    }
    memsetU (tbuf, cU('\0'), LINE_SIZE);
    strcpyU (tbuf, cU("***   TID MANAGEMENT   ***\n"));
    if (fputsU (tbuf, fp) < 0)
    {
      fclose(fp);
      fprintfU(stderr, cU("init_TID\n")); exit(1);
    }
  }
  else
  {
    while ((ptr = fgetsU (tbuf, LINE_SIZE+1, fp)) != NULL)
    { /* Replace CREATED with ROLLBACK                 */
      if (memcmpU (tbuf+52, cU("CREATED"), 7) == 0)
      {
        memcpyU (TransID,   tbuf+26, 24);
        data_file[0] = 0; TransID[24] = 0;
        tid_rc = update_TID(
          TransID, ROLLBACK, tid_file, data_file);
        if (tid_rc != TID_OK)
        {
          fprintfU(stderr, cU("init_TID")); exit(1);
        }
      }
```

```
      }
    }
    fclose(fp);
    return;
} /* init_TID */
```

Listing 3.40 "init_TID" Function

Check TID The check_TID function (Listing 3.41) searches for the transferred TID in the TID file. If it finds the TID and if its state is not equal to ROLLBACK (i.e., EXECUTED), it returns the TID_FOUND message. In this case, the calling function (TID_check in Listing 3.38 earlier) returns a value not equal to "0" to the RFC library, which then doesn't call the requested functions again. If check_TID does not find the transferred TID, it appends the TID at the end of the TID file in the CREATED state.

```
/* Check TID                                                  */
static TID_RC check_TID(RFC_TID tid, rfc_char_t* tid_file,
                        rfc_char_t *datafile)
{
  TID_RC        tidrc;
  TID_STATE     tid_state;
  FILE          *fp;
  rfc_char_t    *ptr, tbuf[MAXBUFF+1];
  /* Open for update                */
  fp = fopenU (tid_file, cU("rb+"));
  if (fp == NULL)
    tidrc = TID_ERROR_UPDATE;
  /* Search TID    */
  while ((ptr = fgetsU (tbuf, LINE_SIZE, fp)) != NULL)
  {
    if ((memcmpU (tbuf+26, tid, 24) == 0) &&
        (memcmpU (tbuf+52, cU("ROLLBACK"), 8) != 0))
      break;
  }
  if (ptr != NULL)
  {
    fclose(fp);
    return TID_FOUND;
  }
  /* Append new TID at the end                               */
  tid_state = CREATED;
  if (write_TID(fp, tid, tid_state, datafile))
    tidrc = TID_ERROR_UPDATE;
```

```
    else
      tidrc = TID_OK;
    fclose(fp);
    return tidrc;
}/* check TID */
```

Listing 3.41 "check_TID" Function

The `update_TID` TID management function (Listing 3.42) searches the TID file for the specified TID that is not in the `ROLLBACK` state. If it finds the TID, it writes the new state of the TID to the file. This function is used by the functions, `init_TID`, `TID_commit`, `TID_rollback`, and `TID_confirm`.

Change TID state

```
/* Change TID state in TID file                         */
static TID_RC update_TID(RFC_TID tid, TID_STATE tid_state,
             rfc_char_t *tid_file, rfc_char_t * datafile)
{
  TID_RC         tidrc;
  long           offset = 0;
  FILE           *fp;
  rfc_char_t     *ptr, tbuf[MAXBUFF+1];
  /* Open TID file for update     */
  fp = fopenU (tid_file, cU("rb+"));
  if (fp == NULL)
    return TID_ERROR_UPDATE;
  /* Search TID */
  while ((ptr = fgetsU (tbuf, LINE_SIZE+1, fp)) != NULL)
  {
    if ((memcmpU (tbuf+26, tid, 24) == 0) &&
        (memcmpU (tbuf+52, cU("ROLLBACK"), 8) != 0))
      break;
    offset = offset + strlenU (tbuf);
  }
  /* Write new state                        */
  if ((ptr != NULL) &&
      (fseek(fp, offset, SEEK_SET) == 0) &&
      (write_TID(fp, tid, tid_state, datafile) == 0))
    tidrc = TID_OK;
  else
    tidrc = TID_ERROR_UPDATE;
  fclose(fp);
  return tidrc;
} /* update_TID */
```

Listing 3.42 "update_TID" Function

3 | Remote Function Call with C

The TID management function, write_TID, which is used by check_TID and update_TID, is identical to the tRFC client shown earlier in Listing 3.22 (Section 3.3.2, Transactional RFC).

Create a purchase order

You now know the functions for managing TIDs in the server. The actual functionality for writing purchase orders is implemented by the server using the z_ifp_order_create function (Listing 3.43). Initially, it defines the orderid variable for returning the newly created purchase order number, the type handles for the ZIFPORDER and ZIFPORDERPOS structures, the orderheader structure, and the itorderpos internal table for receiving purchase order data from the RFC client, as well as the parameters and tables arrays for transferring the RFC parameters.

```
/* Z_IFP_ORDER_CREATE                                     */
RFC_RC DLL_CALL_BACK_FUNCTION z_ifp_order_create(
                                  RFC_HANDLE rfc_handle)
{
  RFC_RC              rfc_rc = RFC_OK;
  RFC_CHAR            orderid[10];
  RFC_CHAR            testrun;
  RFC_CHAR            commit;
  RFC_TYPEHANDLE      typeHandleZifporder;
  ZIFPORDER           orderheader;
  RFC_TYPEHANDLE      typeHandleZifporderpos;
  ITAB_H              itorderpos;
  RFC_PARAMETER       parameters[4];
  RFC_TABLE           tables[2];
  /* Install structures                                   */
  ...

  /* Initialize parameter                                 */
  testrun = cU(' ');
  commit  = cU(' ');
  parameters[0].name = cU("IM_ORDERHEADER");
  parameters[0].nlen = 14;
  parameters[0].type = typeHandleZifporder;
  parameters[0].leng = ZIFPORDER_LN;
  parameters[0].addr = &orderheader;
  parameters[1].name = cU("IM_TESTRUN");
  parameters[1].nlen = 10;
  parameters[1].type = RFCTYPE_CHAR;
  parameters[1].leng = sizeofR(testrun);
  parameters[1].addr = &testrun;
```

```
  parameters[1].name  = cU("IM_COMMIT");
  parameters[1].nlen  = 9;
  parameters[1].type  = RFCTYPE_CHAR;
  parameters[1].leng  = sizeofR(commit);
  parameters[1].addr  = &commit;
  parameters[3].name  = NULL;
  tables[0].name      = cU("TA_ORDERPOS");
  tables[0].nlen      = 11;
  tables[0].type      = typeHandleZifporderpos;
  tables[0].leng      = ZIFPORDERPOS_LN;
  tables[0].ithandle  = ITAB_NULL;
  tables[0].itmode    = RFC_ITMODE_BYREFERENCE;
  tables[0].newitab   = 0;
  tables[1].name      = NULL;
  rfc_rc = RfcGetData (rfc_handle, parameters, tables);
  if (rfc_rc != RFC_OK)
    rfc_error (cU("RfcGetData"));
  itorderpos = tables[0].ithandle;
  /* Initialize parameter                             */
  parameters[0].name  = cU("EX_ORDERID");
  parameters[0].nlen  = 10;
  parameters[0].type  = RFCTYPE_CHAR;
  parameters[0].leng  = sizeofR(orderid);
  parameters[0].addr  = &orderid;
  parameters[1].name  = NULL;
  tables[0].name      = NULL;
  /* Write data to data file                          */
  if(write_order(orderid, testrun, commit,
                 &orderheader, itorderpos)!=0)
  {
    rfc_rc = RfcRaise(rfc_handle, cU("INSERT_FAILURE"));
    if (rfc_rc != RFC_OK)
      rfc_error (cU("RfcSendData"));
  }
  else
  {
    rfc_rc = RfcSendData (rfc_handle, parameters, tables);
    if (rfc_rc != RFC_OK)
      rfc_error (cU("RfcSendData"));
  }
  return rfc_rc;
} /* z_ifp_order_create */
```

Listing 3.43 "z_ifp_order_create" Function

3 Remote Function Call with C

Then, the function installs the ZIFPORDER and ZIFPORDERPOS structures whose descriptions have been generated with the genh program in the *zifporder.h* and *zifporderpos.h* header files so far.

In the next step, the z_ifp_order_create function initializes the orderheader import parameter and then receives the data from the client using RfcGetData. The purchase order items are available in an internal table whose handle can be found in tables[0].ithandle.

This handle is copied to itorderpos, and the received data is written to a file using write_order.

Finally, the function returns the orderid export parameter via RfcSendData.

Saving data Listing 3.44 shows the write_order function. This function writes the received data to the data_file file. Moreover, it generates a new purchase order number by simply counting up the static variable id.

```
/* Write data to file                                    */
int write_order(RFC_CHAR *orderid, RFC_CHAR testrun,
                RFC_CHAR commit, ZIFPORDER* orderheader,
                ITAB_H itorderpos)
{
  int             rc = 0;
  rfc_char_t      tbuf[MAXBUFF+1], strid[11];
  FILE            *fp;
  static unsigned id=0;
  int             i;
  ZIFPORDERPOS    *pos;
  float           price;
  id = id + 1;
  sprintfU(strid,cU("%010u"),id);
  memcpyU(orderid,strid,10);
  if(testrun == cU('X'))
    return 1;
  fp = fopenU (data_file, cU("a"));
  memcpyU(tbuf, orderheader, LINE_SIZE_ORDER);
  memcpyU(tbuf+3,orderid,10);
  tbuf[LINE_SIZE_ORDER] = cU('\n');
  if(fwriteU(tbuf,1,LINE_SIZE_ORDER+1,fp)<LINE_SIZE_ORDER+1)
      rc = 1;
  for(i=1;i<=ItFill(itorderpos);i++)
  {
      pos = (ZIFPORDERPOS*) ItGetLine(itorderpos, i);
```

```
      memcpyU(tbuf, pos, 78);
      memcpyU(tbuf+3,orderid,10);
      sprintfU(tbuf+78,cU("%10u"),pos->Ordercount);
      price =           (pos->Price[0] & 0xF) * 1000.00;
      price = price + (pos->Price[1] >> 4)  *  100.00;
      price = price + (pos->Price[1] & 0xF) *   10.00;
      price = price + (pos->Price[2] >> 4)  *    1.00;
      price = price + (pos->Price[2] & 0xF) *     .10;
      price = price + (pos->Price[3] >> 4)  *     .01;
      sprintfU(tbuf+88,cU("%#7.2f"), price);
      memcpyU(tbuf+95, pos->Currency, 5);
      tbuf[LINE_SIZE_ORDERPOS] = cU('\n');
      fwriteU (tbuf, 1, LINE_SIZE_ORDERPOS+1, fp);
    }
    fclose(fp);
    return rc;
} /* write_order */
```

Listing 3.44 "write_order" Function

The RFC server is now complete. To test it, you can use the Z_IFP_ORDER_CREATE ABAP program from Listing 2.7 (Section 2.2, Transactional RFC). Here, you must remember to use Transaction SM59 to create a suitable destination for your tRFC server, which you then specify in the selection screen of the Z_IFP_ORDER_CREATE program.

In this chapter, you will learn various ways to write RFC programs in Java. We will show you how to use different libraries both outside of and within SAP infrastructures, such as SAP NetWeaver Application Server Java or SAP NetWeaver Portal.

4 Remote Function Call with Java

In Java, there are various convenient ways in which to implement RFC programs. SAP *Java Connector* is the basic option for programming outside of SAP servers and the SAP development environment (Section 4.1, SAP Java Connector). Even more convenient are developments using Enterprise Connector (ECo) (Section 4.2, Enterprise Connector), for which you require SAP NWDS (NWDS). In Section 4.3, RFC Server, we will discuss the implementation of RFC servers, before concluding with a description of RFC programming within SAP NetWeaver AS Java and SAP NetWeaver Portal.

4.1 SAP Java Connector

SAP Java Connector (JCo) forms the interface between a Java-based system and the ABAP backend. JCo facilitates bidirectional communication. In other words, it is possible to access ABAP functions from Java applications and Java functions from ABAP applications. In the following scenario, we will assume that the application is not developed in an SAP development environment such as SAP NWDS. Instead, we will use the free development environment Eclipse.

4.1.1 Installation

Java Connector is installed in two steps. In the first step, you download JCo from the SAP Service Marketplace (*http:service.sap.com/connectors*, Version 3.0 for Windows). After the download, a file called *sapjco3-nitel-3.0.0.zip* is located on your hard drive. Then, after you extract the contents of the ZIP file, the files *sapjco3.jar* and *sapjco3.dll* are located on your hard drive. In addition to these two runtime files, the ZIP file also contains the JCo documentation in Javadoc format.

In the second installation step, you include the file *sapjco3.jar* in the class path of your development environment. To ensure that the installation runs smoothly, we recommend that you place the JAR file and the library *sapjco3.dll* in the same directory.

Windows and UNIX libraries

If you want to use JCo on Linux or UNIX, download the relevant version for your operating system from SAP Service Marketplace. This file contains almost the same files as stored on Windows, with the only difference being the library. On Linux, the file *libsapjco3.so* is the equivalent to *sapjco3.dll*.

> **Note on Java Connector Versions**
>
> In addition to the JCo versions stored on SAP Service Marketplace, SAP always delivers a version of JCo in SAP NetWeaver Developer Studio. On SAP NetWeaver 7.0, this is Connector Version 2.0, which differs greatly from Version 3.0 discussed here. Version 3.0 is an extract of the JCo API contained in the API provided in SAP NetWeaver 7.1. In the SAP world, versions that can be downloaded directly from SAP Service Marketplace are known as *standalone* versions. These standalone versions are used outside of the SAP development environment. If you use SAP NWDS to develop applications, make sure that you use the version delivered together with the development environment. This is particularly important if you are working with SAP NetWeaver Developer Infrastructure.
>
> In Version 3.0, not only have errors been removed but also extensive changes have been made to the API. These changes are so extensive that software changes are necessary when switching from an older version of JCo to Version 3.0.
>
> On the one hand, this involves a great deal of effort. On the other hand, however, Version 3.0 provides you, for the first time, with an API that corresponds to the common programming conventions in Java.

4.1.2 Architecture of SAP Java Connector

Now that we have successfully completed the installation, we will now discuss the use of JCo.

Essentially, the architecture of JCo can be divided into two areas. One part is pure Java and facilitates simplified communication (via an API) between the developer and the backend. The other part is a native layer provided via the *Dynamic Link Library* (DLL). The *Java Native Interface* (JNI) facilitates communication between the Java API and the C RFC library. However, communication between the JNI and the DLL is irrelevant for the developer. The advantage of this is that he can fully concentrate on the Java part without having to concern himself with implementations in C. Figure 4.1 shows possible communication options as well as the basic architecture of JCo.

Java Native Interface

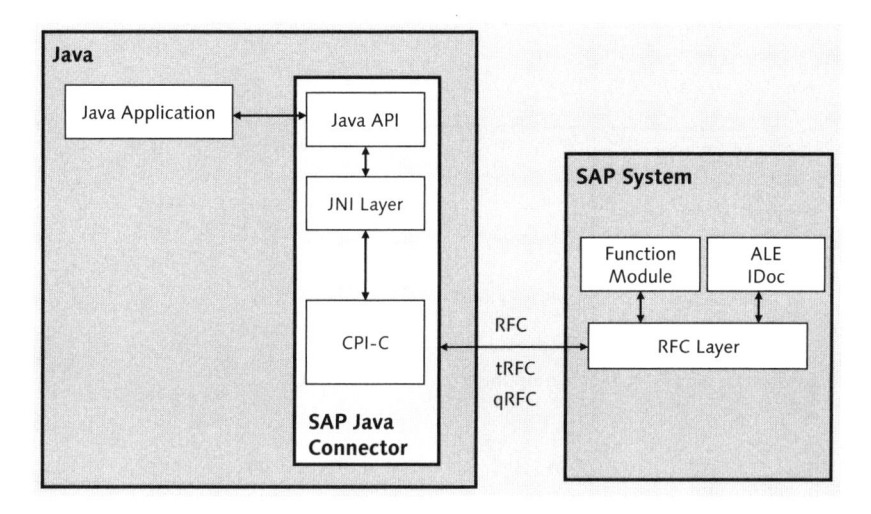

Figure 4.1 Architecture of Java Connector

JCo supports inbound (server-side) and outbound (client-side) communication. Traditional RFC communication as well as transactional RFC (tRFC) and queued RFC (qRFC) are supported in both directions.

Because the API is very basic, the developer must assume some tasks himself, for example, storing metadata temporarily *(caching)* and managing unique connection pools.

Let's take another look at processing an ABAP function module call in Java. As you can see in Figure 4.2, the developers of JCo have ensured

Middleware interface

that other possible facets of communication between JCo and the ABAP backend are conceivable in the future. For this reason, they have implemented a *middleware interface* that represents the abstraction layer between the JCo API and the actual C RFC library. It is therefore entirely conceivable that other communication options could be used (e.g., SOAP calls) instead of calling the JNI and the underlying DLL. However, only SAP can integrate other communication types in place of native communication.

Java
Java Application
SAP JCO Java API
Middleware Interface
RFC Middleware
JNI Layer
RFC Library
↕
RFC
SAP System

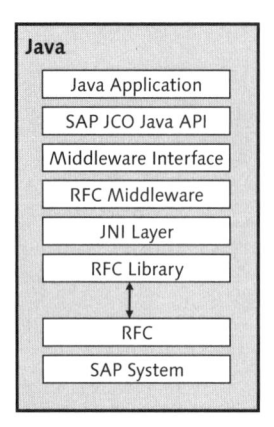

Figure 4.2 Communication Components when Processing an RFC

4.1.3 Programming with SAP Java Connector

Java client

For simple synchronous calls, programming with SAP JCo essentially comprises three steps. Figure 4.3 shows the relevant classes from the JCo API and their communication interfaces in a sequence diagram. As you can see, the `JavaClient` Java class initiates the scenario. In the first step, the Java client is responsible for establishing the connection to the required SAP backend. In the second step, a function module proxy must be generated within the Java client. This proxy is used to provide metadata for the required function module. The metadata plays an important role when filling in import parameters (including table parameters) and when reading export parameters and table parameters.

We will now discuss each step of the sequence diagram shown in Figure 4.3.

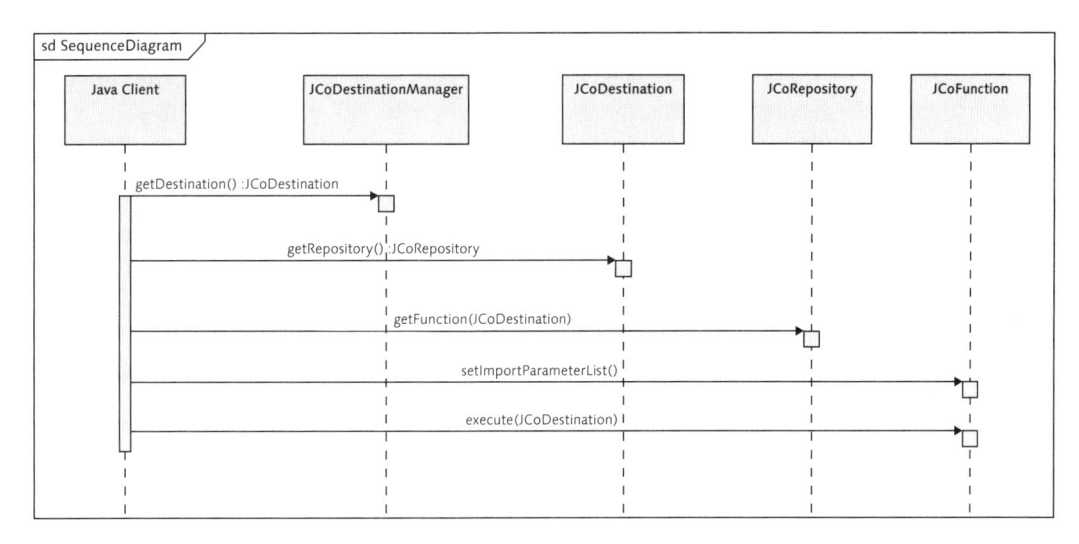

Figure 4.3 Processing a Function Module Call

Establishing a Connection

The `JCoDestinationManager` class is used to establish a connection with an ABAP backend. This class makes the `getDestination` factory methods available, which are used to generate objects of the type `JCoDestination`. The object generated is used to provide the connector with connection information concerning the backend system.

Connection parameters

Two forms of the `getDestination` method are provided. One form of this method receives only one string, which includes the name of a file that contains the connection parameters. In each case, JCo searches the base directory of the project for this file. You cannot actually specify a directory by default. Instead, you must implement a separate destination information provider class via the implementation. The destination name is used as the file name and *.jcoDestination* is the mandatory file extension. Listing 4.1 shows the creation of a `JcoDestination` instance.

```
public static JCoDestination getJCoDestination(
  String destinationName) throws JCoException {
  JCoDestination lclJCoDestination =
    JCoDestinationManager.getDestination(destinationName);
  return lclJCoDestination;
}
```

Listing 4.1 Creating a "JCoDestination" Object

The structure of the property file follows known rules for defining the `java.util.Property` class. You do not have to know all of the property keys by heart. The `DestinationDataProvider` interface defines the properties expected by JCo as constants. Listing 4.2 shows the structure of a simple configuration. Each property has the prefix `jco.client` and is therefore self-explanatory.

```
jco.client.client=001
jco.client.user=men
jco.client.passwd=password
jco.client.lang=en
jco.client.sysnr=01
jco.client.ashost=192.168.126.128
jco.client.r3name=DEV
```

Listing 4.2 Connection Definition of the "MYDESTINATION.jcoDestination" Destination

Providing your own "Destination-Provider"

In many cases, however, it is not useful nor is it even possible to rigidly store connection data in Java binary files. Generally, flexibility is preferred when choosing the storage location of the connection parameters. The `DestinationDataProvider` interface has been implemented for this purpose. If you want another configuration type for your JCo connection data, simply implement this interface, which defines the following three methods: `getDestinationProperties`, `supportEvents`, and `setDestinationDataEventListener`.

Session management

As we already know, two forms of the `getDestination` method are available. One form contains just one string to which only the destination name is transferred, while the other form obtains not only the destination name but also an additional parameter called `scopeType`, which describes the Java documentation. This parameter is not necessarily evaluated. It is only processed if an underlying session management infrastructure is provided. The use of the `scopeType` parameter is processed via an implementation of the `SessionReferenceProvider` interface. Consequently, you can provide your own *session management* in your JCo-based application. To register your implementation, use the `registerSessionReferenceProvider` method in the `Environment` class.

To put it simply, the `scopeType` parameter is used to divide parts of the current Java-side transaction into smaller units. An appropriate level of support by the infrastructure is a prerequisite for using this function.

Frequently, it is necessary to call several function modules in a logical unit of work. JCo provides the `JCoContext` class for this purpose. *Stateful calls* use the same connection for communication with a specific backend. However, the developer must explicitly select "stateful" communication. For this purpose, you must call the `begin` static method in the `JcoContext` class to start communication and then explicitly call the `end` method to end communication.

"JCoContext" class for stateful calls

Connection Types for Communication with the Backend

Two different connection types are available for establishing a connection. You can establish a *direct connection*, or you can use *pooled connections*. The advantage of pooled connections is that connection objects require very little time and effort before use because they can be sourced from a pool. However, the disadvantage of pooled connections is that the same user is used to establish all connections. In many systems, both connection types are used. If, for example, we consider a catalog system in which customers want to view and purchase items, pooled connections are used to load the item master data from the ABAP backend, and a direct connection is used to place an order (to post the purchase order to ERP), so that it is clear which customer sent which purchase order and when. Like direct connections, pooled connections are created using destination files whereby the parameters contain not only traditional connection information but also information about the pool. In Listing 4.3, we will now add three properties to the configuration file introduced in Listing 4.2.

Pooled versus direct connection

```
jco.destination.peak_limit=10
jco.destination.pool_capacity=20
jco.destination.max_get_client_time=100
```

Listing 4.3 Configuration Parameters for a Connection Pool

The `peak_limit` property defines the maximum number of connections that can be active simultaneously for a destination. The second parameter, `pool_capacity`, defines the pool size while `max_get_client_time` specifies the number of milliseconds JCo should wait until sending a timeout if all of the connections in the pool are already in use. Using a pooled destination within an application works in the same way as programming with direct connections.

"JCo" Factory Class

"JCo" central class

In addition to pure SAP system data processing, other administration tasks are extremely important. If we compare the API for JCo Version 3.0 with its predecessors, we can safely say that the current API has many more possible administration tasks than older versions. The `JCo` class is the central class for using these functions. It is implemented as an abstract class and only makes static class methods available.

You can use the methods provided to implement your own monitoring tools for the JCo infrastructure and to integrate them into your own applications. This is exactly what we will do now for our sample application. Throughout this chapter, we will make frequent reference to the use of the `JCo` class. First of all, however, we want to implement an option that will query the way in which a destination is configured.

Destination monitoring

To do this, we will implement a management class that will retrieve and make available the corresponding information for all destinations used. You can use the `JCoDestinationMonitor` class for work with destinations. When you specify the destination name, you obtain a reference to an instance of this class. The class itself provides all of the destination information needed to query the state of a backend at runtime. Listing 4.4 shows how this information can be queried by calling different getter methods.

```
public void showCurrentConnectionData(String destination) {
  JCoDestinationMonitor destinationMonitor =
    getDestinationMonitor(destination);
  long lastActivity =
    destinationMonitor.getLastActivityTimestamp();
  Date lastActivityAsDate = new Date(lastActivity);
  int maxUsedCount = destinationMonitor.getMaxUsedCount();
  long peakLimit = destinationMonitor.getPeakLimit();
  int poolCapacity = destinationMonitor.getPoolCapacity();
  int pooledConnectionCount =
    destinationMonitor.getPooledConnectionCount();
  int usedConnectionCount =
    destinationMonitor.getUsedConnectionCount();
  //TODO print info;
}
```

Listing 4.4 Querying the Current Pool Information for a Destination

In addition to pure pool information, any information concerning specific connection objects within the pool may also be of interest. You can use the `JCoConnectionData` class to read such information. JCo manages an instance of this type for each connection to the backend. The `DestinationMonitor` is used to manage and request such instances. You can obtain a list of current connection information instances by calling the `getConnectionsData` method. This method returns an instance of the `java.util.List` class.

Information about pool objects

Listing 4.5 shows a reading of such data. As you can see, a simple iterator is used to read the list in a loop, and each instance is processed separately.

```
public void showDestinationData(String destination) {
  JCoDestinationMonitor destinationMonitor =
    JCo.getDestinationMonitor(destination);
  List<?> connectionData =
    destinationMonitor.getConnectionsData();
  for (Iterator iterator = connectionData.iterator();
              iterator.hasNext();) {
    JCoConnectionData currentConnectionData =
      JCoConnectionData) iterator.next();
    //TODO get info and print info
  }
}
```

Listing 4.5 List of Transferred Destination Information

Executing an SAP Function

Now that we have successfully established a connection with the backend, we can actually start a synchronous call of the function module. For this purpose, we will use two function modules introduced earlier, namely `Z_IFP_ORDER_CREATE` and `Z_IFP_ORDER_GETDETAILS`.

sRFC

When calling a function module, you must follow these steps:

1. Create a function proxy object for the function module that you want to call.
2. Fill in the import parameter list.
3. Call the function module, and evaluate the return values.

4 | Remote Function Call with Java

Creating a function proxy object

In the first step, you have to create a *proxy* for the remote-enabled function module implemented in the ABAP stack. Because JCo represents a purely generic API and does not provide any support by means of a code generator, the JCo API defines a generic class called JCoFunction. Objects of this type represent the Java-side ABAP function. Therefore, the function module metadata, as defined in the ABAP Dictionary, must be known. This is made possible by using an object from the JCoRepository class. As Listing 4.6 shows, an object from the JCoDestination class is used as a factory for repository objects, which, in turn, is used as a factory for creating JcoFunction objects.

```
private JCoFunction createFunction(
  JCoDestination destination,
  String functionName) throws JCoException {
  JCoFunction function =
    destination.getRepository().getFunction(functionName);
  if (function == null)
    throw new RuntimeException(functionName +
      " not defined!");
  else
    return function;
}
```

Listing 4.6 Creating a Function Module Proxy

Using "JCoImportParameterList"

The second step involves filling in the import parameter list of the function module. The import parameters of the module Z_IFP_ORDER_CREATE contain the field IM_ORDERHEADER as the structure and the fields IM_TESTRUN and IM_COMMIT as scalar parameters. In addition, the module defines a table parameter called TA_ORDERS. As already discussed, the JcoFunction object is the Java-side representation of the function module, which means that this object can also be used to ensure access to the import parameters and table parameters. You can obtain a reference to the import parameter list by calling the getImportParameterList method. The return value of this method is of the type JCoParameterList and is derived from the JCoRecord base interface. The base class provides a number of setValue methods for filling in the import parameters. The method parameters follow the usual Java convention for setting name/value pairs, which means that the first parameter is the name of the field, and the second parameter receives the typed value.

You must ensure that the correct data types are used. Otherwise, runtime errors may occur. Table 4.1 provides an overview of the ABAP-Java-datatype mapping.

ABAP versus Java data types

ABAP	Short Description	Java	JCo Metadata
B	1-byte integer	Int	TYPE_INT1
S	2-byte integer	Int	TYPE_INT2
L	4-byte integer	Int	TYPE_INT
C	Character	String	TYPE_CHAR
N	Numeric character	String	TYPE_NUM
P	Binary coded decimal point	BigDecimal	TYPE_BCD
D	Date	Date	TYPE_DATE
T	Time	Date	TYPE_TIME
F	Floating point number	Double	TYPE_FLOAT
X	Pure data	Byte[]	TYPE_BYTE
G	String of variable length	String	TYPE_STRING
Y	Pure data	Byte[]	TYPE_XSTRING

Table 4.1 Mapping ABAP Data Types to Java Data Types

After the scalar parameters have been set, you can transfer structures and tables to the import parameters. Here, you can use the `getStructure` or `getTable` methods defined in the `JCoRecord` interface to obtain structures or tables from the import parameter list or table parameter list. Two forms of both methods exist. You can use the index or field label to address the field. For the function module `Z_IFP_CREATE_ORDER`, this means that the `getStructure` method receives the value `IM_ORDERHEADER`. The method in Listing 4.7 shows how the fields in the structure are filled using the `createOrderHeaderStructure` method.

Processing complex data types

```
private void createOrderHeaderStructure(
  Orderheader orheader,
  JCoStructure orderheader) {
  orderheader.setValue(IFieldNames.ZIFPORDER_ORDERID,
    orheader.getOrderid());
```

```
    orderheader.setValue(IFieldNames.ZIFPORDER_BUYER,
      orheader.getBuyer());
    orderheader.setValue(IFieldNames.ZIFPORDER_SELLER,
      orheader.getSeller());
    orderheader.setValue(IFieldNames.ZIFPORDER_MANDT,
      orheader.getClient());
    orderheader.setValue(IFieldNames.ZIFPORDER_REFID,
      orheader.getRefid());
    orderheader.setValue(IFieldNames.ZIFPORDER_TYPE,
      orheader.getType());
}
```

Listing 4.7 Filling in the Structure "IM_ORDERHEADER"

Working with the "JCoTable" class

You can now set the table parameter TA_ORDERPOS. We will implement a helper method for this purpose (Listing 4.8). The method obtains, as its call parameters, a list of objects of the user-defined type Orderpos as well as the table parameter object that has been read. The JCoTable class provides the appendRow method for adding a new row. After you have added a new row, you can use setValue to set values for the fields in the new row. Both the field label and the value to be set as an argument are transferred to the setValue method. The user-defined IFieldNames interface is used as a central location for defining string constants for field labels.

```
private void createOrderPosTbl(
  List<Orderpos> orderposList, JCoTable orderTbl) {
  for (Orderpos orderPos : orderposList) {
    orderTbl.appendRow();
    orderTbl.setValue(IFieldNames.TA_ORDERPOS_MANDT,
      orderPos.getClient());
    orderTbl.setValue(IFieldNames.TA_ORDERPOS_ORDERID,
      orderPos.getOrderid());
    orderTbl.setValue(IFieldNames.TA_ORDERPOS_ORDERPOS,
      orderPos.getOrderpos());
    orderTbl.setValue(IFieldNames.TA_ORDERPOS_MATID,
      orderPos.getMaterialid());
    orderTbl.setValue(IFieldNames.TA_ORDERPOS_MATTEXT,
      orderPos.getMaterialtext());
    orderTbl.setValue(IFieldNames.TA_ORDERPOS_ORDERCOUNT,
      orderPos.getOrdercount());
    orderTbl.setValue(IFieldNames.TA_ORDERPOS_PRICE,
      orderPos.getPrice());
```

```
    orderTbl.setValue(IFieldNames.TA_ORDERPOS_CURRENCY,
      orderPos.getCurrency());
  }
}
```

Listing 4.8 Filling in the Table Parameter "TA_ORDERPOS"

After all of the call parameters have been set, you can execute the function. The `JCoFunction` class provides the `execute` method for executing an sRFC. This method obtains the destination (where you want to execute the function) as a parameter. After the function has been successfully processed on the ABAP stack, the `getExportParameterList` method can be used to respond to the return of the function module. To read the values from a parameter list, the `JCoRecord` interface provides two forms of a `getter` method for each data type supported. In each case, there is a method that reads the field via the field index and a method that reads the name of the field as a call parameter. Therefore, when reading all fields in a loop, it is possible to simply work with the field index, while the field name can be used to specifically access a special field. Listing 4.9 shows the call for the function `Z_IFP_CREATE_ORDER` as well as processing of the scalar export parameter `EX_ORDERID`.

Return values for function module

```
try {
  function.execute(destination);
  int orderID = function.getExportParameterList().getInt(
    IFieldNames.EX_ORDERID);
  System.out.println("Order created with the ID "+ orderID);
  order.getOrderheader().setOrderid(orderID);
} catch (AbapException e) {
  System.out.println(e.toString());
  return;
}
```

Listing 4.9 Executing the Function "Z_IFP_CREATE_ORDER"

4.1.4 Processing Tables and Structures

Now that we have successfully created a purchase order, the next step is to read this purchase order from the ABAP system. The function module `Z_IFP_ORDER_GETDETAILS` has been written for this purpose. Here, we will focus less on actually calling the function module and more on processing the complex return values of the function module. As already

Processing complex return values

described at the start of the chapter, the function module defines the export parameter EX_ORDERHEAD and the table parameter TA_ORDERPOS.

Similar to setting complex parameters, the system returns complex parameters via the parameter list for the function and uses the corresponding getter method to make them available. The JCoParameterList interface provides the getStructure method for querying structures from the export parameter list. Either the field index or field name can be used to call the method. After the structure parameter has been read, the structure can be processed further. The getOrderHead method shown in Listing 4.10 obtains, as a call argument, the structure to be processed. If we compare the JCoStructure interface with the JCoTable interface, we see that both enhance the JCoRecord interface in such a way that the process of reading values from the structure is subject to the same rules as those already discussed for table processing. It is possible to read the value from the structure as a typed value by using getter methods and by specifying the field or index.

```
private Orderheader getOrderHead(JCoStructure orderhead) {
  Orderheader orheader = new Orderheader();
  orheader.setClient(
    orderhead.getInt(IFieldNames.ZIFPORDER_MANDT));
  orheader.setOrderid(
    orderhead.getInt(IFieldNames.ZIFPORDER_ORDERID));
  orheader.setType(
    orderhead.getString(IFieldNames.ZIFPORDER_TYPE));
  orheader.setRefid(
    orderhead.getString(IFieldNames.ZIFPORDER_REFID));
  orheader.setBuyer(
    orderhead.getString(IFieldNames.ZIFPORDER_BUYER));
  orheader.setSeller(
    orderhead.getString(IFieldNames.ZIFPORDER_SELLER));
  orheader.setOrderdate(
    orderhead.getDate(IFieldNames.ZIFPORDER_ORDERDATE));
  return orheader;
}
```

Listing 4.10 Processing Information from the Structure "EX_ORDERHEAD"

Reading table rows in a loop

Listing 4.11 introduces the getOrderPos method, which shows how a server-side object model is mapped to a client-side object model. On the client side, order items are regarded as instances of the Orderpos class. The method reads the table in a loop, uses getter methods to read the values, and transfers them to the corresponding fields in the Java model. A simple `for` loop is used for the iteration. Also note the call for the `setRow` method. When called, the method places the cursor on the next row in the table.

```
private List<Orderpos> getOrderPos(JCoTable orderposTbl) {
  List<Orderpos> orderPosList = new ArrayList<Orderpos>();
  for (int i = 0; i < orderposTbl.getNumRows(); i++) {
    Orderpos orderpos = new Orderpos();
    orderposTbl.setRow(i);
    orderpos.setClient(
      orderposTbl.getString(IFieldNames.TA_ORDERPOS_MANDT));
    orderpos.setOrderid(
      orderposTbl.getInt(IFieldNames.TA_ORDERPOS_ORDERID));
    orderpos.setOrderpos(
      orderposTbl.getInt(IFieldNames.TA_ORDERPOS_ORDERPOS));
    orderpos.setMaterialid(
      orderposTbl.getString(IFieldNames.TA_ORDERPOS_MATID));
    orderpos.setMaterialtext(
      orderposTbl.getString(IFieldNames.TA_ORDERPOS_MATTEXT));
    orderpos.setOrdercount(
      orderposTbl.getInt(IFieldNames.TA_ORDERPOS_ORDERCOUNT));
    orderpos.setPrice(
      orderposTbl.getDouble(IFieldNames.TA_ORDERPOS_PRICE));
    orderpos.setCurrency(
      orderposTbl.getString(
        IFieldNames.TA_ORDERPOS_CURRENCY));
    orderPosList.add(orderpos);
  }
  return orderPosList;
}
```

Listing 4.11 Processing the Table Parameter "TA_ORDERPOS"

In addition to using a simple `for` loop, it is also possible to use the `JCoFieldIterator` class or to use a `foreach` method to read a `JcoTable` instance in a loop. Listing 4.12 contrasts the use of both options. Ultimately, the developer decides which option is best. The only thing that may help the developer make this decision is the readability of the code because, in terms of performance, the `while` and `foreach` loops are identical. As you can see, the `JCoField` class is used to access a field. The advantage of using this class, when compared with calling the getter method directly, is that you can access the metadata and field value directly.

Iterators

```
private void printTable(JCoTable orderposTbl) {
  JCoFieldIterator fieldIter =
    orderposTbl.getFieldIterator();
  while(fieldIter.hasNextField()) {
    JCoField currentField = fieldIter.nextField();
    //print field content
  }
  for (JCoField currentField : orderposTbl) {
    // print table content
  }
}
```

Listing 4.12 Using the "JCoFieldIterator" Class

The function module is executed using the `execute` method on the `JcoFunction` instance. Three forms of this method are available, and each form represents a proxy for the three communication types between Java and ABAP.

4.1.5 Transactional RFC

Using Java Connector for tRFC communication

In addition to the traditional synchronous call for a remote-enabled function module, SAP JCo also provides the option of *transactional RFC* communication. tRFCs and synchronous function module calls are almost identical, with the only difference being the way in which the external Java application manages transaction IDs (TIDs). You use the `createTID` method in the `JCoDestination` class to generate the TID provided by the SAP system. A TID provided as a string object is the result of this method call. After the TID and the `JcoFunction` object are available, the function can be called using its `execute` method. Both the destination and the TID created earlier are transferred. Listing 4.13 shows the `main` method of the `TRFCDemo` class.

```
public static void main(String[] args) {
  try {
    TRFCDemo tRFCDemo = new TRFCDemo();
    JCoDestination currentDestination =
      ConnectionManager.getJCoDestination(
        ConnectionManager.SINGLECONNECTION);
    String transactionID = currentDestination.createTID();
    List<Order> listOfOrders = OrderFactory.createOrders();
    for (Order order : listOfOrders) {
```

```
      tRFCDemo.createorder(
        order, transactionID, currentDestination);
    }
    currentDestination.confirmTID(transactionID);
    TRFCHandlerIF transactionIDHandler =
      TRFCFactory.getTIDRegistration ();
    transactionIDHandler.removeTransactionData(
      transactionID);
    } catch (JCoException e) {
      // invoke function with given transaction
    }
  }
}
```

Listing 4.13 Using tRFC to Create a List of Purchase Orders

JCo does not provide any options for managing transaction numbers in the external Java application. Consequently, the developer must ensure that any transactional function module calls not processed correctly are repeated accordingly.

In listing 4.13, an implementation of the `TRFCHandlerIF` interface is used to store TIDs. A factory class is used for this particular implementation, so that its use is fully "abstracted." In the programming examples that you can download for this book, you will find a class called `TRF-CHashHandler`, which is based on the `java.util.Hashtable` class. The hash table uses the transaction number to store the `JcoFunction` object. As shown in Listing 4.14, an instance of the `TRFCHandlerIF` interface is created during actual processing of the function module. The fact that the `JcoFunction` object has been stored in the hash table means that if an error occurs, you can execute the function by specifying the TID again.

Managing transaction numbers

```
private void createorder(Order order, String transactionID,
  JCoDestination destination) {
  TRFCHandlerIF transactionIDHandler =
    TRFCFactory.getTIDRegistration();
  try {
    JCoFunction function =
      ABAPTypeHandler.createFunction(destination,
        IFunctionNames.Z_IFP_CREATE_ORDER);
    transactionIDHandler.storeTransactionData(
      transactionID, function);
    // code for rfc execution
}
```

Listing 4.14 Storing Transaction Numbers

4 | Remote Function Call with Java

4.1.6 Queued RFC

Using Java Connector for qRFC communication

Finally, this section describes the use of *queued RFCs* (qRFC). qRFC programming is very similar to developing tRFC-based processing. As already described, a qRFC defines an asynchronous update process. This means that a qRFC for a function module does not retrieve any results in an export parameter list, even if these have been written to an export parameter in the function module. Moreover, the calls linked to a queue are also queued until the queue is activated. After the queue is activated, it can be emptied. The queued orders are then processed.

We will use the now-familiar function module Z_IFP_CREATE_ORDER to demonstrate the use of qRFC with JCo. Here, we will focus on the differences between qRFC and tRFC. The programming example in Listing 4.15 shows these differences in the code.

```
public void createorder(Order order, String transactionID,
  JCoDestination destination) {
  TRFCHandlerIF transactionIDHandler =
    TRFCFactory.getTIDRegistration();
  try {
    //create function object
    transactionIDHandler.storeTransactionData(transactionID,
      function);
    // set parameters
    // call function
    function.execute(destination, transactionID,"EAIQUEUE");
  } catch (JCoException ex) {
    ex.printStackTrace();
  }
}
```

Listing 4.15 qRFC Processing of the Function Module "Z_IFP_CREATE_ORDER"

After the function module has been processed, we can use Transaction SMQ2 to view the EAIQUEUE that we have just created. As shown in Figure 4.4, this transaction provides an overview of the current queues.

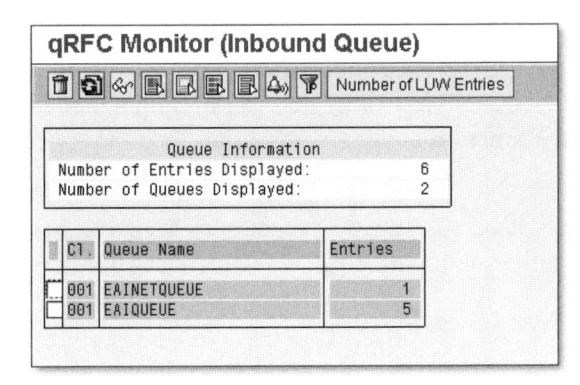

Figure 4.4 Overview of the Queues in the System

You can double-click any queue to view its contents. As you can see in Figure 4.5, five entries are displayed. Therefore, five purchase orders are created in the system. Because the queue is still open, the function calls are yet to be processed. Each entry is assigned to a TID. To unlock the queue, you can press F5 or choose EDIT • UNLOCK from the context menu. The system then processes the entries in the queue.

Figure 4.5 qRFC Monitor for the "EAIQUEUE" Queue

We have already discussed the importance of the repository concept when executing function modules. *Repositories* are used to provide interface descriptions of function modules. They are also the central location for caching these descriptions. Function module metadata is not deleted immediately after you call the function module. Instead, it is retained until the repository object no longer exists. Each repository object is assigned to exactly one destination. Next we will discuss working with objects in the `JCoRepository` class in greater detail.

Managing repositories For our work with repository objects, we will expand the previously discussed administration functions to include aspects for working with the repositories available. Possible functions that can be implemented include reading the cached function module descriptions or using function module metadata.

There are several ways in which to access the repositories available. For example, you can use the destination or the JCo factory class to query the repository.

In the example discussed here, we will use the JCo class and the getRepository method implemented there. The method obtains, as a parameter, the ID of the repository to be evaluated. A repository ID is a character string that is automatically generated by SAP JCo. For this reason, it is not actually possible to address a specific repository, which means that getRepository cannot be called unless the ID is requested. Therefore, our work with repositories comprises two steps. In the first step, the system reads the IDs of the repositories available, and, in the second step, it calls the getRepository method.

4.1.7 Metadata Processing

In addition to using a function module for pure data processing, the *metadata description* of the function module interface is very interesting for your day-to-day work. For example, the column headings of a table parameter can be used when displaying data in a frontend. Metadata is displayed in the JCoMetaData interface. In addition, the JCo API provides the JCoListMetaData interface, which is derived directly. This interface is always used if the entire interface is required, in other words, the import, export, and changing parameters as well as the list of exceptions for a function module.

Accessing metadata There are several ways in which to access the previously mentioned objects. The information can be accessed directly via the parameter list objects of the function module and the getMetaData method defined there or by calling the getFunctionTemplate method. This method returns an object of the type JCoFunctionTemplate. The class provides the complete metadata description of the entire function module, and it is the template for creating the specific JcoFunction object. On closer examination, exactly one instance of the type JCoFunctionTemplate is stored in the destination repository as long as the metadata cache is not invalidated. The object for the `JCoFunctionTemplate` instance of the function module represents the template for creating the function proxy.

The proxy class defines the following five methods for accessing metadata: `getImportParameterList`, `getExportParameterList`, `getChangingParameterList`, `getTableParameterList`, and `getFunctionInterfaceList`. The first four methods deliver specific metadata for the underlying parameter list type while the `getFunctionInterfaceList` method returns all of the metadata for parameter lists, irrespective of the parameter type currently being read. Listing 4.16 shows metadata processing for all cached function module metadata.

Accessing metadata

```
public void getCachedMetaDataForRepository(
  String repositoryID) throws JCoException {
  JCoRepository repository =
    JCo.getRepository(repositoryID);
  String[] listOfCachedMetadataFunctions =
    repository.getCachedFunctionTemplateNames();
  for (int i=0;i<listOfCachedMetadataFunctions.length;i++){
    JCoFunctionTemplate functionTemplate =
      repository.getFunctionTemplate(
        listOfCachedMetadataFunctions[i]);
    JCoListMetaData metaDataOfFunction =
      functionTemplate.getImportParameterList();
    int fieldCount = metaDataOfFunction.getFieldCount();
    for(int o = 0; o < fieldCount; o++) {
      String fieldName = metaDataOfFunction.getName(o);
      String description =
        metaDataOfFunction.getDescription(o);
      int fieldLength = metaDataOfFunction.getLength(o);
      //process metadata
    }
  }
}
```

Listing 4.16 Metadata Processing for All Cached Function Modules in a Repository

4.2 Enterprise Connector

Up to now, we have discussed the use of JCo in detail. We have shown that you can use this technology to integrate standalone Java applications.

No tool support is required here because we assume that no SAP development tools are being used. However, this can often by very laborious, especially if the function modules are highly complex. If you implement applications within the SAP NetWeaver platform (e.g., a web application executed on SAP NetWeaver AS Java), excellent tool support is available. Such applications can be programmed in SAP NetWeaver Developer Studio, which includes code generators that support the developer when consuming function modules. *Enterprise Connector* (ECo) is the name of the code generator used in the context of web programming.

Code generation   Enterprise Connector implements a wizard that supports the developer when creating call classes for a function module. ECo generates the corresponding wrapper classes for all complex data types. Moreover, it generates proxy classes for the consumption of the function module, thus making programming much easier. Essentially, ECo is not a new technology because the JCo API is used within the ECo API. JCo API Version 2.x, and not Version 3.x, is used in SAP NWDS 7.0.

We now want to use ECo to create a list of posted purchase orders. To do this, start SAP NWDS. If you have not yet installed NWDS, you can download a version from SAP Service Marketplace. When discussing ECo, we will assume that you already have extensive knowledge of Java and therefore we will not discuss how to create a Java project.

4.2.1 Generating Proxy Classes

Now that you have created a Java project, you can start to generate proxy classes. To do this, select the relevant project, and then choose NEW • OTHER • SAP CONNECTIVITY from the context menu. The wizard that opens (as shown in Figure 4.6) requires information about the proxy classes to be generated. In the two upper fields, you can specify the location for the classes generated. In our example, choose the Source Folder field. Then, in the Package field, enter a package name that corresponds to your programming guidelines. In the Name field, enter the name of the proxy class used as a communication façade for the function module. In keeping with convention, the class name has the extension _PortType.

Enterprise Connector | 4.2

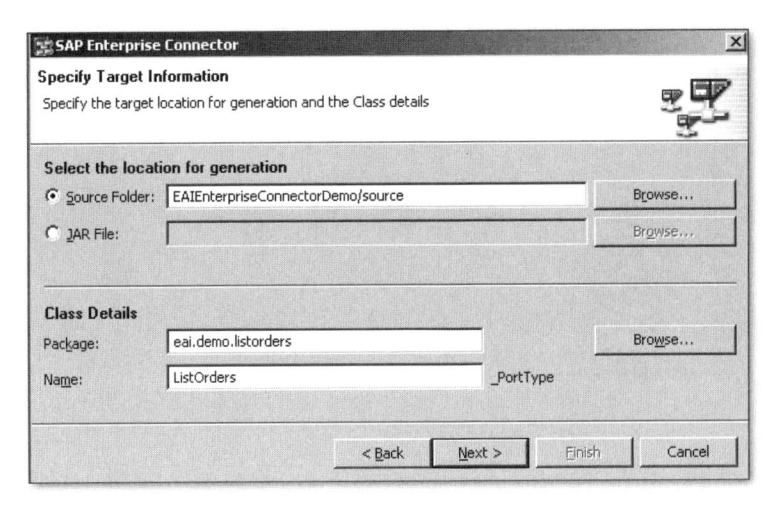

Figure 4.6 Specifying the Proxy Class

Now that all of the fields have been filled, choose Next to move to the next screen. As shown in Figure 4.7, you now enter the connection information for generating the proxy. This information is used for generation purposes only. For subsequent communication, you must configure the parameters separately. It is not possible to transfer this information from the wizard. When generating proxy classes, there are two ways in which you can establish communication with the backend. You can use *load balancing*, or you can establish single-server contact with your SAP system. Select your current configuration on the relevant tab. In the example discussed here, we are using Single Server, and we have entered our communication parameters (see Figure 4.7). These parameters remind us of the connection parameters for JCo, which is not surprising because ECo wizards use familiar JCo classes.

Proxy class

Now that you have entered the connection parameters, choose Next to confirm your entries. In rare cases when using an SAP router, the system may issue a message indicating that it was not possible to reach the backend system. After you have ensured that your entries are correct, copy the SAP router string from the field, so that you can paste it into the field again. Click Next again. You should now be able to continue with the next step.

Connection parameters

239

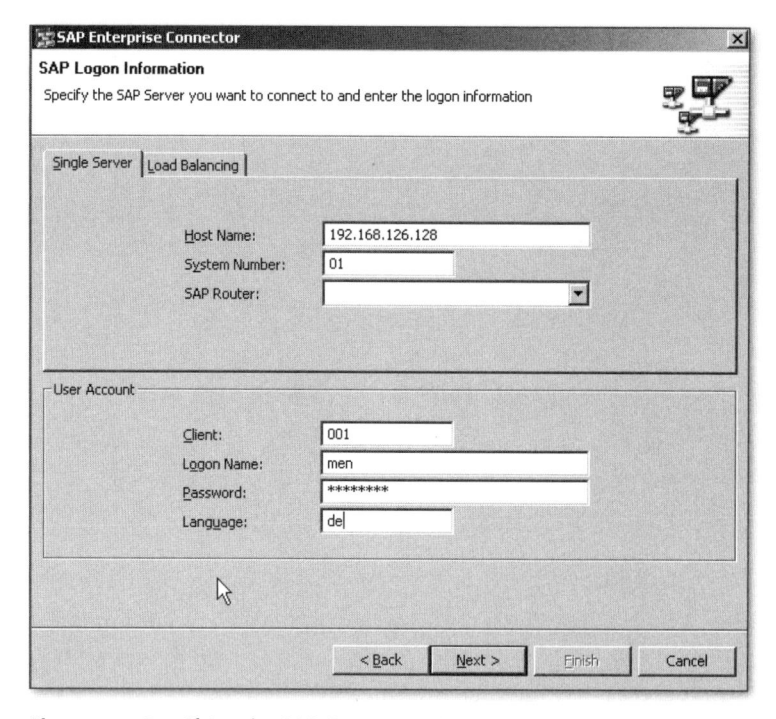

Figure 4.7 Specifying the SAP Connection Parameters

Finding function modules

On the next screen, you can now use the search screen to find function modules for which you want to generate ECo proxy classes (Figure 4.8). As already discussed, we will use ECo to call the function module Z_IFP_ORDER_GETDETAIL. Enter the function module name in the Function Name field, and choose Search. Now select the function module, and choose Finish. The generation process for proxy classes starts, and, a few moments later, you return to the Java perspective of your SAP NWDS.

As you can see, you obtain numerous compiler error messages in the task output for the development environment. The reason for this is that after the proxy classes have been generated, SAP NWDS is not able to automatically include the correct Java libraries in the class path for the Java project. To continue programming, you must maintain the correct JAR files manually.

Enterprise Connector | 4.2

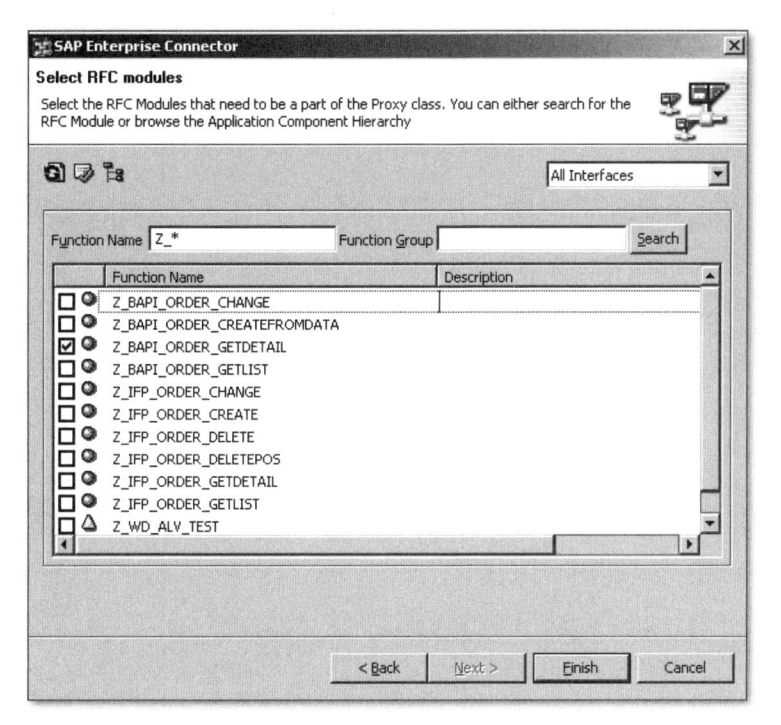

Figure 4.8 Selecting Function Modules

To add libraries, open the properties of your project and then switch to the Java Buildpath menu entry. Now switch to the Libraries tab, and choose Add Variable. In the next dialog box, select the ECLIPSE_HOME variable, and choose Extend. Now add the following JAR files:

Adding Java archives to the project structure

- *<plugins>/com.sap.idb.jcb.core_2.0.0/lib/aii_proxy_rt.jar*
- *<plugins>/com.sap.idb.jcb.core_2.0.0/lib/aii_util_misc.jar*
- *<plugins>/com.mdi_2.0.0/lib/SAPmdi.jar*
- *<plugins>/com.sap.mw.jco_2.0.0/lib/sapjco.jar*

Replace *<plugins>* with *ECLIPSE_HOME/plugins*. Now that the project no longer contains any errors, we will turn our attention to the classes that have been generated.

ECo generates a separate Java class for each structure-like dictionary type referenced by a calling RFC function module. Proxy generation follows

Java classes for ABAP structures

241

the standard conventions for Java Bean programming. The same procedure is adopted when working with tables. Table parameters are handled as lists. Here, ECo generates a class that is based on the table's metadata. Table 4.2 provides a brief overview of the classes generated.

Class Description	Short Description
ListOrders_PortType	Proxy class of function module
Z_Ifp_Order_Getdetail_Fault_Exception	Exception class triggered by the backend if an error occurs
Z_Ifp_Order_Getdetail_Fault	Error text class
Z_Ifp_Order_Getdetail_Input	Import parameter
Z_Ifp_Order_Getdetail_Output	Export parameter
ZifporderposType_List	Table type as a list

Table 4.2 Overview of the Classes Generated

As you can see in the table, not only ABAP Dictionary classes are created but also a class for input processing; a class for processing import, changing, and table parameters; and an output class for export, changing, and table parameters. When naming the input or output class generated, you use the name of the function module (e.g., Z_Ifp_Order_Getdetail for the module discussed here), followed by the extension _Input or _Output.

We have not neglected error processing. Table 4.2 lists two classes for processing exceptions. On the one hand, the class Z_Ifp_Order_Getdetail_Fault is available. This *fault type* represents function module exceptions. In the Java client, you can use the getText method to access the technical name of the error that has occurred. Fault type instances are encapsulated in the exceptions defined in the function module. For this purpose, the code generator generates classes with the suffix _Exception. As you can see in Listing 4.17 in the next section, the exception Z_Ifp_Order_Getdetail_Fault_Exception is processed via a try-catch block, and the method getZ_Ifp_Order_Getdetail_Fault can be used to read the error message.

Establishing a connection

ECo uses the JCo.Client class to establish a connection. The createClient method in the JCo factory class is used to generate instances. Various forms of this method are available. Because we do not want to store the configuration parameters directly in the code, we will transfer an object from the class `java.util.Properties`. Similar to using JCo 3.0, a property file is used here to configure the instance. After the instance has been successfully configured, a connection can be established with the backend. The `connect` method is used for this purpose.

4.2.2 Programming the Client

In the next step, we can prepare the actual function module call. To do this, we will instantiate the `ListOrders_PortType` proxy class and use the `setJCoClient` method, first and foremost, to set the communication client. As you can see, ECo allows you to use various `setter` methods to configure communication between the Java client and the ABAP backend. In the example shown, we want to use only a simple sRFC without any other aspects of communication, so that only the `JCo.Client` instance is transferred.

In Listing 4.17, we will set the import parameters of the function module. The code generator has typed classes for all required backend parameter types. For the import parameters, we will use the class `Z_Bapi_Order_Getdetail_Input`. After we have instantiated the class, we can use the `setIm_Orderid` method to enter the `orderid` parameter and transfer it to the method `z_Bapi_Order_Getdetail`. When the function module can be called without errors, we can use the `getEx_Orderhead` method to access the export parameters. As you can see in the listing, we will use the model classes already discussed in Section 4.1.3, Programming with SAP Java Connector, to manage the purchase order information. The `getter` methods that were generated are now used to read the individual fields in the purchase order header from the returned export structure.

Finally, we will call the `getTa_Orderpos` method for processing purchase order items and then process the data in accordance with our model definition. To complete the process, we will use the `disconnect` method to terminate the connection to the backend.

Processing purchase order items

```
public static void main(String[] args) {
  try {
    Properties connectionProperties = new Properties();
    InputStream is = new
      FileInputStream("c:\\jco.properties");
    connectionProperties.load(is);
```

```
            JCo.Client jcoClient =
              JCo.createClient(connectionProperties);
            jcoClient.connect();
            //ListOrders_PortType proxy = new ListOrders_PortType();
            eai.demo.rfc.listorders.ListOrders_PortType proxy =
              new eai.demo.rfc.listorders.ListOrders_PortType();
            proxy.messageSpecifier.setJcoClient(jcoClient);
            Z_Ifp_Order_Getdetail_Input inputParameter =
              new Z_Ifp_Order_Getdetail_Input();
            inputParameter.setIm_Orderid("43");
            Z_Ifp_Order_Getdetail_Output output =
              proxy.Z_Ifp_Order_Getdetail(inputParameter);
            ZifporderType order = output.getEx_Orderhead();
            Orderheader orderheader = getOrderHeader(order);
            ZifporderposType[] orderpos = output.getTa_Orderpos();
            List orderposes = getOrderpos(orderpos);
            Order currentOrder = new Order();
            currentOrder.setOrderheader(orderheader);
            currentOrder.setOrderpos(orderposes);
            System.out.println(currentOrder.toString());
            jcoClient.disconnect();
        } catch (Z_Ifp_Order_Getdetail_Fault_Exception e) {
            Z_Ifp_Order_Getdetail_Fault orderfault =
              e.getZ_Ifp_Order_Getdetail_Fault();
            System.out.println(orderfault.getText());
        } catch (SystemFaultException e) {
            e.printStackTrace();
        } catch (ApplicationFaultException e) {
            e.printStackTrace();
        } catch (FileNotFoundException e) {
            e.printStackTrace();
        } catch (IOException e) {
            e.printStackTrace();
        }
    }
}
```

Listing 4.17 Calling the Function Module "Z_BAPI_ORDER_GETDETAIL"

4.3 RFC Server

Now that we have described the development of external Java client applications in detail, we will turn our attention to programming JCo servers. Here, ABAP applications are given the option of calling external program code in Java.

4.3.1 Server-Side and Client-Side Repository

Processing a call by an ABAP client in a Java server involves steps similar to those used for communication between a Java client and the ABAP server. As you saw during client programming, a repository is used to store interface metadata in an ABAP stack so that a system can check whether consumers will adhere to the interface before actually processing a call. This ensures that type-safe data is transferred to communication partners. A Java server receives functions in the same way. Consequently, Java servers must be equipped with a repository. The dilemma here is that this is a very complex and laborious development step. In this section, we do not want to provide in-depth information about implementing a specific repository but rather discuss the basic principles of repository programming.

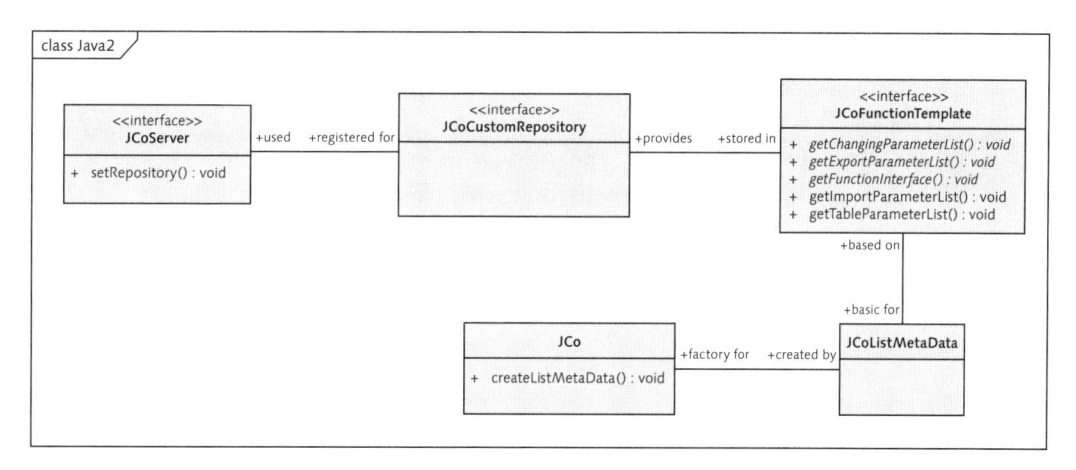

Figure 4.9 Overview of the Classes Relevant for Repository Programming

JCo makes some classes available for the creation of specific repository objects. Figure 4.9 shows a simplified class diagram of the classes relevant for repository programming. In the center, you see the `JCoCustomRepository` interface, which defines, as was already discussed in client programming, a number of methods that can be used to query the metadata of functions that the server will provide later. Because we want to

Classes for JCo Java server programming

implement our own repository, we must provide a class that will implement the interface. This means that we have to describe all of the repository functions that we want the SAP system to call. These functions are described in the `JCoFunctionTemplate` interface. For this purpose, the interface defines some `getter` methods that return a metadata list as a return value. This list is then displayed in the now-familiar `JCoListMetaData` interface.

Complexity of the function description

Providing your own function description, which is required for the `JCoFunctionTemplate` interface, is quite a challenge. In the case of complex functions provided by the SAP system, each individual field, structure, and table must be described in the `JCoListMetaData` interface and in other related metadata interfaces, such as `JCoRecordMetaData`. The programming example in Listing 4.18 represents a simple implementation of the `getExportParameterList` method, which describes export parameters. In the first line, you see that an instance of the type `JCoRecordMetaData` is generated to describe a complex type. The interface provides some `add` methods, which essentially contain the following parameters:

▸ **Parameter name**
Here, you define the parameter name that will be used later to address the parameter.

▸ **Parameter data type**
The data types provided by each metadata characteristic are used here. All data type names have the prefix `TYPE_`.

▸ **Symbol length of parameter**
This specifies the permitted number of characters in a parameter.

▸ **Symbol length of parameter for Unicode**
This specifies the permitted number of characters in a parameter when using Unicode.

▸ **Offset for internal JCo data buffer**
This is the field distance from the start of the structure.

▸ **Offset for internal JCo data buffer when using Unicode**
This is the field distance from the start of the structure when using Unicode.

Metadata list

Now that we have created the structure, we can include it in the list of metadata for the export parameter list. We will use the `JCoListMetaData` interface for this purpose. The `add` method obtains, as its parameters, the name of the structure, the data type, the recently created structure object, and the parameter type. The example shown here concerns an export parameter.

```
public JCoListMetaData getExportParameterList() {
  JCoRecordMetaData structure =
    JCo.createRecordMetaData("Orderhead");
  structure.add("orderid", JCoRecordMetaData.TYPE_STRING,
                8, 8, 0, 0);
  structure.add("buyer", JCoRecordMetaData.TYPE_STRING,
                50,50,0,0);
  JCoListMetaData exportMetaData =
     JCo.createListMetaData("export");
  exportMetaData.add("Orderhead",
    JCoListMetaData.TYPE_STRUCTURE, structure,
    JCoListMetaData.EXPORT_PARAMETER);
  return exportMetaData;
}
```

Listing 4.18 Implementing the "getExportParameterList" Method for the "JCoFunctionTemplate" Interface

Now that we have defined the `JcoFunctionTemplate` implementation, we must now register the metadata in your own repository. The repository provides the `addFunctionTemplateToCache` method for this purpose. The final step in repository programming involves registering the new autonomous repository on the server. To do this, call the `setRepository` method, and transfer an instance of your own repository.

4.3.2 Programming a Simple JCo Server

The JCo API provides the `JCoServer` interface and the `JCoServerFactory` factory class for the purposes of programming a Java server for an SAP system. The factory class is used to return an instance of the interface implementation to the calling program. During this generation process, an attempt is made to establish a connection with the SAP system and to register the Java server accordingly. To establish a connection, the factory class requires the connection information provided by an implementation of the `ServerDataProvider` interface.

To demonstrate server programming, we will generate a class called `EAIServerDemo` and implement a private helper method called `startServer`. Listing 4.19 shows the first steps toward starting a synchronous RFC (sRFC) server.

Getting started

```
private void startServer() {
  JCoServer eaiServer;
  try {
      eaiServer = JCoServerFactory.getServer("EAIServer");
  } catch (JCoException ex) {
    throw new RuntimeException(
        "Unable to create server. Error message is:" +
        ex.getMessage(), ex);
  }
  // register ServerFunctionHandler
  registerServerFunctionHandler(eaiServer);
  eaiServer.start();
  System.out.println(
      "Server successful started and registered with " +
      server.getProgramID());
}
```

Listing 4.19 Starting the JCo Server

Configuring inbound communication

Three steps are required to start the RFC server. In the first step, the `JCoServerFactory` class is used to create an instance of the type `JCoServer`. The factory provides the `getServer` method for this purpose. This method obtains the name of a file in which the connection information for the registration process at the SAP backend is defined. In this case, the file name must be stored in the class path for the Java server and have the file extension *.jcoServer*. Listing 4.20 shows a sample configuration file. You can also request access to the parameter names via the `ServerDataProvider` interface.

```
jco.server.connection_count=2
jco.server.gwhost=192.168.126.128
jco.server.progid=EAIJAVASERVER
jco.server.gwserv=sapgw01
jco.server.repository_destination=EAIRepository
```

Listing 4.20 Server Connection Configuration File

Configuring the server connection parameters

The entries `jco.server.progid` and `jco.server.repository_destination` are of particular interest here. The first entry, `jco.server.progid`, is used as a unique identifier for registering the server in the SAP system, while the second entry, `jco.server.repository_destination`, is an optional parameter used to indicate the backend system responsible for providing the repository and thus providing the metadata of the calling functions. As already discussed at the start of this chapter, inbound communication has a similar structure to outbound communication, so it is necessary to provide the functions in the Java server in the same way as you provide the ABAP Dictionary on the ABAP side. Therefore, the parameter `jco.server.repository_destination` simply denotes the name of a configuration file with the extension *.jcoDestination*. You have already seen the structure of this configuration file earlier in Listing 4.2 (Section 4.1.3, Programming with SAP Java Connector). When setting up the server, you will specify a connection that will enable the server to read the metadata of the functions provided.

4.3.3 Registering a Function Handler

After you have implemented the server process, the next step is to implement a function handler and to register it with the server process. The function handler processes inbound function calls. You define the `JCoServerFunctionHandle` interface for this implementation. This interface only defines a `handleRequest` method. The call parameters of the method are one object of the type `JCoServerContext` and one object of the type `JCoFunction`. The `JCoServerContext` object is used to access the flow context of the current inbound call. You can access the repository and server information via the interface. In addition to the flow context, the method still requires the actual call parameters. Similar to processing outbound calls, a `JcoFunction` object is used to describe the parameters. As discussed in Section 4.1.3, Programming with SAP Java Connector, you can use this object to access import, export, and table parameters. Listing 4.21 shows the implementation for the `EAIJavaOrderCreate` class, which is used for Java-side processing of calls associated with the function module `Z_IFP_ORDER_CREATE`.

Registering an instance of the type "JCoServerFunctionHandle"

```
public class EAIJavaOrderCreate
  implements JCoServerFunctionHandler {
  @Override
  public void handleRequest(
    JCoServerContext arg0, JCoFunction arg1)
    throws AbapException {
    // implement incoming requests
  }
}
```

Listing 4.21 Implementing a Function Handler

However, the implementation alone is insufficient. To process inbound function calls, you must register the function handler with each server. You can use the class `DefaultServerHandlerFactory.FunctionHandlerFactory` to register simple server functions. By calling the `registerHandler` method and transferring the function name and function handler instance, the server knows who is responsible for processing inbound calls for the function Z_IFP_CREATE_ORDER. Finally, the `setCallHandlerFactory` method is used to register the new factory object with the server. The following programming example (Listing 4.22) shows the registration process for a function handler.

```
JCoServerFunctionHandler stfcConnectionHandler =
                            new EAIJavaOrderCreate();
DefaultServerHandlerFactory.FunctionHandlerFactory factory =
   new DefaultServerHandlerFactory.FunctionHandlerFactory();
factory.registerHandler("Z_IFP_ORDER_CREATE",
                        stfcConnectionHandler);
server.setCallHandlerFactory(factory);
server.start();
```

Listing 4.22 Registering the Function Handler

Configuring a new TCP/IP destination

Java server programming concludes with the creation of a TCP/IP destination in the SAP system. To do this, switch to destination administration in Transaction SM59. After you have started the transaction, select the entry TCP/IP, and choose Create. Then specify a name for the RFC destination, and provide a brief description to ease subsequent identification. In addition, select the Registered Server program field, and enter the program ID that you used to register the server with the SAP system. In the scenario shown here, the ID is EAIJAVASERVER. Figure 4.10 shows a destination configuration.

Problematic error handling

Now that the server is up and running and it can process requests from the SAP system, there is an additional task. The preceding scenario for creating purchase orders in an external server is implemented as a blocking, synchronous call. In other words, after the SAP system has called the function on the server, the system is blocked until the server is finished processing. Furthermore, it is important to ensure that a purchase order is only ever created on the Java server once, even if an error occurs. To solve this problem, the purchase order must be created in a tRFC. The server must be enhanced for this purpose. In other words, functions that support tRFCs must be implemented.

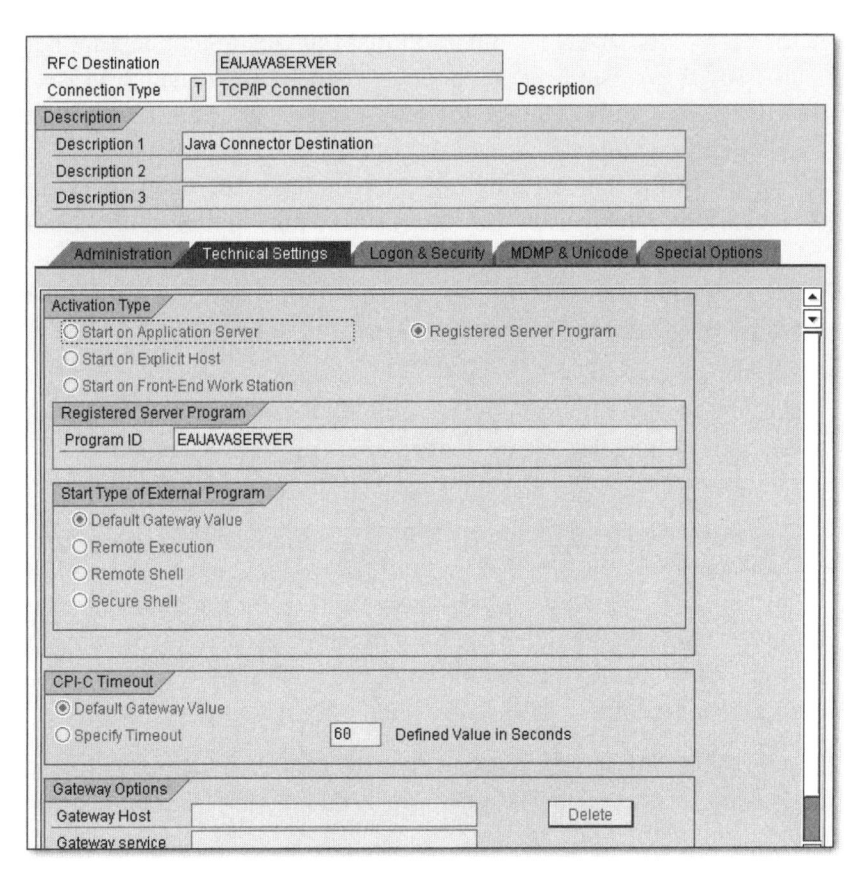

Figure 4.10 Configuring the "EAIJAVASERVER" Destination

4.3.4 Managing Transactions

The first enhancement to our server concerns transactional call processing in accordance with the model for tRFC communication. The JCoServer API provides the JCoServerTIDHandler interface for this purpose, which, in turn, provides the following methods:

- checkTID

  The SAP system calls the checkTID method if an RFC is transferred to the Java server as a tRFC. The method obtains, as its parameters, the server context and the TID used to process the call. This method must ensure that the system executes only one call with a transferred TID.

Methods of the "JCoServerTID Handler" interface

Therefore, it is extremely important that transaction numbers are not lost. For this reason, the method is generally implemented in conjunction with storing the TID in a database or in another persistent medium. In addition to simply storing the TID, it is also necessary to store the processing status of the TID so that transaction numbers can be easily monitored later. The contract for this method states that a `boolean` parameter is returned to the calling program. If the transferred TID has already been processed once, the value `false` must be returned. Otherwise, the value `true` must be returned.

- `commit and rollback`
  The `commit` method is called if all of the RFC functions executed with the same transaction number have been successfully processed. In contrast, the `rollback` method is called if a transaction finishes with errors.

- `confirmTID`
  The `confirmTID` method is used to confirm that a transaction with a specific transaction number has been executed successfully. As a result of this method, the transaction number is either removed from the persistent medium or, at the very least, assigned a suitable status.

Registering the TID handler

Before starting the server, you must register the implementation of the `JCoServerTIDHandler` interface with the server. To do this, call the `setTIDHandler` method and transfer an instance of the `TIDHandler` implementation. After the server has started, the function can be called on the ABAP side with the addition `in background task destination 'EAI-JAVASERVER'`. The server is contacted, and the `checkTID` method checks whether the transaction number is already in use. If the method returns the value `true`, the `handleRequest` method is called.

4.4 JCo RFC Provider Service

You always use the preceding implementation for a server function if you are using the standalone version of JCo. In addition to this type of server implementation, SAP already provides an integrated server function in SAP NetWeaver AS Java. This server function, known as the *JCo RFC Provider Service*, is implemented directly in the application server as a J2EE service. Like all services, this service can be configured using the *Visual Administrator* (VA).

The JCo RFC Provider Service works in the same way as the standalone version of JCo, with the only difference being that the JCo RFC Provider Service is based on J2EE concepts. Therefore, a traditional Java class is not used, but rather *Enterprise Java Beans* (EJB) are used as communication endpoints for processing inbound RFCs. In SAP NetWeaver 7.0, you use JCo Version 2.0, which is delivered in SAP NWDS, for communication between the EJB endpoint and the ABAP stack.

In the JCo RFC Provider Server, both communication and administration follow the same model used for traditional server programming. In contrast to pure server programming, EJB-based server programming involves the registration (in the RFC provider) of one RFC destination for each EJB component. Similarly, Transaction SM59 is used to generate a destination on the ABAP side. Therefore, both sides agree on one program ID.

RFC destination

Following configuration, the following communication steps are processed: The Java-side destination is linked to the repository in SAP NetWeaver AS ABAP. Similar to traditional server programming, the JCo RFC Provider Service is then registered with a gateway under the name specified during configuration. If a function is called by specifying the TCP/IP destination on the ABAP side, the call is forwarded via the gateway to the configured JCo RFC Provider Service. Until now, the EJB was of no further interest. However, the JCo RFC Provider Service must now forward the call to the EJB component responsible for this function call. JNDI registration (*Java Naming and Directory Interface*) of the EJB component identifies which EJB is responsible for which RFC. Consequently, the JNDI entries and the RFC name must be identical. If, for example, you want to call the function module Z_IFP_ORDER_CREATE via the JCo RFC Provider Service, you must register an EJB under the same name in the JNDI. This EJB does not necessarily have to implement the Remote and RemoteHome interfaces, but they must be available for local communication (LocalHome and Local).

After you have found the correct EJB component, you must call the EJB. To perform the call in a standardized procedure, the EJB that you want to call via the JCo RFC Provider Service must implement the processFunction method. Consequently, this method must contain a single parameter of the type JCo.Function and specify an exception of the type java.lang.Exception as an exception in the method signature. Thanks to the transferred function, the EJB can now read the parameter list, execute the required function, and then return it via the JCo.Function object to the calling point of communication.

JCo RFC Provider Service examples

We will now use the function module Z_IFP_ORDER_CREATE to demonstrate how to use the JCo RFC Provider Service. For this purpose, we will assume that you already have sufficient experience in creating and programming J2EE applications in SAP NWDS. The example shown here can also be downloaded for this book under the EJB module project JavaRFCProvider. This project contains a Stateless Session bean (SLSB) called RFCProviderDemoBean, which implements the processFunction method discussed earlier. The programming example in Listing 4.23 shows the main features of the implementation. Here, processing is similar to the concepts that we have discussed up to now; that is, the import parameters can be accessed, or the export parameters returned to the SAP system can be set. As you can see in the programming example provided in Listing 4.23, we will write the order ID 123 to the export parameter list. This value will be returned to the calling program when the processFunction is fully processed.

```
public void processFunction(JCo.Function function)
  throws java.lang.Exception {
  Location rfcLocation =
    Location.getLocation(this.getClass());
  rfcLocation.debugT(
    "start java serverside processing with function " +
    function.getName());
  JCo.ParameterList importParameter =
                    function.getImportParameterList();
  JCo.Structure structure =
        importParameter.getStructure("im_orderheader");

  // save data to database, set a simple orderid
  function.getExportParameterList().setValue(
                                    "EX_ORDERID",123);
  rfcLocation.debugT(
    "java serverside processing finished");
}
```

Listing 4.23 Implementing the "processFunction" Method

Before the application can be distributed, the JNDI name of the component must be set in the deployment descriptor `ejb-j2ee.xml` (see Listing 4.24). After you have opened the file, you can use the wizard to enter the JNDI name. As already discussed, the name must correspond to the function that you want to call from the ABAP stack. This example concerns the function `Z_IFP_ORDER_CREATE`. The EJB component can now be distributed across the associated Enterprise Application Project.

Setting the JNDI name

```
<ejb-j2ee-engine>
  <enterprise-beans>
    <enterprise-bean>
      <ejb-name>RFCProviderDemoBean</ejb-name>
      <jndi-name>Z_IFP_ORDER_CREATE</jndi-name>
      <session-props/>
    </enterprise-bean>
  </enterprise-beans>
</ejb-j2ee-engine>
```

Listing 4.24 Configuring the JNDI Name in the File "ejb-j2ee-engine.xml"

After programming is complete, the next step is to configure the Java-side destination. To do this, start the Visual Administrator. After logon, navigate within the service tree, via the node SERVER • SERVICES, to the entry JCo RFC PROVIDER SERVICE. Enter "EJBRFCPROVIDER" in the Program Id field, and fill in the Gateway Host and Gateway Service fields in accordance with your infrastructure. In addition, enter a value between 1 and 20 in the Server Count field. This value specifies the number of server instances required on the Java side for processing. If you expect a very high and parallel access frequency on your Java server, increase the value in accordance with your requirements.

Configuring the JCo RFC Provider Service

In the next step, fill in the fields for communication with the SAP repository. Once again, enter values in accordance with your backend system. Lastly, choose Set to save the entry. You will obtain an entry similar to the entry shown in Figure 4.11.

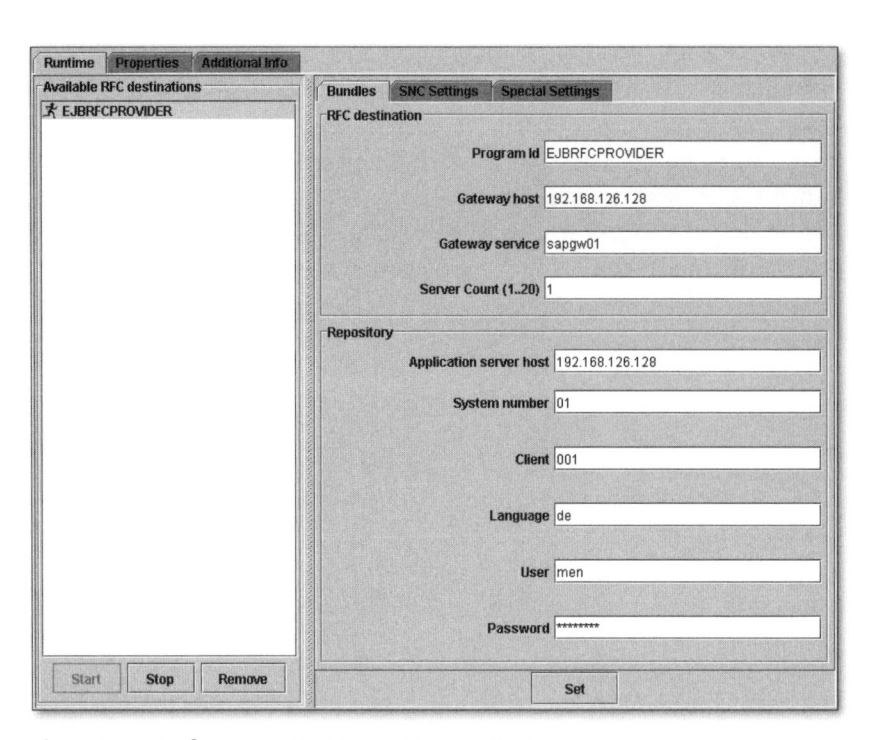

Figure 4.11 Configuring an RFC Destination in a J2EE Server

Configuration in ABAP

You can now configure the ABAP side. Proceed in the same way as you did for configuring a TCP/IP destination (Section 4.3, RFC Server), and specify the corresponding program ID for the destination configuration in the Visual Administrator. Finally, test the configuration. To do this, start the function module Z_IFP_ORDER_CREATE, and enter, as an RFC destination, the TCP/IP destination that you have just configured. After processing, a new order ID is displayed in the SAP system.

4.5 SAP NetWeaver Portal Connector Framework

In addition to known technologies such as JCo and ECo for systems, or SQLJ and JDBC for databases, SAP NetWeaver Portal provides an additional interface technology for access to ABAP-based systems and databases, namely *SAP NetWeaver Portal Connector Framework*. This framework provides an implementation that is based on the JCA standards (*Java Connector Architecture*) for accessing backend systems. The Connector Framework has replaced the JCo Client Service in the portal and raised ABAP communication to J2EE specification standards.

4.5.1 Java Connector Architecture

The *Java Connector Architecture* (JCA) is part of the J2EE specification. It was defined with a view to harmonizing the process of integrating backend systems into *Enterprise Information Systems* (EIS). JCA describes a standard for communication between a J2EE application server and the EIS. If both sides adhere to the standard, such backend systems can be easily integrated in a homogenous manner. Backend manufacturers must implement a *resource adapter* for communication purposes. Because the resource adapter adheres to the standard, it can be installed on J2EE application servers as a plug-in. Users of JCA communication can rely on three integral parts of a contract that exists between the application server manufacturer and the EIS manufacturer:

- Connection management
- Transaction management
- Security management

In addition to these integral parts of a contract, the standard also defines a *Common Client Interface* (CCI), which, in turn, defines the interfaces that a backend manufacturer can implement. These are merely recommendations from Sun Microsystems. The backend manufacturer does not necessarily have to follow them. He can also enhance the CCI. This is particularly useful if it is not possible to express some aspects of backend communication per the approach defined in the CCI. The CCI simplifies the implementation of EIS consumers considerably because, in most cases, the classes accessed are known classes defined in the standard system. Table 4.3 provides an overview of CCI classes.

Common Client Interface

Class Name	Description
ConnectionFactory	Establishes a connection to EIS.
Connection	Represents the connection to EIS.
ConnectionSpec	Describes the necessary communication parameters for communication with the backend (for example, user name).

Table 4.3 Overview of Central JCA Classes

Class Name	Description
Interaction	Represents interaction with EIS. For example, this class is used for the actual BAPI call.
InteractionSpec	Defines interaction parameters, for example, the function module name to be called as a result of this interaction.
Record	Base class for the results of a successful EIS call.
RecordFactory	Used to create records, for example, of ABAP structures transferred to an RFC as import parameters.
LocalTransaction	Creates a local transaction context.

Table 4.3 Overview of Central JCA Classes (Cont.)

4.5.2 System Landscape of the Portal

SAP NetWeaver Portal makes it possible to use various mechanisms to display data from third-party systems in the portal. This does not involve an ounce of programming nor is it necessary to implement a portal component. You must set up a *system* to facilitate the consumption of third-party systems in the portal. This is done in the *system landscape* of the portal.

> **Note**
>
> Note that the system landscape has nothing to do with the *System Landscape Directory* (SLD), which is used, for example, to deploy the adaptive RFC under Web Dynpro for Java.

Communication adapter

Various mechanisms can be used to implement systems in the system landscape of the portal. However, all procedures have one thing in common; each system must have an adapter that facilitates communication with a third-party system. SAP already provides some adapters for integration purposes, for example, integration of an external HTTP-based system to display external content in the portal. In addition, customers or manufacturers of third-party systems can achieve simple integration by implementing a separate system component.

Creating a new ABAP system in the portal

In this chapter, we will use the now-familiar function module Z_IFP_ORDER_GETDETAIL to demonstrate how to use SAP NetWeaver Portal Connector Framework. The first step toward using the framework is the definition of an ABAP system in the portal. Therefore, log on to the portal (to do so, you need higher-level administrative rights). After logon, navigate via SYSTEM ADMINISTRATION • SYSTEM CONFIGURATION • SYSTEM LANDSCAPE to the system landscape of the portal. Before you create the system, create a folder under the *Portal Content* directory by selecting the root directory and then selecting NEW • FOLDER from the context menu. A wizard for creating folders opens. Enter "DemoABAP" in the Folder Name and Folder ID fields, and enter "en.sapeai.fd" in the Folder ID Prefix field. Confirm your entries, and close the next screen.

In the next step, select the folder that you have just created, and select NEW • SYSTEM (FROM TEMPLATE) from the context menu. The system displays a system wizard in which you obtain a list of templates for creating systems. Because you want to create an SAP system, choose SAP System Using Dedicated Application Server.

Dedicated Server for Test Purposes Only

Do not use the system type *dedicated application server* in production environments. It is for test and demonstration purposes only. The reason for this is that the host name and/or IP address of the SAP system are fixed entries. Nevertheless, we chose this variant here because it is easier to configure.

Now confirm your selection, and, on the next screen, enter "DemoABAPSystem" as the System Name and System ID. In addition, enter "en.sapeai.sys" in the System ID Prefix field, and choose Next. When you choose Finish to complete the process, the system will ask you if you want to switch to the object editor. If you choose Yes, you will access the configuration settings of the system that you have just created. Use the Alias property category to switch to the definition of a new alias. For this purpose, enter, for example, "Demo" in the Alias Name field, and then choose Add. Choose Save to save your entries.

In the next step, configure the authentication method at the SAP backend. To do this, select the User Management entry from the Property Category dropdown list. As shown in Figure 4.12, choose the setting that requires users to enter a user name and password for authentication purposes. Choose Save to save your configuration.

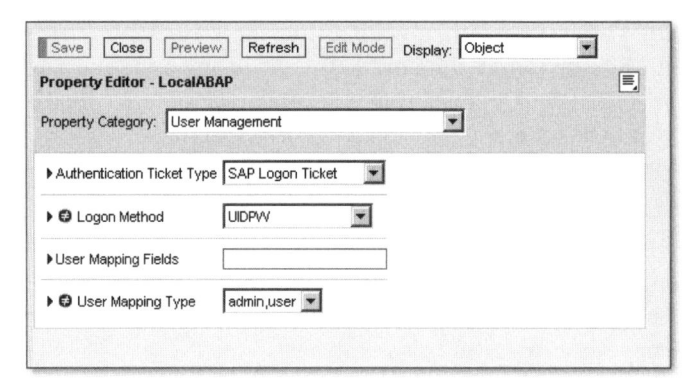

Figure 4.12 Configuring the Authentication Method at the SAP Backend

Defining user mappings

Close the current configuration, and switch to portal user management. User management is available under the User Administration role. Find the user or group for which you want to grant access to the backend system that you have just created, and then select the User Mapping for System Access tab. Select the system called Demo, choose Change, and enter your user name and password. Choose Save to confirm your entry. Figure 4.13 shows the resulting screen.

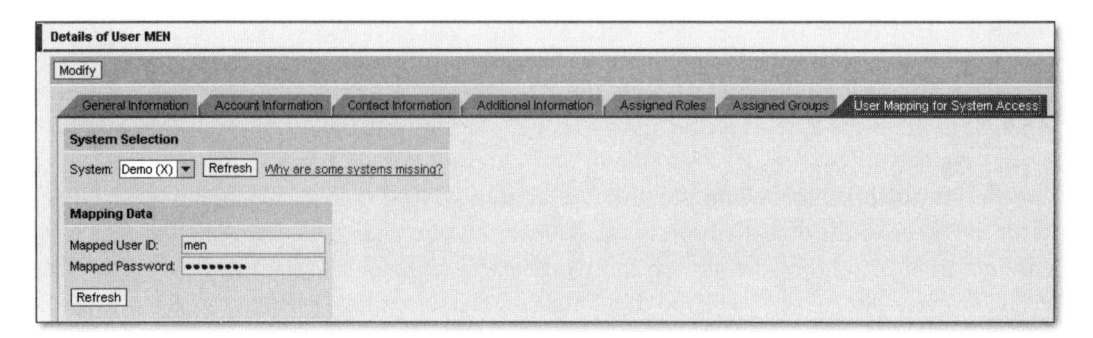

Figure 4.13 Defining User Mappings in the Portal

Now test whether the earlier configuration steps have been successful, and check communication between the portal and the ABAP backend. To do this, switch back to the *System Landscape Editor,* and open the system that you created earlier. Select the Connection Test entry from the View dropdown menu, and, on the next screen, choose the Connection Test for Connectors selection box. Finally, choose Test. You should now receive confirmation that the communication test has been successful (Figure 4.14).

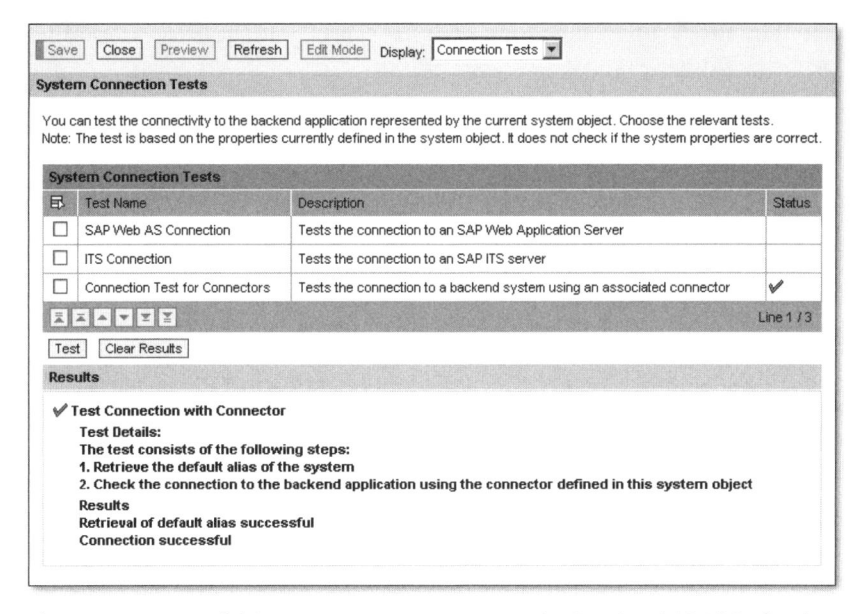

Figure 4.14 Successful Communication Test Between the Portal and ABAP Backend

4.5.3 Introduction to Programming in the Portal

The portal provides various technologies for content development. The programmer can decide on a certain degree of convenience in terms of the implementation and define the extent to which he wants to obtain a clean application architecture. Portal components are created in SAP NWDS. The NWDS provides a separate perspective for this purpose. There are three types of portal components:

- AbstractPortalComponent
- DynPage
- JSPDynPage

Types of portal components

In this section, we will not discuss the pros and cons of using one of these technologies to program portal components. Instead, we want to consider the steps that you must follow the first time you program portal content. After you have started SAP NWDS, follow the menu path WINDOW • OPEN PERSPECTIVE • OTHER. In the next window, select Enterprise Portal. The system opens a perspective of the same name, which is indicated by the fact that the toolbar contains entries for fast access to other aspects of the portal.

Creating a Portal Project

Before you can start to implement a component, you need a project. For this purpose, open the context menu in *Package Explorer*, and select the project type Portal Application under the path NEW • PROJECT. Choose Next to confirm the dialog box. Then, in the next dialog box, enter the name "SAPConnectorDemo" in the Project Name field.

As you can see, the SAP NWDS plug-in does not store the project in the workspace within the development environment. The reason for this is that the plug-in was already provided under Eclipse 1.0, and it has not undergone intensive further development since then. Choose Finish to confirm the dialog box shown in Figure 4.15.

Workspace not used

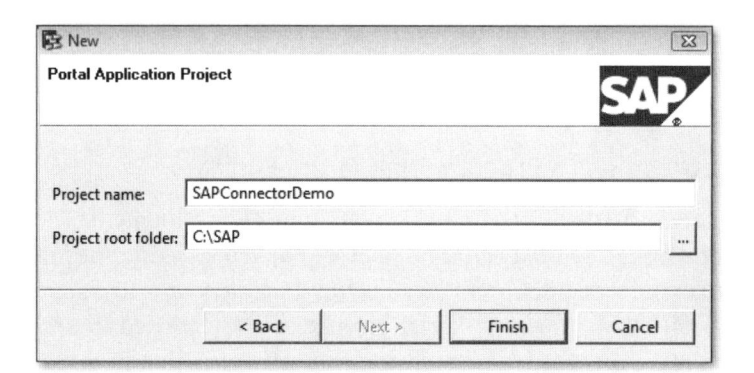

Figure 4.15 Creating a Portal Project

Creating a Portal Component

Figure 4.16 shows the starting point for implementing a simple portal component, which we will describe next. Step by step, this component will be used to call an ABAP function module.

A portal application is always used to incorporate portal components into the portal server.

SAP NetWeaver Portal Connector Framework | 4.5

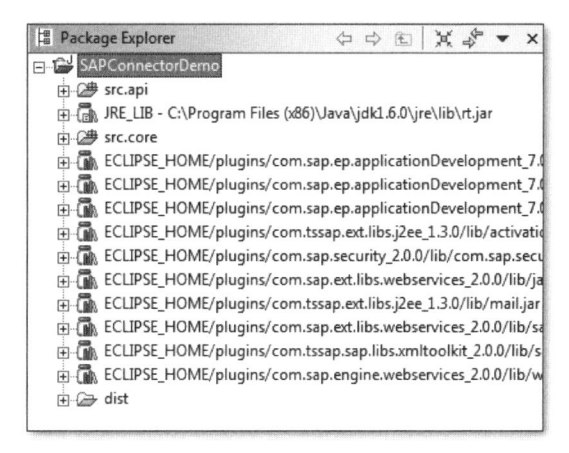

Figure 4.16 Structure of a Portal Project

Adding a Portal Component

Before you start programming, you must add a portal component to the portal project that you have just created. To do this, follow the menu path FILE • NEW • OTHER • CREATE NEW PORTAL APPLICATION OBJECT, and choose Next to confirm the dialog box. On the next screen, select the portal project SAPConnectorDemo, and choose Next. Then expand the Portal Component menu, and select the portal component type AbstractPortalComponent. Choose Next again to reach the last step in the wizard (see Figure 4.17).

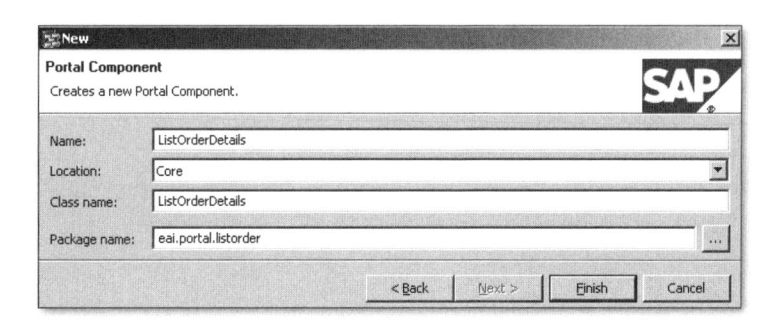

Figure 4.17 Creating a Portal Component

The New dialog box contains four fields. The Name field contains the name of the component. Together with the project name, the component

Unique identifier for portal components

263

name is a unique identifier for accessing the component. The name is used to register the component in the portal infrastructure. Other components can then use this name to reference and use this component later on.

Storage location The Location field reflects the storage location of the component to be created within the project structure. We must distinguish between two storage locations. On the one hand, you can specify API as the storage location. If you select API when creating the component, the component will be stored in the *src.api* directory of the portal project. When deploying the portal application, a separate Java archive is created for the directory. Components stored within *src.api* can be reused by other components and therefore consumed by other components at runtime and dynamically incorporated into a separate structure. Of course, you do not always want this to happen. In such cases, you should choose the second storage location, known as Core. Similar to using API, a separate directory is created for Core in the project structure. This directory is called *src.core,* and, once again, a separate archive is created for this directory during deployment.

You do not require any portal programming knowledge to understand the significance of the Class Name and Package Name fields. Of course, the class name and component name can differ. After you have completed all of the fields, choose Finish to start the creation process.

4.5.4 Application Example of the Connector Framework

After creating the portal project and the associated component, you can start to implement a portal page that will list the details of a purchase order. The implementation comprises numerous classes that originate from different JAR files. These files are available in the ECLIPSE-HOME variable or in the installation directory of your application server. Integrate the following archives:

- *activation.jar*
- *connector.jar*
- *com.sap.portal.ivs.connectorservice_api.jar*
- *GenericConnector.jar*
- *jta.jar*

In the first step, implement a `getConnection` method, as shown in Listing 4.25. The task of this method is to establish a connection with the SAP backend and to return the generated object to the calling program. The Connector Framework handles all communication with the SAP system. This framework is available as a portal service and it is encapsulated by the `IConnectorGatewayService` interface. A reference to portal services is delivered via the central `PortalRuntime` factory class. This is done by calling the `getRuntimeResources` method, which provides a reference to the portal runtime environment, which, in turn, provides the service reference. The associated method is called `getService`. A key is used to store and retrieve portal services. The reference key is made available to the Connector Framework via the `IConnectorService` interface. Save the result of the service request in the `cgService` variable.

Establishing a connection with the SAP backend

Now that a reference to the service exists, you can start to create a backend connection. The framework defines the `IConnection` interface for connections, and the `getConnection` method is used to call the associated objects on the `cgService` instance. The method therefore obtains the alias of the backend system, as defined in the system landscape of the portal, as well as an object of the type `ConnectionProperties`. When establishing a connection, objects of this type specify which user wants to access the backend system. As already mentioned in Section 4.5.2, System Landscape of the Portal, both the alias and the authentication method must be configured correctly on the backend so that the `getConnection` method can successfully establish a connection.

Connection definition

```
private IConnection getConnection(
  IPortalComponentRequest request,
  IPortalComponentResponse response)  throws Exception {
  IConnectorGatewayService cgService =
    (IConnectorGatewayService)
    PortalRuntime.getRuntimeResources().getService(
                        IConnectorService.KEY);
  ConnectionProperties prop =
    new ConnectionProperties(request.getLocale(),
                        request.getUser());
  IConnection client = null;
  client = cgService.getConnection("Demo", prop);
  return client;
}
```

Listing 4.25 Establishing a Connection with the SAP System

4 | Remote Function Call with Java

Calling the function module

Now that the connection has been established, you can call the function module. The Connector Framework follows a very similar approach to JCo. This is not surprising because it works under the API layers of the Connector Framework. Unlike JCo, however, the API layer of the framework is less ABAP-dependent in terms of the method names. This is because the framework implements the JCA specification, which was not defined specifically for ABAP systems, but for any backend communication. For example, you will search in vain for terms such as *import parameter* or *export parameter*. In addition to the absence of almost ABAP-like naming conventions (and as a result of abstraction from a specific backend system), you must follow more lengthy implementation steps when calling a function module.

To communication with the backend, you must first create an instance of the type `IInteraction`. You can use the `createInteractionEx` methods on `IConnection` for this purpose. As already described in Table 4.3, the `IInteraction` instance is used as a communication object for calling a function provided in the backend. You could say that this is a generic proxy object for a backend function.

After the generic object has been created, it must be configured accordingly. This means that the function module must be assigned a name and import parameters before it can be called. The implementation of the `IInteractionSpec` interface is used to specify a function module name as well as other relevant aspects of communication. You obtain an instance of this type from the `getInteractionSpec` method provided by the `IInteraction` object. Save the resulting object in a variable called `ixspec`, and then call the `setPropertyValue` method, which is used to configure communication-relevant information (already discussed earlier in Table 4.3). In the example shown here, we will only set the `Name` parameter, which contains the function module name as a value.

Parameter processing

Because the function module has the `IM_ORDERID` import parameter, it must be filled. The `MappedRecord` class is used for this purpose. This class is derived from the `Record` base type, and it represents a key/value-oriented way in which to save parameters. Record objects cannot be generated using a constructor but rather a factory. This is necessary to enable backend manufacturers to have different interpretations of the record concept. For the SAP Connector Framework, you use the methods in the `RecordFactory` class to obtain instances of the record types supported.

Therefore, in our example, we will call the `createMappedRecord` method and transfer the name for our parameter type to this method. Before we can actually call the function module, we must fill the previously discussed parameter with the value "43."

Lastly, the `execute` method on the `Iinteraction` object is used to initiate execution of the function module. This method obtains not only the information contained in the `IinteractionSpec` object but also the import parameters. The result of the synchronous call is immediately returned as a `MappedRecord` object, which can then be processed using now-familiar methods, thus facilitating access to the names of the return parameters.

This means that the purchase order header `EX_ORDERHEAD` (a structure) and the purchase order items `TA_ORDERSPOS` (a table) must be read for the `Z_IFP_ORDER_GETDETAIL` function module. JCA provides the `IRecord` class for processing structures and the `IrecordSet` class for processing tables. To read the structure, call the `get` methods from the `MappedRecord` class, and transfer the structure name. In type checking, you should use the keyword `instanceof` to check whether the return values really have the correct data types before you convert a corresponding data type (*casting*) for access to the data. After the `cast` has been successful, you can start to read the structure. Suitable `getter` methods are provided for this purpose. Table parameters are also processed in the same way (see Listing 4.26).

Processing structures and tables

To display the purchase order header and the table contents, the portal component implements the `printOrderHeader` and `printOrderDetails` methods. Both the data and metadata from the function module are processed in these methods. The `retrieveMetaData` method is then used to read the metadata from the result.

```
IConnection client = getConnection(request, response);
IInteraction ix = client.createInteractionEx();
IInteractionSpec ixspec = ix.getInteractionSpec();      ixspec.
setPropertyValue(
       "Name",IFunctionNames.Z_IFP_ORDER_GETDETAIL);
RecordFactory rf = ix.getRecordFactory();
MappedRecord importParamter=rf.createMappedRecord("input");
importParamter.put(IFieldNames.IM_ORDERID,"43");
MappedRecord output =
 (MappedRecord) ix.execute(ixspec,importParamter);
```

```
Object result = output.get(IFieldNames.EX_ORDERHEAD);
Orderheader header = null;
if(result instanceof IRecord) {
  IRecord rs = (IRecord) result;
  header = printOrderHeader(rs,response);
}
Object resultOrderDetails =
                    output.get(IFieldNames.TA_ORDERPOS);
List orderdetails = null;
if(resultOrderDetails instanceof IRecordSet) {
  IRecordSet orderDetails = (IRecordSet) resultOrderDetails;
  orderdetails = printOrderDetails(orderDetails);
}
```

Listing 4.26 Calling the Function Module with Subsequent Processing

Deploying components

After you have called the function module and implemented the data display, you can prepare the components for deployment. If you take another look at the implementation steps, you can see that there is a certain dependency between the portal component introduced and the portal service `ConnectorGatewayService`. Consequently, the classes must be known not only at the time of implementation but also at runtime. A classloader reference must be established between the classloader of the component that has been developed and the classloader of the portal service. If this does not happen, the system issues error messages at runtime indicating that the portal service does not exist and no classes could be found. Listing 4.27 shows how to set this dependency in the deployment descriptor `portalapp.xml`. The property is set as an application configuration parameter and is therefore valid for all portal components contained in the portal application.

```
<property name="ServicesReference"
          value="com.sap.portal.ivs.connectorservice"/>
```

Listing 4.27 Setting the "ServicesReference"

Uploading the application

To complete the process, you can upload the application to the portal. To do this, choose PAR-Upload in the portal perspective or use the project's context menu in which you select Export and then PAR File in the next dialog box. You then access the dialog box for uploading portal components. Select the project that you want to upload, and choose Next. On the next screen, you can select the portal server (if it already exists) on which you want to deploy the application. If there is no configuration, choose Configure Server Settings. You can then choose Add to enter the necessary parameters. The configuration result should then look as shown in Figure 4.18.

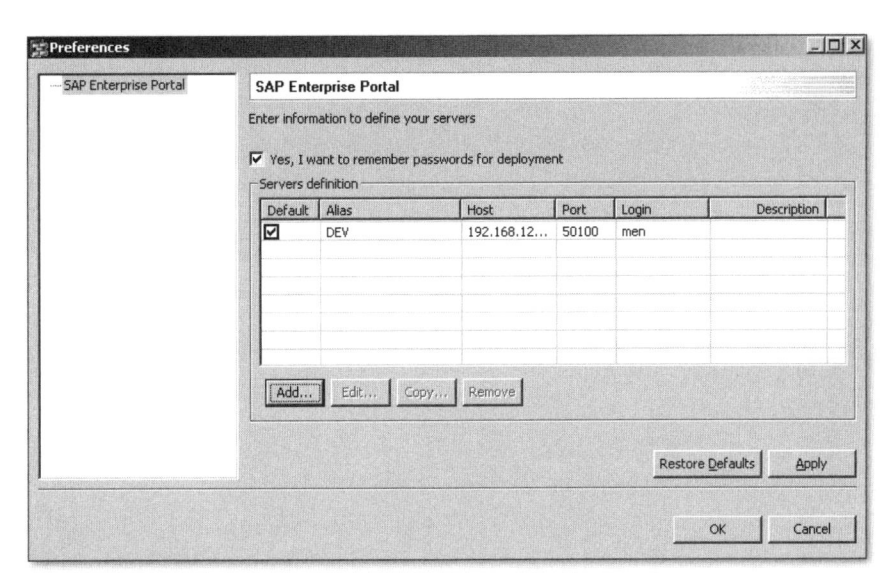

Figure 4.18 Server Configuration

Choose OK, enter your password, and then choose Finish. Make sure that you have chosen the Deploy Par selection field. The system will notify you if the installation process fails.

To test your application, navigate to Package Explorer in your development environment, and double-click the file *portalapp.xml* to open it. Then select the Application tab, and choose Run. The system opens a browser window in which you will see the application that you have developed. In some installations, you must log on to the portal before you can see the end result of your development work.

Testing the application

This chapter presents the tools that are required for developing ALE scenarios in which applications exchange data in the form of IDocs. You learn how to define IDocs, configure the ALE layer, and implement ALE scenarios in ABAP, C, and Java.

5   IDocs and ALE

In the ALE (Application Link Enabling) integration technology, the applications involved exchange data in the form of Intermediate Documents (IDocs). The communication is asynchronous; that is, the sender of a message does not wait for the direct answer of the receiver but continues working after the document has been sent.

We will develop ALE scenarios in the programming languages ABAP, C, and Java. In the first section, we describe IDocs and their development in SAP NetWeaver Application Server ABAP (SAP NetWeaver AS ABAP). Then we outline the ALE subsystem and describe its configuration.

In this scenario, purchase order data of client 001 is sent to client 002 of the same SAP system. In the subsequent sections, we will extend this scenario for external systems. The following steps are required to implement the scenario:

1. **Defining the IDoc type**
   You first define an IDoc type, which determines the structure of the IDoc that is sent.

2. **Developing a report for sending**
   This report retrieves the data from the application tables, sets up the IDoc, and transfers it to the ALE subsystem for sending.

3. **Developing a function module for receiving**
   This function module accepts the received IDoc from the ALE subsystem and writes the data into the application tables.

4. **Customizing the ALE subsystem**
   The ALE subsystem must be set up in such a way that the outbound IDoc is forwarded to the receiving system via the transactional RFC

Four implementation steps

(tRFC), and the inbound IDoc is transferred to the correct function module.

The following sections describe these four steps in detail before we discuss the implementation in ABAP, C, and Java.

5.1 IDocs

In this section, you learn, based on an example, how you can create the necessary definitions, reports, and function modules for the IDoc communication in SAP NetWeaver.

5.1.1 Developing IDocs

Segments IDocs are documents that consist of individual lines referred to as *segments*. The structure of a segment is determined by its segment type. The *segment types* are defined using Transaction WE31. In this transaction, however, SAP does not use the word "segment types" but "segments."

IDoc Segments

For the scenario mentioned, you must define two segments: one for the header data and one for the item data of a purchase order. To define a segment that can accept the header data for a purchase order, you must start Transaction WE31 and enter "Z1ORDHD" as the name of the segment type. The names of the SAP segments start with the abbreviation "E1", and customer-specific segments start with "Z1".

Data elements Select the SEGMENT • CREATE menu path to define the individual field names in the segment definition. For this purpose, you must implement the necessary specifications in the Field Name and Data Element columns (Figure 5.1). The system automatically assigns a name for the segment definition, in this case Z2ORDHD000. The name of the definition starts with the name for the segment and ends with a three-digit version number. Save this segment definition, and assign it to a development package at the same time. After you've completed the definition, you can release it via the EDIT • SET RELEASE menu path.

IDocs | 5.1

```
Development segments: Change segment definition Z2ORDHD
[icons] New Fields

Segment type attributes
Segment type        Z1ORDHD                    ☐ Qualified segment
Short Description   Order header

Segm. definition    Z2ORDHD000                 ☐ Released
Last Changed By     MWE

Pos | Field Name | Data element   | ISO co | Exp
1   | ORDERID    | ZIFPORDERID    | ☐      | 10
2   | TYPE       | ZIFPORDERTYPE  | ☐      | 2
3   | REFID      | ZIFPREFID      | ☐      | 10
4   | BUYER      | ZIFPBUYER      | ☐      | 50
5   | SELLER     | ZIFPSELLER     | ☐      | 50
6   | ORDERDATE  | ZIFPORDERDATE  | ☐      | 8
7   |            |                | ☐      |
```

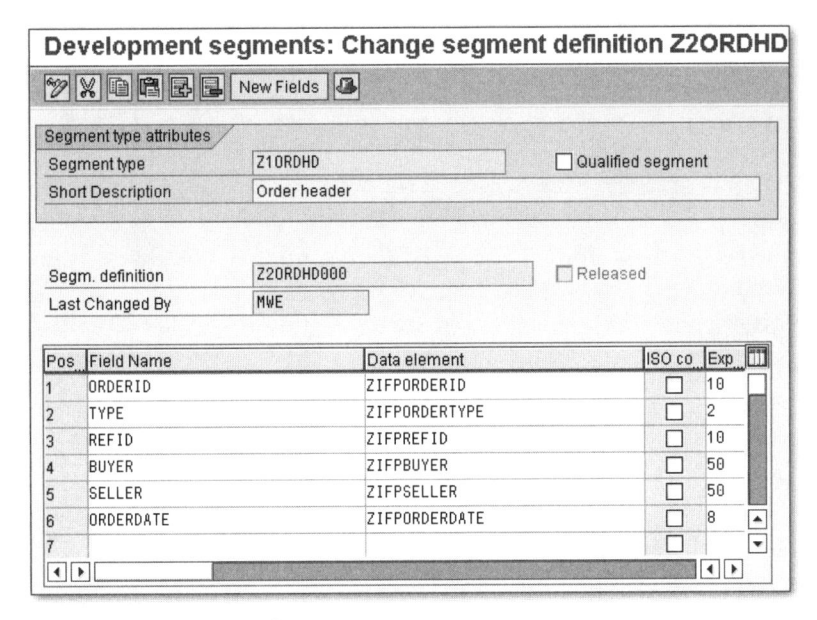

Figure 5.1 Version 000 of the "Z1ORDHD" Segment

Another word about naming conventions that the development environment enforces here: The names of segment types always start with Z1 (for customer-specific segments) or E1 (for SAP-defined segments). The names of segment definitions always start with Z2 or E2.

Versioning of segments

If you want to further develop your IDoc segments in an SAP system with a higher version number later on, you can add another version with an extended segment definition to the segment type. This extended segment definition contains additional fields. Existing fields cannot be removed or changed. Segment type and version of SAP Basis uniquely identify the associated segment definition.

To send data for the item data in IDocs, you must additionally define the Z1ORDPS segment (Figure 5.2).

IDoc Types

After you've defined the segments, you can define the ZORDER01 IDoc type using Transaction WE30. IDocs of this type are used to transport purchase orders.

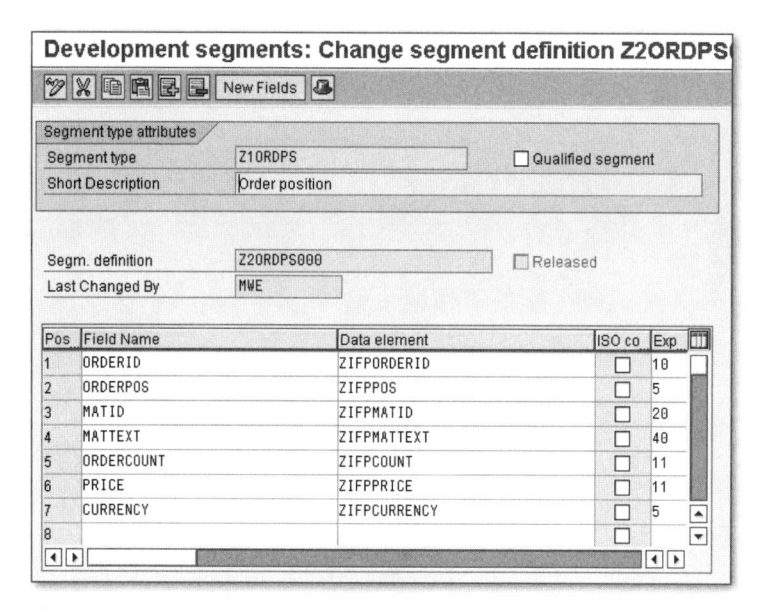

Figure 5.2 Version 000 of the "Z1ORDPS"

In the Object Name field, enter the name for the IDoc type, leave the selection of the option field at Basic Type, and select the path, Development Object • Create (F5). In the subsequent dialog, do not change the Create New selection of the option field, and enter a description for the IDoc type. Then you can create the ZORDER01 basic type. Select Edit • Create Segment (Shift + F6). Specify that it is a mandatory segment, and determine the minimum and the maximum number of occurrences of this segment in the IDoc (Figure 5.3).

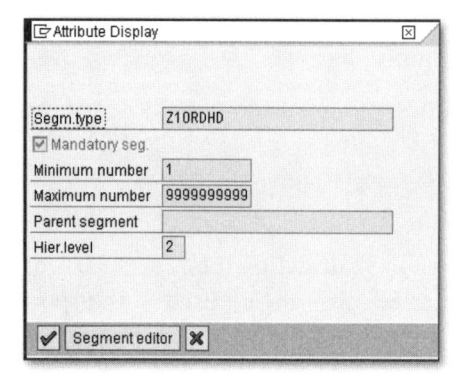

Figure 5.3 Attributes of the "Z1ORDHD" Segment in the "ZORDER01" IDoc

Then click on the newly inserted segment to select it, and add the `Z1ORDPS` segment as the child of the `Z1ORDHD` segment. The `ZORDER01` IDoc type now appears as shown in Figure 5.4.

Hierarchical IDoc structure

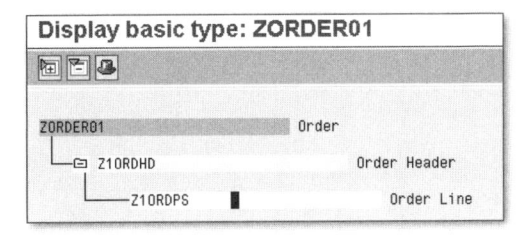

```
Display basic type: ZORDER01

ZORDER01              Order
  └─ Z1ORDHD          Order Header
       └─ Z1ORDPS     Order Line
```

Figure 5.4 "ZORDER01" IDoc Type

After the definition, release the IDoc type in the initial screen of Transaction WE31 by selecting EDIT • SET RELEASE.

Message Type

The next step involves the definition of a message type using Transaction WE81. The message types determine the meaning of a message whose content is transported by an IDoc. Here, different message types can definitely be transported using the same IDoc type. For example, requests for master data to different SAP ERP modules represent different message types. In most cases, however, they are transported via the `ALEREQ01` IDoc type.

For the purposes of the purchase order application, you create the ZORDER message type with Order as the short description.

In the last development step, you must assign an IDoc type to this message type for the SAP Basis release. This is done using Transaction WE82. Assign the `ZORDER01` basic type to the `ZORDER` message type for your current SAP Basis release. Here as well, you can assign a new IDoc type that transports the same message in a subsequent release. Of course, this IDoc type should then be an extension of the previous type.

IDoc type for a message type

5.1.2 Creating IDocs

The application is responsible for creating IDocs and transferring them to the ALE layer. In the simplest case, it provides a report for this purpose in which the user selects the data to be sent. Listing 5.1 shows such a report for our application example.

"ALE_MODEL_
INFO_GET"
function module

Initially, the report checks whether a receiving system exists that is interested in the ZORDER message. For this purpose, it uses the ALE_MODEL_INFO_GET function module and transfers the ZORDER value to the message_type import parameter.

```
REPORT  zifp_send_idoc.
DATA:
  wa_hdr           TYPE zifporder,       " Purchase order header
  wa_pos           TYPE zifporderpos,    " Purchase order item
  rec_control      TYPE edidc,           " Control record
  it_control       TYPE TABLE OF edidc,  " Control records
  it_data          TYPE TABLE OF edidd,  " IDoc lines
  wa_data          TYPE edidd,           " IDoc line
  wa_idoc_hdr      TYPE zlordhd,         " IDoc data header
  wa_idoc_pos      TYPE zlordps,         " IDoc data item
  segnum           TYPE i,               " Segment number
  psgnum           TYPE i.               " Parent segment number
PARAMETERS:
  pa_ord TYPE zifporderid.
START-OF-SELECTION.
* Check whether receiver exists at all
  CALL FUNCTION 'ALE_MODEL_INFO_GET'
    EXPORTING
      message_type            = 'ZORDER'
    EXCEPTIONS
      no_model_info_found     = 1
      own_system_not_defined  = 2
      OTHERS                  = 3.
  IF sy-subrc <> 0.
    MESSAGE ID sy-msgid TYPE sy-msgty NUMBER sy-msgno
            WITH sy-msgv1 sy-msgv2 sy-msgv3 sy-msgv4.
  ENDIF.
*  Create control record
  rec_control-mestyp = 'ZORDER'.
  rec_control-idoctp = 'ZORDER01'.
* Set up IDoc
  segnum = 1.
  SELECT SINGLE * FROM zifporder INTO wa_hdr
    WHERE orderid = pa_ord AND type = 'PO'.
  MOVE-CORRESPONDING wa_hdr TO wa_idoc_hdr.
  CLEAR wa_data.
  wa_data-segnum = segnum.
```

```
   wa_data-psgnum = 0.
   wa_data-segnam = 'Z1ORDHD'.
   wa_data-mandt  = sy-mandt.
   wa_data-sdata  = wa_idoc_hdr.
   APPEND wa_data TO it_data.
   ADD 1 TO segnum.
   psgnum = wa_data-segnum.
   SELECT * FROM zifporderpos INTO wa_pos
     WHERE orderid = wa_hdr-orderid.
     MOVE-CORRESPONDING wa_pos TO wa_idoc_pos.
     wa_data-segnum = segnum.
     wa_data-psgnum = psgnum.
     wa_data-segnam = 'Z1ORDPS'.
     wa_data-mandt  = sy-mandt.
     wa_data-sdata  = wa_idoc_pos.
     APPEND wa_data TO it_data.
     ADD 1 TO segnum.
   ENDSELECT.
*  Send IDoc
   CALL FUNCTION 'MASTER_IDOC_DISTRIBUTE'
     EXPORTING
       master_idoc_control              = rec_control
     TABLES
       communication_idoc_control       = it_control
       master_idoc_data                 = it_data
     EXCEPTIONS
       error_in_idoc_control            = 1
       error_writing_idoc_status        = 2
       error_in_idoc_data               = 3
       sending_logical_system_unknown   = 4
       OTHERS                           = 5.
   IF sy-subrc <> 0.
     MESSAGE ID sy-msgid TYPE sy-msgty NUMBER sy-msgno
             WITH sy-msgv1 sy-msgv2 sy-msgv3 sy-msgv4.
   ENDIF.
   COMMIT WORK.
   WRITE:/ 'IDoc verschickt.'.
```

Listing 5.1 "ZIFP_SEND_IDOC" Program

If successful, the report initially populates the fields, mestyp and idoctp, of the rec_control control record with the values, ZORDER and ZORDER01, respectively. Base on this control record, the ALE subsystem determines the receiver from the distribution model, which is created in ALE Customizing. Table 5.1 lists some fields of the control record. Here, the application only needs to populate a few fields; the rest is done by the ALE subsystem.

Field	Content
MANDT	Client
DOCNUM	IDoc number
DOCREL	IDoc SAP release
STATUS	IDoc status
DOCTYP	IDoc type
DIRECT	Direction of transfer (1 = outbound, 2 = inbound)
RCVPOR	Receiver port
RCVPRT	Partner type of receiver
RCVPRN	Partner number of receiver
SNDPOR	Sender port
SNDPRT	Partner type of sender
SNDPRN	Partner number of sender

Table 5.1 Components of the "EDIDC" IDoc Control Record

Control segment   Then, the report creates the IDoc. For each selected record of the ZIF-PORDERHEADER table, it writes one line to the it_data internal table. This line is of the EDIDD type and contains information on the segment as well as the actual application data (Table 5.2). Here, the SEGNAM field is set to Z1ORDHD, and the data of the purchase order header is copied to the SDATA field.

Field	Content
MANDT	Client
DOCNUM	IDoc number
SEGNUM	Segment number within the document
SEGNAM	Segment name
PSGNUM	Parent segment number
HLEVEL	Hierarchy level
SDATA	Application data

Table 5.2 Components of the "EDIDD" IDoc Data Record

For each purchase order, the report reads all items of this purchase order and writes one line to the IDoc for each item. Here, the SEGNAM field is set to Z1ORDPS, and the item data is copied to the SDATA field. Finally, the report transfers the created IDoc to the ALE subsystem by calling the MASTER_IDOC_DISTRIBUTE function module.

Data segments

5.1.3 Inbound Processing of IDocs

A function module accepts the IDoc from the ALE subsystem on the receiver side. The name of the function module should be Z_IDOC_INPUT_ZORDER. To create it, simply copy the ALE_INPUT_ALEAUD function module directly because it has the right interface (Listing 5.2).

```
FUNCTION z_idoc_input_zorder.
*"----------------------------------------------------------
*"*"Local interface:
*"  IMPORTING
*"     VALUE(INPUT_METHOD) LIKE  BDWFAP_PAR-INPUTMETHD
*"     VALUE(MASS_PROCESSING) LIKE  BDWFAP_PAR-MASS_PROC
*"  EXPORTING
*"     VALUE(WORKFLOW_RESULT) LIKE  BDWF_PARAM-RESULT
*"     VALUE(APPLICATION_VARIABLE) LIKE  BDWF_PARAM-APPL_VAR
*"     VALUE(IN_UPDATE_TASK) LIKE  BDWFAP_PAR-UPDATETASK
*"     VALUE(CALL_TRANSACTION_DONE) LIKE  BDWFAP_PAR-CALLTRANS
*"  TABLES
*"      IDOC_CONTRL STRUCTURE  EDIDC
*"      IDOC_DATA STRUCTURE  EDIDD
*"      IDOC_STATUS STRUCTURE  BDIDOCSTAT
*"      RETURN_VARIABLES STRUCTURE  BDWFRETVAR
*"      SERIALIZATION_INFO STRUCTURE  BDI_SER
*"  EXCEPTIONS
*"      WRONG_FUNCTION_CALLED
*"----------------------------------------------------------
   INCLUDE mbdconwf.             " Constants of ALE subsystem
   DATA:
     wa_data     TYPE edidd,     " IDoc data line
     wa_control  TYPE edidc,     " Control data record
     wa_idoc_hdr TYPE z1ordhd,   " Header data from IDoc
     wa_idoc_pos TYPE z1ordps,   " Item data from IDoc
     wa_hdr      TYPE zifporder, " Header data for DB
     wa_hdr_old  TYPE zifporder, " Old header data
     wa_pos      TYPE zifporderpos. " Item data for DB
```

```abap
* Read control data record
  READ TABLE idoc_contrl INTO wa_control INDEX 1.
  LOOP AT idoc_data INTO wa_data WHERE
    docnum = wa_control-docnum.
    IF wa_data-segnam ='Z1ORDHD'.
* Insert or modify purchase order data record
      wa_idoc_hdr = wa_data-sdata.
      MOVE-CORRESPONDING wa_idoc_hdr TO wa_hdr.
      wa_hdr-refid = wa_hdr-orderid.
      wa_hdr-type  = 'SO'.
* New creation or update?
      SELECT SINGLE * FROM zifporder INTO wa_hdr_old
        WHERE refid = wa_hdr-orderid.
      IF sy-subrc EQ 0.
        wa_hdr-orderid = wa_hdr_old-orderid.
      ELSE.
        CALL FUNCTION 'NUMBER_GET_NEXT'
          EXPORTING
            nr_range_nr = '01'
            object      = 'ZIFPORDER'
          IMPORTING
            number      = wa_hdr-orderid
          EXCEPTIONS
            OTHERS      = 1.
      ENDIF.
      MODIFY zifporder FROM wa_hdr.
      IF sy-subrc NE 0.
        EXIT.
      ENDIF.
    ELSEIF wa_data-segnam = 'Z1ORDPS'.
* Insert or update item data record
      wa_idoc_pos = wa_data-sdata.
      MOVE-CORRESPONDING wa_idoc_pos TO wa_pos.
      wa_idoc_pos = wa_data-sdata.
      MODIFY zifporderpos FROM wa_pos.
      IF sy-subrc NE 0.
        EXIT.
      ENDIF.
    ENDIF.
  ENDLOOP.
* Write confirmation
  IF sy-subrc NE 0.
    idoc_status-status = c_idoc_status_error.
```

```
   idoc_status-msgty  = sy-msgty.
   idoc_status-msgid  = sy-msgid.
   idoc_status-msgno  = sy-msgno.
   idoc_status-msgv1  = sy-msgv1.
   idoc_status-msgv2  = sy-msgv2.
   idoc_status-msgv3  = sy-msgv3.
   idoc_status-msgv4  = sy-msgv4.
   workflow_result    = c_wf_result_error.
   return_variables-wf_param  = c_wf_par_error_idocs.
 ELSE.
   idoc_status-status = c_idoc_status_ok.
   idoc_status-msgty  = 'S'.
   idoc_status-msgid  = 'ZIFP'.
   idoc_status-msgno  = 150.
   workflow_result    = c_wf_result_ok.
   return_variables-wf_param  = c_wf_par_processed_idocs.
 ENDIF.
 idoc_status-docnum = wa_control-docnum.
 idoc_status-repid  = sy-repid.
 APPEND idoc_status.
 return_variables-doc_number  = wa_control-docnum.
 APPEND return_variables.
ENDFUNCTION.
```

Listing 5.2 "Z_IDOC_INPUT_ORDER" Function Module

The interface of the function module has 11 parameters with the following meaning:

Interface

- **IDOC_CONTRL**
  This table contains a control data record for each transferred IDoc. From this table, the function module requires the Docnum and Idoctp columns that contain the numbers and the IDoc types of the transferred IDocs.

- **IDOC_DATA**
  This table contains the segments of the IDocs that have been transferred to the function module. In this table, the Docnum, Segnam, and Sdata columns are relevant that contain the IDoc number, the segment name, and the application data.

Parameters of the interface

- INPUT_METHOD

  If the function module is supposed to be handled in the background, this parameter has its type-specific initial value. If the function module was selected as dialog-enabled, that is, if it displays input screens, it can have the values 'A' or 'E'. In the former case, it will display all input screens, in the latter case, it will only show the screens if an error occurs.

- MASS_PROCESSING

  This parameter is no longer used.

- IN_UPDATE_TASK

  The function module evaluates this export parameter with 'X' if it implements the update via update modules with the IN UPDATE TASK addition.

- CALL_TRANSACTION_DONE

  The function module populates this export parameter with 'X' if it uses CALL TRANSACTION to write the IDoc status.

- WORKFLOW_RESULT

  The function module uses this export parameter to control whether events are supposed to be triggered.

- APPLICATION_VARIABLE

  This is an optional parameter that can be transferred to the workflow.

- IDOC_STATUS

  This table contains an entry for each IDoc that was processed by the function module. The Status field can have the value 53 in case of success and the value 51 in case of error.

- RETURN_VARIABLES

  This table contains the IDoc numbers and the associated numbers of the processed application objects. This information is used to link the IDoc with the corresponding application object.

- SERIALIZATION_INFO

  This parameter is no longer used.

The Z_IDOC_INPUT_ZORDER function module assumes that it only receives an IDoc. It determines the number of this IDoc from the IDOC_CONTRL table using `READ TABLE`. Then, it makes a loop through all segments of the IDoc in the `IDOC_DATA` table. Depending on whether it is a `Z1ORDHD` or `Z1ORDPS` segment, the function modules make changes to the data of the `ZIFPORDER` or `ZIFPORDERPOS` database table. In case of error, the function module cancels the processing of the IDoc. Both in case of error and success, it finally populates the parameters, `IDOC_STATUS`, `RETURN_VARI-ABLES`, and `WORKFLOW_RESULT`.

In addition to the development, you must register the function module as an inbound function module for ALE processing using Transaction BD51. Because it can only process an IDoc, you must set the input type to "1."

Registration

You use Transaction WE57 to specify that the function module is assigned to the `ZORDER` message type and the `ZORDER01` IDoc basic type for the inbound processing (Figure 5.5).

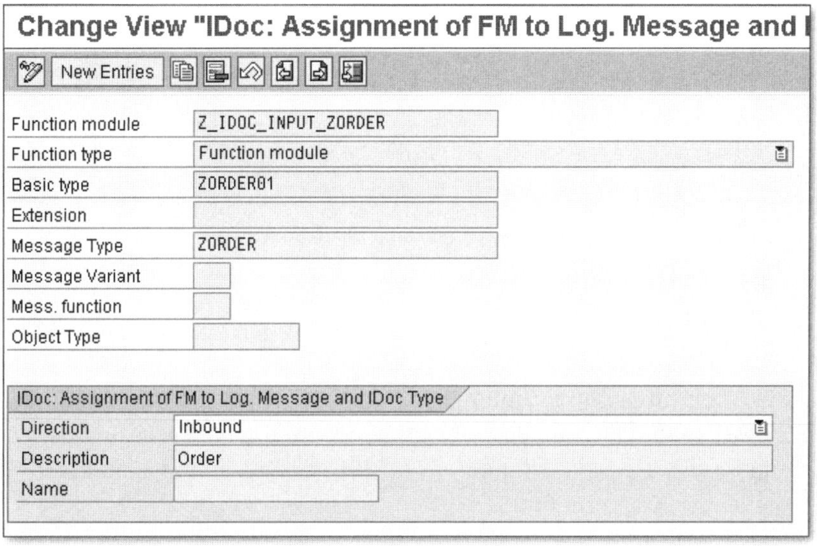

Figure 5.5 Transaction WE57

To ensure that the function module can actually be used for the inbound processing, in the receiving system, you must add a `ZORDER` process code for the inbound using Transaction WE42. As shown in Figure 5.6, the process code defines how the inbound IDoc needs to be processed.

Process codes

Later on in ALE Customizing, the process code is used to specify the inbound parameters for the ZORDER message type (see Section 5.2.1, ALE Configuration).

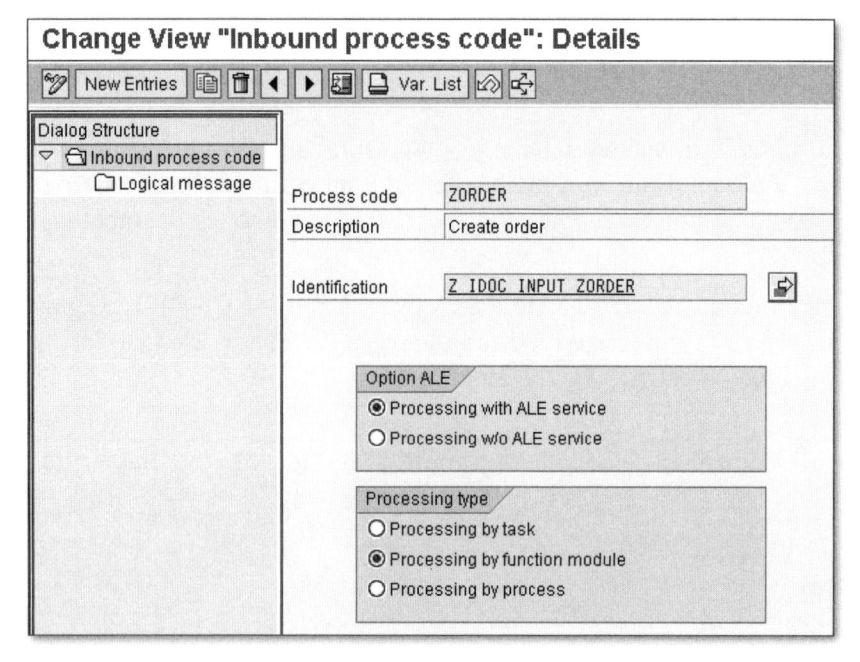

Figure 5.6 Transaction WE42 for Maintaining the Process Code

5.2 ALE

ALE (Application Link Enabling) is a basic service within SAP NetWeaver AS ABAP with which applications can send and receive IDocs. In this section, we discuss the configuration of this subsystem and send an IDoc from client 001 to client 002.

5.2.1 ALE Configuration

Transaction SALE To send and receive IDocs, the ALE subsystem must be configured accordingly. For this purpose, you can use Transaction SALE that lists the necessary steps in the correct sequence, documents them, and provides links to the required transactions. Figure 5.7 shows a section taken from the list displayed by Transaction SALE.

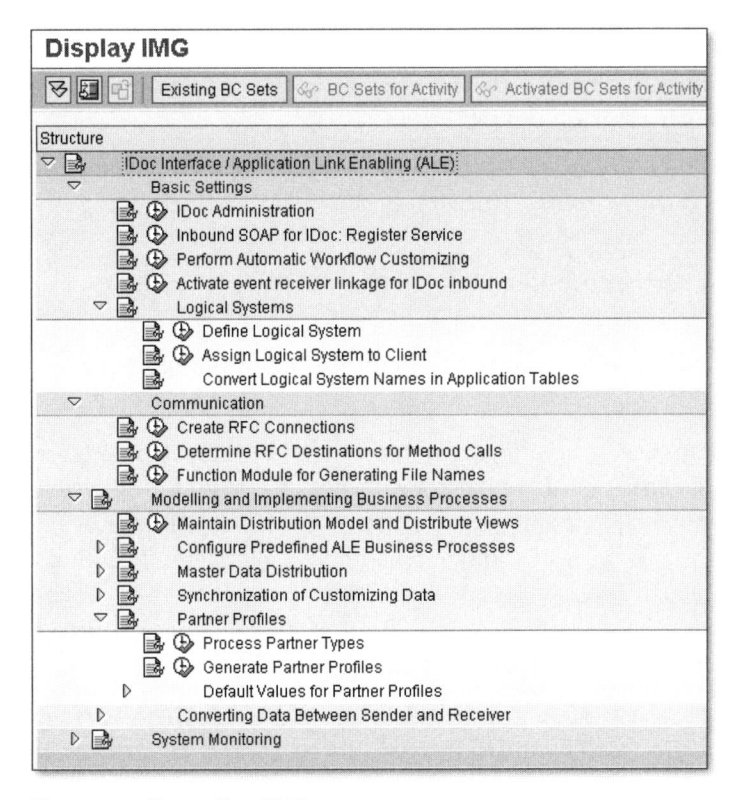

Figure 5.7 Transaction SALE

The following steps are required:

1. **Define logical systems.**

    Each system participating in ALE is identified by a logical name. These names are entered in the TBDLS database table.

2. **Assign logical systems to clients.**

    A logical system is assigned to every client in an SAP system by maintaining the master data of the client.

3. **Define target systems for RFC calls.**

    In the sending system, you must use Transaction SM59 to create tRFC destinations for the target system. If the tRFC destination has the

Configuration steps

same name as the target system, some definitions can be generated automatically in the last step.

4. **Maintain distribution model.**

   Here it is determined which messages the sending system sends to which receiving systems. This step is performed in the sending system.

5. **Maintain partner profiles.**

   Finally, it is determined how outbound IDocs are sent to the receiving systems and how inbound IDocs are processed in the receiving system.

Define logical systems

To enter the names of the logical systems in the TBDLS database table, click on the Define Logical System node in Transaction SALE. The system takes you to the table maintenance of the TBDLS table. For each of the clients involved in the scenario, you enter a logical system, including a name. Typically, the logical system of the client <xxx> in the SAP system is defined with the system ID <SID> <SID>CLNT<xxx>. For our scenario, we require the two logical systems, AOUCLNT001 and AOUCLNT002.

Logical system of a client

To assign the logical system to a client, click on the Assign Logical System to Client node in Transaction SALE. Select the client, and navigate to the detail screen to open the master data maintenance. Here you enter the logical system for the selected client as shown in Figure 5.8. You must implement this assignment of a logical system to a client both for the sending and for the receiving client.

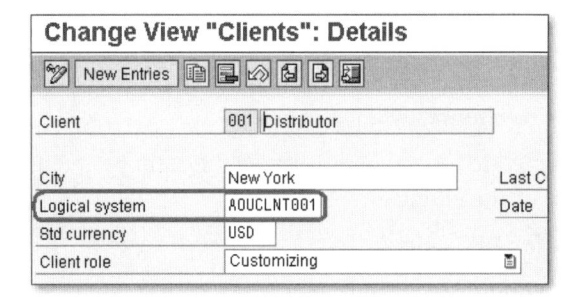

Figure 5.8 Logical System of an SAP Client

In the third step, you maintain a tRFC destination for the receiving system. For this purpose, you select the Create RFC Connections node in Transaction SALE. The system takes you to Transaction SM59 in which you can create a new RFC destination for the target system (Figure 5.9). The RFC destination should have the same name as the logical system of the receiver so that the partner profiles can be generated automatically.

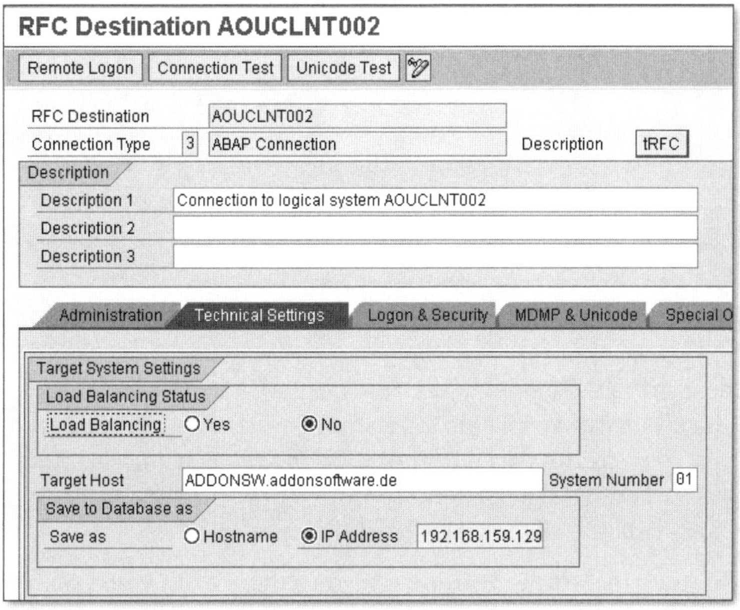

RFC destination for receiver

Figure 5.9 RFC Destination for a Logical System

Make sure that you have an account in the Logon & Security tab with which you can log on to the target system. Moreover, you should maintain the tRFC options in the EDIT • TRFC OPTIONS menu item. If there is a communication error during the transfer of the IDoc to the receiving system, ALE automatically schedules a background job that resends the IDoc. In the tRFC options, you can specify how often the system tries to establish a connection and how much time is supposed to pass between two attempts. But you can also disable the scheduling of this background job completely.

5 | IDocs and ALE

Maintain the distribution model   For this step, you must be logged on to the client for the sending logical system. In Transaction SALE, select the Maintain Distribution Model and Distribute Views node. Create a new model view with the short text "Orders" and the technical name "ZORDER." Insert a message type in this model view. Specify that the AOUCLNT001 sender sends a ZORDER message type to the AOUCLNT002 receiver. Figure 5.10 shows the finalized distribution model.

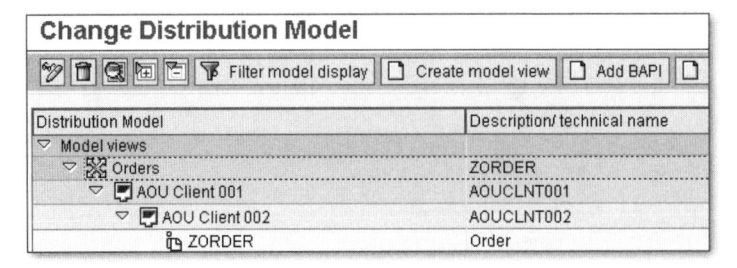

Distribution Model	Description/ technical name
▽ Model views	
▽ 🗒 Orders	ZORDER
▽ 📁 AOU Client 001	AOUCLNT001
▽ 📁 AOU Client 002	AOUCLNT002
📄 ZORDER	Order

Figure 5.10   Distribution Model

Generate partner profiles   From the distribution model, you can select the ENVIRONMENT • GENERATE PARTNER PROFILES menu path to generate partner profiles. In this process, the system creates partner profiles for the sending and the receiving system, a port with the previously created tRFC destination, and the outbound parameters of the ZORDER message type.

Check partner profiles   You can check the creation process by selecting the ENVIRONMENT • CHANGE PARTNER PROFILE menu item from the distribution model. This takes you to Transaction WE20 (Figure 5.11). You can view that both the sending and the receiving system have been entered under the Logical System (LS) partner type. Additionally, outbound parameters for the ZORDER message type were created for the receiving system.

Maintain outbound parameters   Figure 5.12 shows the outbound parameters for the ZORDER message type. Here, the generated port is entered as the receiver port, which in turn references to the previously created tRFC destination.

In the Outbound Options tab, the Transfer IDoc Immediately flag was set as the output mode. Alternatively, you could collect IDocs before transfer and transfer them as a package. In the Package Size input field, you can specify the number of IDocs to be collected. Finally, the IDoc type is defined in the Basic Type field.

To maintain the inbound parameters, you must log on to the receiving system. As already mentioned, you must first add the "ZORDER" process code using Transaction WE42. As already described, the process code defines how the system must process the inbound IDoc (see Figure 5.6).

Maintain inbound parameters

Then call Transaction WE20 to manually maintain the inbound parameters. Initially, create an entry for the logical system of the sender under the Partner Type LS node.

Then add an entry for the ZORDER message type in the inbound parameters. Double-click this entry to navigate to the maintenance of the inbound parameters. Enter "ZORDER" as the process code, that is, the process code that you previously created in the transaction.

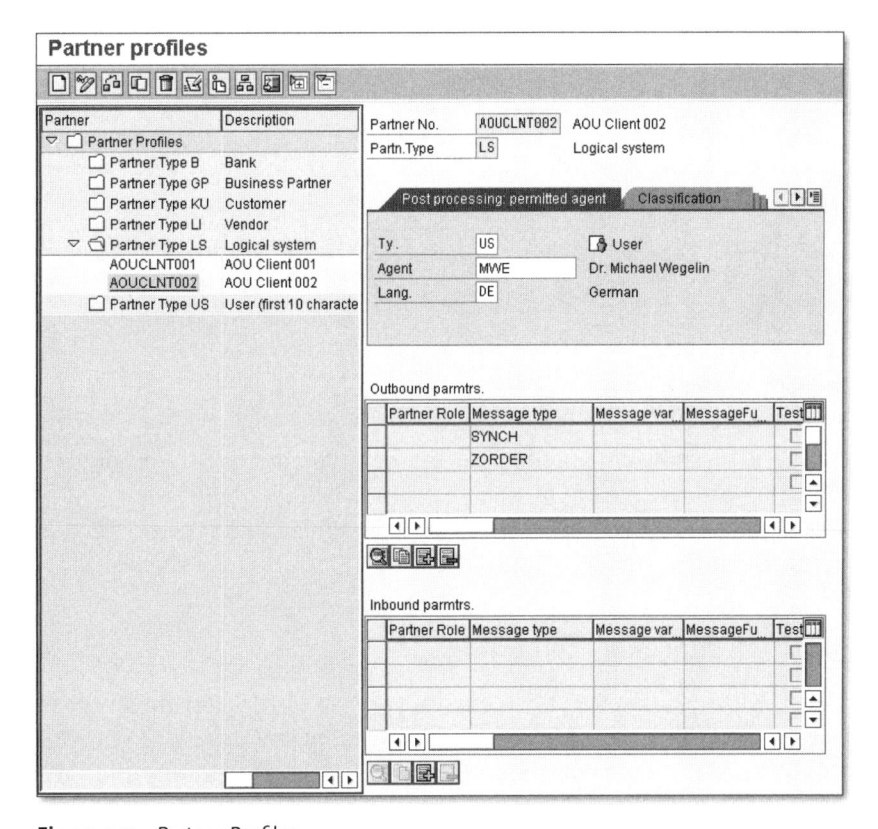

Figure 5.11 Partner Profiles

5 | IDocs and ALE

Partner profiles: Outbound parameters

Partner No.	AOUCLNT002	AOU Client 002
Partn.Type	LS	Logical system
Partner Role		

Message Type	ZORDER		Order
Message code			
Message function		☐ Test	

Outbound Options | Post Processing: Permitted Agent | Telephony | EDI Standard

Receiver port: A000000001 — Transactional RFC — Connection to logical system AO
Pack. Size: 1
☐ Queue Processing

Output Mode
◉ Transfer IDoc Immed.   Output Mode   2
○ Collect IDocs

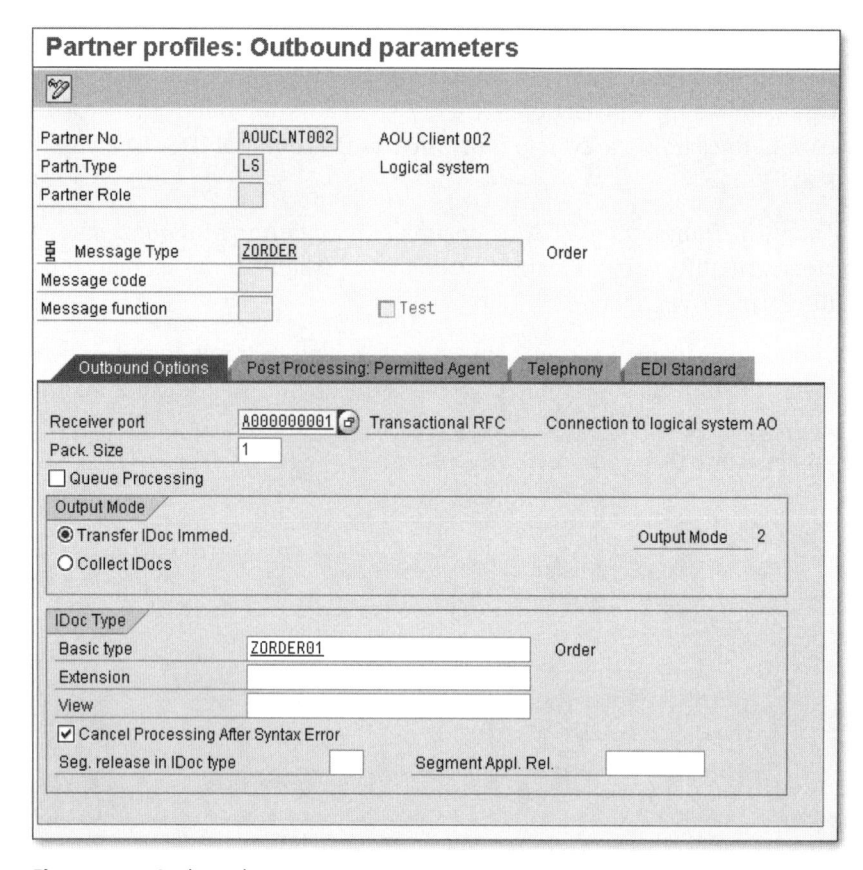

IDoc Type
Basic type: ZORDER01   Order
Extension:
View:
☑ Cancel Processing After Syntax Error
Seg. release in IDoc type: Segment Appl. Rel.:

Figure 5.12 Outbound Parameters

Figure 5.13 shows the configured inbound parameters. If you double-click the process code, you can see that it is linked with the `Z_IDOC_INPUT_ZORDER` function code that serves for the individual processing of inbound IDocs.

5.2.2 Testing and Monitoring

Test the scenario

After you've completed this scenario, you can test it. For this purpose, log on to the client to which the sending system is assigned. Execute the `ZEAI_SEND_IDOC` report to send information about the authors and their books to the receiving system.

Figure 5.13 Inbound Parameters

If the report notifies an error, you can use the status monitor for ALE messages (Transaction BD87) to display a list of the IDocs (Figure 5.14). This list is sorted by the status of the IDocs. By double-clicking an entry, the transaction displays the list of the corresponding IDocs. By double-clicking an IDoc, you can view the IDoc details (Figure 5.15).

You can use Transaction BD87 to reprocess IDocs after an error has been removed. If you log on to the client of the receiving system, you should find the transferred data if the processing was error-free. Here again, you can use Transaction BD87 to display a list of the received IDocs, find errors, and reprocess IDocs after error removal.

Post-processing in case of errors

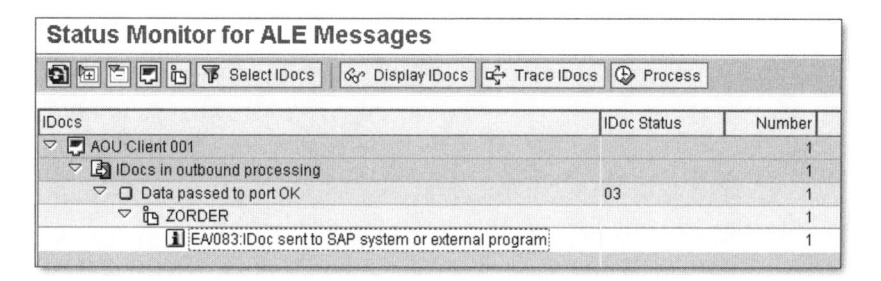

Figure 5.14 Status Monitor for ALE Messages (Transaction BD87)

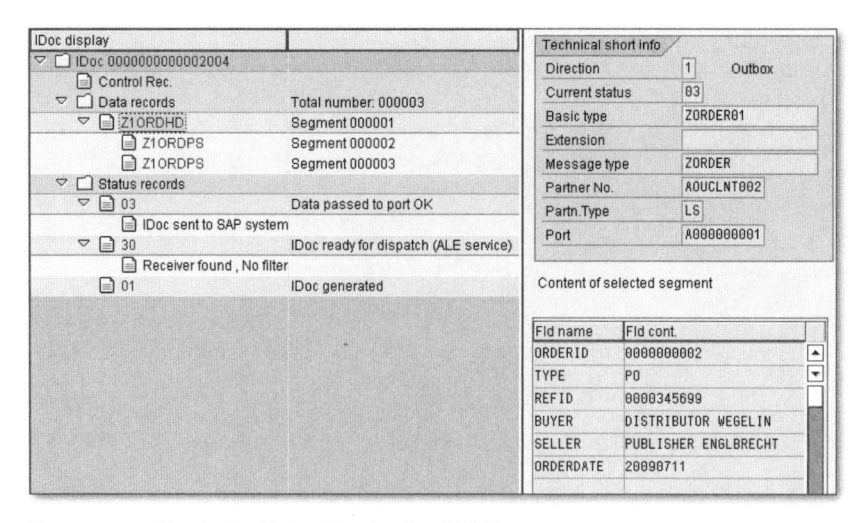

Figure 5.15 IDoc in the Status Monitor for ALE Messages

5.2.3 ALE Interface for BAPIs

To enable you to use the ALE infrastructure when calling BAPIs in another system, Transaction BDBG provides the option to generate and maintain an ALE interface for a BAPI.

In the initial screen of Transaction BDBG, you specify the object type and the method for which you want to generate an ALE interface.

Create interface objects

The transaction generates the following objects, which are also shown in Figure 5.16:

- **Message type**
  You can use this message type in ALE scenarios to enable the call of the corresponding BAPI in the target system.

- **IDoc type**
  IDocs of this type can accept the export and table parameters of the BAPI and transport them to the target system. The corresponding segment types are automatically generated for the IDoc type. You only need to release them after they've been generated. The IDoc type is also linked with the generated message type.

- **Function module for the ALE outbound processing**
  This function module is called by the sending application. Its interface corresponds to the interface of the BAPI; that is, the sending

application calls this function module almost like the BAPI. Only ALE-specific parameters on the object type and the receivers are added. After a successful call, the function module returns a table, including the numbers of generated IDocs.

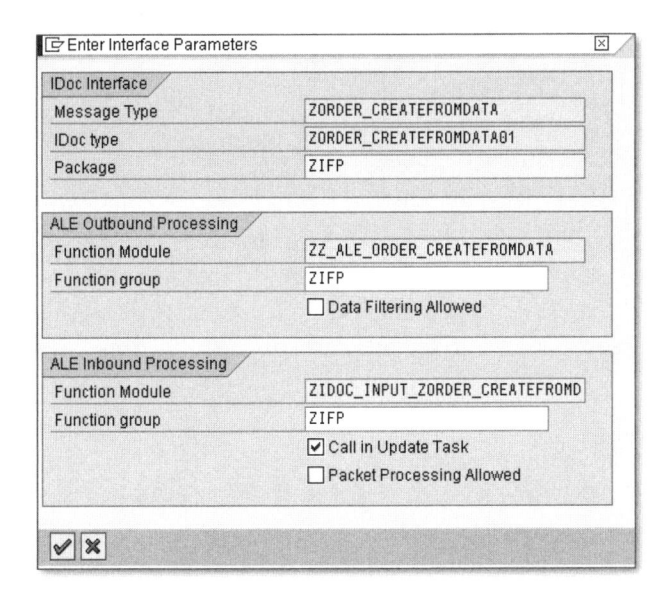

Figure 5.16 Generating an ALE Interface for the "CreateFromData" BAPI

- **Function module for the ALE inbound processing**
  This function module is used by the receiving system to process the inbound IDoc. The function module extracts the data from the IDoc and uses this data to call the BAPI in the receiving system.

With this ALE interface for BAPIs, you can use the functions that ALE provides for distributed processes. However, you don't obtain the return parameters of the called BAPIs because the communication is asynchronous.

To use the created ALE interface, you must maintain an ALE distribution model — as previously. In this ALE distribution model, you don't add a message type but a BAPI (Figure 5.17). After you've saved the distribution model, you can have the system generate the partner profiles as usual. A new outbound parameter to the created message type is generated for the target system.

Distribution model with BAPI

5 | IDocs and ALE

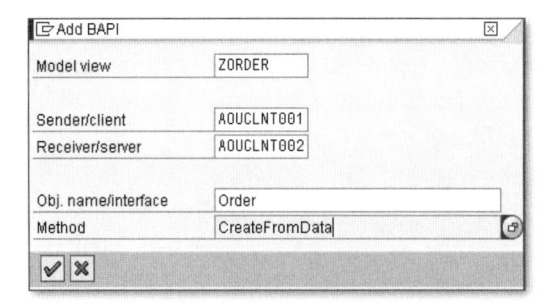

Figure 5.17 ALE Distribution Model for a BAPI

Inbound parameters

In the receiving system, you must re-add inbound parameters to the generated message type for the sending system. In the inbound parameters, you link the message type with the BAPI process code as shown in Figure 5.18. This process code references to the function module BAPI_IDOC_INPUT1.

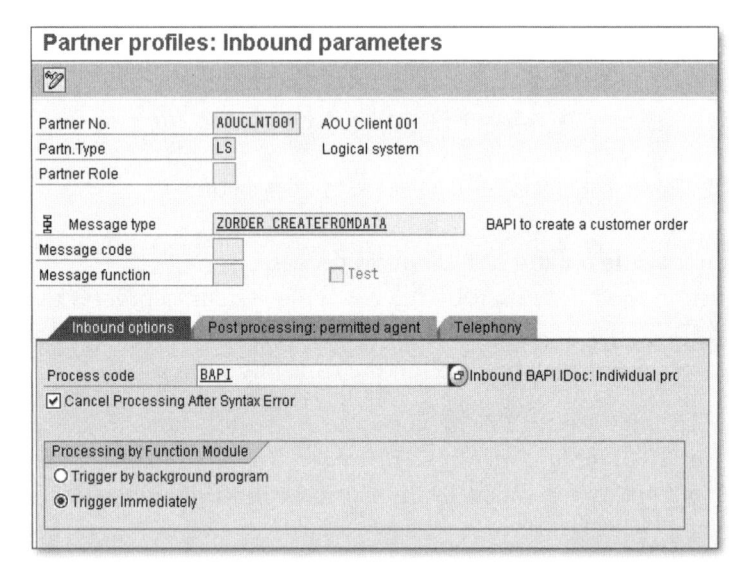

Figure 5.18 Inbound Parameters for a BAPI

So when the IDoc is received, it is transferred from the ALE subsystem to this function module. It refers to the TBDE table to determine the name of the generated function module. The message type is used as the selection criterion. When the ALE interface is generated, Transaction BDBG has added a corresponding line in the TBDBE table.

The IDoc is now transferred to the determined function module, and it calls the BAPI using the transferred data. This has already been described.

Receiver determination

Listing 5.3 shows a report that uses the generated function module to create purchase orders in the target system. To determine the target systems, the report initially calls the `ALE_BAPI_GET_MODEL_DATA` function module. The returned `bapi_model_data` table parameter lists the receiving systems in the `rcvsystem` column; these systems are interested in this data coming from the sending system due to the distribution models. Using this information, the report creates the `it_receivers` internal table, which it then transfers in the subsequent call of the generated outbound function module.

Determining target systems

```
REPORT   zifp_send_bapi_idoc.
DATA:
  it_model_data TYPE STANDARD TABLE OF bdi_bmodel,
  wa_model_data TYPE bdi_bmodel,
  it_log_system TYPE STANDARD TABLE OF bdi_logsys,
  it_receivers  TYPE STANDARD TABLE OF bdi_logsys,
  wa_receivers  TYPE bdi_logsys,
  orderheader   TYPE zifporder,
  it_orderpos   TYPE STANDARD TABLE OF zifporderpos,
  msg_text(80)  TYPE c.
PARAMETERS:
  pa_id TYPE zifporder-orderid.
AT SELECTION-SCREEN.
  SELECT SINGLE * FROM zifporder
  INTO orderheader
  WHERE
    orderid  = pa_id AND
    type     = 'PO'.
  IF sy-subrc <> 0.
    MESSAGE e001(zifp).
  ELSE.
    orderheader-refid = pa_id.
    orderheader-type = 'SO'.
ENDIF.
START-OF-SELECTION.
  SELECT * FROM zifporderpos INTO TABLE it_orderpos
  WHERE
    orderid = pa_id.
  CALL FUNCTION 'ALE_BAPI_GET_MODEL_DATA'
    EXPORTING
```

```
                object                        = 'Z_BUS4500'
                method                        = 'CREATEFROMDATA'
            TABLES
                log_system                    = it_log_system
                bapi_model_data               = it_model_data
            EXCEPTIONS
                own_logical_system_not_defined = 1
                OTHERS                        = 2.
        IF sy-subrc <> 0.
            MESSAGE ID sy-msgid TYPE sy-msgty NUMBER sy-msgno
                    WITH sy-msgv1 sy-msgv2 sy-msgv3 sy-msgv4.
        ENDIF.
        LOOP AT it_model_data INTO wa_model_data.
            APPEND wa_model_data-rcvsystem TO it_receivers.
        ENDLOOP.
        CALL FUNCTION 'ZZ_ALE_ORDER_CREATEFROMDATA'
            EXPORTING
                imorderheader      = orderheader
            TABLES
                taorderpos         = it_orderpos
                receivers          = it_receivers
            EXCEPTIONS
                error_creating_idocs = 1
                OTHERS               = 2.
        IF sy-subrc <> 0.
            MESSAGE ID sy-msgid TYPE sy-msgty NUMBER sy-msgno
                    WITH sy-msgv1 sy-msgv2 sy-msgv3 sy-msgv4.
        ENDIF.
        COMMIT WORK.
```

Listing 5.3 Report for Testing the ALE Interface for a BAPI

5.3 IDoc Programming with the C RFC Library

To implement ALE scenarios using C programs, you must write a tRFC server and a tRFC client. The tRFC server must provide the IDOC_INBOUND_ASYNCHRONOUS function module. This function module receives an IDoc as an internal table. This IDoc can be written into a file or a database by the implementing C function. The tRFC client must generate an IDoc as an internal table from a file or the data in the database and send it to the IDOC_INBOUND_ASYNCHRONOUS function module via tRFC.

5.3.1 IDoc Receiver

The IDoc receiver is a tRFC server that implements the `IDOC_INBOUND_ASYNCHRONOUS` function module as a C function. Listing 5.4 shows this function. It defines type handles for the two structure types, `EDI_DC40` and `EDI_DD40`. As we already discussed in Chapter 3, Section 3.2.3, Structured Parameters, with regard to the RFC programming using the C RFC library, a type handle uniquely identifies a data type through its unsigned number.

Defining type handles

```
/* IDOC_INBOUND_ASYNCHRONOUS                                  */
RFC_RC DLL_CALL_BACK_FUNCTION idoc_inbound_asynchronous(
  RFC_HANDLE rfc_handle)
{
  RFC_RC             rfc_rc = 0;
  RFC_TYPEHANDLE     typeHandleEdiDc40;
  RFC_TYPEHANDLE     typeHandleEdiDd40;
  RFC_PARAMETER      parameters[1];
  RFC_TABLE          tables[3];
  /* Install structures                                       */
  rfc_rc = RfcInstallUnicodeStructure(
      cU("EDI_DC40"), Description_U_EDI_DC40,
         ENTRIES_OF_U_EDI_DC40,0,NULL, &typeHandleEdiDc40);
  if (rfc_rc != RFC_OK)
    rfc_error(cU("RfcInstallUnicodeStructure"));
  rfc_rc = RfcInstallUnicodeStructure(
      cU("EDI_DD40"), Description_U_EDI_DD40,
         ENTRIES_OF_U_EDI_DD40,0 NULL, &typeHandleEdiDd40);
  if (rfc_rc != RFC_OK)
    rfc_error(cU("RfcInstallUnicodeStructure"));
  /* Initialize parameter                                     */
  parameters[0].name = NULL;
  tables[0].name     = cU("IDOC_CONTROL_REC_40");
  tables[0].nlen     = 19;
  tables[0].type     = typeHandleEdiDc40;
  tables[0].leng     = EDI_DC40_LN;
  tables[0].ithandle = ITAB_NULL;
  tables[0].itmode   = RFC_ITMODE_BYREFERENCE;
  tables[0].newitab  = 0;
  tables[1].name     = cU("IDOC_DATA_REC_40");
  tables[1].nlen     = 16;
  tables[1].type     = typeHandleEdiDd40;
  tables[1].leng     = EDI_DD40_LN;
  tables[1].ithandle = ITAB_NULL;
```

```
            tables[1].itmode   = RFC_ITMODE_BYREFERENCE;
            tables[1].newitab  = 0;
            tables[2].name     = NULL;
            /* Receive data                                          */
            rfc_rc = RfcGetData (rfc_handle, parameters, tables);
            if (rfc_rc != RFC_OK)
              rfc_error (cU("RfcGetData"));
            /* Initialize parameter                                  */
            tables[0].name     = NULL;
            /* Write IDoc into data file                             */
            if(write_idoc(tables[0].ithandle, tables[1].ithandle)!=0)
              rfc_rc = 1;
            else
            {
              rfc_rc = RfcSendData (rfc_handle, parameters, tables);
              if (rfc_rc != RFC_OK)
                rfc_error (cU("RfcSendData"));
            }
            return rfc_rc;
        } /* idoc_inbound_asynchronous */
```

Listing 5.4 "idoc_inbound_asynchronous" Function

"idoc_inbound_asynchronous" function

The function module uses table parameters with these line types to receive the IDoc control data records and the IDoc data records. The server installs these two structures. The C definitions required for this purpose have been generated previously using the genh program. Then the server initializes the two table parameters, IDOC_CONTROL_REC_40 and IDOC_DATA_REC_40, and calls the RfcGetData function to receive the control data record and the IDoc.

The server calls the write_idoc function to write the IDoc and its control data record into a file. The server function concludes with the RfcSend-Data function. Listing 5.5 shows the write_idoc function, which receives the handles to the two internal tables, including the control data records and the IDoc lines. It first writes the control data records and then the IDocs into the data file.

```
/* Write IDoc into file                                  */
int write_idoc(ITAB_H itControl, ITAB_H itData)
{
    int           rc = 0;
    unsigned      i;
    unsigned      it_leng;
```

```
  rfc_char_t      tbuf[MAXBUFF+1];
  FILE            *fp;
  fp = fopenU (data_file, cU("a"));
  if(fp == NULL)    return 1;
  it_leng = ItLeng(itControl)/sizeofR(SAP_UC);
  for(i=1;i<=ItFill(itControl);i++)
  {
     memcpyU(tbuf,ItGetLine(itControl, i), it_leng);
     tbuf[it_leng] = cU('\n');
     if (fwriteU (tbuf, 1, it_leng+1, fp) < it_leng+1)
     {
        fclose(fp);  return 1;
     }
  }
  it_leng = ItLeng(itData)/sizeofR(SAP_UC);
  for(i=1;i<=ItFill(itData);i++)
  {
     memcpyU(tbuf,ItGetLine(itData, i), it_leng);
     tbuf[it_leng] = cU('\n');
     if (fwriteU (tbuf, 1, it_leng+1, fp) < it_leng+1)
     {
        fclose(fp);  return 1;
     }
  }
  fclose(fp);  return 0;
}/* write_idoc */
```

Listing 5.5 "write_idoc" Function

To test the receiver, you must use Transaction SALE to implement the corresponding Customizing in the ALE subsystem. Initially, you define a logical system for the external C program, for instance, `CTSERV`. Then you maintain a tRFC destination for this system. To facilitate the generation of the partner profiles later on, the name of the destination should be identical to the name of the logical system.

ALE Customizing

Finally, use Transaction BD64 to create or extend an ALE distribution model in such a way that `ZORDER` messages are sent from an SAP client to your external C program (Figure 5.19). From this transaction, you can also generate the partner profiles.

You can now use the `ZIFP_SEND_IDOC` ABAP program to test your IDoc receiver. If everything works properly, the receiver writes the IDoc that was sent by this transaction into a file with the name <TID>.dat.

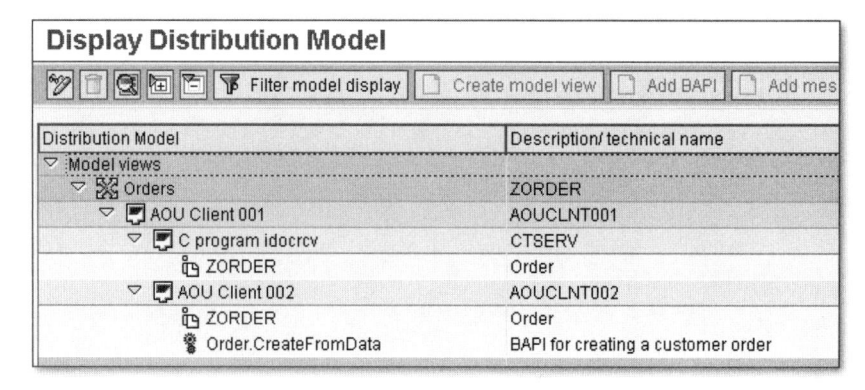

Display Distribution Model	
Distribution Model	Description/ technical name
▽ Model views	
▽ 🔲 Orders	ZORDER
▽ 🖥 AOU Client 001	AOUCLNT001
▽ 🖥 C program idocrcv	CTSERV
🗋 ZORDER	Order
▽ 🖥 AOU Client 002	AOUCLNT002
🗋 ZORDER	Order
🎯 Order.CreateFromData	BAPI for creating a customer order

Figure 5.19 Extending the ALE Distribution Model

5.3.2 IDoc Sender

The IDoc sender looks exactly like the tRFC client, which we've already discussed in Chapter 3, Section 3.3, More Complex RFC Clients. Like the IDoc receiver, the IDoc sender installs the `EDI_DC40` and `EDI_DD40` structure types. Then, it generates the two internal tables for the IDoc control data record and the IDoc lines.

Read IDoc The `read_idoc` function shown in Listing 5.6 reads the IDoc and its control data record from a file whose name is transferred as a command-line argument to the sender. The function assumes that the first line of the file contains the control data record and appends this control data record to the `itControl` internal table in the first loop run. The remaining lines are appended to the `itData` internal table.

```
/* Copy file content to IDoc                                   */
int read_idoc(FILE *fp, ITAB_H itControl, ITAB_H itData)
{
  int         rc = 0;
  int         fCtrl = 1;
  rfc_char_t  *ptr, buf[MAXBUFF+1];
  unsigned    it_leng;
  while ((ptr = fgetsU (buf, MAXBUFF, fp)) != NULL)
  {
    if(fCtrl)
    {
      ptr = (rfc_char_t *) ItAppLine(itControl);
      it_leng = ItLeng(itControl)/sizeofR(SAP_UC);
      fCtrl = 0;
```

```
    }
    else
    {
      ptr = (rfc_char_t *) ItAppLine(itData);
      it_leng = ItLeng(itData)/sizeofR(SAP_UC);
    }
    if (ptr != NULL)
    {
      size_t leng = strlenU (buf);
      if ((leng > 0) && (buf[leng-1] == cU('\n')))
        leng = leng - 1;
      if (leng == 0)
      {
        memsetU (ptr, BLANK, it_leng);
        continue;
      }
      if (leng < it_leng)
        memsetU (buf+leng, BLANK, it_leng-leng);
      memcpyU (ptr, buf, it_leng);
    }
    else
    {
      rc = 1; break;
    }
  }
  return rc;
} /* read_idoc */
```

Listing 5.6 "read_idoc" Function

To create a test file for the IDoc sender, simply copy a file that was received by the sender, and change the first line (in the control data record) as follows:

Creating a test file

- **"DIRECT" column (Offset 37)**
  Change the direction specification from 2 (outbound) to 1 (inbound).

- **"SNDPRN" column (Offset 163)**
  Change the specification of the sending system to your external system (CSERV).

- **"RCVPRN" column (Offset 278)**
  Change the specification of the receiving system to your receiving system (AOUCLNT001).

To ensure that the IDoc, which is sent by your IDoc sender, is processed properly, you must maintain a partner profile for your sending system using Transaction WE20 (refer to Figure 5.13).

5.4 IDoc Programming with Java and JCo

In this section, we discuss programming with the Java IDoc library. Now that we've presented the IDoc client programming, we turn our attention to the implementation steps that are necessary to send IDocs to a receiving Java system.

5.4.1 Preparation for the Use of IDoc Libraries

For programming Java-based applications that use IDocs, you initially need to download the SAP IDoc library from the SAP Service Marketplace. The library used in this book corresponds to Version 3.0 and is currently the latest version that works with Java Connector 3.0 (JCo 3.0) and the subsequent implementations of the connector. The file is named *sapidoc-3.0.0.zip* for the Windows platform.

Integrating the programming environment

The library is available both for Windows and for numerous other environments such as UNIX or HP-UX. After you've downloaded and extracted the ZIP file, a new folder is available on your hard disk that contains the Java documentation, examples for programming the IDoc client and IDoc server, as well as a Java archive called *sapidoc3.jar*. Readers who have already worked with Java-based IDoc applications will determine that there is only one library (instead of two) in comparison to the older versions. Besides this innovation, many classes have been renamed and restructured. Moreover, Java 5 language constructs have found their way into the new IDoc library.

As already indicated, the use of the JCo library is necessary for the use of the IDoc library. The JCo library is responsible for communication with the backend, whereas the IDoc library contributes the classes for creating and processing IDocs. For programming, you therefore put the *sapidoc3.jar* Java archive, which we just mentioned, into the class path of your development environment in addition to your possibly already existing JCo library.

5.4.2 Client Application for IDocs

After you've integrated your Java project into your development environment, you can start with the programming of the first IDoc application. The application sends an IDoc of the `ZORDER` type to client 002. As in traditional Java client programming, you first need to establish a connection to the SAP system. Establishing a connection is identical to pure JCo programming. That is, you generate a new `JCoDestination` object above the `JCoDestinationManager` factory class. As you can see in the sequence diagram shown in Figure 5.20, the next step instantiates the access to the metadata of IDocs. Here, metadata is described via an instance of the `IDocRepository` type. Because it is an interface, the object must be generated via a factory. The `JCoIDoc` class is the central class for generating all relevant types. As you can see in the simplified class screen of the `JCoIDoc` class in Figure 5.20, the class implements the `getIDocRepository` method for working with repositories. You can use the repository object to access the entire metadata structure of the IDocs. As in pure JCo programming, in IDoc programming, the repository is the starting point for validating the specified actual values against the metadata defined in the ABAP stack. Therefore, the metadata must also be the starting point for generating the IDoc. IDocs are represented via the `IDocDocument` interface in the Java IDoc library.

Two steps are necessary to generate such objects. In the first step, you must generate a specification of the `IDocFactory` interface. For this purpose, call the `getIDocFactory` method on the central factory class, `JCoIDoc`. The generated factory instance is the key element for providing an IDoc object. The IDoc object is represented by the `IDocDocument` interface. To generate an instance of this class, call the `createIDocDocument` method. The method receives two parameters: The first parameter is the already-generated repository object, and the second parameter specifies the name of the IDoc for which a proxy representation is required. The sequence diagram in Figure 5.20 gives information on the individual method calls for which you need to generate an `IDocDocument` object.

After you've generated the proxy object, you can start with the actual processing of the IDoc-relevant information. Here, we use the IDoc called `ZOrder`, which we already introduced and discussed in Section 5.1.1, Developing IDocs. The IDoc consists of two segments, `Z1ORDHD` and `Z1ORDPS`. Segments are processed as `ISegment` in the Java IDoc library.

Processing segments

5 IDocs and ALE

To populate the individual segment types with data, you must make a reference to the root segment of the IDoc proxy representation.

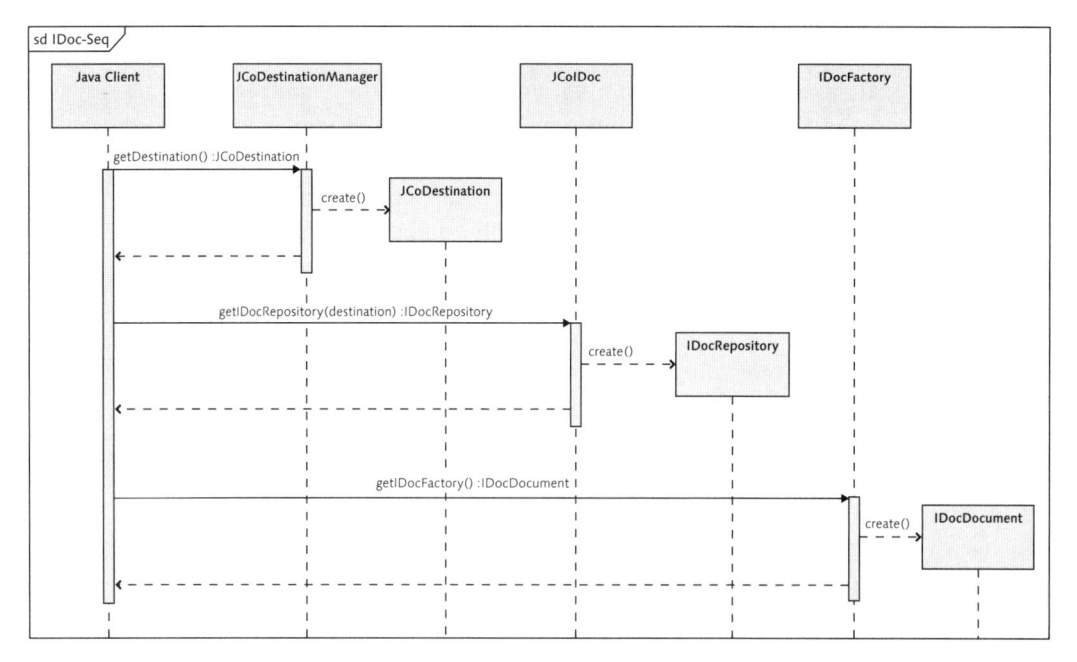

Figure 5.20 Communication Dependencies for Generating an Object of the "IDocDocument" Type

The root segment is retrieved using the `getRootDocument` method. Because the purchase order header information must be considered as child elements from the root perspective, the `addChild` method is called on the root segment. The method gets the name of the segment and returns a new `ISegment` object. This object can now be populated with the corresponding values using the `setValue` method. The method follows the Java standard and obtains the field label as the first parameter and the value to be set as the second parameter.

After you've populated the purchase order header with data, you can set the purchase order items. For this purpose, call the `addChild` method on the `ISegment` object of the header data, and transfer the corresponding values for the purchase order items.

Finally, the IDoc is sent. For this purpose, the central IDoc class, `JCoIDoc`, provides the `send` method. The method is available in four different forms. The method forms can be roughly subdivided into two types: One form is used if only one single IDoc is supposed to be sent to the ABAP system. The second form of the method is called using a list of IDocs (of the `IDocDocumentList` type). All methods have in common that they not only receive the IDoc objects but also the IDoc version, an object of the `JCoDestination` type, and the transaction number with which the IDoc is supposed to be processed. Analogous to the JCo programming, the transaction number is called on the `JCoDestination` class via the `createTID` method. After the necessary information of the sending and the receiving system has been set in the IDoc proxy object, you can use the `send` method to transfer the IDoc to the ABAP system (Listing 5.7).

Sending the IDoc to the ABAP system

```
public static void main(String[] args) {
  try {
    JCoDestination lcoDestination =
      ConnectionMan-ager.getJCoDestination("MYDESTINATION");
    IDocRepository repository =
      JCoIDoc.getIDocRepository(lcoDestination);
    IDocFactory idocFactory = JCoIDoc.getIDocFactory();
    IDocDocument iDocument =
      idocFactory.createIDocDocument(repository,IDOCNAME);
    //Add the root segments
    IDocSegment rootSegement = iDocu-ment.getRootSegment();
    //Create the purchase order header segment
    IDocSegment orderheader =
      rootSegement.addChild(IDOC_ORDER_HEADER);
      orderheader.setValue(ORDER_HEADER_ORDERID , 122);
      orderheader.setValue(ORDER_HEADER_BUYER,
        "Michael Wegelin");
     orderheader.setValue(ORDER_HEADER_TYPE, "A0");
     orderheader.setValue(ORDER_HEADER_REFID, "2");
    //Add a purchase order segment
    IDocSegment orderpos =
      orderheader.addChild(IDOC_ORDER_POS);
    orderpos.setValue(ORDER_POS_ORDERID,"122");
    orderpos.setValue(ORDER_POS_ORDERPOS,1);
    orderpos.setValue(ORDER_POS_MATID, "M1");
    orderpos.setValue(ORDER_POS_MATTEXT,
      "Screws and anchors");
```

```
            orderpos.setValue(ORDER_POS_ORDERCOUNT, "23");
            orderpos.setValue(ORDER_POS_PRICE, 12.30);
            orderpos.setValue(ORDER_POS_CURRENCY, "EUR");
            String tid = lcoDestination.createTID();
            iDocument.setMessageType("ZORDER");
            iDocument.setRecipientPartnerNumber("AOUCLNT002");
            iDocument.setRecipientPartnerType("LS");
            iDocument.setSenderPort("SAPBSP");
            iDocument.setSenderPartnerType("LS");
            iDocument.setSenderPartnerNumber("AOUCLNT001");
            JCoIDoc.send(iDocument,IDocFactory.IDOC_VERSION_DEFAULT,
                    lcoDestination , tid);
            lcoDestination.confirmTID(tid);
        } catch (JCoException e) {
            e.printStackTrace();
        } catch (IDocMetaDataUnavailableException e) {
            e.printStackTrace();
        } catch(IDocIllegalTypeException e) {
            e.printStackTrace();
        } catch (IDocSyntaxException e) {
            e.printStackTrace();
        } catch (IDocConversionException e) {
            e.printStackTrace();
        } catch(IDocFieldNotFoundException e) {
            e.printStackTrace();
        }
    }
}
```

Listing 5.7 Sending an IDoc with Java

Checking the IDoc consistency

To check the consistency and syntax of the `IDocument` object, you can call the `checkSyntax` method. If the syntax is damaged or faulty, an exception of the `IDocSyntaxException` type is raised. Therefore, you must position the method call in a `try/catch` block. If no error exists in the syntax, you can send the IDoc to the SAP system.

Processing IDocument objects

The processing of the pure `IDocument` objects is often not sufficient both for sending and for receiving Java systems. For example, in many cases, it is necessary to convert the received document into another format and process it accordingly. Likewise, in infrastructures in which messages are exchanged, it can occur that an `IDocument` object is initialized from an intermediate format and transferred to the SAP system. Experience has shown that the XML format (*Extensible Markup Language*) is particularly beneficial, although other formats are comparably convenient. One possible benefit of using XML is the easier conversion into different formats using XSLT (*Extensible Stylesheet Language for Transformations*). This enables a convenient communication in heterogeneous landscapes.

For XML-based processing, the Java IDoc library offers the IDocXMLProcessor interface as the starting point. It provides various method forms with the name, parse and render. The parse methods are used to create IDocument objects or a list of IDocument objects (as IDocumentList implementation); the same applies to render methods. They enable you to generate IDocument objects as XML presentations.

XML-based processing

You obtain an instance of an SAP implementation of this interface via the central IDoc factory class, IDocFactory. The required method is called getIDocXMLProcessor. The programming example in Listing 5.8 shows the option to save an IDoc as an XML document.

```
private void processIDoc(IDocDocument document) {
  try {
    IDocFactory idocFactory = JCoI-Doc.getIDocFactory();
    IDocXMLProcessor xmlProcessor =
      idocFactory.getIDocXMLProcessor();
    FileWriter fileWriter =
      new FileWriter("c:\\temp\\purchaseorder.xml");
    xmlProcessor.render(document, fileWriter);
  } catch (IOException e) {
    e.printStackTrace();
  }
}
```

Listing 5.8 XML Processing of an "IDocument" Object

5.4.3 IDoc Server

Now that you've sent an IDoc, the following section describes how you can receive an IDoc. In this scenario, we write the received IDoc as an XML file to the hard disk. The project configuration in the development environment is similar to the programming of an IDoc sender. The class path includes the libraries of the JCo and the Java IDoc library.

To implement the IDoc server, we create a class called EAIIDocServer. You can find this class in the programming examples for the book in the JCoServerProgrammierung Eclipse project in the de.eai.javaserverprg.idoc package. The JCoIDocServer interface is the starting point.

Implementing an IDoc server

The interface inherits from the JCoServer interface. This means that it is possible to establish a Java-based infrastructure that enables both a pure RFC communication and an IDoc-based communication with the SAP system. The JCoIDocServer interface introduces four new methods in JCo programming. These involve the methods, getIDocHandlerFactory, getIDocRepository, setIDocHandlerFactory, and setIDocRepository.

At the beginning of the implementation, you generate a new JCoIDocServer object. The object is initialized with the communication parameters for the SAP system. As you can see in the programming example of Listing 5.9, this is enabled via the getServer factory method in the JCoIDoc class. Moreover, you must inform the Java server which inbound IDocs are supposed to be processed by whom. This is done by registering an implementation of the JCoIDocHandlerFactory interface. In the example presented here, this is done by the EAIIDocHandlerFactory class. As you have already seen, the IDocs are transferred via tRFC. Therefore, you must inform the server object about who manages the transaction numbers in the Java system. They register an implementation of the JCoServerTIDHandler interface. The implementation of this interface is identical to the pure JCo server programming.

```
public class EAIIDocServer {
  public static void main(String[] args) {
    try {
      JCoIDocServer eaiServer =
        JCoIDoc.getServer("EAIIDocSample");
      eaiServer.setIDocHandlerFactory(
        new EAIIDocHandlerFactory());
      eaiServer.setTIDHandler(new EAITIDHandler());
      EAIIDocErrorListener listener =
        new EAIIDocErrorListener();
      eaiServer.addServerErrorListener(listener);
      eaiS-erver.addServerExceptionListener(listener);
      eaiServer.setConnectionCount(1);
      eaiServer.start();
    } catch (JCoException e) {
      System.out.println(
        "Problems while starting the IDoc server " +
        e.getMessage());
    }
  }
}
```

Listing 5.9 Implementing an IDoc Receiver in Java

As already indicated, a Java IDoc server can implement different processors for inbound IDoc objects. The decisive component here is an implementation of the `JCoIDocHandlerFactory` interface. This interface provides a method called `getIDocHandler`. It obtains an object of the `JCoIDocServerContext` type as the call parameter. The context can be used to decide who carries out the actual processing of an IDoc. The IDoc version from the context can be a decision criterion, for example. The `getIDocHandler` method returns implementations of the `JCoIDocHandler` interface. Ultimately, the interface forms the basis for the actual processing of the IDoc and offers the `handleRequest` method for this purpose.

Processing inbound IDocs

The method receives two parameters: The first parameter is of the `JCoServerContext` type, and the second one, of the `IDocDocumentList` type, represents a list of received IDocs. The programming example in Listing 5.10 shows how received IDocs can be saved as XML documents using `IDocXMLProcessor`.

```java
public void handleRequest(JCoServerContext serverCtx,
   IDoc-DocumentList idocList) {
  String filepath = "c:\\idocoutput\\";
  FileOutputStream fileOS = null;
  OutputStreamWriter objectOS = null;
  try {
    IDocXMLProcessor xmlProcessor =
      JCoIDoc.getIDocFactory().getIDocXMLProcessor();
    fileOS = new FileOutputStream(filepath +
      serverCtx.getTID()+ "Document.xml");
    objectOS=new OutputStreamWriter(fileOS, "UTF8");
    xmlProcessor.render(idocList, objectOS,
      IDocXMLProces-sor.RENDER_WITH_TABS_AND_CRLF);
    objectOS.flush();
  } catch (FileNotFoundException e) {
    e.printStackTrace();
  } catch (UnsupportedEncodingException e) {
    e.printStackTrace();
  } catch (IOException e) {
    e.printStackTrace();
  }
}
```

Listing 5.10 Implementing the "handleRequest" Method

5.4.4 Configuration for the Dispatch of IDocs

After the implementation of the external Java IDoc server, you must configure the SAP system accordingly. For this purpose, log on to your SAP system, and call Transaction SALE. Initially, define a logical system for the Java server, which was previously presented, by selecting the BASIC SETTINGS • LOGICAL SYSTEMS • DEFINE LOGICAL SYSTEM menu path. Now, add a new entry. Then use Transaction WE20 to configure the newly defined logical system. Subsequently, start Transaction SM59, and maintain a tRFC destination for the receiving Java server, as we've already described for the traditional JCo server programming. To facilitate the generation of the partner profiles, the name of the destination should be identical to the name of the logical system.

Extending the distribution model

After you've successfully created the destination, you need to change the distribution model that was presented at the beginning of this chapter so that ZORDER messages are sent from an SAP client to your external Java program (Figure 5.21). From this transaction, you can also generate the partner profiles.

Finally, start your Java IDoc server. You can now use the ZIFP_SEND_IDOC ABAP program to test your IDoc receiver. If everything works properly, the receiver writes the IDoc that was sent by this transaction into the directory that you've specified during programming.

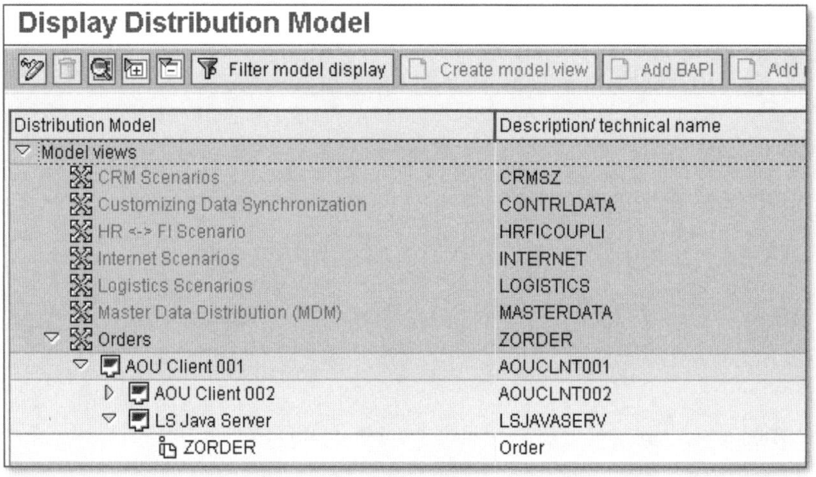

Distribution Model	Description/ technical name
▽ Model views	
CRM Scenarios	CRMSZ
Customizing Data Synchronization	CONTRLDATA
HR <-> FI Scenario	HRFICOUPLI
Internet Scenarios	INTERNET
Logistics Scenarios	LOGISTICS
Master Data Distribution (MDM)	MASTERDATA
▽ Orders	ZORDER
▽ AOU Client 001	AOUCLNT001
▷ AOU Client 002	AOUCLNT002
▽ LS Java Server	LSJAVASERV
ZORDER	Order

Figure 5.21 Extending the ALE Distribution Model

This chapter shows how you can easily and quickly develop SOAP clients and servers in ABAP and Java on the SAP NetWeaver AS. The third section discusses how you can use the SOAP services of C#.

6 Service-Oriented Architecture Protocol

The Service-Oriented Architecture Protocol (SOAP) has established itself as an important standard of inter-process communication within a very short period of time. This is particularly due to its high platform independence and the use of Internet standards: The messages between two processes are transported as XML messages, and the transport is usually carried out via HTTP. Today, both standards are supported by many platforms, including SAP NetWeaver. Many programming examples show how SOAP components that have been developed in different programming languages can exchange messages.

6.1 Web Services and Clients with SAP NetWeaver AS ABAP

The ABAP Workbench provides a wizard for developing web services and clients that helps developers to quickly reach their goal in just a few steps. First, we will describe the development of an ABAP web service that you can call from an ABAP client.

6.1.1 ABAP SOAP Web Service

It is very simple to develop a SOAP web service on an ABAP stack. For this purpose, start the Object Navigator (Transaction SE80). Have the system display the package that will contain your web service. In the context menu of the package, select CREATE • ENTERPRISE SERVICE/WEB SERVICE • WEB SERVICE to start the web service wizard, which guides you through the following six steps to complete a web service:

Web service in six steps

1. **Provide an overview.**
   In the first step, the wizard provides an overview of the options to create a web service:
   - RFC-enabled function modules
   - Function groups
   - BAPIs
   - Message interfaces

   Click Continue to go to the next screen.

2. **Create service.**
   Enter the name of the web service, for instance, "ZIFP_ORDER_SERVICE," in the Service Definition input field. You can enter a short description in the Short Text input field. Select one of the four options from the Endpoint Type dropdown list. We choose the BAPI entry for our example.

3. **Choose endpoint.**
   In the third step, you choose the endpoint. Depending on the endpoint type that you've selected in the previous step, you now enter the name of a function module, a function group, a business object, or an inbound SAP NetWeaver XI interface. We choose the Z_BUS4500 (Order) business object type for our example.

4. **Choose operations.**
   In this step, you choose the operations that your web service will provide. It is only displayed for the endpoint types, Function Group and BAPI because a function group can contain multiple function modules, or a business object can contain multiple BAPIs. In our example, we decide to provide all four BAPIs also as operations in the web service. Additionally, we use the BAPI Commit/Rollback button to specify that the `TransactionCommit` and `TransactionRollback` methods of the `BapiService` business object are supposed to be added to web service as operations. Figure 6.1 shows this step.

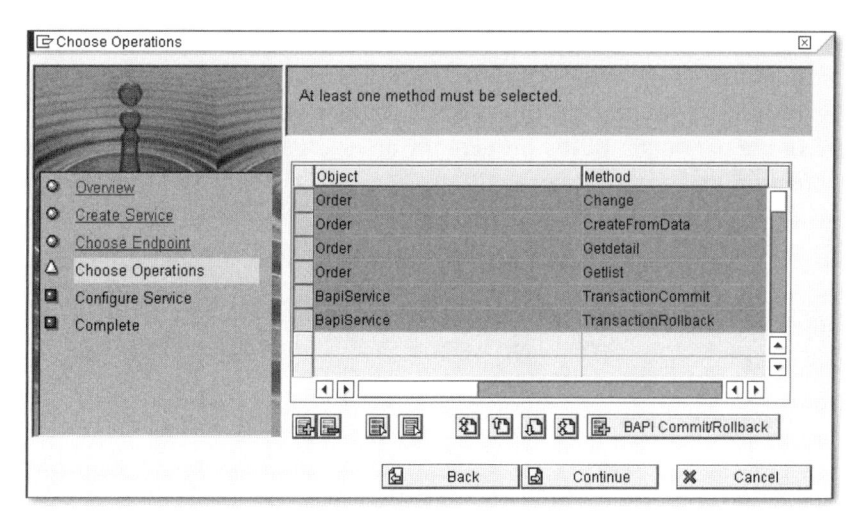

Figure 6.1 Choosing Operations of the Web Service

5. **Configure service.**
   In the second to last step, you select a profile for the security settings. In the Profile dropdown list, you can select between Basic Authorization: SOAP Profile and Secure SOAP Profile. The first one is a profile for SOAP 1.1 with stateless HTTP communication and simple authentication; the second one is a profile for SOAP 1.1 with stateless HTTP communication, strong authentication, and secure transfer.

   Additionally, you can select the Release Service for Runtime checkbox. In this case, the web service is immediately released upon completion. If you don't select this field, you can release the web service later on using Transaction WSCONFIG.

6. **Complete the wizard.**
   In the last step, the wizard displays which web service is created. Click the Complete button, confirm the selected package (or choose a new one), and assign the new object to a development order.

Figure 6.2 show the service interface of the web service. You can see that an operation was created for each BAPI. Each operation has an `Input` import parameter and an `Output` export parameter. In the import parameter, you find equivalents to the import and table parameters of the function module, in export parameter equivalents to its export and table parameters. The reason why the table parameters occur twice is that

Interface of a web service

they can be used both as import and as export parameters in function modules. If you click on such a parameter in the structure overview of the service interface, on the right hand side you can see the assignment of the parameter of the End Point (top) to the corresponding parameter within the Service Interface (bottom).

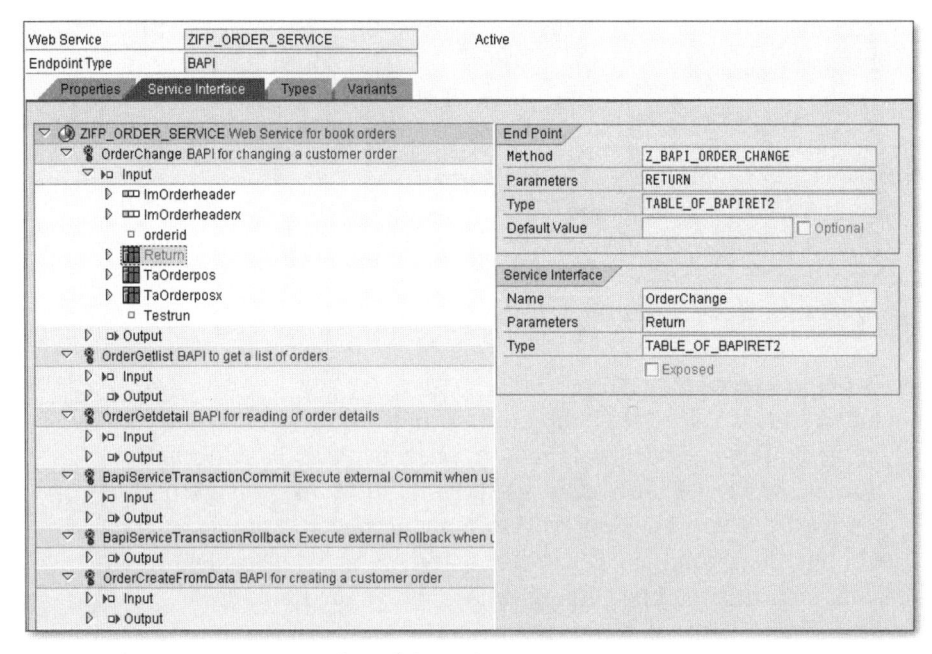

Figure 6.2 Service Interface of the Web Service

By selecting Exposed, you can determine whether the corresponding parameter is supposed to appear in the service interface at all. In Figure 6.2, for example, we removed the `Return` table parameter from the input parameter because this table parameter definitively is a return parameter.

Chapter 1, Section 1.4.5, SOAP, already discussed that you can change the configuration settings for the web service later on using Transaction WSCONFIG. We also referred to Transaction WSADMIN, which you can use to test the web service. This is the first thing you should do after you've generated the web service.

WSDL file   However, Transaction WSADMIN is particularly important to call the file that writes the service in the *Web Service Description Language* (WSDL).

The WSDL file is an XML document that precisely describes the web service. Figure 6.3 shows sections of the WSDL file for our web service. Normally, you wouldn't take a look at such a WSDL file, but you need it now to generate code for clients that want to use the web service.

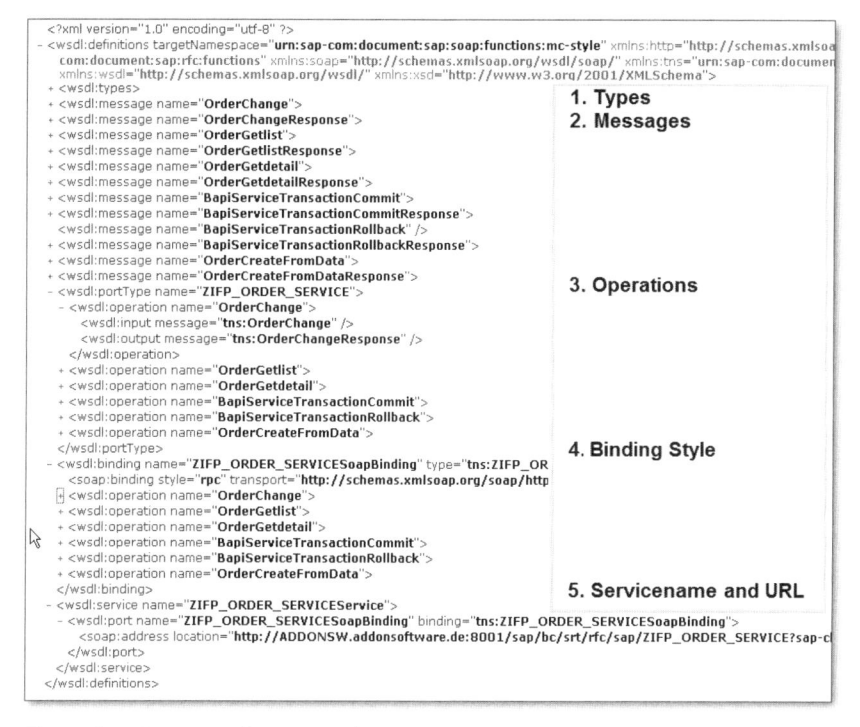

```
<?xml version="1.0" encoding="utf-8" ?>
- <wsdl:definitions targetNamespace="urn:sap-com:document:sap:soap:functions:mc-style" xmlns:http="http://schemas.xmlsoa
    com:document:sap:rfc:functions" xmlns:soap="http://schemas.xmlsoap.org/wsdl/soap/" xmlns:tns="urn:sap-com:documen
    xmlns:wsdl="http://schemas.xmlsoap.org/wsdl/" xmlns:xsd="http://www.w3.org/2001/XMLSchema">
  + <wsdl:types>
  + <wsdl:message name="OrderChange">                          1. Types
  + <wsdl:message name="OrderChangeResponse">                  2. Messages
  + <wsdl:message name="OrderGetlist">
  + <wsdl:message name="OrderGetlistResponse">
  + <wsdl:message name="OrderGetdetail">
  + <wsdl:message name="OrderGetdetailResponse">
  + <wsdl:message name="BapiServiceTransactionCommit">
  + <wsdl:message name="BapiServiceTransactionCommitResponse">
    <wsdl:message name="BapiServiceTransactionRollback" />
  + <wsdl:message name="BapiServiceTransactionRollbackResponse">
  + <wsdl:message name="OrderCreateFromData">
  + <wsdl:message name="OrderCreateFromDataResponse">
  - <wsdl:portType name="ZIFP_ORDER_SERVICE">                  3. Operations
    - <wsdl:operation name="OrderChange">
        <wsdl:input message="tns:OrderChange" />
        <wsdl:output message="tns:OrderChangeResponse" />
      </wsdl:operation>
  + <wsdl:operation name="OrderGetlist">
  + <wsdl:operation name="OrderGetdetail">
  + <wsdl:operation name="BapiServiceTransactionCommit">
  + <wsdl:operation name="BapiServiceTransactionRollback">
  + <wsdl:operation name="OrderCreateFromData">               4. Binding Style
    </wsdl:portType>
  - <wsdl:binding name="ZIFP_ORDER_SERVICESoapBinding" type="tns:ZIFP_OR
      <soap:binding style="rpc" transport="http://schemas.xmlsoap.org/soap/http
  + <wsdl:operation name="OrderChange">
  + <wsdl:operation name="OrderGetlist">
  + <wsdl:operation name="OrderGetdetail">
  + <wsdl:operation name="BapiServiceTransactionCommit">
  + <wsdl:operation name="BapiServiceTransactionRollback">
  + <wsdl:operation name="OrderCreateFromData">               5. Servicename and URL
    </wsdl:binding>
  - <wsdl:service name="ZIFP_ORDER_SERVICEService">
    - <wsdl:port name="ZIFP_ORDER_SERVICESoapBinding" binding="tns:ZIFP_ORDER_SERVICESoapBinding">
        <soap:address location="http://ADDONSW.addonsoftware.de:8001/sap/bc/srt/rfc/sap/ZIFP_ORDER_SERVICE?sap-cl
      </wsdl:port>
    </wsdl:service>
  </wsdl:definitions>
```

Figure 6.3 Structure of a WSDL File

As you can see in the figure, the WSDL file consists of five parts:

Components of the WSDL file

▶ **Definition of simple and complex data types**
The data types used by the web service are described in the `<wsdl:types>` XML element in the *XML Schema Definition Language* (XSD).

▶ **Description of the message types**
This is done in the `<wsdl:message>` XML elements. Here, each operation of the web service has an input and an output message, for instance, `OrderChange` and `OrderChangeResponse`. Of course, the message definitions refer to the previous type definitions in `<wsdl:types>`.

315

- **Description of the operations**
  Within the `<wdsl:portType>` elements, the WSDL file describes which operations the web service provides and which input and output message is respectively expected and returned by an operation.

- **Binding style and SOAP action**
  In the `<wsdl:binding>` section, the SOAP actions the operations are bound to and the binding style the messages have are both defined. The *SOAP action* is transferred in the HTTP header when it is called via HTTP and helps the web service select the proper operation. The binding styles are detailed in the box following this list.

- **Servicename and URL**
  Within a `<wsdl:service>` element, the web service receives a name, and the URL is specified that is used to call the web service via HTTP.

Binding Styles

In the *document style*, the input and output parameters of the operations are considered documents that can have any structure. The exchanged messages are considered messages that cannot be subdivided any further; so they consist of only one part:

```
<wsdl:message name="OrderChange">
  <wsdl:part name="parameters" element="tns:OrderChange" />
</wsdl:message>
```

For the *RPC style (Remote Procedure Call)*, it is assumed that the input and output parameters can be subdivided into individual, named parameters. So the exchanged messages comprise several different parts:

```
<wsdl:message name="OrderChange">
  <wsdl:part name="ImOrderheader" type="tns:Zifporder" />
  <wsdl:part name="ImOrderheaderx" type="tns:Zifporderx" />
  <wsdl:part name="TaOrderpos"
         type="tns:TableOfZifporderpos" />
  <wsdl:part name="TaOrderposx"
         type="tns:TableOfZifporderposx" />
  <wsdl:part name="Testrun" type="n0:char1" />
  <wsdl:part name="orderid" type="n0:numeric10" />
</wsdl:message>
```

When you click the WSDL button (Ctrl + F1) in the application toolbar of Transaction WSADMIN, the SAP GUI starts a web browser in which the URL for calling the WSDL file from SAP NetWeaver AS ABAP is entered. Before the browser is started, you must select whether the

WSDL file is supposed to be displayed in document style or in RPC style. You can then save the WSDL file from the browser in a file and forward it to the client developers. It contains all of the information required for calling the web service.

Although the WSDL file is very impressive at first glance, the exchanged documents have a very simple structure. When you test the web service from Transaction WSADMIN, the test tool also displays the XML files that are exchanged via HTTP POST. Listing 6.1 shows the request document.

SOAP documents

```
<?xml version="1.0" encoding="UTF-8" ?>
<SOAP-ENV:Envelope
  xmlns:SOAP-ENV="http://schemas.xmlsoap.org/soap/envelope/"
  xmlns:xsi="http://www.w3.org/2001/XMLSchema-instance"
  xmlns:xs="http://www.w3.org/2001/XMLSchema">
  <SOAP-ENV:Header>
    <!-- ... -->
  </SOAP-ENV:Header>
  <SOAP-ENV:Body>
    <ns1:OrderGetlist xmlns:ns1='urn:sap...'>
      <ImRefid></ImRefid>
    </ns1:OrderGetlist>
  </SOAP-ENV:Body>
</SOAP-ENV:Envelope>
```

Listing 6.1 SOAP Request

The root element is a *SOAP envelope* that contains an optional SOAP header and a SOAP body. In the SOAP body, you can view the request message, `OrderGetList`. The SOAP header contains SAP-specific information about the session's management.

SOAP envelope

Listing 6.2 shows the server's response. Again, the response document, in this case `OrderGetlistResponse`, is embedded into the SOAP body element with the SOAP envelope element.

```
<?xml version="1.0" encoding="UTF-8" ?>
<soap-env:Envelope
 xmlns:soap.env="http://schemas.xmlsoap.org/soap/envelope/"
>
  <soap-env:Body>
    <n0:OrderGetlistResponse xmlns:n0="urn:sap... ">
      <Return>
```

```xml
            <Type>S</Type>
            <Id></Id>
            <Number>000</Number>
            <Message></Message>
            <LogNo></LogNo>
            <LogMsgNo>000000</LogMsgNo>
            <MessageV1></MessageV1>
            <MessageV2></MessageV2>
            <MessageV3></MessageV3>
            <MessageV4></MessageV4>
            <Parameter></Parameter>
            <Row>0</Row>
            <Field></Field>
            <System></System>
          </Return>
          <TaOrders>
            <item>
               <Mandt>001</Mandt>
               <Orderid>0000000040</Orderid>
               <Type>SO</Type>
               <Refid>0000000002</Refid>
               <Buyer>Buyer</Buyer>
               <Seller>Seller</Seller>
               <Orderdate>2008-12-19</Orderdate>
            </item>
            <item>
               <Mandt>001</Mandt>
               <Orderid>0000000053</Orderid>
               <Type>SO</Type>
               <Refid>0000000001</Refid>
               <Buyer>Distributor Wegelin</Buyer>
               <Seller>Wholesaler Englbrecht</Seller>
               <Orderdate>2009-01-31</Orderdate>
            </item>
          </TaOrders>
       </n0:OrderGetlistResponse>
    </soap-env:Body>
</soap-env:Envelope>
```

Listing 6.2 SOAP Response

You can clearly identify the `Return` export parameter and the `TaOrders` table with two entries. The SOAP header is completely missing in the response.

6.1.2 ABAP SOAP Web Client

It's not very difficult and only takes two steps to write an ABAP client that calls the operations of the web service. First, you have the system generate a proxy class from the WSDL file, and then you write a program that instantiates the proxy class and uses its methods.

Start the Object Navigator (Transaction SE80). Have the system display the package that will contain your proxy class. In the context menu of the package, select CREATE • ENTERPRISE SERVICE/WEB SERVICE • PROXY OBJECT to start a wizard that generates the proxy class.

In the first step of the wizard, you specify whether the WSDL file will be retrieved via HTTP, from a local file, via a *Universal Description and Discovery Interface Service* (UDDI), or from the SAP NetWeaver XI repository. For our own web service, which we generated in Section 6.1.1, ABAP SOAP Web Service, we specify the URL that we've previously copied from the browser when we discussed the WSDL file from Transaction WSADMIN. If you've stored the WSDL file in a local file, specify this file.

Specifying the WSDL file

In the second step, you select the package in which the generated objects will be stored. Furthermore, you enter a prefix that is to be put in front of all generated object names. Here, we've selected ZIFP as the package and ZIFP_ as the prefix. You possibly receive a warning that your package has no use access for the SAI_TOOLS package. You can add this use access later by opening the Object Navigator of your package, selecting the Use Accesses tab, and creating a new use access for the SAI_TOOLS package. Moreover, you probably receive a warning that name collisions and name truncations occurred. But you have the option to change the generated names in the Name Problems tab before you activate the generated proxy.

Selecting the package and the prefix

Figure 6.4 shows the generated web service client proxy. You can see that the generated proxy class, ZIFP_CO_ZIFP_ORDER_SERVICE, has six methods — one for every operation of the web service. Every operation has an import and an export parameter. The individual components of this parameter correspond to the import and export parameters of the web service.

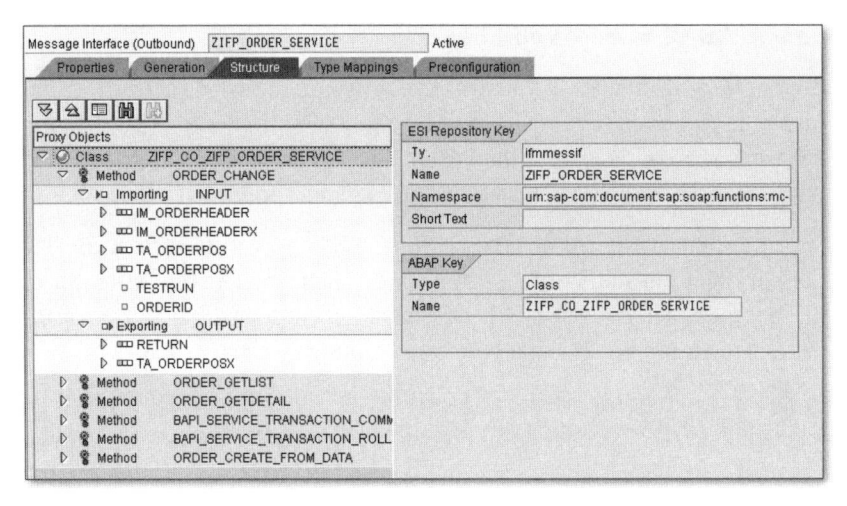

Figure 6.4 Generated Web Service Client Proxy

Logical ports   Before you can test and use the proxy, you still need to create a *logical port* for the generated class in Transaction LPCONFIG because the generated proxy class doesn't yet contain any information about the URL, which can be used to call the web service. This information is stored in a logical port, which is transferred in the constructor when the proxy class is instantiated. For a proxy class, you can create multiple ports in Transaction LPCONFIG. This enables you to flexibly reference to different URLs for which the same web services are accessible. You can omit the transfer of a port in the instantiation if you select one of the ports as the default port.

Start Transaction LPCONFIG to create a new port. Enter the name of the generated proxy class in the Proxy Class input field and any name for the logical port that you want to create in the Logical Port input field. Additionally, select the Default Port checkbox to select the port that you currently create as the default port. In the application toolbar, click on Create ([F5]), and then enter a description for the port you just created. If you now go to the Call Parameters tab, you can see that the URL of the web service was entered there. If this is not the case, you must copy it from the WSDL file into the URL input field. You can now save and activate the newly created port.

Instead of specifying the URL in the port, you can also use Transaction SM59 to create an RFC destination of the H type (an HTTP destination) and reference to this destination in the logical port. For this destination, you can store the user name and the password or even a certificate for the logon to the web service in the Logon & Security tab. The technical settings of such a destination are shown in Figure 6.5.

Now go back to the Object Navigator to test the proxy. Click on Test Interface (F8) in the application toolbar. The system displays a dialog in which you select the XML option so that you can view and edit the XML document later which is sent via HTTP to the web service. Select Execute (F8), and double-click the operation you want to test in the following dialog. The system then displays the XML request with the generated data.

Testing the proxy

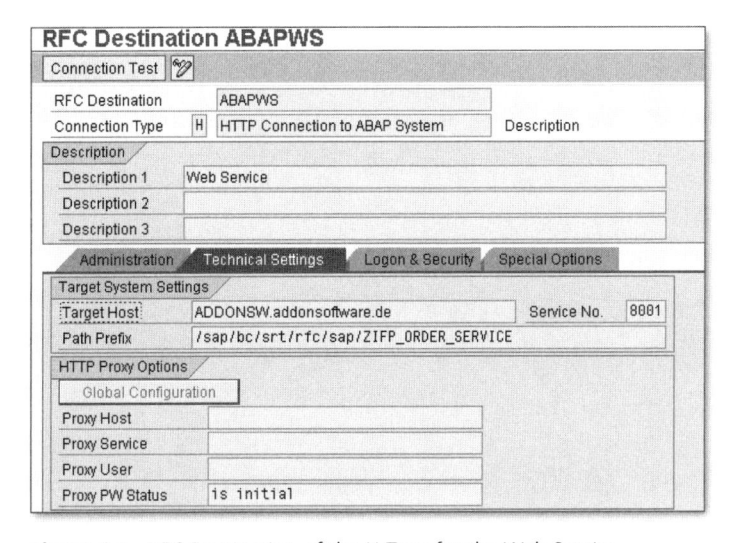

Figure 6.5 RFC Destination of the H Type for the Web Service

Replace the generated REFID (customer purchase order number) with an ID that you know exists in the target system so that the system returns meaningful data. Again, click on Execute (F8), and the system displays a success or error message in the next screen. There, you can have the system display the request and response message.

After the successful test, you can write a program that calls the web service. Listing 6.3 shows an ABAP program that calls the `order_getlist` method of the generated proxy class and then outputs the returned purchase order details in an ABAP list.

Client program

```
REPORT  zifp_test_webservice.
DATA:
  r_proxy TYPE REF TO zifp_co_zifp_order_service,
  output TYPE zifp_order_getlist_response,
  input TYPE zifp_order_getlist,
  wa TYPE zifp_zifporder.
TRY.
    CREATE OBJECT r_proxy
*   EXPORTING
*     LOGICAL_PORT_NAME  =
      .
  CATCH cx_ai_system_fault.
ENDTRY.
TRY.
    CALL METHOD r_proxy->order_getlist
      EXPORTING
        input  = input
      IMPORTING
        output = output.
  CATCH cx_ai_system_fault.
  CATCH cx_ai_application_fault.
ENDTRY.
LOOP AT output-ta_orders-item INTO wa.
  WRITE:/ wa-orderid, wa-type, wa-refid,
          wa-buyer, wa-seller, wa-orderdate.
ENDLOOP.
```

Listing 6.3 ABAP Program That Calls a Web Service

First, the program generates an object of the proxy class. Because the `order_getlist` method has no relevant input parameters, you don't have to populate them prior to the call. After the call of the method, the system outputs the internal table, `output-ta_orders-item`, with the purchase order headers.

Call of an external web service

As soon as you have a WSDL file, you can have the system generate an ABAP proxy for calling the web service that is described in the WSDL file. Unfortunately, in real life, it is not possible to reuse the proxy that you previously generated for the ABAP web service because the WSDL files for the ABAP service and for the Java service show subtle and possibly less subtle differences even though both services do the same. The WSDL file was not the starting point for development, but the WSDL file was generated from the ABAP or Java code. In Chapter 7, SAP NetWeaver Process Integration, we will describe the opposite approach to first create the interface description and then have the system generate a server proxy from the interface description for different programming languages.

6.2 Web Services and Clients with SAP NetWeaver AS Java

As part of the new orientation of the SAP infrastructure toward a service-oriented platform, customers have been provided with numerous options to provide and implement services on the basis of SOAP-oriented services on SAP NetWeaver AS Java. The following section describes this and illustrates the web service infrastructure, the paths of provision, and the consumption of SOAP web services.

6.2.1 Web Service Infrastructure in SAP NetWeaver AS Java

Already in very early versions of the SAP J2EE engine, the infrastructure provides the option to consume web services. Although Version 6.20 did not allow you to select individual components (*session beans*) as a web service in the SAP AS, Version 6.30 enables you to finely restrict which functionality of a component is provided as a web service to the outside world. Here, the web service framework not only supports the provisioning of session beans as web services but also default Java classes and SAP NetWeaver Portal services.

When implementing a Java-based web service, SAP provides developers with the SAP NetWeaver Developer Studio. This is a tool with which you can create web services very easily. Of course, this is a big advantage initially, but on the other hand, it provides functionality to the outside world that is not intended as such if you don't consider the consequences. For example, if the security topic has not been considered sufficiently for publishing a web service method, this could have the result that a security-critical service is provided to the outside world without any security restrictions. This provision of a web service is broken down into two significant parts: the *web service interface part* and the *web service binding part*.

Parts of a web service

| Web service interface | The *web service interface* is used to abstract the web service from its concrete runtime definition. Consequently, it does not depend on a concrete transport binding or a concrete protocol implementation. An interface part of a Java web service can be divided into two areas: On the one hand, there is the *Virtual Interface* (VI). Imagine that you want to provide a Java class as a web service to the outside world, but your Java class not only contains the method that is supposed to be called through a web service but also many other methods. To publish one method only, it would be necessary to introduce a new Java interface. If it is many Java classes, however, this can become very confusing. Here, the VI can help. It describes which methods are provided in the web service and how this method can be accessed from the outside. It is possible to change the name of the methods, the parameter names, or similar for outside use. |

Besides the VI, another part in the web service interface part plays an important role: the *Web Service Definition* (WSD). The WSD is used to determine the runtime aspects that are supposed to be used by the web service's runtime environment. Note, however, that no concrete implementation is described here but only that the web service is supposed to be stateful (and not how it is actually implemented). The WSDL interface is generated from these two parts of the web service interface. The web service interface comprises the areas of *type*, *message*, and *port type*.

| Web service binding | The abstract method to describe the web service via the WSD must be concretely defined for the runtime. The specific properties that are used by the runtime environment of the web service must be specified. For this purpose, you must know the runtime environment of the web service. The implementation of the abstract WSD is instantiated via web service configurations. By generating the definition and the configuration, you generate the web service binding in the WSDL file later on. For example, a web service configuration specifies |

- Which transport binding is supposed to be used
- How the WSD requirements are implemented concretely at runtime
- How security is defined at runtime

| Inbound and outbound web services | The SAP Web AS supports both inbound and outbound web service calls. Here, the entire call processing is supported by the web service framework. |

Processing Inbound Calls Through the Web Service Framework

The processing of inbound web service calls is ensured via the web service runtime in the application server. In this process, inbound calls are encapsulated in a *transport object* and transferred to the web service runtime after it has been received by the server. The transport object enables the runtime environment to identify the receiver of the inbound call and to implement the call of the service. In addition to the receiver information, one or more configurations are provided for each web service that is offered by the application server. A configuration determines which runtime properties must be loaded to execute the web service. Runtime properties could be, for example, whether the service is to be called stateless or stateful or whether the service can only be called if the authentication characteristics are set. For example, you can specify in the configuration whether the consumer must authenticate to the server via the user name and password or via an *X509 certificate*.

At runtime, the previously described configuration properties are linked with *protocol implementations*. Ultimately, a protocol is nothing but a Java service that is executed in the application server and assumes a specific task in processing. The individual protocol steps are processed by the *protocol handler*. It is responsible for the sequential processing of the individual steps for request, response, and error messages.

The protocol phase is followed by the *transport binding* or the *WSDL binding*. The main task is to process the inbound call and to generate the resulting Java objects for further processing. So you can say that the transport binding is that part of the processing that actually "knows" how to process inbound requests. Because inbound information can ultimately use any type of format, the correct processing must be ensured in the transport binding. Finally, the generated Java objects are forwarded to the *Implementation Container* (IC) for further processing, and the web service is called. The result of the web service call is returned as a Java object to the transport binding. The object is serialized and returned to the caller via the entire stack.

Processing Outbound Calls Through the Web Service Framework

The communication as a web service consumer entails that the client communicates with the web service via a *Service Endpoint Interface* (SEI).

Service endpoint interface

The SEI is generated through a generated proxy on the basis of the WSDL port type and represents the web service on the client side. The proxy uses a concrete transport binding. This means that after the generation of the proxy, you cannot change the communication type any longer. The proxy is generated by a corresponding proxy generator; the generator reads the WSDL document and generates the SEI for all port types and schema classes. Then, the WSDL binding elements are generated (the suitable transport binding is used for each found element). The transport binding is responsible for generating the message (request) that is sent to the web service. If the web service provides a response, it is the task of the transport binding to generate type-safe Java objects from the received information.

6.2.2 Web Service Provider with J2EE

Now that we've presented the basic terminology and considered the infrastructure, we will discuss the programming of a web service in this section. In the example presented, we want to implement a web service that enables other retail enterprises to read all articles from our catalog system. For this purpose, we implement a web service that is based on the J2EE technology. As already discussed in Chapter 1, Section 1.1.3, SAP NetWeaver Application Server Java, SAP NetWeaver AS Java is a product that implements the J2EE standard. The standard that is implemented in Release 7.0 does not extensively describe the web service communication, so all application server manufacturers have a lot of freedom in how SOAP-oriented services are implemented and processed on the concrete platform.

Now let's discuss how you can turn an Enterprise Java Bean into a SOAP-oriented service interface with just a few steps.

Creating an EJB module project

To create a web service that is based on J2EE, you generate an *EJB module project* in the SAP NetWeaver Developer Studio. After you've entered a name for your project (e.g., ArticleManagement) and successfully completed the creation, you receive an overview of the project content in the J2EE perspective in the J2EE Explorer view. There are two XML files and a folder called *EJBModule*. The icons indicate that this is the source code folder in which all Java-relevant source code files are stored. One of the two XML files, the *ejb-jar.xml* file, will look familiar to you because it is a standard J2EE deployment descriptor as it is described in the J2EE specification. Before we start with the actual programming, we first generate an enterprise application project called "EAIArticleApplication" and add the newly created "ArticleManagement" project as a *references project*.

Now that we've created the project, the first step is to program the class that represents the articles from our catalog system. The programming example from Listing 6.4 shows the `Article` class. As you can see, the class implements an interface called `IArticle`. The interface only defines the three `getter` methods that are implemented in the class. The attributes are defined as strings intentionally. If you use other data types, a consumer might not be able to consume the service due to incompatibility. Here, we only want to enable a read access to the articles; therefore, the implementation of the `setter` methods was omitted. The `Serializable` interface was implemented in addition to the `IArticle` interface. This is mandatory because otherwise the J2EE application server cannot transfer the article objects to the consumer.

Implementing the data model

```
public class Article implements IArticle, Serializable {
  private String articleID;
  private String articlename;
  private String articlelongtext;
  public Article() {
  }
  public String getArticleID() {
    return articleID;
  }
  public String getArticlelongtext() {
    return articlelongtext;
  }
  public String getArticlename() {
    return articlename;
  }
  public void setArticleID(String artid){
    articleID = artid;
  }
  public void setArticlelongtext(String articlelgtxt){
    articlelongtext = articlelgtxt;
  }
  public void setArticlename(String name){
    articlename = name;
  }
}
```

Listing 6.4 "Article" Class

6 Service-Oriented Architecture Protocol

Creating the EJB   In the next step, we'll create a new stateless EJB. For this purpose, select the *EJBModule* folder, and choose NEW • EJB from the context menu. In the subsequent screen, enter the class name of the class to be generated in the EJB Name field, and select the Stateless Session Bean entry from the Bean Type selection list.

After you've specified a Java package in the Default EJBPackage field, you can go to the next dialog by selecting Next. You see an overview of those interfaces and classes that are created by the wizard. Click the Next button to go to the dialog for defining the methods that are supposed to be provided by the EJB. Figure 6.6 shows that a method called `listArticles` is created in our example. This method returns an array of `IArticle` objects to the caller. Click Finish to confirm the dialog, and implement the newly generated `listArticles` method in the `ArticleServiceBean` class.

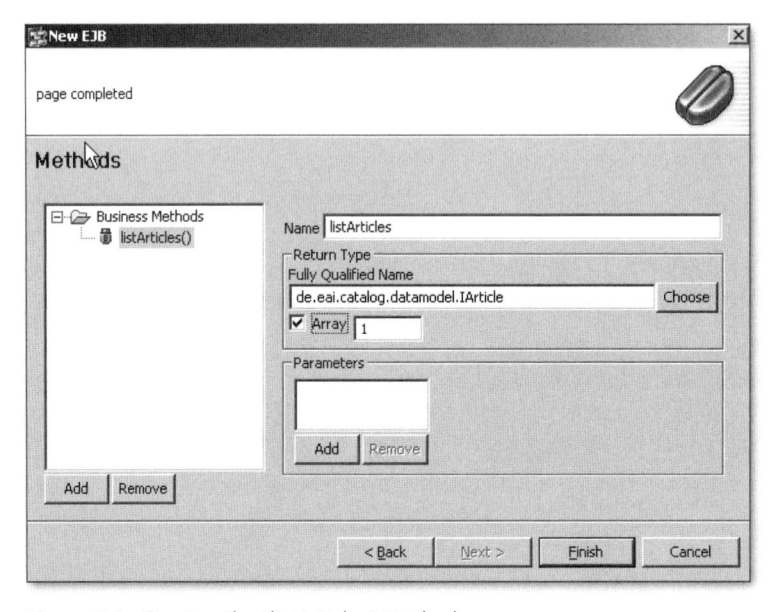

Figure 6.6 Creating the "listArticles" Method

Supported data types of a web service endpoint   In the implementation of web service endpoints, for example, the previously mentioned method, `listArticles`, you must take into account that not all data types are supported. Table 6.1 provides an overview of those data types that may be used as request or response parameter data type in a web service endpoint.

Description	Data Types
Simple wrapper data types	`java.lang.Void`, `java.lang.Boolean`, `java.lang.Byte`, `java.lang.Short`, `java.lang.Integer`, `java.lang.Long`, `java.lang.Float`, `java.lang.Double`, `java.lang.String`
Marker interfaces	`java.io.Serializable`, `java.lang.Cloneable`, `java.lang.Comparable`
Array classes	`java.util.HashSet`, `java.util.Vector`, `java.util.List`, `java.util.Stack`, `java.util.ArrayList`
Date and time specifications	`java.util.Calendar`, `java.util.Date`, `java.util.GregorianCalendar`, `java.sql.Date`, `java.sql.Time`
Big numbers	`java.math.BigInteger`, `java.math.BigDecimal`
Exception	`java.lang.Throwable`, `java.lang.Exception`, `java.rmi.RemoteException`
	`java.lang.Object`

Table 6.1 Supported Data Types for Web Service Endpoints

As you can see in Table 6.1, you should only use object types in the area of SAP web services. You should not process simple data types in the interface. If you return — as in our case — a class such as `Article` as the return parameter type via a web service to the consumer, you must note that the known specifications for the programming of Java beans are implemented. Therefore, the class must have a default constructor as well as `getter` and `setter` methods and implement the `java.io.Serializable` interface.

6 | Service-Oriented Architecture Protocol

Implementing the web service

After the implementation, you can start with the generation of the web service. For this purpose, expand the `ejb-jar.xml` deployment descriptor in the J2EE Explorer view. You see an overview of all EJBs that have been created within the project. To generate a web service, select the EJB, and open the context menu. In the New menu entry, you can find two selection options called Virtual Interface and Web Service. In this context, select the Web Service entry. Enter the name of your web service in the Web Service Name field and a name for your web service configuration in the Configuration Name field. Figure 6.7 shows this dialog with the values for our example.

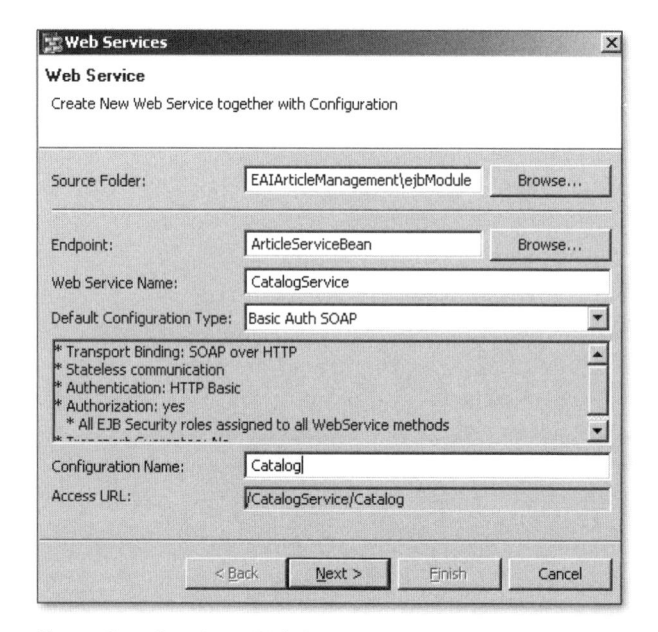

Figure 6.7 Creating a Web Service

After you've clicked Next, you'll see an overview of the methods of your EJB. In our case, only the `listArticle` method is included. The next dialog step prompts you to specify the class that implements the `IArticle` interface. Select the `Article` class, and click Next to confirm. Finally, you must select the enterprise application project that includes the enterprise module project. Figure 6.8 shows the last dialog step for generating the web service. As you can see, the EJB ArticleServiceBean is specified as the endpoint, and the name of the VI and the name of the WSD are indicated.

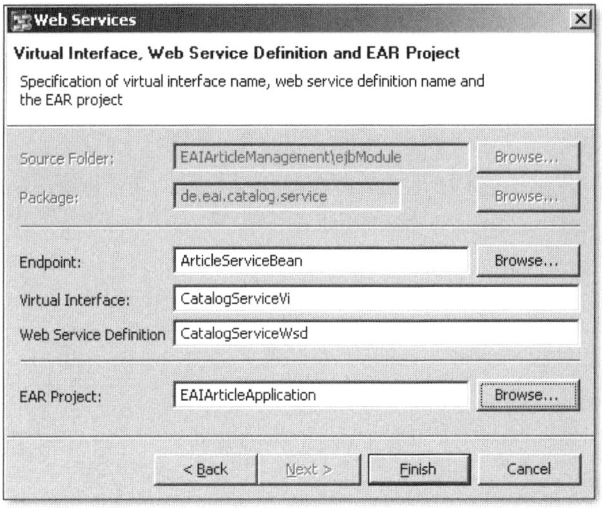

Figure 6.8 Final Dialog for the Web Service Generation

The web service implementation is concluded with the deployment of the enterprise application project. We assume that you've already configured the SAP NetWeaver Developer Studio in such a way that you can install the project on your server. Prior to the deployment, right-click the enterprise archive project to open the context menu, and select the Build entry. After you've successfully created the project, start the deployment process by selecting the Deploy button in the context menu. Enter the SDM password. Use the Web Service Navigator to test the web service after a successful deployment.

The Web Service Navigator is a Java web application that is executed on the J2EE server. The application itself can be called not only via the Internet browser using the /wsnavigator alias but also directly from the SAP NetWeaver Developer Studio. In the Developer Studio, go to the web service view from where you can access the Web Service Navigator view. Click the Refresh button so that you can find the newly installed web service in the list of installed services. After the successful refresh, expand the server node.

Web Service Navigator

Double-click the relevant web service to select it. The Web Service Navigator opens. Figure 6.9 shows the `CatalogService` web service.

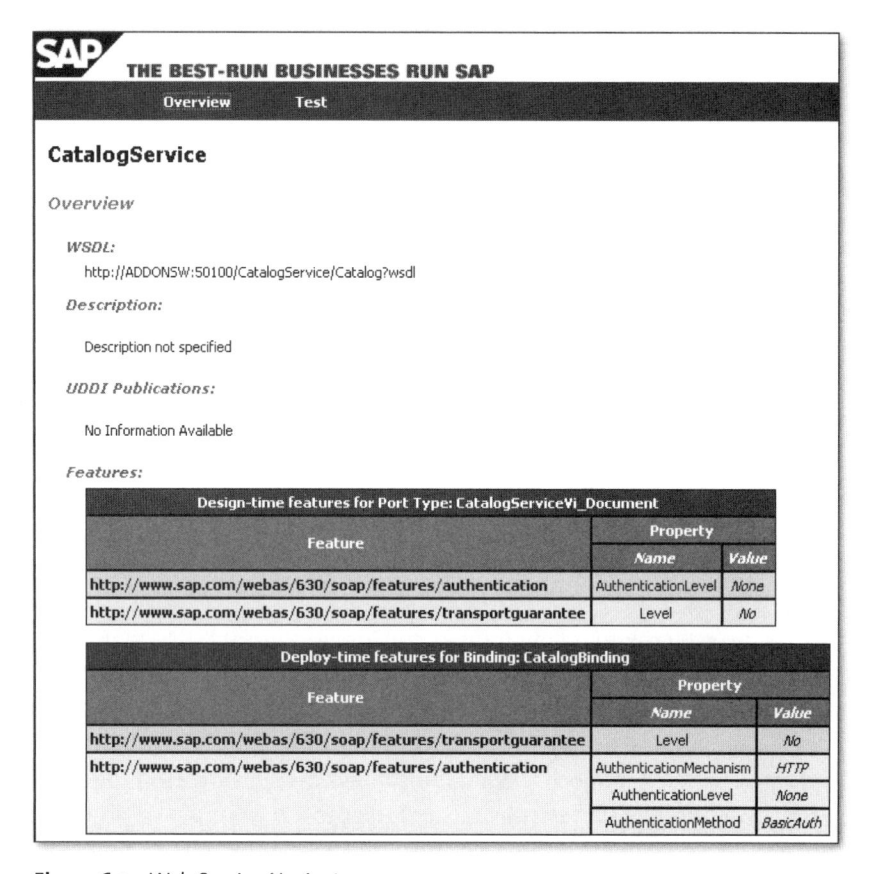

Figure 6.9 Web Service Navigator

Services of the web service
Using the Test link shown in Figure 6.9, you see an overview of the services that the web service provides. In the example presented here, you are only provided with the listArticles service. When you've followed the link, the system prompts you to enter the timeout value for the execution of the web service, and you possibly need to enter a user name and password. After you've entered all of the information and confirmed it, the web service is executed (Figure 6.10).

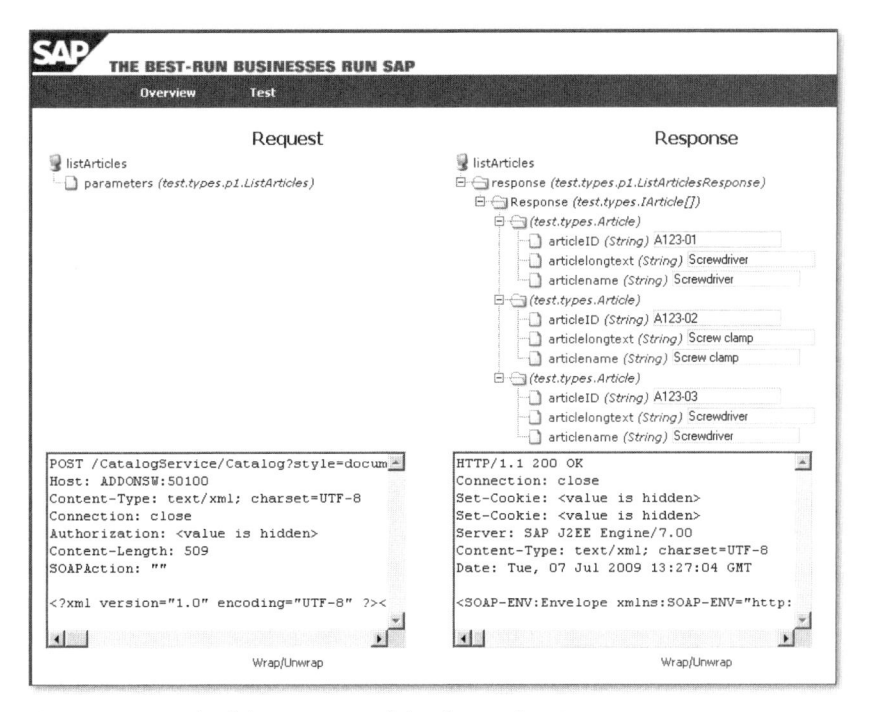

Figure 6.10 Result of the Execution of the "listArticles" Service

6.2.3 Web Service Clients

The SAP NetWeaver Developer Studio supports developers in the use of web services quite well. So not only is it very easy to generate a web service from an EJB, a Java class, or a portal service, it is also easy to consume web services quickly. In general, there are three different options to generate the web service proxy:

1. **Standalone Java proxies**
   This type of proxy generation is used if the user of the proxy classes is a standard Java application.

2. **Deployable Java proxies**
   The deployable Java proxy is required to use web services within enterprise module projects or web module projects. Here, the generated proxy classes are provided in such a way that they can be included in the J2EE server via a deployment.

Options for generating proxies

3. **Adaptive web service with Web Dynpro**
   The adaptive web service is used as a communication means in Web Dynpro for Java.

The following discusses the use of standalone Java proxies. We want to call the `ordergetlist` web service that we generated in Section 6.1.1, ABAP SOAP Web Service, and read the list of purchase orders.

Standalone Java Proxies

Implementing the Java consumer

The generation of a simple Java project is the starting point for programming a Java client. In the example presented here, the Java project has the name `JavaStandaloneWebservice`. A simple Java class called `EAIOrderClient` is added to the project. Before we can start with the implementation of the Java consumer, it is necessary to generate the proxy classes. For this purpose, you create a standalone proxy project, which you can find under FILE • NEW • PROJECT • WEBSERVICE • STANDALONE PROXY PROJECT. Enter a meaningful name for the project (e.g., EAIOrderWebservices), click Next to confirm, and configure your Java project settings. Now select the newly generated project, and choose NEW • OTHER • WEBSERVICES • STANDALONE PROXY. Then a wizard opens in which you enter the package and the name of the proxy. This specification of the package and the proxy uniquely identifies the classes and configuration files that will be generated in the subsequent steps. Because in this example we want to consume a web service that runs on the ABAP stack, we select the Local File System or URL entry under Select WSDL Source. Figure 6.11 shows the fields just described.

Now click the Next button to navigate to the next dialog. The system prompts you to enter the URL for the WSDL file. As described, you get the WSDL file of the ABAP web service using Transaction WSADMIN. Copy the URL path for the web service into the corresponding field. The path is not yet sufficient to successfully obtain the WSDL information; you still need to specify the user and the password with which the user authenticates in the SAP system.

So add the `sap-user` and `sap-password` fields to the WSDL URL. Listing 6.5 shows the URL with the previously described fields.

```
http://server:port/sap/bc/srt/rfc/sap/ZIFP_ORDER_SERVICE?sap-
client=001&sap-user=men&sap-password=passwort&wsdl=1.1
```

Listing 6.5 Path to the WSDL File

6.2 Web Services and Clients with SAP NetWeaver AS Java

Figure 6.11 Creating a Web Service Proxy

In the next dialog, the system displays an overview of the port types of the web service. Click Finish to close the dialog. When you are in the web service perspective and in the Client Explorer tab, you can view all generated files from the proxy generation process. Figure 6.12 shows an overview of the individual elements of the standalone proxy. When you expand the Proxy Classes node, you can view all parameter types of the web services as Java classes. You can see the classes that are relevant for the call under the SEIs node. There, you can find the classes that are instantiated within the consumer and perform the web service call.

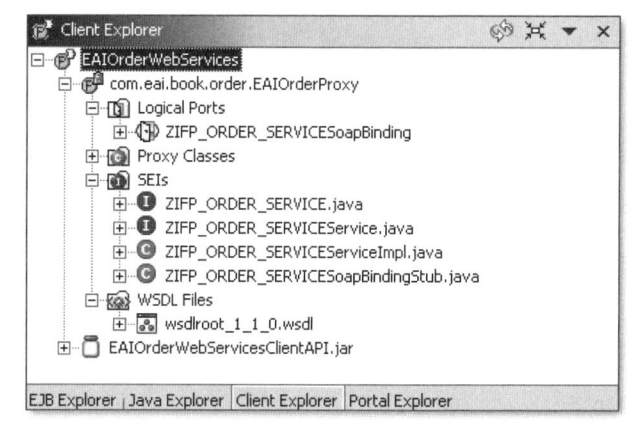

Figure 6.12 Overview of the Result of the Proxy Generation

As mentioned at the outset, the corresponding Java project for this example has the name JavaStandaloneWebservice. To ensure that the proxy classes are available in this project, we set a project reference between the Java project and the standalone proxy project. Of course, you can also add the JAR archive, which was automatically created during the proxy generation, to the class path. In addition to the pure proxy classes, you require further Java archives. Add the following libraries to the class path of your project:

- *ECLIPSE_HOME/plugins/com.sap.engine.webservices_2.0.0/lib/ webservices_lib.jar*
- *SAP_WEBSERVICES_EXT_LIBS_HOME/lib/jaxrpc-api.jar*

Creating a Java class

Conclude the project configuration, and create a new Java class with a `main` method. In the example presented here, the class has the name, `EAIOrderClient`, and the programming example in Listing 6.6 shows the programming of this class. The instantiation of the `ZIFP_ORDER_SERVICEService` class is the starting point, and you need this class to obtain the logical port of the web service by calling the `getLogicalPort` method. Later on, the web service is called through the logical port. In the run-up of the call, you must set the call parameters and two communication parameters. As you can see in the listing, the user name and the password of the web service caller is set via the `_setProperty` method. In addition, you generate a request object of the `OrderGetList` type. This class encapsulates the import parameters of the web service call. Using the `orderGetlist` method, you can ultimately call the web service and evaluate the return parameters of the service.

```
public class EAIOrderClient {
  public static void main(String[] args) {
    try {
      ZIFP_ORDER_SERVICEService orderService =
        new ZIFP_ORDER_SERVICEServiceImpl();
      ZIFP_ORDER_SERVICE lpOrderService =
        OrderService.getLogicalPort();
      lpOrderService._setProperty(
        ZIFP_ORDER_SERVICE.USERNAME_PROPERTY,
        "men");
      lpOrderService._setProperty(
        ZIFP_ORDER_SERVICE.PASSWORD_PROPERTY,
        "passwort");
      OrderGetlist requestParameters =
```

```
      new OrderGetlist();
    OrderGetlistResponse orderList =
      lpOrderService.orderGetlist(requestParameters);
    Zifporder[] orders = orderList.getTaOrders();
    for (int i = 0; i < orders.length; i++) {
      System.out.println(orders[i].getBuyer());
    }
  } catch (Exception e) {
    // handle Exceptions
  }
 }
}
```

Listing 6.6 Calling the "OrderGetList" Web Service

Deployable Java Proxies

In addition to the standalone Java proxies just described, the SAP NetWeaver Developer Studio also supports *deployable Java proxies*. Deployable proxies are used whenever the consumer of a web service is a component that is executed directly in the J2EE application server. This particularly includes *enterprise module projects* as well as *web module projects*.

The use of enterprise module projects has already been presented in the previous sections. Web module projects, however, are used when data is to be presented within a web application in the browser. So they are implemented whenever the developer decided against the use of Web Dynpro for Java as the UI framework and instead implements integration scenarios using other techniques, such as *Struts* or *Java Server Faces* (JSF) on the J2EE server. Deployable proxies are not directly instantiated in the consumer but are obtained via a JNDI call. In this context, the JNDI entry has the `java:comp/env/` prefix followed by the name of the web service.

Web module projects

In the following, we don't describe the use of this type of proxy step by step because the procedure is very similar to the standalone variant. The difference during creation is that you use a *deployable proxy project*. You can find it under the following path: FILE • NEW • PROJECT • WEBSERVICE • DEPLOYABLE PROXY PROJECT. After you've made the project settings, you create a new web service via NEW • CLIENT PROXY DEFINITION. When the proxy has been generated, you can deploy the project on the application server.

6.2.4 Adaptive Web Service with Web Dynpro

Model View Controller

Web Dynpro was defined as a UI framework for developing web interfaces. The primary focus of Web Dynpro is to standardize the interfaces and the interface components used there. The goal is to provide applications that share and reuse the UI components. For this purpose, Web Dynpro uses a stringent interpretation of the Model View Controller pattern. The model as a data definition and data container represents the central component. In this process, Web Dynpro for Java provides different model types; web services are supported in addition to Java bean and RFC models. The central question that arises for all integration options is about the configurability of the different endpoints of the communication in a three-system landscape. In comparison to the predecessors, the adaptive web service can be configured in such a way that the endpoints that were used for creating the proxy classes can be changed using a corresponding runtime configuration. For this purpose, you link the classes that were generated via the proxy generator with a *destination name*. This name references a URL via which the WSDL file can be consumed. One of the many advantages is that the endpoint is not fixed and can be changed.

6.3 SOAP Programming with Java

Now that we've discussed working with web services in the SAP environment, we turn our attention to using the tools that are common in the standard Java 6 environment. Here, we discuss both the tools and the Java classes to be used. For this purpose, we use the web service that we've generated in Section 6.2.2, Web Service Provider with J2EE. This web service was generated on the basis of an EJB and runs in SAP NetWeaver AS.

6.3.1 Java API for XML Web Services

Java API for XML web services

The support of web services under Java was not directly available for a very long time. This has changed with the Java Platform Enterprise Edition 5 (JEE 5) and Version 6 of the standard Java edition. In the JEE standard, a separate specification for working with web services was introduced; as a result, the API is now delivered within the standard edition. This API is called *Java API for XML Web Services* (JAX-WS). The

JAX-WS uses annotations that enable the provision of Java methods as web services. Moreover, the following features are available:

- Use of the *wsimport* and *wsgen* tools to generate web service proxy classes
- Simplification of the call of web services through the endpoint API and integration of a lightweight HTTP server in the *Java Development Kit* (JDK)
- Integration of *Java Architecture for XML Binding 2.0* (JAXB 2.0) as part of JDK 6 for converting XML data types into Java-conforming data types
- As already mentioned, the JAX-WS is part of the JEE-5 specification and therefore represents an innovation. Now, the web services are part of the specification for the first time, and we hope that the different application servers have found a way to ensure a very good integration of the inter-server communication. SAP implements the JEE-5 specification as of the application server of SAP NetWeaver Composition Environment 7.1 (SAP NetWeaver CE 7.1). Under SAP NetWeaver CE, the developers are supported by the SAP NetWeaver Developer Studio for the generation of both the web service consumers and the web service providers.

The web service client programming using Java Development Kit 6 starts with the generation of proxy classes. Proxy classes are generated using the *wsimport* tool. This involves a simple console application that can be configured via numerous switches. Listing 6.7 shows the switch p, which causes the system to store the generated files in the specified directory. Additionally, you can use the keep switch to specify that the generated source code files are not to be deleted after compiling. Finally, we also indicate the URL to the WSDL file.

Proxy class generation with "wsimport"

```
wsimport -p ejbservice -keep http://192.168.126.128:50100/
CatalogService/Catalog?wsdl&style=rpc
```

Listing 6.7 Generating the Web Service Proxy Classes Using the "wsimport" Tool

The generated proxy classes should be packed in a Java archive for easier handling so that the consumption of the web service is simplified later on. Unfortunately, the *wsimport* tool cannot process all specified WSDL

6.3.2 Implementing a Web Service Client

To implement a web service client, we again use Eclipse as the development tool. We generate a new project called `WSClient` and add the newly generated JAR file to the class path of our project. Additionally, we create a simple Java class and can now start with the programming of a simple Java web service client. The two central classes that were generated by the generator are called `CatalogService` and `CatalogServiceViDocument`.

As you can see in Listing 6.8, the `CatalogService` class is instantiated first. As usual, you first need to request the list of the services provided. This is done using the `getCatalogPortDocument` method, which returns an object of the `CatalogServiceViDocument` type. This ultimately involves the virtual interface of the EJB web service. Now call the `listArticles` web service method to receive a wrapper for the array of `IArticle` objects. Finally, read the list of returned articles using `getIArticle`, and write them to the console.

```
private void callWebservice() {
   CatalogService catalogService = new CatalogService();
   CatalogServiceViDocument serviceVI =
     catalogService.getCatalogPortDocument();
   BindingProvider bp = ((BindingProvider)serviceVI);
   bp.getRequestContext().put(
     BindingProvider.USERNAME_PROPERTY, "men");
   bp..getRequestContext().put(
     BindingProvider.PASSWORD_PROPERTY, "password");
   ArrayOfIArticle articleListProx =
     serviceVI.listArticles();
   List<IArticle> articleList =
     articleListProx.getIArticle();
   for (IArticle article : articleList) {
     printArticle(article);
   }
 }
 private void printArticle(IArticle article) {
   System.out.println(article.getArticleID().getValue());
   }
 }
```

Listing 6.8 Calling the Web Service with JAX-WS

6.3.3 Implementing a Web Service Provider

The provision of services via web service is implemented using annotations in Java 6 and JEE. This way, you can quickly consume simple Java classes and, for example, session beans via the SOAP protocol. Classes are selected as web service implementation using the `Webservice` annotation. You can configure the web service in more detail using the `name`, `portName`, or `endpointInterface` attributes. For example, the `endpointInterface` attribute is used if you want to export a session bean as a web service. This way, you determine which interface (remote or local) is supposed to be used as the communication interface for the web service. The `SOAPBinding` annotation can be used to specify the style of the message. Here, the two values, `Style.RPC` or `Style.Document`, are permitted.

After you've configured the class, you can select those methods in the class that is selected as the web service provider class using the `WebMethod` annotation. You can extend the annotation via the `operationName` attribute. It is used whenever the consumer of the method is supposed to be addressed via another name. The programming example in Listing 6.9 shows a simple web service.

```
@Webservice(name="EAIJava6Service")
@SOAPBinding(style = Style.RPC)
public class ArticleService {
  @WebMethod(operationName="listArticles")
  public ArrayList<IArticle> getArticles() {
    return createArticleCollection();
  }
  private ArrayList<IArticle> createArticleCollection() {
    return ArticleFactory.createArticles();
  }
}
```

Listing 6.9 Providing the "getArticles" Method as a Web Service

In addition to the annotations just described, there are further annotations, for instance, `WebParam` for describing the parameter of a service method in more detail, `WebResult` for configuring the return value, or `OneWay` for specifying an asynchronous processing of the web service call.

Additional annotations

Listing 6.10 shows the publishing of the web service that was implemented in Listing 6.9. This publishing can be done in a simple `main` method via the `Endpoint` class.

```
Endpoint endPoint =
   Endpoint.publish("http://localhost:8080/eaiService",
                    new ArticleService());
```

Listing 6.10 Publishing "ArticleService"

6.4 SOAP Programming with C#

This section discusses the consumption of web services in C# using Visual Studio 2008.

.NET and web service

As a relatively young platform for developing and executing enterprise applications, .NET provides numerous options to simply integrate applications with the .NET infrastructure. The capabilities that .NET provides in the remoting area are impressive if you compare them with the integrated functions of other platforms. Together with a programming environment such as Visual Studio, the implementation is very convenient and comfortable. Web service providers can be selected quickly via corresponding attributes, and web service consumers can be provided with the necessary proxy classes by the generator using wizards in the development tool.

.NET strategy of SAP

Some time ago, the use of the *.NET Connector* (NCO) was intended as the framework for both inbound and outbound communication with the SAP system. In the meantime, however, SAP has decided to not continue to maintain the NCO. According to the information provided in SAP Notes 856863 and 943349, the strategy is now oriented in such a way that .NET only communicates with the SAP system via web services. Not only is the NCO not further developed but also the maintenance and support of subsequent Visual Studio versions is no longer supported by SAP.

The programming of web service consumers under .NET essentially involves having Visual Studio generate proxy classes.

To consume the web services created in the SAP system, we generate a new *solution* in Visual Studio and add a new project (e.g., a console project). You can start with the generation of the proxy classes when the project is created. For this purpose, select the project you just generated, and click the Add Service Reference entry in the context menu. Visual Studio opens a dialog as illustrated in Figure 6.13. Enter the WSDL URL of your web service in the Address field. Remember: You get the WSDL URL via Transaction WSADMIN. After you've confirmed the dialog by clicking OK, Visual Studio tries to load the WSDL file. If you omitted the transfer of the `sap-user` and `sap-password` parameters into the URL, the system prompts you to enter the user name and password. After successful authentication, the WSDL file is loaded. You receive an overview of all methods that are provided in the SAP system by the service. You cannot select methods individually but must always have all methods of the service generated. As you can see in Figure 6.13, the web service only provides the `ZIFPOrderGetlist` method. Finally, enter the name of the namespace in the Namespace field under which the generated proxy classes will be created. In the example presented here, we use the name `ORDERGETLIST`. Click OK to conclude the generation of the proxy classes.

Consuming web services

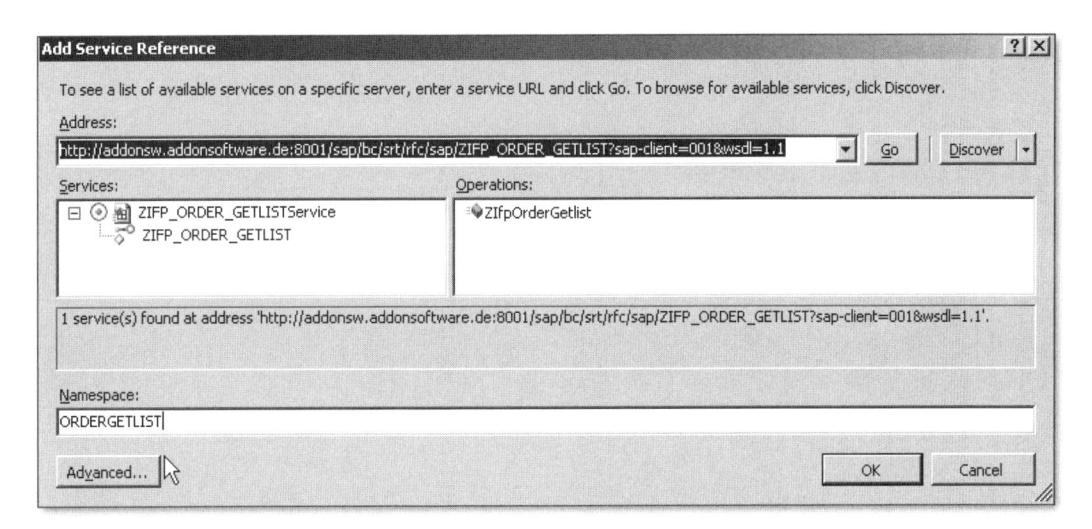

Figure 6.13 Adding a Service Reference

Implementing web services

Now, the implementation of the web service client is not too difficult. The class that has the name of web service with the "Client" addition is the central class for the call. In name assignment, all name fragments of the web service that start with a capital letter are provided with a prefixed underscore. We instantiate the class, `ZIFP_ORDER_GETLISTClient`. The next program step is to authenticate in the backend system using the user name and the password. For this purpose, you assign the user and the password via the `ClientCredentials` property.

Calling web services

Then, calling the web service is only a mere formality. We provide the `ZIfpOrderGetlist` method with the corresponding call parameters for the purchase order type and the reference number. In addition to the import parameters, the web service proxy also requests the table parameters for the purchase order headers. Because the list of purchase order headers is a table, we transfer it as reference parameters and output the result on the console. The following programming example (Listing 6.11) presents the web service client.

```
class Program
{
    static void Main(string[] args)
    {
        ORDERGETLIST.ZIFP_ORDER_GETLISTClient orderClient =
            new ORDERGETLIST.ZIFP_ORDER_GETLISTClient();
        orderClient.ClientCredentials.UserName.Password =
          "password";
        orderClient.ClientCredentials.UserName.UserName =
          "men";
        ORDERGETLIST.Zifporder[] listOfOrders =
          new ORDERGETLIST.Zifporder[100];
        orderClient.ZIfpOrderGetlist("", "100",
                                    ref listOfOrders);
        for (int i = 0; i < listOfOrders.Length; i++)
        {
            Console.WriteLine(listOfOrders[i].Buyer);
        }
    }
}
```

Listing 6.11 Web Service Consumer with C#

Unfortunately, this web service client cannot be executed yet. If you started this application now, you would receive a runtime error with a message that you do not have anonymous HTTP access to the SAP system. The message is definitely correct even if you've already assigned the user name and password using the `Username` and `Password` properties. The error can be found in the configuration file, *app.config*. This file has been provided as a configuration center in every application since .NET 2.0. The code generator for web services has added some entries to this file without any user intervention. Unfortunately, the entries are not completely correct for the use of an SAP backend system; many attributes are provided that are not supported by the SAP system and therefore result in runtime errors.

Runtime error

To ensure a successful logon to the backend system, you must add a separate binding to the *app.config* file. Self-defined bindings are added using the `customBinding` entry. As you can see in the programming example of Listing 6.12, we introduce a new binding with a freely selectable name using the `binding` entry. The concrete configuration then contains information on the SOAP version and on the type of transport. Because SAP currently supports SOAP Version 1.1 only, enter this version in the `textMessageEncoding` field, and additionally specify that you want to use HTTP as the transport protocol with basic authentication.

```
<binding>
  <customBinding>
    <binding name="ABAPBinding">
      <textMessageEncoding messageVersion="Soap11" />
      <httpTransport authenticationScheme="Basic" />
    </binding>
  </customBinding>
</bindings>
```

Listing 6.12 Configuring a "CustomBinding"

A `CustomBinding` is used to implement customer-specific configuration settings for the communication between the web service consumer and the web service producer. So the configuration just describes the implementation of technical aspects, for instance, security, for this consumer. To ensure that the `CustomBinding` is actually used at runtime, you must adapt the endpoint configuration. The `bindingConfiguration` field and the `name` attribute must be adapted to the new `CustomBinding`. Listing 6.13 shows the necessary adaptation measures.

```
<client>
  <endpoint
    address="http://ADDONSW.addonsoftware.de:8001/
       sap/bc/srt/rfc/sap/ZIFP_ORDER_GETLIST?sap-client=001"
    binding="customBinding"
    bindingConfiguration="ABAPBinding"
    contract="ORDERGETLIST.ZIFP_ORDER_GETLIST"
    name="ABAPBinding" />
</client>
```

Listing 6.13 Configuring the Use of the Binding

Finally, start the application, and the SAP system returns a list of purchase orders.

This final chapter explains how to use the Integration Repository within SAP NetWeaver Exchange Infrastructure or the Enterprise Services Repository within SAP NetWeaver Process Integration for interface development. In both repositories, you can generate proxy classes that implement the SAP NetWeaver XI or SOAP communication protocols.

7 SAP NetWeaver Process Integration

In SAP NetWeaver Process Integration (SAP NetWeaver PI), formerly SAP NetWeaver Exchange Infrastructure (SAP XI), you can describe interface metadata before you implement the software that provides these interfaces. Only after you have described the interfaces in the Enterprise Services Repository (known as the Integration Repository before SAP NetWeaver PI 7.1), do you generate server-side and client-side proxy classes for use when implementing servers and clients.

We will first describe this process for SAP NetWeaver XI 3.0 (later known as SAP NetWeaver PI 7.0), followed by a description for SAP NetWeaver PI 7.1 and SAP Composition Environment 7.1 (SAP CE 7.1). Sometimes, this approach to interface development is also known as the *outside-in* approach because the external interfaces are described before the inner workings of the application are implemented.

Outside-in approach

We will not discuss the use of adapters or the many other features of SAP NetWeaver PI here because they are already described in detail in the book *SAP Exchange Infrastructure* (SAP PRESS, 2005). Instead, we will use examples to illustrate the outside-in approach.

7.1 SAP NetWeaver Exchange Infrastructure 3.0

SAP NetWeaver Exchange Infrastructure 3.0 is a middleware server that relays messages between senders and receivers. SAP NetWeaver XI is

7 | SAP NetWeaver Process Integration

based on an SAP NetWeaver AS dual-stack system (ABAP and Java). Figure 7.1 shows the structure of SAP NetWeaver XI, which comprises the following four components:

Components

- **System Landscape Directory**
  Here, you maintain information about the software components, technical systems, and business systems in your system landscape.

- **Integration Repository**
  At design time, you save a description of all inbound and outbound interfaces for software components here, along with any mappings between these interfaces.

- **Integration Directory**
  At configuration time, you specify the receivers of incoming documents here, along with the inbound interfaces to be used when forwarding messages and the way to reach receivers.

- **Integration Server**
  This server receives incoming documents via HTTP, determines the receivers, executes the mappings, and forwards the converted document to the receivers.

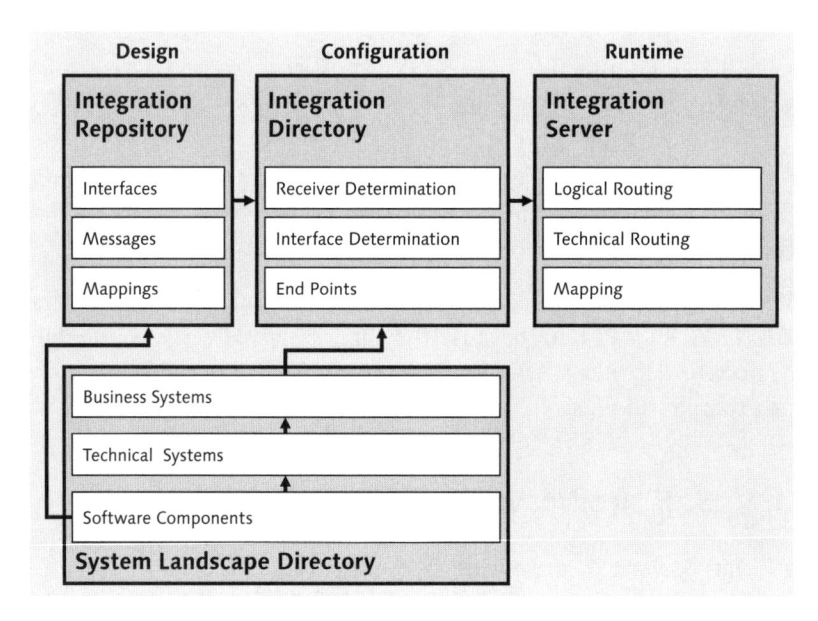

Figure 7.1 Architecture of SAP NetWeaver XI

To access the various different components in SAP NetWeaver XI, log on to your SAP NetWeaver PI system in the Integration Server client, and call Transaction SXMB_IFR, which starts the web browser. You will then see a page containing links to the individual components, as shown in Figure 7.2.

Figure 7.2 SAP NetWeaver XI Components

7.1.1 System Landscape Directory

The *System Landscape Directory* (SLD) stores information about the system and software landscape of an enterprise. This information is also used by other components on the SAP NetWeaver platform (e.g., SAP Solution Manager). Here, we will describe only those functions used by SAP NetWeaver PI.

The SLD stores information about software products, their manufacturers, and versions. SAP APO (*Advanced Planning & Optimizing*) 3.0 is just one example of the many software product versions stored in the SLD. Software product version SAP APO 3.0 corresponds to Version 3.0 of the APO product manufactured by SAP. A 1:n relationship exists between a software product and its versions.

Software products

Software components A software product version comprises one or more software component versions. Software components and their versions are maintained irrespective of the software products. Consequently, an m:n relationship exists between software product versions and software component versions. In other words, one software component version can be contained in several software product versions. For example, software component version SAP Basis 4.6D is contained in many of the SAP software product versions (SAP APO 3.0, among others).

For our scenario, we will create software product version SP_IFP 1.0 in the SLD with just one software component version SC_IFP 1.0. To start the SLD, click the link System Landscape Directory (refer to Figure 7.2). Figure 7.3 shows the initial screen displayed after you have successfully logged on to the SLD.

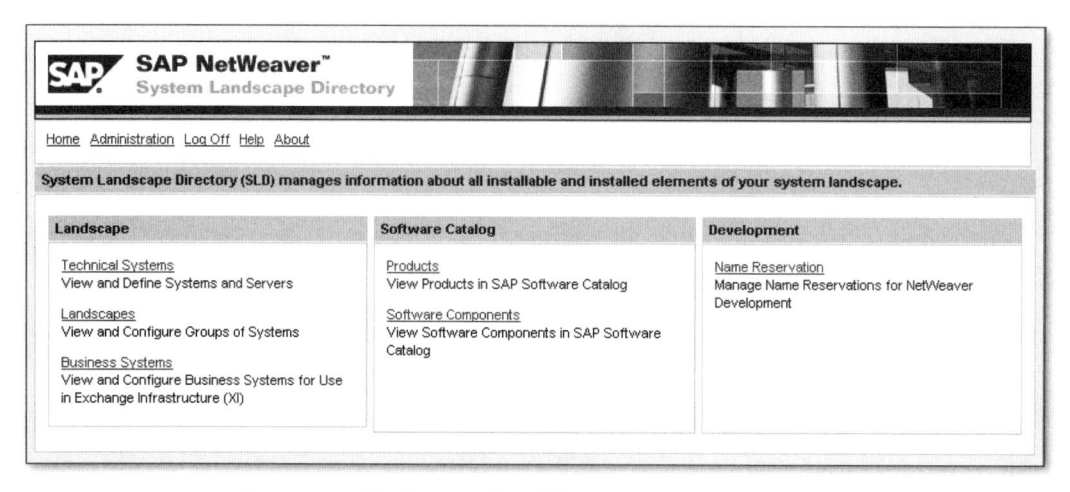

Figure 7.3 Initial Screen of the SLD

To create the software component version that you will later require in the Integration Repository, choose Products, and create a new software product version there. To do this, enter the name of the manufacturer, the name of the software product, and the version. The system will then prompt you to create a software unit and a software component version within the product version. Figure 7.4 shows the outcome of this action.

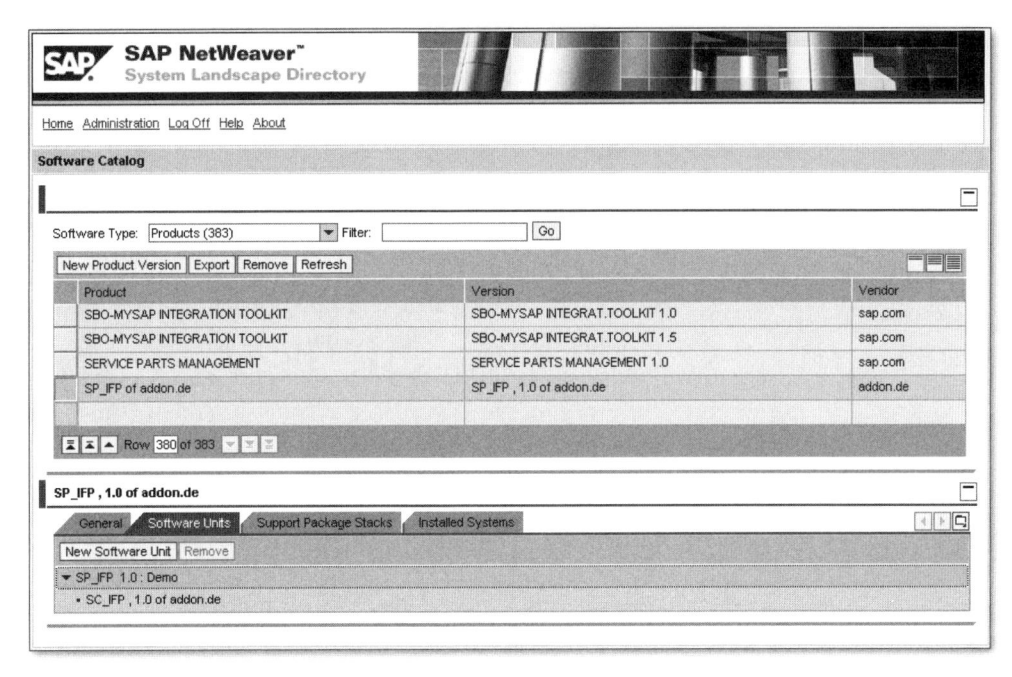

Figure 7.4 Software Product and Software Component

In addition to information about software products and components, the SLD also stores information about technical systems and business systems. The SLD recognizes five types of technical systems:

Technical systems

- **SAP NetWeaver AS ABAP**
  For these systems, the SLD stores, among other things, the name, host name, system number and release, message server, the products installed, and the clients. Exactly one business system is assigned to each client.

- **SAP NetWeaver AS Java**
  For these systems, the SLD stores, among other things, the name, instances, and the products installed. Exactly one business system is assigned to each SAP NetWeaver AS Java.

- **Standalone system**
  For these systems, the SLD stores only a technical name and the host name. It does not store the products installed. Several business systems can be assigned to a standalone system.

- **Third-party system**
  In addition to a technical name and a host name, the products installed can also be stored here. Several business systems can be assigned to a third-party system.

- **SAP NetWeaver XI**
  In our development system, we have only two technical systems: SAP NetWeaver AS ABAP and SAP NetWeaver AS Java. SAP NetWeaver XI 3.0 is installed on these two technical systems. The central Integration Server runs on client 001. In the two scenarios described in this section, we will first use client 002 as the sender and the Java server as the receiver, followed by the Java server as the sender and client 003 as the receiver. We will assign software product version SP_IFP 1.0 with software component version SC_IFP 1.0 to both of these technical systems.

Business systems are logical names used to identify the communicating servers and clients at configuration time and runtime. Several business systems can run on a technical system. For example, each client in SAP NetWeaver AS ABAP corresponds to a business system. For each business system, the SLD stores the associated technical system, an ALE name, and the assigned Integration Server.

For our scenario, we will create the following three business systems in the SLD: `MWEPublisher` (client 002), `MENDistributor` (client 003), and `IntegrationServerJava`.

7.1.2 Integration Repository

The *Integration Repository* stores information about the interface objects in software component versions. For this purpose, the software component versions from the SLD are imported at design time into the Integration Repository, and namespaces are created for the software component versions. The interface objects are then maintained below the namespaces.

For our scenario, we will import software component version SC_IFP 1.0 into the Integration Repository. To do this, we will click the link Integration Repository to start the Integration Repository (refer to Figure 7.2). This uploads a Java application (via *Java Web Start*) to the development server, which can be used to manage repository objects. Choose the menu path TOOLS • TRANSFER FROM SYSTEM LANDSCAPE DIRECTORY • IMPORT SOFTWARE COMPONENT VERSIONS to import the software component version that you created earlier in the SLD. Create the namespace `urn:addon.de:ifp` in this software component version, and then create the necessary interface objects in this namespace. The Integration Repository recognizes four types of interface objects:

- **Integration scenarios and integration processes**
  Integration scenarios document distributed business processes while integration processes coordinate them.
- **Interface objects**
  These include message interfaces, message types, and data types.
- **Mapping objects**
  These include interface mappings, message mappings, and imported archives with XSL transformation (XSLT) and Java class files.
- **Adapter objects**
  These include metadata for various different adapter types and templates for adapters, both of which are used by the Integration Directory.

Interface objects

Integration scenarios document the sequence of actions in distributed business processes. The actions are process steps that send information to other actions (via outbound interfaces) or receive information from other actions (via inbound interfaces). At configuration time, this information in the Integration Repository can be used to generate the necessary configuration objects.

Integration scenarios

Message interfaces describe the inbound and outbound interfaces for the software component version. A sender or client uses an outbound interface while a receiver or server uses an inbound interface. Interfaces can be *synchronous* or *asynchronous*.

Message interfaces

A *synchronous* interface contains references to the following three message types:

Synchronous and asynchronous interfaces

- The outgoing message (sent from the client to the server)
- The incoming message (which transports the server response to the client)

▶ The (optional) error message, which is sent to the client if an error or exception occurs

If a sender uses a synchronous interface, it does not continue its work until it receives a response from the receiver.

An *asynchronous* interface contains only one reference to a message type: the message sent from the sender to the receiver. If a sender uses an asynchronous interface, it continues its work immediately after sending the message and does not wait for a response from the receiver.

Message type and data type

Each *message type* references a data type. SAP NetWeaver XI distinguishes between ordinary message types and *fault message types*, which are only sent if an error occurs.

A *data type* describes the structure of an SAP NetWeaver XI document. This structure is created in a graphical editor and saved as an XML schema.

For our example, we will create two message interfaces. Later on, a server will implement the inbound message interface `MI_Order_Getlist_In` to return a list of purchase orders to a client. The client uses the outbound message interface `MI_Order_Getlist_Out` to send its request to the server. Both interfaces are synchronous and refer to the same request message `MT_OrderlistRequest` and the same response message `MT_OrderlistResponse`. The structure of the message `MT_OrderlistRequest` is described by the data type `DT_ORDERTYPEREF` while the structure of the message `MT_OrderlistResponse` is described by the data type `DT_ORDERLIST`, which, in turn, references the data type `DT_ORDERHEAD` in one of its components. Figure 7.5 shows the message type `MT_OrderlistResponse` in the Integration Repository. Furthermore, the navigation area on the left-hand side of this figure shows the software component version, namespace, message interfaces, message types, and data types.

Interface mapping

An *interface mapping* stores information about the mapping between outbound and inbound message interfaces, which use different message types. For this purpose, it references a mapping program for each pair of related messages. A mapping program is either a *message mapping*, an XSL transformation, or a Java class that can make the structure transformation.

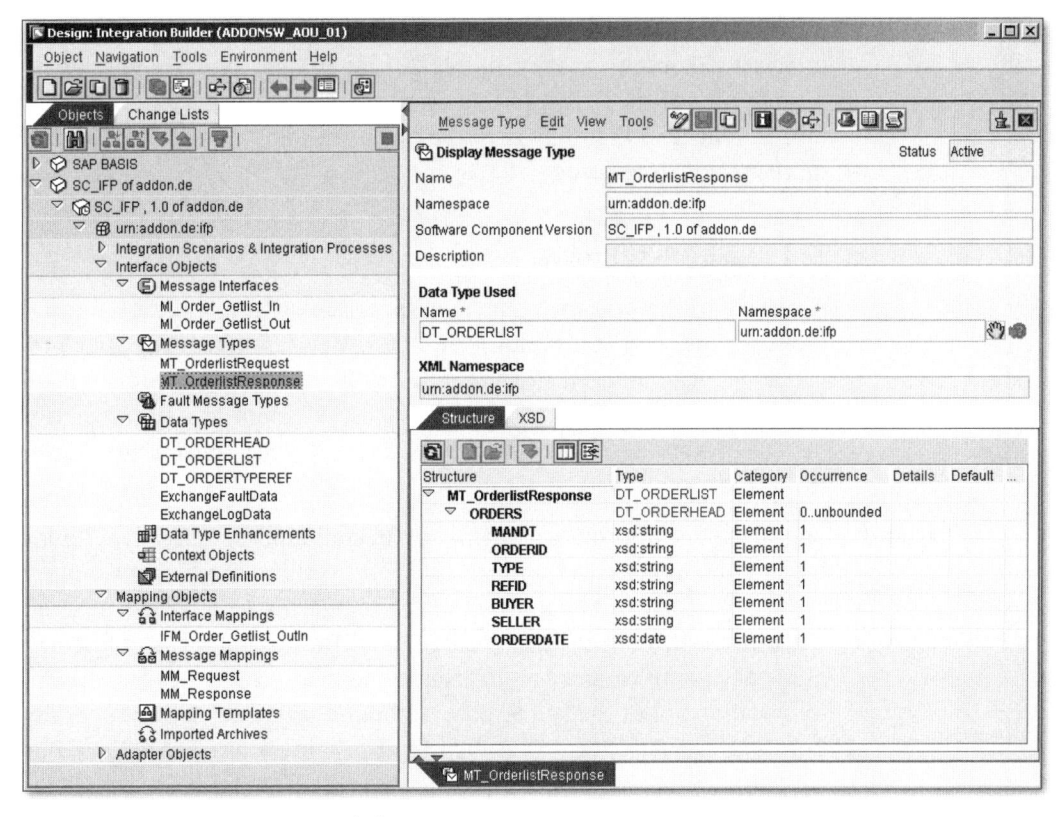

Figure 7.5 Message Type "MT_OrderlistResponse"

A *message mapping* is a transformation between two message types. The transformation is created in a graphical editor in the Interface Repository. As an alternative to message mappings, interface mappings can also use XSL transformations or Java classes (mentioned earlier). *XML Style Sheet Language for Transformations* (XSLT) is an XML-based programming language that can be used to write highly compact transformation programs. These programs are saved to files with the file extension *.xsl*. You can pack XSL files with XSL transformations or CLASS files with compiled Java classes into JAR archives and import them into the Integration Repository.

Message mapping

As you can see in Figure 7.5, we have also created an interface mapping for our scenario, along with a message mapping for the request message and a message mapping for the response message. Because the message types are identical, the message mappings referenced by this interface mapping are very simple 1:1 mappings. Even though we do not require the mappings in this simple scenario, we have nevertheless inserted them so that they exist once as placeholders and reminders for more complex scenarios.

7.1.3 ABAP XI Proxies

Adapters are helpful for connecting programs that already have interfaces. If you want to develop completely new interfaces for your programs, you can proceed as follows: In the Integration Repository, generate proxies for the programming languages ABAP and Java from message interface objects. These proxies require the local *Integration Engine* (BC-XI), which is available as of SAP Web AS 6.20.

XI SOAP — The advantage of proxies is that they can communicate directly with the Integration Server in its protocol *XI SOAP*, without the use of adapters. the SAP protocol is an extension of the standard SOAP. The client sends a two-part MIME document via HTTP POST to the server. The first part of the document contains a SOAP envelope whose SOAP header contains information about the sender, the outbound interface, the communication type (synchronous or asynchronous), and so on. The SOAP body contains a reference to the second part of the document, known as the *payload*. This payload contains the actual business document as an attachment to the SOAP envelope.

Client proxies — *Outbound* or *client proxies* are classes that provide a method for sending data. The sender instantiates the proxy class, calls this method, and transfers the data to be sent. The proxy compresses this data into XI XML documents and sends them via the local Integration Engine of SAP NetWeaver AS.

Server proxies — *Inbound* or *server proxies* are Java or ABAP object interfaces that define a method for receiving data. The developer of inbound interfaces must provide a class that implements this method. At runtime, the document that arrives via the local Integration Engine is transferred to the proxy runtime. This runtime searches for the corresponding implementing class and calls the method provided. Here, the proxy runtime transfers the data from the incoming document to the parameters for the implemented method.

Next, we will show you how to generate server and client proxies in ABAP, implement server proxies, and use client proxies.

Server Proxy

To generate a server proxy, log on to the receiving system. In our example, this is client 003 in system AOU. Transaction SPROXY contains the software component versions and the interfaces (described in these versions) for the Integration Repository in the SAP NetWeaver XI system to which your application system is assigned. Navigate to the inbound message interface MI_Order_Getlist_In. Double-click the message interface to start proxy generation. You must specify a package (e.g., ZIFP) and a prefix (e.g., ZIFP) here. All of the objects generated (ABAP interface, ABAP class, several structures, and other global data types) start with the same prefix (as chosen by you) and are assigned to the package that you have specified. The interface generated (ZIFP_II_MI_ORDER_GETLIST_IN) defines the EXECUTE_SYNCHRONOUS method with the INPUT import parameter and the OUTPUT export parameter. The class generated (ZIFP_CL_MI_ORDER_GETLIST_IN) implements the interface, but the method is still empty and must be implemented by you. Figure 7.6 shows the structure of the proxy generated.

Transaction SPROXY

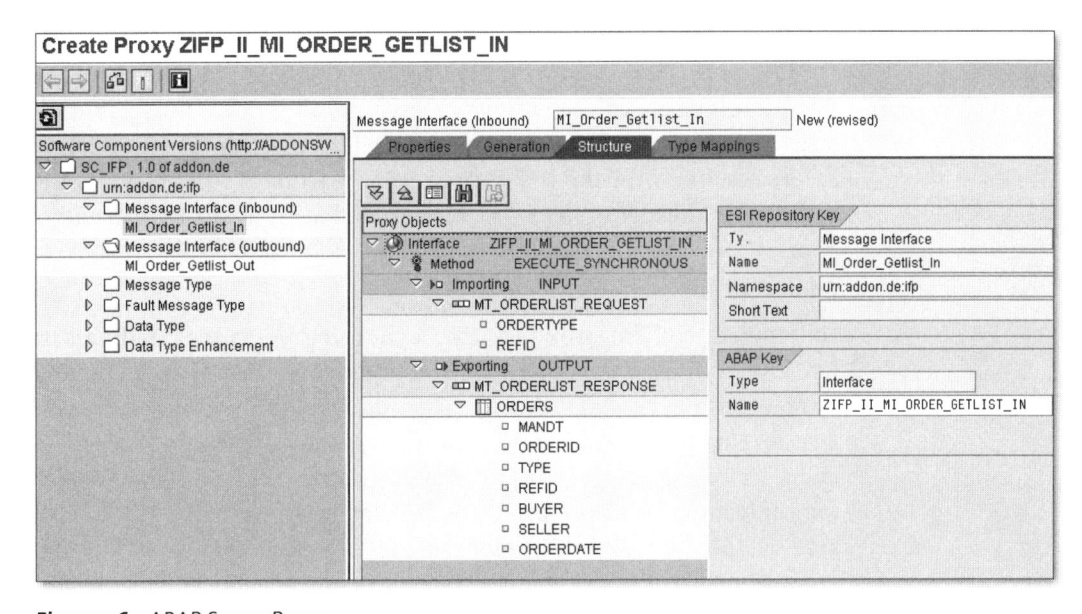

Figure 7.6 ABAP Server Proxy

357

After this preparatory work is complete, it is quite easy to implement the EXECUTE_SYNCHRONOUS method as shown in Listing 7.1. The ordertype and refid fields from the parameter input-mt_orderlist_request are easily forwarded to the function module Z_IFP_ORDER_GETLIST, the result of which is copied to the internal table output-mt_orderlist_response.

```
METHOD zifp_ii_mi_order_getlist_in~execute_synchronous.
  DATA:
    orders TYPE STANDARD TABLE OF zifporder,
    wa TYPE zifporder,
    waout TYPE zifp_dt_orderhead.
  wa-type  = input-mt_orderlist_request-ordertype.
  wa-refid = input-mt_orderlist_request-refid.
  CALL FUNCTION 'Z_IFP_ORDER_GETLIST'
    EXPORTING
      im_ordertype  = wa-type
      im_refid      = wa-refid
    TABLES
      ta_orders     = orders.
  LOOP AT orders INTO wa.
    MOVE-CORRESPONDING wa TO waout.
    APPEND waout TO output-mt_orderlist_response-orders.
  ENDLOOP.
ENDMETHOD.
```

Listing 7.1 Implementing the Server Proxy

Testing the server proxy

Even at this stage, you can test your server proxy by choosing Test Interface ([F8]). Here, the system creates an XML file, which you can still edit before sending it to the proxy runtime environment. The result is the payload and header of the SOAP request and SOAP response messages.

Client Proxy

To generate a client proxy for the sender, log on to the sending system and call Transaction SPROXY. From there, navigate to the outbound interface MI_Order_Getlist_Out. Then double-click the message interface to start proxy generation. You must specify a package (e.g., ZIFP) and a prefix (e.g., ZIFP) here. You can, of course, choose different names for the package and prefix. All of the objects generated (ABAP class, several structures, and other global data types) start with this prefix and are assigned to the package that you have specified. The class generated (ZIFP_CO_MI_ORDER_GETLIST_OUT) defines the EXECUTE_SYNCHRONOUS method with the INPUT import parameter and the OUTPUT export parameter. Even at this stage, you can test the generated proxy by choosing Test Interface ([F8]). However, the system will issue an error message because the request message has been sent to the Integration Server, but a receiver cannot be determined there. We will fully configure this scenario in Section 7.1.5, Integration Directory.

However, you can already write the simple program shown in Listing 7.2, which creates an instance of the client proxy, calls the EXECUTE_SYNCHRONOUS method, and then writes the returned purchase orders to a list.

```
REPORT   zifp_test_XI.
DATA:
  r_proxy TYPE REF TO zifp_co_mi_order_getlist_out,
  output TYPE zifp_mt_orderlist_request,
  input TYPE zifp_mt_orderlist_response,
  wa TYPE zifp_dt_orderhead.
TRY.
    CREATE OBJECT r_proxy.
  CATCH cx_ai_system_fault.
ENDTRY.
output-mt_orderlist_request-ordertype = 'SO'.
output-mt_orderlist_request-refid = '1234567890'.
TRY.
    CALL METHOD r_proxy->execute_synchronous
      EXPORTING
        output = output
      IMPORTING
        input  = input.
  CATCH cx_ai_system_fault.
  CATCH cx_ai_application_fault.
ENDTRY.
LOOP AT input-mt_orderlist_response-orders INTO wa.
  WRITE:/
    wa-orderid, wa-type, wa-refid, wa-buyer,
    wa-seller, wa-orderdate.
ENDLOOP.
```

Listing 7.2 Using the Client Proxy

7.1.4 Java XI Proxies

In SAP NetWeaver XI 3.0, you generate Java proxies directly from the Integration Repository. To do this, navigate to the message interfaces in software component version SC_IFP 1.0, and choose the menu option Java Proxy Generation from the context menu. The system will then display a dialog box prompting you to create a new archive or open an existing archive. Enter the name of a new archive, and choose Continue. In the second step, make sure that you have actually selected software component version SC_IFP 1.0, and choose Continue again. In the third step, check that you have selected the right message interfaces. For our scenario, select the two message interfaces from software component version SC_IFP 1.0, and choose Continue. In the final step, check all of your entries one last time, and choose Finish.

The result is a JAR file containing generated Java source text for your proxies. You must now compile these proxies and publish them on your SAP NetWeaver AS Java.

Server Proxy

Proxy EJB project

To implement the Java server proxy and publish it on SAP NetWeaver AS Java, create an EJB project in SAP NetWeaver Developer Studio. The project requires various libraries for compilation purposes. These libraries are listed in Table 7.1. To add these libraries to your EJB project, choose the menu path PROJECT • PROPERTIES, navigate to JAVA BUILD PATH • LIBRARIES, and choose Add External JARs to select the libraries from the directory system.

Library	Directory
aii_proxy_xirt.jar	<server>/bin/ext/com.sap.aii.proxy.xiruntime
aii_msg_runtime.jar	<server>/bin/ext/com.sap.aii.messaging.runtime
aii_utilixi_misc.jar	<server>/bin/ext/com.sap.xi.util.misc
guidgenerator.jar	<server>/bin/ext/com.sap.guid

Table 7.1 Libraries Required for Compilation Purposes

Now that you have created the project, select the *ejbModule* directory, and choose FILE • IMPORT to import the JAR file that contains the generated proxy code. In the import dialog box, select the entry ZIP File.

The imported code contains a file with the extension *.template*. This is the template for the server proxy. Double-click the file to open it in J2EE Explorer, and then save it with the extension *.java*. If you need to regenerate the proxy later, your JAVA file will not be overwritten because the generated file has the extension *.template*. Now implement the method mIOrderGetlistIn in the class as shown in Figure 7.7.

Implementing a server proxy

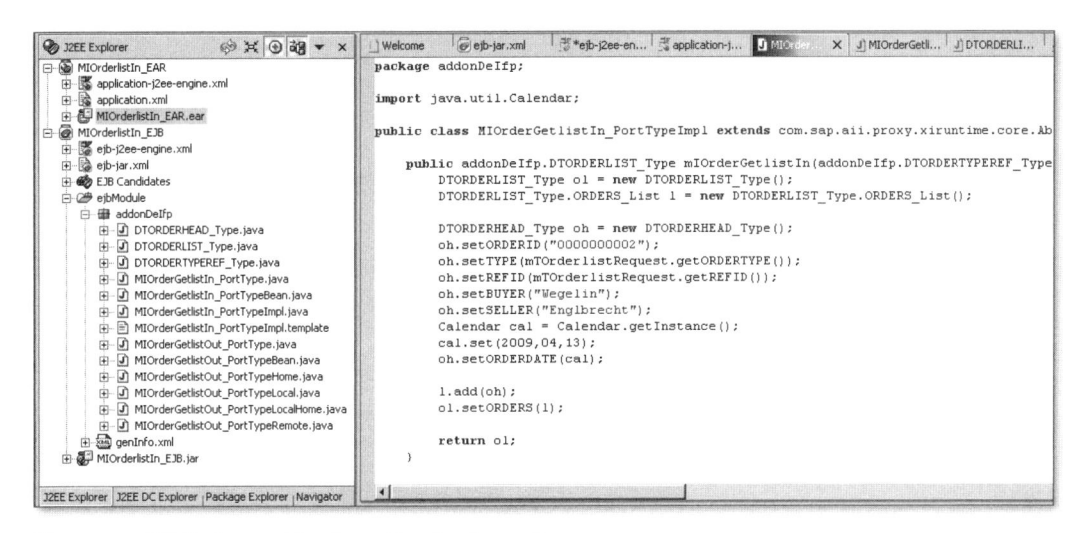

Figure 7.7 EJB Project and Implementing the Server Proxy

As a result of the comments contained in the files generated, SAP NetWeaver Developer Studio automatically recognizes those classes that follow EJB conventions and lists them under the EJB Candidates node. Unfortunately, this is not always reliable, which means that, if necessary, you must have the development environment to parse the sources again, for example, by adding a new session bean and then deleting it again. Then select the two beans MIOrderGetlistIn_PortTypeBean and MIOrderGetlistOut_PortTypeBean from the EJB Candidates node, and select the entry Add to ejb-jar.xml from the context menu.

Because the server proxy only provides an implementation but no interface classes (these are defined generically for all server proxies in the library *aii_proxy_xirt.jar*), the Developer Studio contains an error (Bean problem: No interface classes found). Switch to Package Explorer, close

Server proxy doesn't define interfaces

7 | SAP NetWeaver Process Integration

Building an EJB archive

the project in the context menu, reopen it in the context menu, and return to J2EE Explorer. This should resolve the error.

Now double-click the node ejb-j2ee-engine.xml, and assign the JNDI names "OrderGetlistIn" and "OrderGetlistOut" to the server or client proxy bean (Figure 7.8). Finally, build your EJB archive by selecting the entry Build EJB Archive from the context menu for the project in J2EE Explorer.

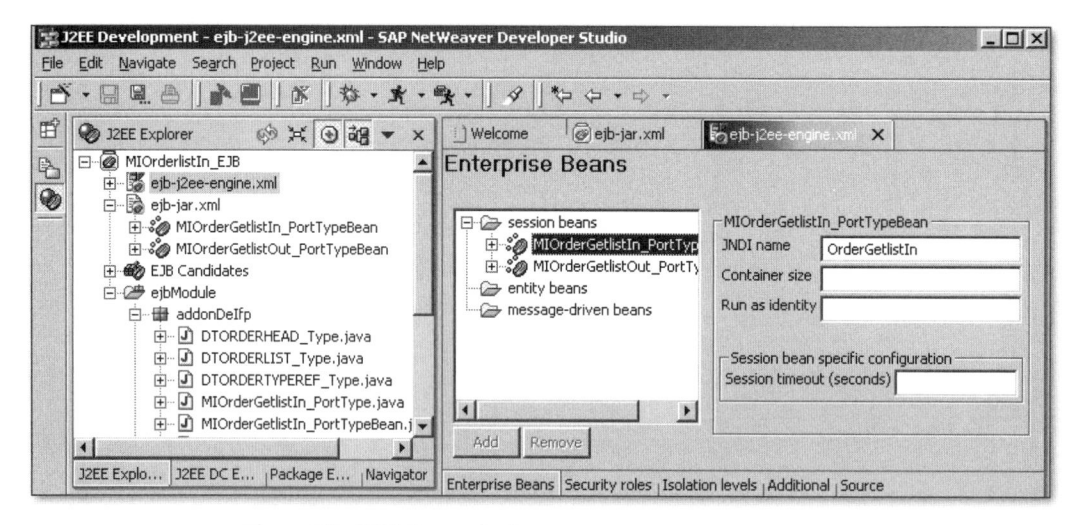

Figure 7.8 JNDI Names for Beans

You must now add this archive to an EAR project (*Enterprise Archive*), which you will then publish on SAP NetWeaver AS Java. Create a new EAR project, and reference the EJB project when creating this new EAR project. Then double-click the node application-j2ee-engine.xml to add weak references to the four libraries shown earlier in Table 7.1, as shown in Figure 7.9.

To conclude development, generate the application archive by selecting the entry Build Application Archive from the context menu for the EAR project. To publish the archive on SAP NetWeaver AS Java, choose Deploy to J2EE engine from the context menu for the EAR file that you have created.

SAP NetWeaver Exchange Infrastructure 3.0 | 7.1

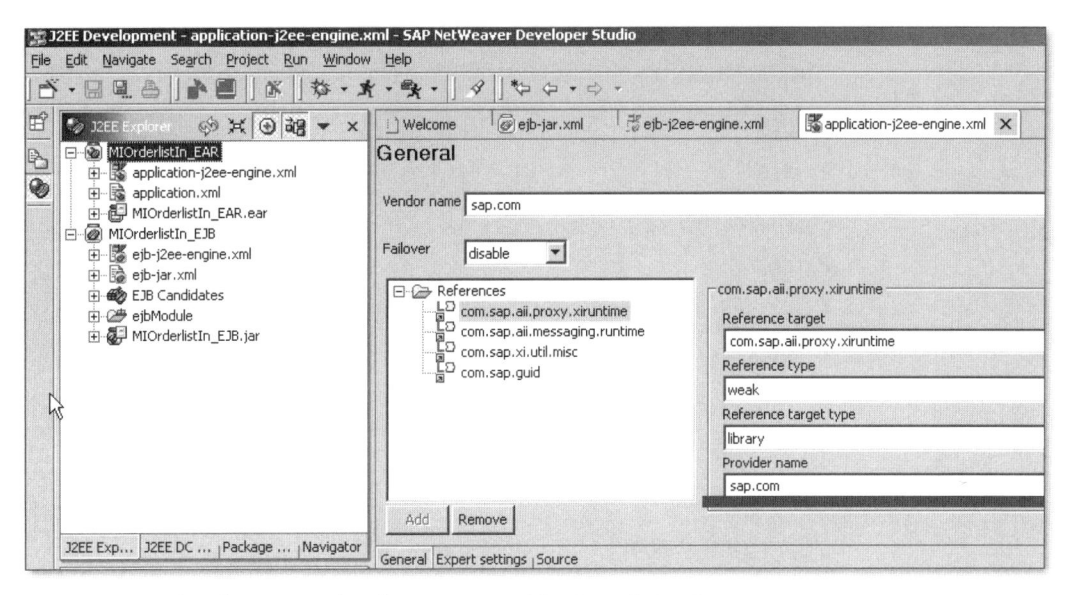

Figure 7.9 Weak References to the Libraries Required for Compilation Purposes

You now have to register the bean during proxy runtime. To do this, open a web browser, and enter the following URL:

Registration during proxy runtime

http://<server>:<port>/ProxyServer/register?ns=urn:addon.de:ifp& interface=MI_Order_Getlist_In&bean=OrderGetlistIn&method= mIOrderGetlistIn

This concludes our development of the server proxy, so we will now turn our attention to the client proxy.

Client Proxy

For the server proxy project, you also published the client proxy on SAP NetWeaver AS Java. For this proxy, you can now write a client that uses the Stateless Session Bean (SLSB) `OrderGetlistOut` to send a message to the Integration Server. Of course, you can use various technologies (J2SE, JSP, Web Dynpro) for this implementation. Here, we will show you a J2SE client.

To compile and publish the Java client proxy on SAP NetWeaver AS Java, create a Java project to which you will add the EJB archive from the server proxy project, the generated proxy classes, and the following libraries, which you gather on the server:

- *aii_adapter_xi_svc.jar*
- *aii_af_cci.jar*
- *aii_af_cpa.jar*
- *aii_af_mp.jar*
- *aii_af_ms_api.jar*
- *aii_af_ms_spi.jar*
- *aii_af_service_message_security.jar*
- *ejb20.jar*
- *exception.jar*
- *guidgenerator.jar*
- *jARM.jar*
- *jperflib.jar*
- *jta.jar*
- *log_api.jar*
- *logging.jar*
- *sapj2eeclient.jar*
- *sapni.jar*
- *sapxmltoolkit.jar*
- *aii_proxy_xirt.jar*
- *aii_msg_runtime.jar*
- *aii_utilxi_misc.jar*
- *guidgenerator.jar*

Implementing a client

Add to your project a class with a `main` method in which you will implement the client as shown in Listing 7.3.

```
public class OrderlistOut {
  public static void main(String[] args) {
    MIOrderGetlistOut_PortTypeHome queryOutHome;
    MIOrderGetlistOut_PortTypeRemote queryOutRemote;
```

```java
try{
 // Get name context
 Properties p = new Properties();
 p.put(Context.INITIAL_CONTEXT_FACTORY,
"com.sap.engine.services.jndi.InitialContextFactoryImpl"
 );
 p.put(Context.PROVIDER_URL, "addonsw:50104");
 p.put(Context.SECURITY_PRINCIPAL, "mwe");
 p.put(Context.SECURITY_CREDENTIALS, "addon99");
 Context ctx = new InitialContext(p);
 // Look up JNDI name of client proxy
 Object ref = ctx.lookup("OrderGetlistOut");
 // Get home interface
 queryOutHome = (MIOrderGetlistOut_PortTypeHome)
 PortableRemoteObject.narrow(ref,
 MIOrderGetlistOut_PortTypeHome.class);
 // Get remote interface
 queryOutRemote = queryOutHome.create();
}
catch (Exception e) {
  System.out.println("RemoteException :" +
                     e.getMessage());
  e.printStackTrace();
  return;
}
try{
  queryOutRemote.$messageSpecifier();
  DTORDERTYPEREF_Type req = new DTORDERTYPEREF_Type();
  req.setORDERTYPE("SO");
  req.setREFID("0000000000");
  DTORDERLIST_Type res =
    queryOutRemote.mIOrderGetlistOut(req);
  DTORDERLIST_Type.ORDERS_List list =
    res.get_as_listORDERS();
  for(int i=0;i<list.size();i++){
    DTORDERHEAD_Type oh = list.getORDERS(i);
    System.out.println(oh.getORDERID());
    System.out.println(oh.getTYPE());
    System.out.println(oh.getREFID());
    System.out.println(oh.getBUYER());
    System.out.println(oh.getSELLER());
    System.out.println(oh.getORDERDATE().getTime());
```

```
      }
    }
    catch (Exception e) {
      System.out.println("Exception occurred: " +
                           e.getMessage());
      e.printStackTrace();
      return;
    }
  }
}
```

Listing 7.3 Java XI Client

The client in Listing 7.3 obtains a reference to its home interface via the JNDI name of the client proxy and a reference to the remote interface via the home interface, and then calls the method via the remote interface.

7.1.5 Integration Directory

In the Integration Directory, you configure the parameters that control the Integration Server at runtime. For our scenario, these include the following objects:

Configuration scenario

- **Business system**
  Business systems are created in the SLD and imported into the Integration Directory. They identify senders and receivers.

- **Receiver channel**
  Here, you define the technical connection parameters for the receiver, including the user name and password.

- **Receiver determination**
  Here, you specify the receiver to which you want incoming documents to be forwarded. The sending business system as well as the namespace and name of the outbound interface are used to determine the receiver. In addition, you can still define filter criteria for the document content.

- **Interface determination**
  Here, you configure your chosen inbound receiver interfaces as well as interface mappings between the outbound and inbound interfaces. The sending and receiving business systems as well as the namespace

and name of the outbound interface are used to determine the inbound interfaces.

▶ **Receiver agreement**
Here, you specify the receiver channel through which you want to send the message to the receiver. A receiver agreement is determined by the sending and receiving business systems, as well as the namespace and names of the inbound and outbound interfaces.

In the integration client in your SAP NetWeaver XI system, call Transaction SXMB_IFR to start the Integration Builder, as already shown in Figure 7.2. Start the Integration Directory by clicking the link Integration Directory. To make it easier for you to later find the objects that you will create now, you can create a configuration scenario under the menu path OBJECT • NEW and assign all objects to this configuration scenario.

First, import the business systems into the Integration Directory. To do this, go to the Objects tab, and select the entry Assign Business System from the context menu for the node SERVICE WITHOUT PARTY • BUSINESS SYSTEM. Choose Continue to skip the first two screens in the dialog box. Then select the three business systems involved in both scenarios. For our development system, the three systems are `MWEPublisher`, `MENDistributor`, and `IntegrationServerJava`. Make sure that you remove the checkmark from the Create Communication Channels Automatically selection box before you choose Finish.

The next step is to create a receiver channel of the type XI for each of the three business systems (Figure 7.10). To do this, select the entry New from the context menu for the Communication Channel node below the business systems. Assign a name to the communication channel (e.g., "ProxyIn"), and choose XI as the adapter type. Make sure that you select the Receiver option field and XI 3.0 from the Message Protocol dropdown list.

Communication channel

You must also specify the host name of the receiver, the HTTP port number, and the path for the local Integration Engine. The path is */sap/xi/engine?type=receiver* for the two ABAP servers and */MessagingSystem/receive/JPR/XI* for the Java server. To conclude your configuration of the receiver channels, enter the user name, password, and client (you only require the client for the two ABAP servers).

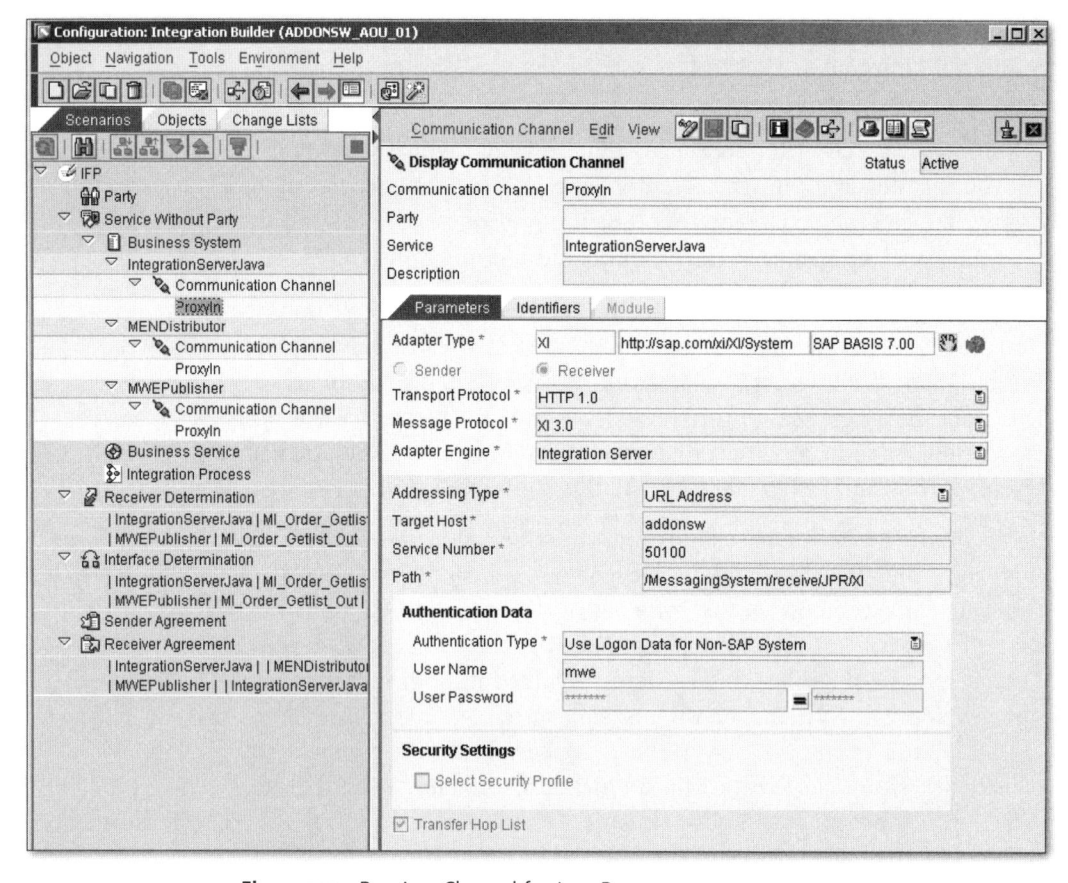

Figure 7.10 Receiver Channel for Java Proxy

> **Note**
>
> For the communication channel for the Java server, you must select the entry Use Logon Data for Non-SAP System from the Authentication Type dropdown list even though the Java server is clearly an SAP system! The entry in the dropdown list should actually be Logon Data for Non-ABAP Systems.

Receiver determination

Now create a receiver determination for each of the two scenarios (ABAP client for Java server and Java client for ABAP server). To do this, select the entry New from the context menu for the Receiver Determination node. Specify the sending Service ("MWEPublisher" or "Integration-

ServerJava"), the Interface "MI_Order_Getlist_Out", and the Namespace "urn:addon.de:ifp". Then choose Create. For the configured Receiver, specify "IntegrationServerJava" for the first scenario and "MENDistributor" for the second scenario. Figure 7.11 shows these specifications for the MWEPublisher sender and the IntegrationServerJava receiver.

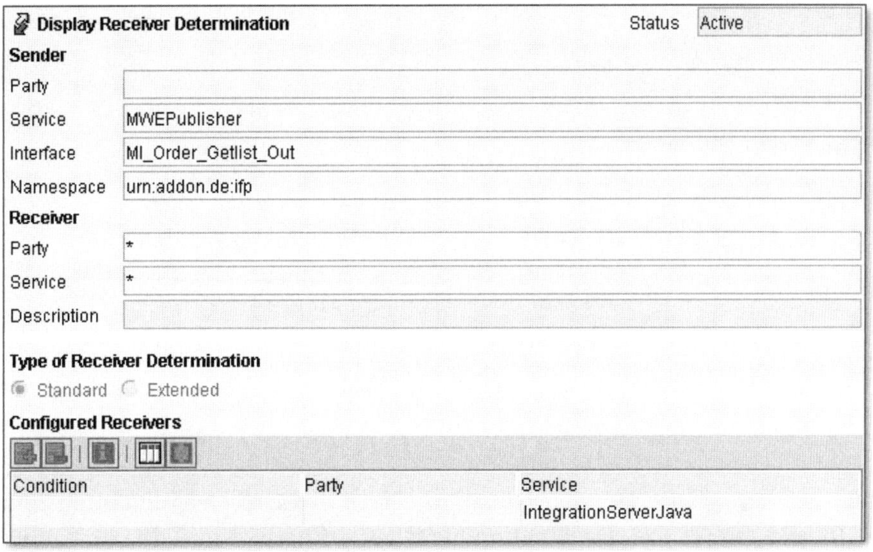

Display Receiver Determination		Status	Active
Sender			
Party			
Service	MWEPublisher		
Interface	MI_Order_Getlist_Out		
Namespace	urn:addon.de:ifp		
Receiver			
Party	*		
Service	*		
Description			

Type of Receiver Determination
⦿ Standard ○ Extended

Configured Receivers

Condition	Party	Service
		IntegrationServerJava

Figure 7.11 Receiver Determination for the "ABAP Client for Java Server" Scenario

You still have to create an interface determination and receiver agreement for both scenarios. The fastest and easiest way to do this is in the Configuration Overview for Receiver Determination area of the receiver determination that you have just created. Any configured inbound interfaces, interface mappings, and receiver channels that already exist in the Integration Directory are displayed here. However, because they have not been created yet, you will see three notes here (written in a red font) indicating that the corresponding objects do not exist yet. Now choose the menu option New Specific from the context menu for the first note. Create an interface determination into which you only have to enter the inbound interface and the interface mapping to be used (Figure 7.12).

Interface determination

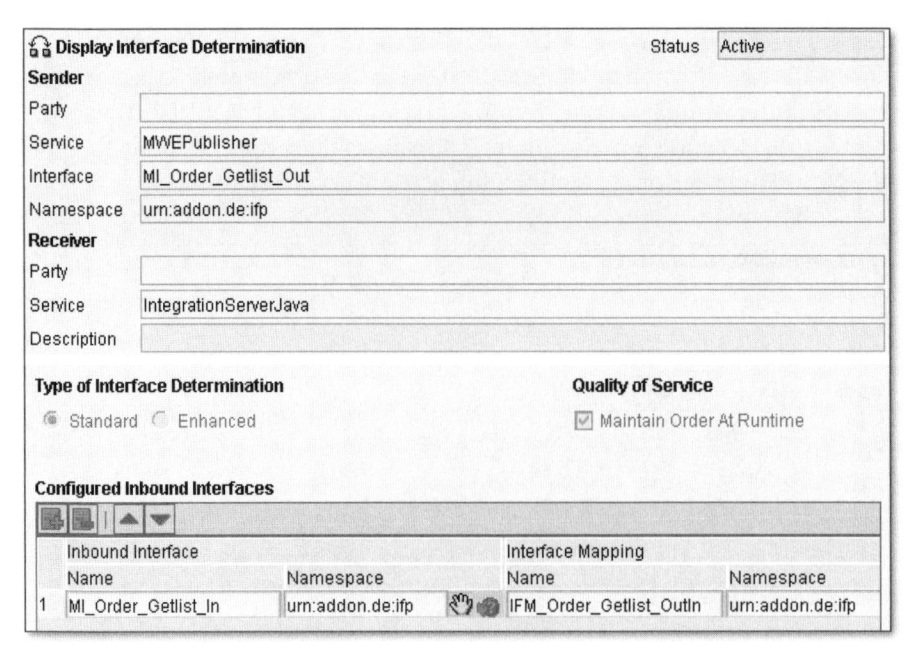

Figure 7.12 Interface Determination for the "ABAP Client for Java Server" Scenario

Receiver agreement
Save your interface determination, return to the receiver determination, and refresh the configuration overview for the receiver determination. You will now see the inbound interface and interface mapping that you have just configured. Now choose the menu option New Specific from the context menu for the remaining red note. Create a receiver agreement into which you only have to enter the receiver channel (Figure 7.13).

Proceed in the same way for the second scenario (Java client for ABAP server). Now save all of your objects, and activate the change list. You are now ready to start the test.

Log on to the sending ABAP client (002, business system MWEPublisher), and start the report shown earlier in Listing 7.2. The request is initially forwarded to the central Integration Server and, from there, to the inbound Java proxy shown in Figure 7.7. For the second scenario, start the Java program shown earlier in Listing 7.3. Once again, the request is initially forwarded to the central Integration Server and, from there, to the inbound ABAP proxy shown previously in Listing 7.1.

Figure 7.13 Receiver Agreement for the "ABAP Client for Java Server" Scenario

In the Integration Server client, you can now use Transaction SXMB_MONITOR to track the individual processing steps within the pipeline in detail. Figure 7.14 shows an extract of successful and unsuccessful messages on our development system. You can double-click any entry to display the corresponding message and to view detailed information about the individual processing steps in the Integration Server.

Monitoring

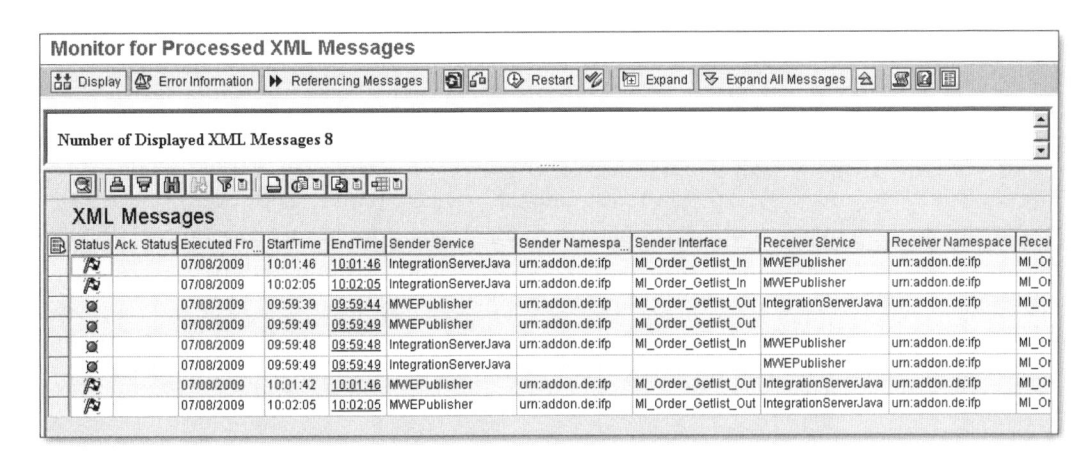

Figure 7.14 Message Monitor

7.2 SAP NetWeaver Process Integration 7.1

SAP NetWeaver Process Integration 7.1 (SAP NetWeaver PI 7.1) is considerably different from SAP NetWeaver XI 3.0 or SAP NetWeaver PI 7.0. The most important changes are as follows:

- The Integration Repository is now called the *Enterprise Services Repository* (ES Repository) because it primarily describes the service interfaces of Enterprise Services.

- Message interfaces no longer exist. They have been replaced with service interfaces, which can provide several operations.

- The proxies generated from service interfaces are now SOAP proxies and no longer SAP NetWeaver XI proxies.

- With *SAP NetWeaver Composition Environment 7.1* (SAP NetWeaver CE 7.1), the ES Repository is now used by another component (in addition to SAP NetWeaver PI).

In this section, we will use two examples (one in ABAP and one in Java) to illustrate some of these new features.

7.2.1 Service Interfaces

To enable you to implement both examples, first go to the SLD and create software product version SP_IFP 2.0 with the software unit Server Unit and software component version SWC_IFP 2.0. Import this software component version into the repository.

Data types and message types

In the next step, create the necessary data types for the messages that are to replace the operations provided by our service interfaces. These include data types for the purchase order header, purchase order item, purchase order, purchase order number, and purchase order reference. As message types, we now require separate request and response messages for each operation. Figure 7.15 shows sample message type MT_ORDER-CREATE_REQ. This message type references the data type DT_IFP_ORDER with the two components ORDERHEAD and ORDERPOS, which, in turn, reference the more simple data types DT_IFP_ORDERHEAD and DT_IFP_ORDERPOS. Additional data types and message types are listed on the left-hand side of Figure 7.15.

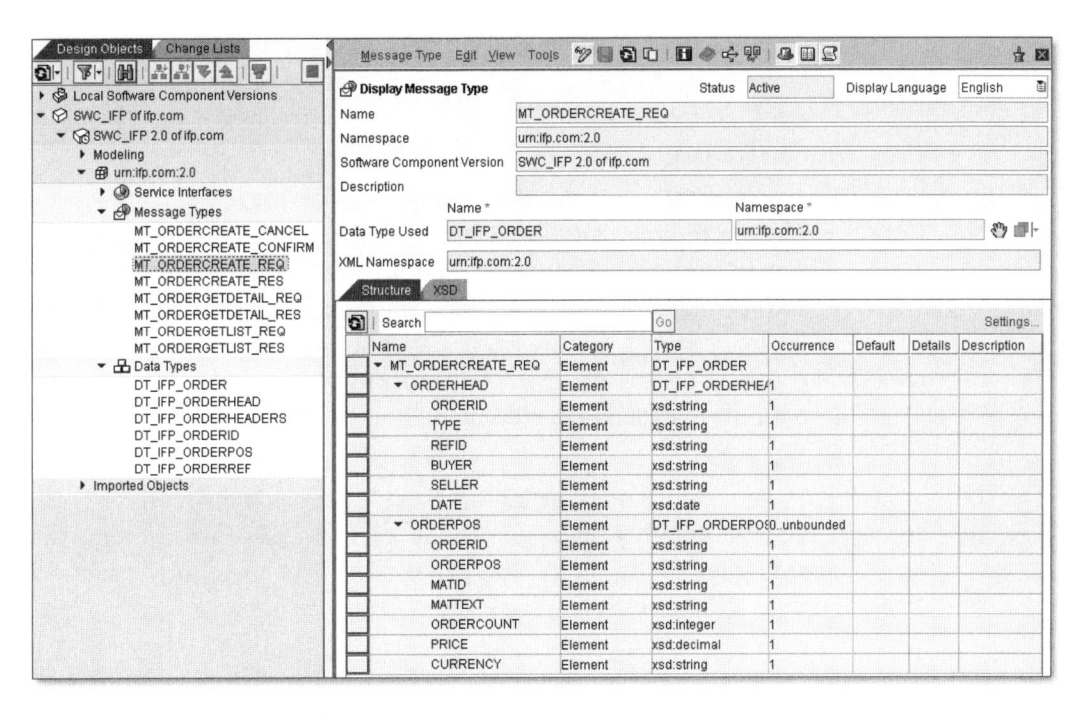

Figure 7.15 Message Type in ES Repository

To conclude your work in the ES Repository, create the required service interfaces. As is the case with a message interface in the Integration Repository, a service interface of a sender (client) belongs to the category *outbound,* and a service interface of a receiver (server) belongs to the category *inbound*. Unlike message interfaces, however, service interfaces can provide not only one but several operations. Each individual operation has the mode *synchronous* or *asynchronous*.

Service interfaces

Another new feature are the interface patterns to which a service interface can be assigned. There are four interface patterns as follows:

Interface patterns

- **Stateless**

    The operations on these interfaces do not leave a state on the server that can be used by other operations on the same interface when calling the same client in the future. This is by far the most important interface pattern.

▶ **Stateless (SAP NetWeaver XI 3.0-compatible)**
These interfaces behave in the same way as the former message interfaces. They have exactly one operation, which has the same name as the interface.

▶ **Tentative Update & Confirm/Compensate (TU&C/C)**
These interfaces comprise four operation types. Synchronous *tentative update operations* tentatively create or change data on the server. An asynchronous *confirm operation* confirms and commits the changes, while an asynchronous *compensate operation* rejects and undoes the changes. Finally, there are synchronous *standard operations* that do not change data on the server.

▶ **Stateful**
The operations on these interfaces leave a state on the server that can be used by other operations on the same interface when calling the same client in the future. This pattern is only required for very special technical purposes.

For our example, create the two service interfaces SI_IFP_ORDER_IN and SI_IFP_ORDER_OUT with the two operations GetList and GetDetail. Figure 7.16 shows the GetList operation for the interface SI_IFP_ORDER_IN. The message type for the request message is MT_ORDERLIST_REQ, and the message type for the response message is MT_ORDERLIST_RES. For both interfaces, we will generate server and client proxies in ABAP and Java, and then use these proxies to develop web services (providers) and web service clients (consumers).

7.2.2 ABAP SOAP Proxies

The service interface SI_IFP_ODERCREATE_IN, provided as an example in this section, illustrates the Tentative Update & Confirm/Compensate pattern (Figure 7.17). It has the synchronous tentative update operation Create, which only tentatively creates a purchase order. This purchase order is only confirmed when the confirm operation Confirm is used. If the client that used the tentative update operation to create a tentative purchase order now wants to cancel this order, it can use the compensate operation Cancel.

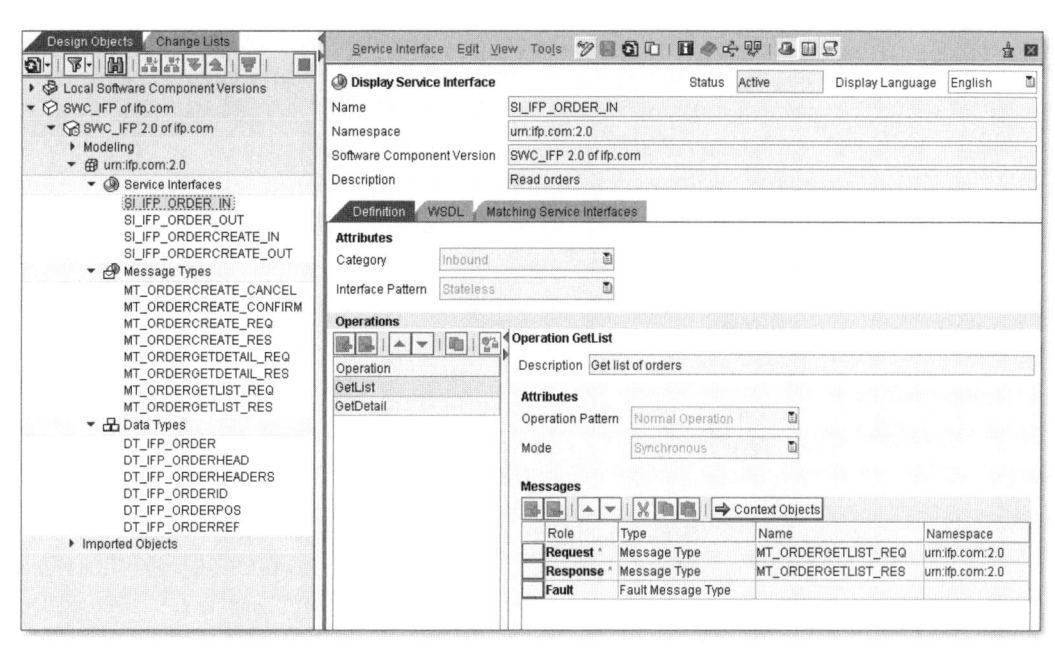

Figure 7.16 Service Interface with Two Operations

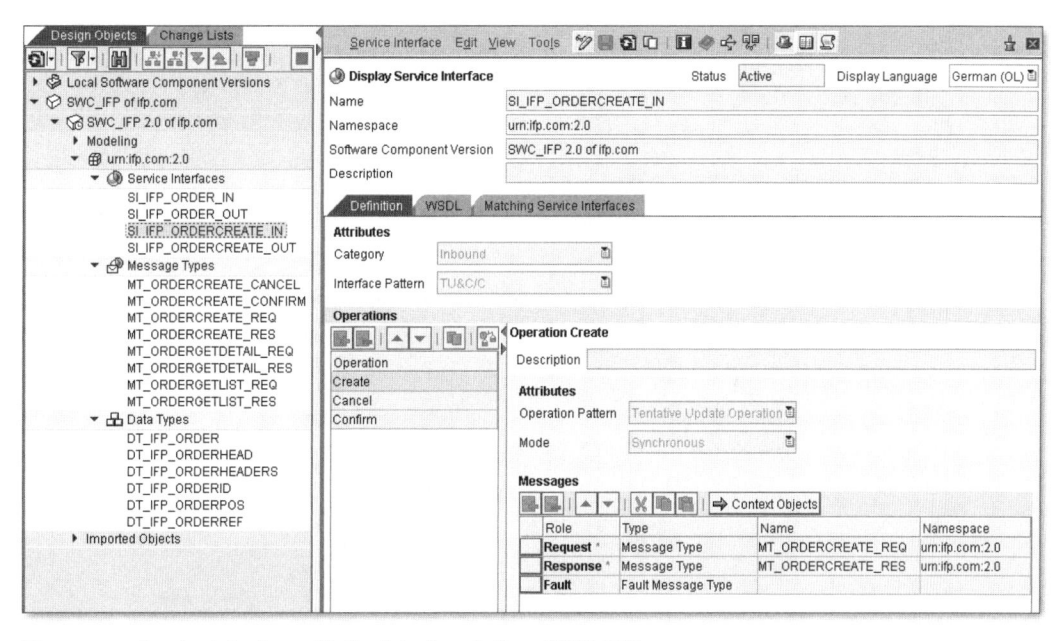

Figure 7.17 Service Interface with the Interface Pattern "TU&C/C"

7 | SAP NetWeaver Process Integration

Generating proxies In this section, we will generate a server or provider proxy for the inbound service interface `SI_IFP_ORDER_IN` and a client or consumer proxy for the outbound service interface `SI_IFP_ORDER_OUT`. We will write an ABAP report that the consumer proxy will use to call the web service implemented by the provider proxy. You can either create the proxies in Transaction SPROXY (as before) or you can use Transaction SE80 (Object Navigator).

Providers

Log on to the receiving system, and create a new package in Transaction SE80 (Object Navigator). In this package, create a new object of the type *Enterprise Service*. This will start a wizard that will guide you through the steps associated with generating a provider proxy.

In the first step after the overview, choose the option Object Type Service Provider. In the next step, choose the option ESR Service Interface (Outside-in). Then select the ES Repository interface `SI_IFP_ORDER_IN`, and specify a package, prefix, and workbench order. Choose Finish, and activate your proxy. Figure 7.18 shows the result.

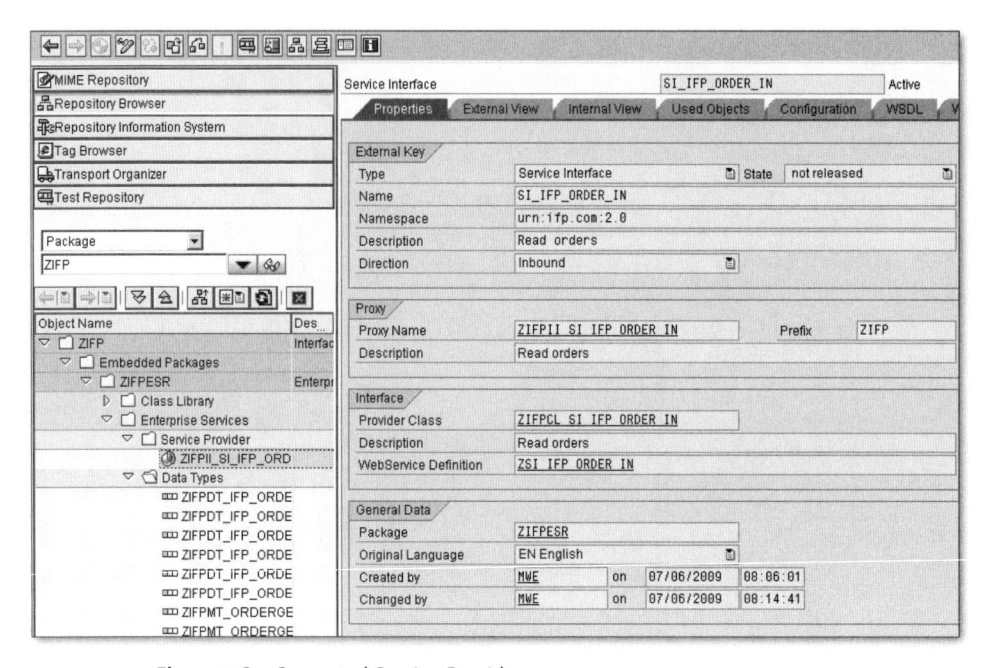

Figure 7.18 Generated Service Provider

A server proxy called `ZIFPII_SI_IFP_ORDER_IN` has been generated and is implemented by the class `ZIFPCL_SI_IFP_ORDER_IN`. The web service definition `ZSI_IFP_ORDER_IN` has also been created. Because you have defined two methods in the service interface, the proxy generated also has two methods (Figure 7.19) called `GET_DETAIL` and `GET_LIST`. Each of these methods has an `INPUT` import parameter and an `OUTPUT` export parameter. The corresponding ABAP structures have been generated for the parameters (in accordance with the request and response message types).

Server proxy

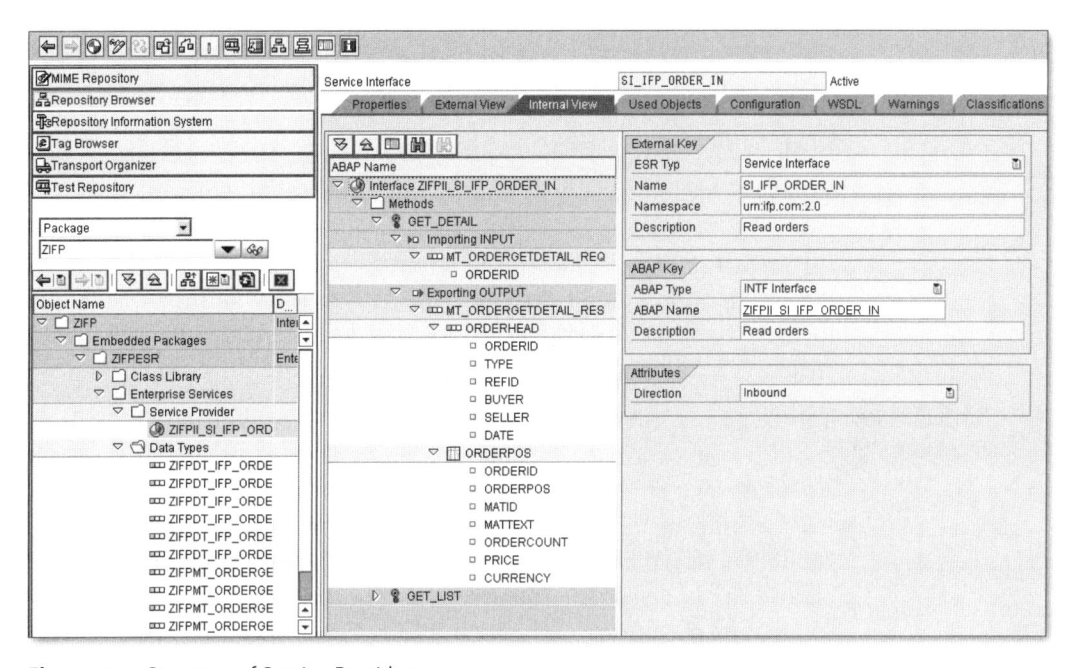

Figure 7.19 Structure of Service Provider

Of course, you have to provide the code for both methods yourself. Listing 7.4 shows the sample method `GET_LIST`.

```
METHOD zifpii_si_ifp_order_in~get_list.
  DATA:
    orders TYPE STANDARD TABLE OF zifporder,
    wa_orders TYPE zifporder,
    wa TYPE zifpdt_ifp_orderhead,
    ordertype TYPE zifpordertype,
    refid TYPE zifprefid.
```

```
            ordertype = input-mt_ordergetlist_req-type.
            refid     = input-mt_ordergetlist_req-refid.
            IF ordertype IS INITIAL.
              ordertype = 'SO'.
            ENDIF.
            CALL FUNCTION 'Z_IFP_ORDER_GETLIST'
              EXPORTING
                im_ordertype = ordertype
                im_refid     = refid
              TABLES
                ta_orders    = orders.
            LOOP AT orders INTO wa_orders.
              MOVE-CORRESPONDING wa_orders TO wa.
              APPEND wa TO output-mt_ordergetlist_res-orderheader.
            ENDLOOP.
          ENDMETHOD.
```

Listing 7.4 Implementing the Method "get_list" in the Service Provider Class

In the final step, you must use Transaction SOAMANAGER to create a web service and a binding, so that you can also use your proxy. Note that the configuration that you make in Transaction SOAMANAGER is client-specific. You must therefore start the transaction in the right client.

Transaction SOAMANAGER — Transaction SOAMANGER starts a web browser with an ABAP Web Dynpro application. In this application, navigate to the area BUSINESS ADMINISTRATION • WEB SERVICE ADMINISTRATION. Here, select the entry Service from the Search By dropdown list, and enter the search pattern "SI_IFP*". Start the search, select your proxy from the search results, and choose Apply Selection. You can now choose Create Service to create a service and a binding, as shown in Figure 7.20.

As soon as you have created the service, select the authentication type User ID/Password, and save the service. If you navigate from the details of the service definition ZSI_IFP_ORDER_IN back to the overview, you can test your web service by clicking the relevant link to open the Web Service Navigator for the binding that you have just created.

Executing a service — Select the GetList operation, enter the request parameters, and choose Execute. Figure 7.21 shows the result of executing your service in Web Service Navigator.

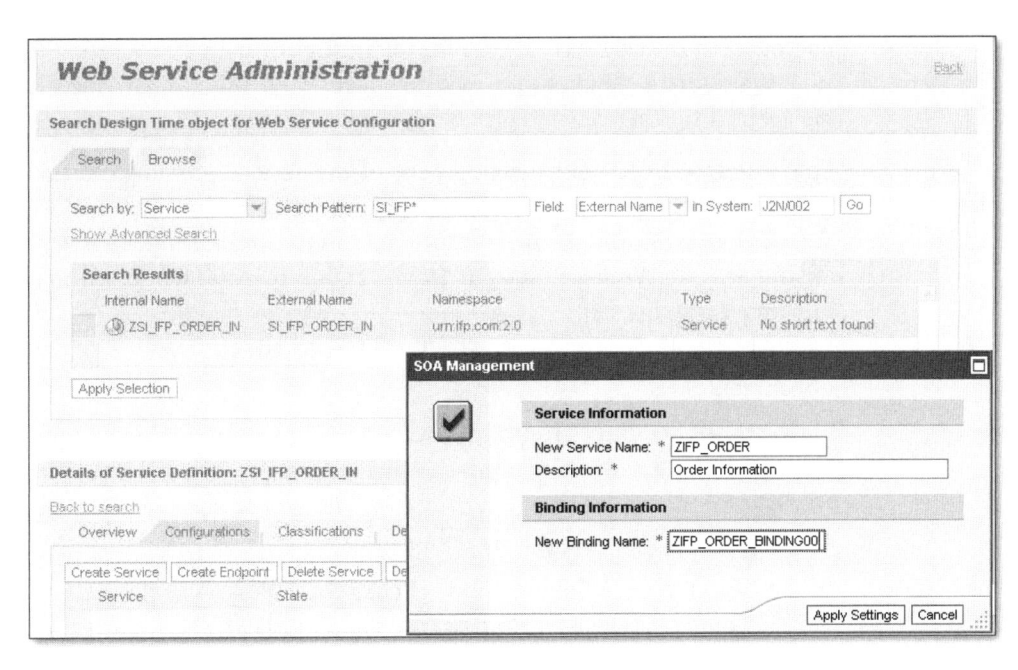

Figure 7.20 Creating a Web Service in Transaction SOAMANAGER

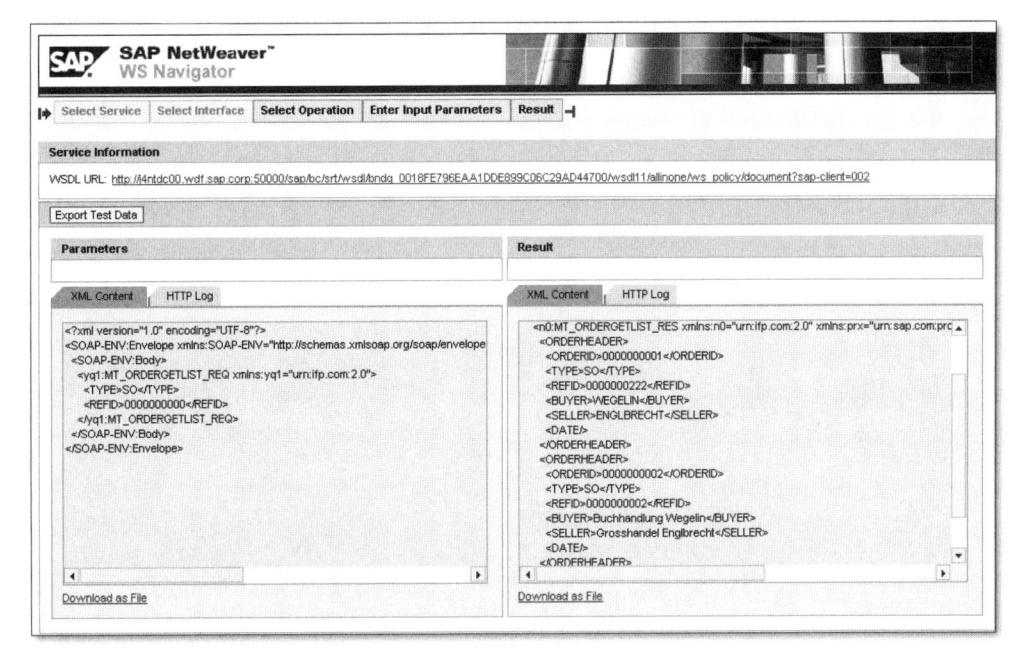

Figure 7.21 Testing the Web Service in Web Service Navigator

The detailed overview of the service definition contains a URL for the WSDL file for the service. You will need this URL if you later create a logical port for the consumer.

This test concludes your development of the service provider, so you can now turn your attention to the consumer. Before that, you can use Transaction WSPUBLISH to publish your service in the service registry of your SAP NetWeaver PI system. However, our scenario works without implementing this step.

Consumers

Log on to the sending system, and create a new object of the type Enterprise Service in a development package in Transaction SE80 (Object Navigator). This will start a wizard that will guide you through the steps associated with generating a consumer proxy.

Service consumers In the first step after the overview, choose the option Object Type Service Consumer. In the next step, choose the option ESR Service Interface (Outside-in). Then select the ES Repository interface SI_IFP_ORDER_OUT, and specify a package, prefix, and workbench order. Choose Finish, and activate your proxy. Figure 7.22 shows the result. A proxy called ZIFPCO_SI_IFP_ORDER_OUT has been created with two operations.

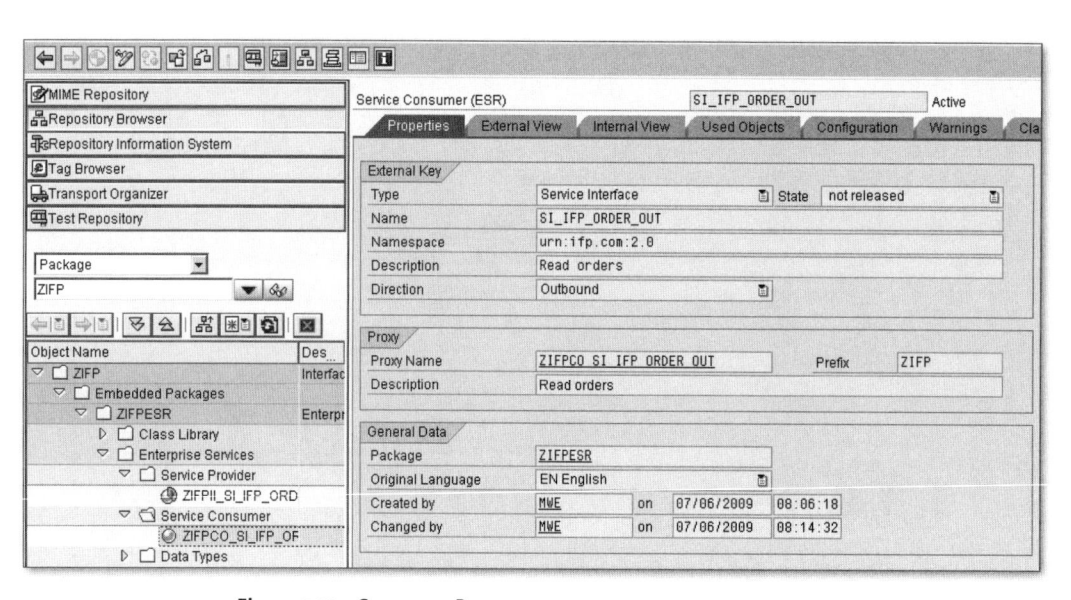

Figure 7.22 Consumer Proxy

To enable you to use this proxy from an ABAP program, you still have to create a logical port in Transaction SOAMANAGER. In SOAMANGAGER, navigate to the area BUSINESS ADMINISTRATION • WEB SERVICE ADMINISTRATION. Here, select the entry Consumer Proxy from the Search By dropdown list, and enter the search pattern SI_IFP*. Start the search, select your proxy from the search results, and choose Apply Selection. You can now choose Create Logical Port to create a logical port that references the service provider. Here, you must specify the URL for the WSDL file for the service as well as a user name and password for WSDL access (Figure 7.23).

Logical port

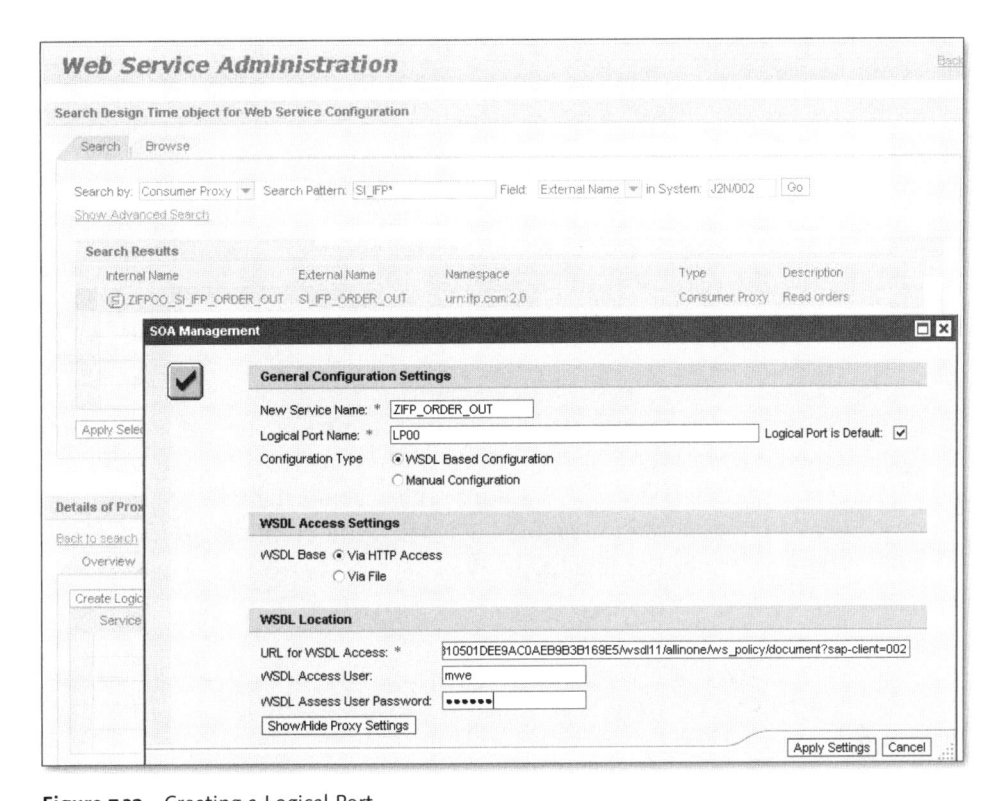

Figure 7.23 Creating a Logical Port

As soon as you have created the logical port, you must specify the user name and password for actual web service access and then save your port. You may quickly forget this particular piece of information, so we will show it again in Figure 7.24.

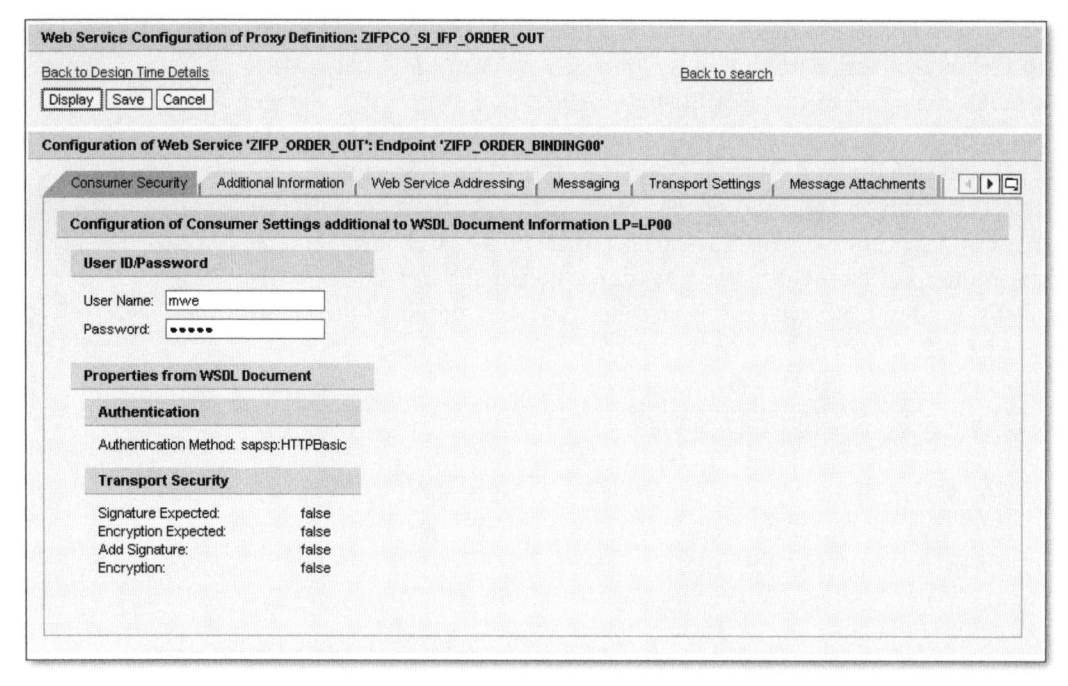

Figure 7.24 Specifying a User Name and Password in the Logical Port for Web Service Access

As soon as you have created the logical port, you can test your consumer proxy in Transaction SE80. However, you can also write the small test report shown in Listing 7.5. In this report, you instantiate the consumer proxy and then call the method `get_list`. You output the returned purchase order headers in a loop.

```
REPORT  zifp_test_esr.
DATA:
  rp TYPE REF TO zifpco_si_ifp_order_out,
  input TYPE zifpmt_ordergetlist_res,
  output TYPE zifpmt_ordergetlist_req,
  wa TYPE zifpdt_ifp_orderhead.
START-OF-SELECTION.
  TRY.
      CREATE OBJECT rp
        EXPORTING
          logical_port_name = 'LP00'.
```

```
      CATCH cx_ai_system_fault.
    ENDTRY.
    TRY.
        CALL METHOD rp->get_list
          EXPORTING
            output = output
          IMPORTING
            input  = input.
        LOOP AT input-mt_ordergetlist_res-orderheader INTO wa.
          WRITE:/
            wa-orderid,
            wa-type,
            wa-refid,
            wa-buyer,
            wa-seller,
            wa-date.
        ENDLOOP.
      CATCH cx_ai_system_fault.
      CATCH cx_ai_application_fault.
    ENDTRY.
```

Listing 7.5 Web Service Consumer in ABAP

This concludes our work with the ABAP scenario, so we will now turn our attention to the Java scenario.

7.2.3 Java SOAP Proxies

In this final section, we will develop a service provider and service consumer in Java for the same service interfaces used in the previous section. For this purpose, we will use SAP NetWeaver Developer Studio in SAP NetWeaver CE 7.1.

Providers

Start SAP NetWeaver Developer Studio in SAP CE 7.1, and create a new EJB project called "IFPOrders_EJB". At the same time, add this project to an EAR project called "IFPOrders_EAR", as shown in Figure 7.25. Choose Next, and remove the checkmark from the Create an EJB Client JAR selection box. Then choose Finish to create the project.

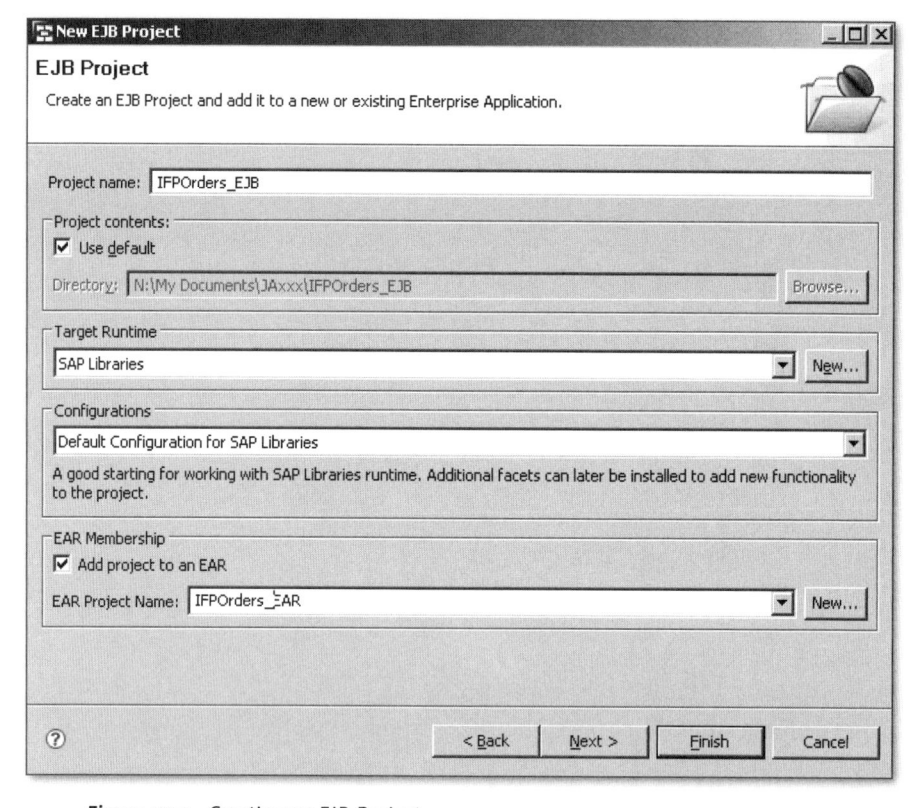

Figure 7.25 Creating an EJB Project

Enterprise Service Browser — Choose the menu path WINDOW • PREFERENCES to open the dialog box for user settings, and follow the menu path WEB SERVICES • ENTERPRISE SERVICE BROWSER. Here, enter the connection data for your ES Repository. Then choose the menu path WINDOW • SHOW VIEW • OTHER to open the dialog box for the views, and select the view WEB SERVICES • ENTERPRISE SERVICE BROWSER.

The upper-right section of the view contains a plug-and-socket connection icon, which you can use to establish a connection to the ES Repository. Enter your user name and password for the ES Repository here. Figure 7.26 shows the Enterprise Service Browser in SAP NetWeaver Developer Studio.

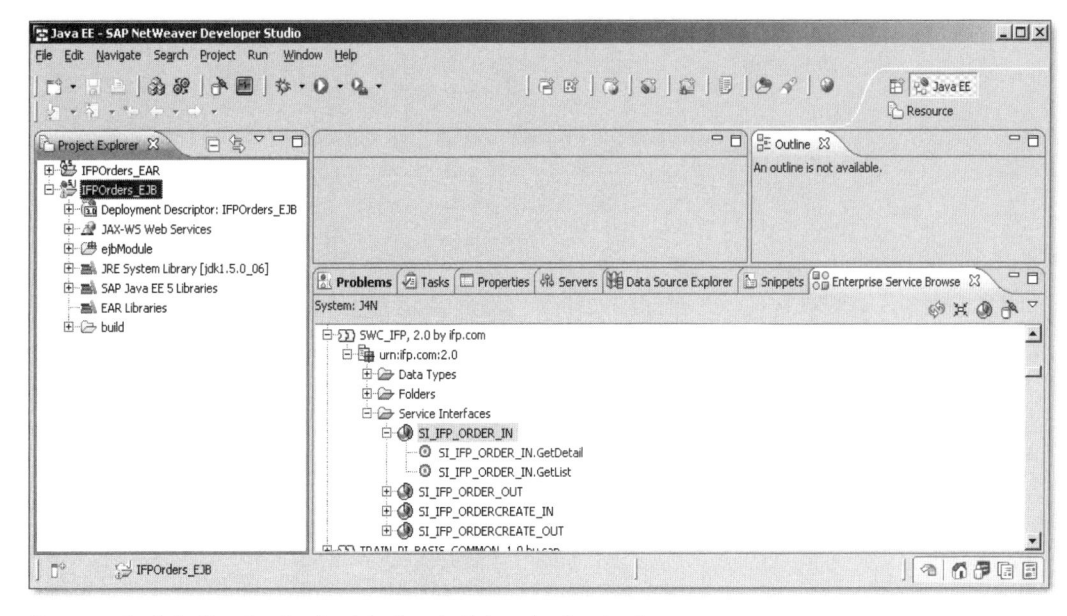

Figure 7.26 Selecting the Service Interface in Enterprise Service Browser

In the Enterprise Service Browser, select the entry Generate Java-Bean Skeleton from the context menu for the service interface `SI_IFP_ORDER_IN`. The system opens the dialog box shown in Figure 7.27. In this dialog box, move the top-left slider down to level 1. Develop Service is displayed next to the slider. Then use the exact same configuration settings shown in the upper part of the figure (under Configuration):

Java-bean skeleton

▸ Server: SAP Server

▸ Web Service Runtime: SAP NetWeaver

▸ Service Project: IFPOrders_EJB

▸ Service EAR Project: IFPOrders_EAR

As soon as you choose Finish to close this dialog box, the system will generate the classes for the provider proxy in the *ejbModule* folder of your EJB project. The generated class `SIFPORDERINImplBean` contains the provider proxy implementation.

385

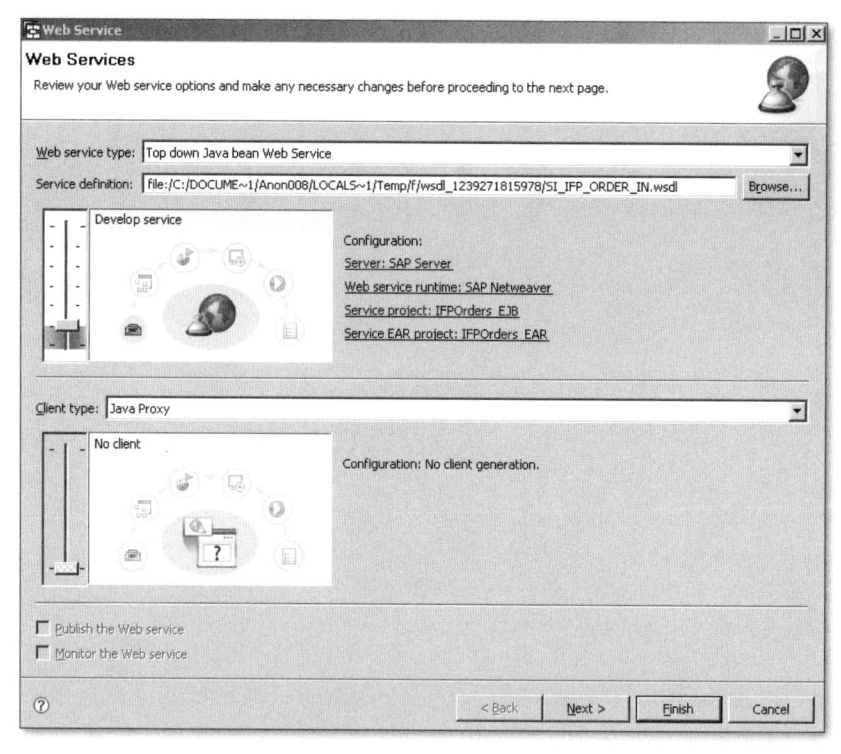

Figure 7.27 Developing a Web Service

Implementation You still have to implement the two methods `getList` and `getDetail` in this class (Figure 7.28 and Listing 7.6).

```
@RelMessagingNW05DTOperation(enableWSRM=false)
public  com.ifp._2.DTIFPORDERHEADERS getList(
    com.ifp._2.DTIFPORDERREF MT_ORDERGETLIST_REQ) {
  DTIFPORDERHEADERS ohs = new DTIFPORDERHEADERS();
  DTIFPORDERHEAD oh = new DTIFPORDERHEAD();
  oh.orderid = "0000000002";
  oh.type = "SO";
  oh.refid = "0000000002";
  oh.buyer = "Wegelin";
  oh.seller = "Englbrecht";
  oh.date = XMLGregorianCalendarImpl.createDate(
            2009, 4, 10, 0);
  ohs.getORDERHEADER().add(oh);
  return ohs;
}
```

Listing 7.6 Implementing the "getList" Method of the Provider

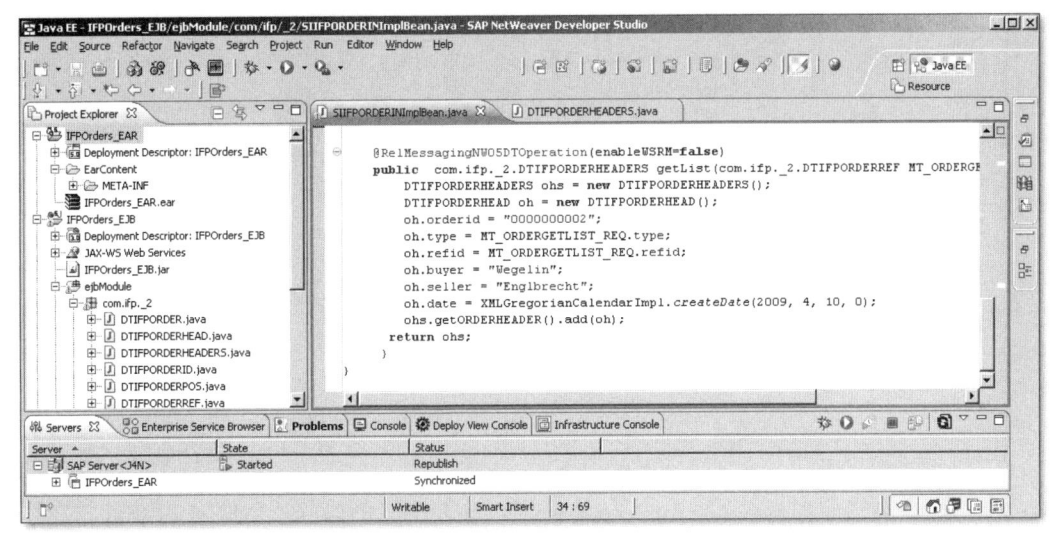

Figure 7.28 Implementing the "getList" Method

Save your implementation, and then publish the provider proxy. To do this, enter the connection data for SAP NetWeaver AS Java in the Preferences dialog box, and open the server view. Move the EAR project to the server in the server view. It will be displayed as a node below the server in the server view. Then select the entry Publish from the context menu for this node.

Publishing the proxy

You still have to create the web service and a binding. This is done in exactly the same way as the ABAP scenario (Section 7.2.2, ABAP SOAP Proxies). However, you do not use Transaction SOAMANAGER to access the configuration but rather SAP NetWeaver Administrator. Navigate to the area SOA MANAGEMENT • BUSINESS ADMINISTRATION • WEB SERVICE ADMINISTRATION, and create an endpoint for your service there. As already described in the ABAP scenario, you can now use Web Service Navigator to test your service.

Creating a Web service and a binding

Consumers

It is now very easy to develop a consumer. Create a new Java project with a class that contains a `public static void main` method.

Then select the entry Create Client from the context menu for the outbound service interface `SI_IFP_ORDER_OUT` in the Enterprise Service

Generating proxy classes

Browser. Proxy classes are generated in your project (Figure 7.29). Now code the consumer as shown in Listing 7.7.

```
public class IFPClient {
  public static void main(String[] args) {
    try{
      SIIFPORDEROUTService svc = new SIIFPORDEROUTService();
      SIIFPORDEROUT prt = svc.getSI_IFP_ORDER_OUT_Port();
      BindingProvider bp = (BindingProvider) prt;
      Map<String,Object> ctx = bp.getRequestContext();
      ctx.put(BindingProvider.ENDPOINT_ADDRESS_PROPERTY,
              "...");
      ctx.put(BindingProvider.USERNAME_PROPERTY,"zifp-00");
      ctx.put(BindingProvider.PASSWORD_PROPERTY, "addon99");
      DTIFPORDERREF ref = new DTIFPORDERREF();
      ref.setTYPE("SO");
      ref.setREFID("0000000000");
      DTIFPORDERHEADERS hdrs = prt.getList(ref);
      for(int i=0;i<hdrs.getORDERHEADER().size(); i++) {
        DTIFPORDERHEAD hd = hdrs.getORDERHEADER().get(i);
        System.out.println(hd.getORDERID());
        System.out.println(hd.getTYPE());
        System.out.println(hd.getREFID());
        System.out.println(hd.getBUYER());
        System.out.println(hd.getSELLER());
        System.out.println(hd.getDATE());
      }
    }
    catch(MalformedURLException e){
    }
  }
}
```

Listing 7.7 Java Web Service Client

The web service client in Listing 7.7 first instantiates the service class SIIFPORDEROUTService and obtains a port from this instance. This port is an instance of the BindingProvider class, which the interface SIIF-PORDEROUT implements. To enable you to access the methods for setting an endpoint, user name, and password, which are provided by this class, you must convert the interface reference prt into a reference to the BindingProvider class. As an endpoint, use the address of the web service that you want to call. This address is contained in the WSDL document for the web service. The client now calls the getList method for the port and outputs the results of the call on the console.

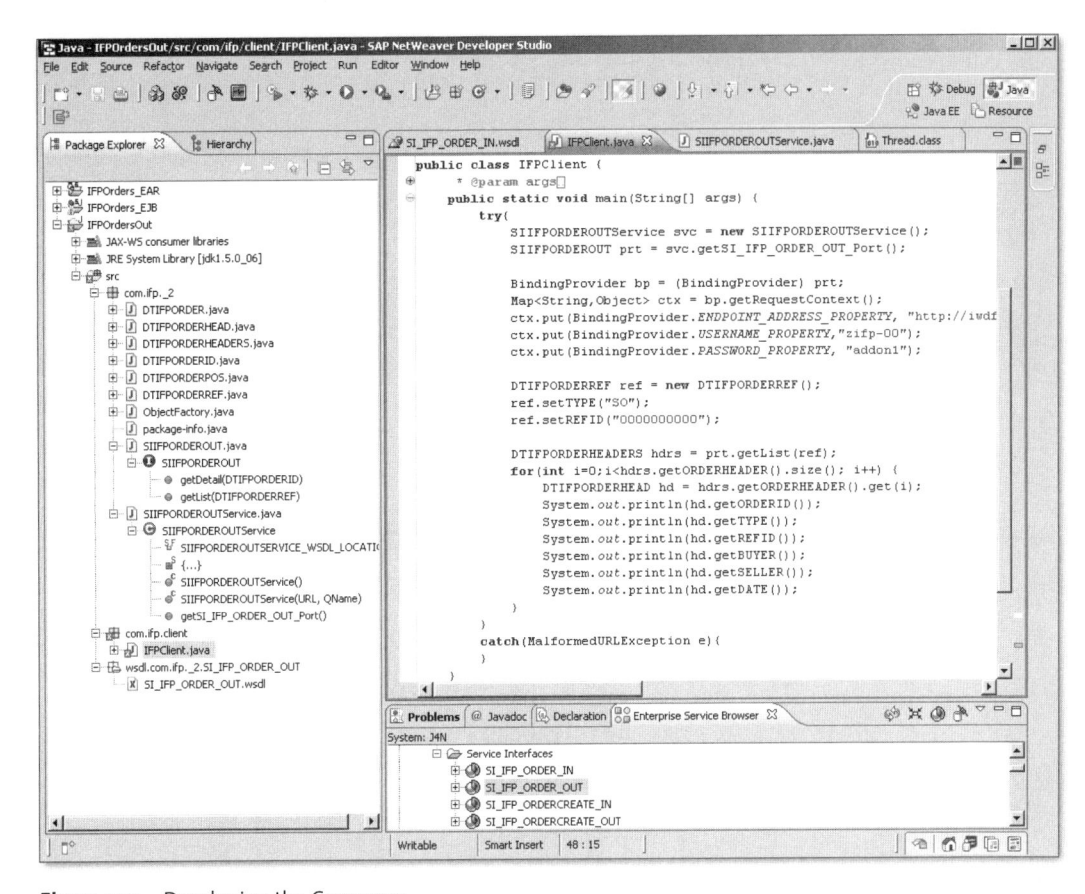

Figure 7.29 Developing the Consumer

This concludes our use of an SAP NetWeaver PI proxy to develop a Java SOAP client. If you compare Listing 7.7 for this Java client with Listing 3.16 for a C-RFC client in Chapter 3, Remote Function Call with C, you see that nowadays it is much easier to program interfaces for SAP systems. Added to this is the fact that SOAP is a web-based standard, whereas RFC is SAP's own protocol.

A Bibliography

Andrew Nash, Bill Duane, William Duane, *PKI: Implementing & Managing E-Security* (New York: McGraw-Hill Professional, 2001).

Dominik Ofenloch, Roland Schwaiger, *Getting Started with Web Dynpro ABAP* (Boston: SAP PRESS, 2010).

Frédéric Heinemann, Christian Rau, *Web Programming in ABAP with the SAP Web Application Server*, 2nd ed. (Boston: SAP PRESS, 2005).

Horst Keller, Sascha Krüger, *ABAP Objects*, 2nd ed. (Boston: SAP PRESS, 2007).

Jens Stumpe, Joachim Orb, *SAP Exchange Infrastructure* (Boston: SAP PRESS, 2005).

Ulli Hoffman, *Web Dynpro for ABAP* (Boston: SAP PRESS, 2006).

B   The Authors

Dr. Michael Wegelin studied physics at the Karlsruhe Technical University, Germany, and at the Tübingen University, Germany. During his studies, he worked as a C++ developer for Schärfe System Reutlingen and developed graphical user interfaces on Windows for measuring devices, among other things.

After finishing his studies, he worked as a software developer for Think Tools GmbH in Starnberg, Germany; K.I.S. Krankenhaus-Informationssysteme GmbH in Pliezhausen, Germany; and h/m systemtechnik GmbH & Co. KG in Reutlingen, Germany.

Since 1998, he has been the managing director of AddOn Software GmbH in Neu-Ulm, Germany. Here, he is responsible for the ABAP and SAP NetWeaver Process Integration area. His work focuses on the following areas:

- Consulting and implementing projects with SAP NetWeaver PI and ABAP
- Integrating external systems with C, C++, and C#
- Conducting trainings in the areas of ABAP programming and SAP NetWeaver PI

Michael Englbrecht, who holds a degree in computer science, studied at the University of Applied Sciences in Augsburg, Germany. He worked as a software developer and consultant for Tiscon Infosystems Ulm and MATHEMA AG.

Since 2002, he has been a senior consultant at AddOn Software GmbH in Neu-Ulm, Germany. Here, he is responsible for the Enterprise Java and SAP NetWeaver J2EE/JEE area. His work focuses on the following areas:

- Consulting and implementing SAP NetWeaver Portal projects and in the SAP NetWeaver Knowledge Management and Collaboration area
- Integrating systems with the SAP Java landscape
- Planning and implementing service-oriented infrastructures
- Conducting trainings in the areas of Java programming as well as Knowledge Management and Collaboration in the SAP environment

Index

.NET, 342
.NET Connector (NCO), 342

A

ABAP, 16
   ABAP Dictionary, 58, 73, 119, 242
   ABAP Workbench, 13, 58
   Short dump, 81
   SOAP proxy, 374
   SOAP web client, 319
   SOAP web service, 311
   Stack, 15
   Transaction concept, 27
   Web Dynpro, 69
   XI proxy, 356
Access
   Security, 33
ACL (Access Control List), 42
   Entry, 42
   Maintenance, 43
Active Server Pages .NET (ASP.NET), 69
Adapter object, 353
Adaptive web service, 338
ALE, 84, 271
   Architecture, 85
   Configuration, 284
   Customizing, 86
   Distribution model, 87, 277, 286, 288, 293, 299, 310
   Inbound function module, 283, 293
   Inbound parameter, 289, 294
   Outbound function module, 292
   Partner profile, 88
   Process code, 283
   Receiver determination, 295
   Receiver port, 288
   Status monitor, 291
Annotation, 31, 341
   SOAPBinding, 341
   WebMethod, 341

API (Application Programming Interface), 30
Application
   wsnavigator, 91
Application bar, 19
Application component, 29
Application layer, 13, 14, 16, 31
Application Link Enabling (ALE), 84
Application protocol, 20
Application security, 33
Application server, 14, 19, 29, 73, 149
   Dedicated, 259
Application server, 29
Architecture
   Client-server, 14
Array, 67
Array insert, 67, 122
ASP.NET, 69
Asymmetric procedures, 33
Authentication, 32, 40, 259
Authorization, 32, 41, 63, 80
   Check, 97, 104, 141
   Object, 63, 80

B

Background
   Work process, 22
BAdI, 120
BAPI, 82, 118
   ALE interface, 88, 292
   BAPI_TRANSACTION_COMMIT, 83, 134
   BAPI_TRANSACTION_ROLLBACK, 84
   Conventions, 119
   Error message, 130
   GetSearchhelp, 141
   Input help, 141
   Instance-dependent, 84, 129
   Instance-independent, 84, 136
   Interface, 82

Release, 127
RETURN parameter, 120, 122
Transaction model, 83, 110, 174
Update, 122
Batch input, 71
Best Effort (BE), 92
Binding, 345, 378, 387
    Custom, 345
Binding style
    Document, 316
    RPC, 316
BOR, 82
Browser, 15
BSP, 69
Buffer area, 23
Business Add-In (BAdI), 120
Business application, 14
Business Application Programming Interface (BAP), 82
Business object, 82, 118
    Helpvalues, 141
Business Object Builder, 118
Business Server Pages (BSP), 69
Business system, 352, 366

C

Cast, 267
CCI, 257
CE (SAP NetWeaver Composition Environment), 372
Certificate, 52, 56, 325
    Export, 43
    Import, 45
    X509, 325
Changing parameter, 66, 158, 242
Check field, 60
Check table, 60
Class
    BindingProvider, 389
    JCo.Client, 242
    JCoConnectionData, 225
    JCoContext, 223
    JCoDestination, 226
    JCoDestinationManager, 221

JCoDestinationMonitor, 224
JCoFieldIterator, 231
JCoFunction, 226
JCoRepository, 226
JCoServerFactory, 247, 248
JCoTable, 228
PortalRuntime, 265
RecordFactory, 266
Client, 17
    Proxy, 356, 358, 363
    Server architecture, 14
Client, 17
Collective search help, 61
Command field, 18
Commit, 100
Common Client Interface (CCI), 257
Communication
    Asynchronous, 30
    Façade, 238
Compile, 152
Compiler, 152
Composite application, 31
Confidentiality, 33
Configuration scenario, 367
Connection, 265
    Direct, 223
    Establish, 242
    Management, 257
    Parameter, 239
    Pooled, 223
Consumer, 380, 388
    Proxy, 380, 388
C RFC library, 145, 220
Cryptography
    Private key, 33
    Provider, 38, 47
    Public key, 33

D

Data
    Security, 33
Data access layer, 32
Database, 14

Database Logical Unit of Work
   (DB LUW), 27
Data element, 58
Data layer, 14
Data type, 354, 372
DB LUW, 27
Deployable Java proxy, 337
Deployment descriptor, 31, 268, 327
Design by contract, 30
Destination, 98, 215, 255, 286, 287, 320
   ‚BACK';destination Ba, 100
   Name, 338
   ‚NONE';destination No, 100
   SPACE;destination Sp, 100
DIAG, 16, 20
Dialog
   Processing, 25
   Step, 26
   Transaction, 25
   Work process, 22
Digital
   Certificate, 35
   Signature, 34
Direct input, 71
Dispatcher, 21, 24
Dispatching, 202
Distribution model (ALE distribution model), 286
DLL, 219
Double stack, 14
Dynamic Information and Action Gateway (DIAG), 16
Dynamic Link Library (DLL), 219
Dynpro Screen, 26

E

EAR, 362
   Project, 362, 383
ECo, 238
EIS, 257
EJB, 29, 253, 326
   Container, 32
   Project, 326, 360, 383
Encryption, 32, 33

Endpoint API, 339
Enqueue, 23
   Work process, 28
Enterprise application project, 327, 337
Enterprise Archive (EAR), 362
Enterprise Connector (ECo), 238
Enterprise Information System (EIS), 257
Enterprise Java Bean (EJB), 29
Enterprise Service, 376
   Browser, 384
Enterprise Services Repository (ES Repository), 372
Entity bean, 29
Error handling, 242
ES Repository, 372, 384
Exactly Once (EO), 92
Exactly Once In Order (EOIO), 92
Exception, 66, 100, 159
   Communication_failure, 100
   system_failure, 100
Export parameter, 66, 158, 230, 242, 243, 266
Extensible Markup Language (XML), 306
Extensible Stylesheet Language for Transformations, 306

F

Fault message type, 354
Fault type, 242
File
   app.config, 345
   Interface, 70
   saprfc.h, 155
   saprfc.ini, 151, 193
   Services, 21
Firewall, 24
Flagged for changing, 28
Foreign key dependency, 60
Function
   ItAppLine, 171
   ItCreate, 171
   ItFill, 171

Index

  ItGetLine, 171
  RfcAccept, 189, 194
  RfcCallEx, 160, 172
  RfcCallReceiveEx, 160, 172
  RfcCancelRegisterServer, 193
  RfcCheckRegisterServer, 193
  RfcConfirmTransID, 177
  RfcCreateTransID, 177, 186
  RfcDispatch, 190, 202
  RfcGetData, 196, 197, 198
  RfcGetNameEx, 204
  RfcIndirectCallEx, 177, 186
  RfcInstallFunction, 190, 194, 202
  RfcInstallTransactionControl, 205, 207
  RfcInstallUnicodeStructure, 174
  RfcLastErrorEx, 164
  RfcListen, 161, 203
  RFC_ON_CHECK_TID, 205
  RFC_ON_COMMIT, 205
  RFC_ON_CONFIRM_TID, 205
  RFC_ON_ROLLBACK, 205
  RfcOpenEx, 155, 160
  RfcQueueInsert, 188
  RfcRaise, 196, 200
  RfcReceiveEx, 160, 172
  RfcSendData, 196, 197
  RfcWaitForRequest, 202
  TID_check, 208
  TID_commit, 208
  TID_rollback, 208
Function Builder, 65, 77, 119
Function group, 65
Function handler, 249
  Register, 250
Function module, 28, 64
  ALE_INPUT_ALEAUD, 279
  ALE_MODEL_INFO_GET, 276
  BALW_BAPIRETURN_GET2, 126
  BAPI_TRANSACTION_COMMIT, 174
  IDOC_INBOUND_ASYNCHRONOUS, 86, 296
  IN BACKGROUND TASK addition, 106
  Interface, 66
  IN UPDATE TASK statement, 67

  MASTER_IDOC_DISTRIBUTE, 279
  QIWK_REGISTER, 117
  TRFC_QIN_RESTART, 117, 189
  TRFC_SET_QIN_PROPERTIES, 115
  Update, 28

G

Gateway, 21, 73, 189, 192, 253
  Host, 75
  Monitor, 81
  Service, 75
Generic Security Services Application Programming Interface Ver, 52
GSS-API V2, 52

H

Hash function, 34
Hash value, 34
Home interface, 366
Hook method, 30
Host name, 19, 20
HTTP (Hypertext Transfer Protocol), 22, 311

I

IC, 325
ICF, 90
ICM, 22, 90
Identity, 37
IDoc, 84, 86, 271
  Basic Type, 274
  Client, 303
  Control record, 277, 278, 281, 298, 300
  Creation, 275
  Data record, 279, 298, 300
  Number, 282
  Post-processing, 291
  Programming with C, 296
  Programming with Java, 302

Receiver, 297
Segment, 86, 272, 303
Segment definition, 272
Segment type, 272
Sender, 300
Server, 307
Status, 282
XML processing, 307
IDoc type, 87, 271, 273, 292
 ALEREQ01, 275
Implementation Container (IC), 325
Import parameter, 66, 158, 226, 242, 243, 266
Inbound queue, 112, 116
Input check, 60
Instance, 19
 IDocRepository, 303
 IInteraction, 266
Integration
 Directory, 348, 366
 Engine, 92, 356
 Repository, 92, 348, 352
 Server, 348
Integration process, 353
Integration scenario, 353
Integrity, 33, 34
Interface, 13
 Agreement, 30
 DestinationDataProvider, 222
 Determination, 366, 369
 IConnection, 265
 IConnectorGatewayService, 265
 IDocDocument, 303
 IDocFactory, 303
 IDocXMLProcessor, 307
 IInteractionSpec, 266
 IUser, 37
 IUserMaint, 37
 JCoCustomRepository, 245
 JCoFunctionTemplate, 246
 JCoIDocHandlerFactory, 308, 309
 JCoIDocServer, 307
 JCoListMetaData, 236, 246
 JCoMetaData, 236
 JCoRecord, 226
 JCoServer, 247

 JCoServerFunctionHandle, 249
 JCoServerTIDHandler, 252, 308
 Mapping, 354, 369
 Object, 353
 Pattern, 373
 ServerDataProvider, 247
 Technology, 70
 Virtual <Pfeil>R<Normal> Virtual Interface (VI, 324
Intermediate Document (IDoc), 271
Internet Connection Framework (ICF), 90
Internet Connection Manager (ICM), 22
ISO standard, 36
Iterator, 231

J

J2EE, 29
 KeyStore service, 39
JAAS, 50
Java
 Java 2 Enterprise Edition (J2EE), 29
 Java API for XML Web Services (JAX-WS), 339
 Java Architecture for XML Binding (JAXB), 339
 Java Authentication and Authorization Service, 50
 Java Connector Architecture, 256
 Java Connector (JCo), 217
 Java Cryptography Architecture, 38
 Java Cryptography Extension (JCE), 38
 Java Development Kit, 339
 Java Enterprise Edition (JEE), 31
 Java key store (JKS), 49
 Java Message Service (JMS), 30
 Java Naming and Directory Interface (JNDI), 253
 Java Native Interface (JNI), 47
 Java Server Faces (JSF), 337
 Java Server Pages (JSP), 31
 Library, 241
 SOAP proxy, 383

Stack, 15, 29, 31
Web Dynpro, 69, 338
Web Start, 352
XI proxy, 360
Java proxy
   Deployable, 337
JAXB, 339
JAX-WS, 339
JCE, 38
JCo, 217, 302
   Architecture, 219
   Factory class, 224
   Installation, 217
   RFC Provider Service, 253
   Session management, 222
JEE, 31
JKS, 49
JMS, 30
JNDI, 253, 362, 366
JNI, 47, 219
JSF, 337
JSP, 31, 69

K

Key, 33
   Field, 60
   Management, 35
   Private, 33
   Public, 33
KeyStore, 38, 48
KeyStore content
   JKS, 38
   PKCS12, 38
KeyStore file
   verify.der, 39

L

LDAP, 36
Library
   SAPSSOEXT, 47
Lifecycle, 30
Lightweight Directory Access Protocol (LDAP), 36
Linker, 152
Linking, 152
Load balancing, 16, 49, 73, 78, 149, 239
Load distribution, 23
Lock, 27, 104
   List, 35
   Module, 63
   Object, 63
Lock management
   Work process, 23
Login module, 51
Logon, 17
   Client, 19
   Group, 23
   Language, 17
   Language (Logon language), 17
   Ticket, 42, 49
LUW, 27, 107, 114

M

Management, 257
Mapping
   Object, 353
   Program, 354
Mass data, 67, 123
Mass updating, 67
Menu bar, 17
Message, 30, 100
   Class, 126
   Interface, 92, 353, 354, 357
   Mapping, 354
   Number, 126
   Server, 16, 23, 73, 149
   Type, 87, 275, 292, 315, 354, 372
Message-driven bean, 29
Message-Oriented Middleware (MOM), 30
Metadata, 236, 246, 303, 347
Method
   getFunctionTemplate, 236
   JCoParameterList, 226
Middleware

Interface, 220
Server, 347
MIME, 92
Mode, external, 19
Module pool, 69
MOM, 30
Multipurpose Internet Mail Extensions (MIME), 92

N

Name collision, 319
NCO, 342
Non-repudiation, 33
Number range, 64

O

Object
  JCoDestination, 221
  JCoFunction, 249
  JCoFunctionTemplate, 236
  JCoIDocServerContext, 309
  JCoServerContext, 249
Object type, 119
One-way function, 34
Open SQL, 32
Operation, 373
Outbound queue, 112, 116, 373
Outside-in approach, 347

P

Package, 58, 238
  Use access, 319
Package Explorer, 262
PAI module, 26
PAM, 50
Parameter
  Export, 66, 158, 230, 242, 243, 266
  IDOC_CONTROL_REC_40, 298
  IDOC_DATA_REC_40, 298
  Import, 66, 158, 226, 242, 243, 266

Scalar, 98
Structured, 98
Partner profile, 286, 287, 288, 299
Pass by value, 98
Password, 17
Payload, 356
PBO module, 26
Performance, 31
Persistence, 30
Personal Security Environment (PSE), 40
PKI, 35
Pluggable Authentication Model (PAM), 50
Port
  Default, 320
  Logical, 320, 336, 380
  Number, 21
Portal
  Application, 262
  Component, 261, 262, 264
  Project, 262
Presentation layer, 14
Principal API, 36
Private-key cryptography, 33
Process After Input module (PAI module), 26
Process Before Output module (PBO module), 26
Process code, 289
Processing sequence, 80
Profile, 64
  Parameter, 43
Program
  genh, 147, 167
  rfcping, 146, 148
  sapinfo, 146, 148
  ZSSF_TEST_PSE, 57
Program ID, 75, 250, 256
Protocol
  Handler, 325
  Implementation, 325
Provider, 376, 383
  Proxy, 385
Proxy, 226, 303, 326
  Class, 238, 243, 266, 319, 336, 339, 342

Runtime, 363
PSE, 40, 52
  Central, 52
  File, 49
  Individual, 53
Public-key cryptography, 33
Public-key infrastructure (PKI), 35
Purchase order, 58

Q

QIN Scheduler, 117, 189
  SMQR, 117
QOUT Scheduler, 114
qRFC monitor
  For inbound queues, 116
  For outbound queues, 114
Quality of service, 92
Queue, 234
  Name, 188

R

Receiver
  Agreement, 367, 370
  Determination, 366, 368
Receiver channel, 366, 367
References project, 327
Registration, 193
Relationship of trust, 47, 48
Remote Function Call (RFC), 21
Remote interface, 366
Report, 69
Repository, 235, 253
  Server-side, 245
Repudiation, 34
Resource adapter, 257
Resources
  Consumption, 27
Responsibility, 30
RFC, 21, 72, 95
  Asynchronous, 78, 117
  Client, 154, 220
  Data types, 156, 227
  Debugging, 150
  Destination, 73
  Error handling, 162
  For changing, 101
  For creating, 107
  For deleting, 101
  Function module, 95
  Handle, 196
  Parameter, 164, 167
  Queued, 80, 111, 188, 234
  Registered server, 75, 189, 250
  Return code, 157
  Server, 189, 244
  Synchronous, 77, 95, 106, 225
  Table parameter, 171
  Tracing, 82, 150
  Transactional, 79, 106, 109, 177, 205, 232
  Type handle, 170
  Unicode library, 157
  With C, 145
  With Java, 217
RFC Software Development Kit, 146
Roll area, 23
Route, 24
Router string, 25

S

Sales order, 58
Sample application, 57
SAP
  Gateway, 149
  IDoc library, 302
  Instance, 73
  menu, 19
  Router, 24, 149
  Router string, 239
  SAP CRM, 14
  SAP Cryptolib, 53
  SAP Crypto Toolkit, 46
  SAP ERP, 14
  SAP GUI, 15, 16, 20, 24
  SAP Implementation Guide, 88
  SAP Java Connector (JCo), 217
  SAP Logical Unit of Work (SAP LUW), 27

Index

SAP logon ticket, 39, 46
SAP NetWeaver Administrator, 39, 387
SAP NetWeaver AS, 13
SAP NetWeaver AS ABAP, 16, 57
SAP NetWeaver AS Java, 29
SAP NetWeaver BW, 14
SAP NetWeaver Composition Environment (CE), 31, 339
SAP NetWeaver Developer Studio (SAP NWDS), 261
SAP NetWeaver Exchange Infrastructure (SAP XI), 14
SAP NetWeaver Master Data Management, 14
SAP NetWeaver Mobile, 14
SAP NetWeaver PI, 92, 347, 372
SAP NetWeaver Portal, 14, 42, 258
SAP NetWeaver Portal Connector Framework, 256
SAP NetWeaver XI, 14, 92, 347
SAP NWDS, 13, 218, 238, 261, 323
SAP PLM, 14
SAP SCM, 14
SAP SRM, 14
System, 20
Scheduler
    QIN, 117, 189
    QOUT, 114
Screen, 19, 26
Search help, 61, 62
Secure Network Communication (SNC), 51
Secure Socket Layer (SSL), 34
Security, 32
    Access, 33
    Data, 33
    Infrastructural, 32
    Integration, 46
    Management, 257
    System, 33
    Transport layer, 51
SEI, 326
Selection, 137
Selection method, 61
Self-registration, 37
Separation of concerns, 29

Server proxy, 356, 360, 377
Service Endpoint Interface (SEI), 326
Service interface, 372, 373
Service-oriented architecture (SOA), 31
Service-Oriented Architecture Protocol (SOAP), 90
Service Provider Interface (SPI), 30
Services file, 21
Servlet, 31, 69
Session bean
    Stateful, 29
    Stateless, 29, 254, 328
Session management (JCo), 31
SID, 20, 149
Single point of access, 42
Single sign-on (SSO), 41
Single stack, 14
Size category, 61
SLD, 258, 348, 349, 372
SNC, 51
SNC PSE container, 55
SOA, 31
SOAP, 90, 311
    Action, 316
    Body, 317
    Document, 92
    Envelope, 317
    Header, 92, 317
Software
    Component, 350, 352
    Product, 349
SPI, 30
Spool
    Work process, 22
SSL, 34, 51
SSO, 41
Standalone Java proxies, 334
Standard
    BAPI, 84
    Destination, 100
    Toolbar, 18
Stateful, 223
Stateless, 29, 254, 328, 373, 374
Statement
    AUTHORITY CHECK, 80
    CALL FUNCTION, 64
    CALL TRANSACTION, 70

Index

  COMMIT WORK, 27, 28, 67, 107
  DELETE, 28
  INSERT, 28
  ROLLBACK WORK, 27, 28, 67, 106
  UPDATE, 28
Status bar, 19
Structure parameter, 230
Struts, 337
Symmetric procedure, 33
System
  External, 74
  Logical, 86, 285, 286, 299, 310
  Message, 19
  Number, 20, 73, 149
  PSE, 45
  Security, 33
  Technical, 351
System ID (SID), 149
System Landscape, 258
  Editor, 260
System Landscape Directory (SLD), 258

T

Table
  ARFCSDATA, 106
  ARFCSSTATE, 106
  BAPIF4T, 141
  Maintenance, 60
  Parameter, 66, 159, 228, 230, 242
  T100, 122, 129
  TBDBE, 294
  Transparent, 58
  TWPSSO2ACL, 43
TCP, 20
Ticket issuer, 42
TID, 79, 106, 177, 188, 208, 232, 305
  Management, 178, 206, 233, 251, 308
Title bar, 18
Tool
  Keytool, 39
  sapgenpse, 40, 53
  wsgen, 339
  wsimport, 339
Transaction, 18, 19

BD51, 283
BD64, 299
BD87, 291
BDBG, 292, 294
LPCONFIG, 320
Management, 257
RZ10, 43, 54
SA16, 60
SALE, 86, 88, 284, 299, 310
SE11, 58
SE16, 60
SE37, 65, 77
SE80, 58
SICF, 90
SM30, 43, 141
SM35, 71
SM58, 106
SM59, 73, 98, 193, 215, 250, 286, 287, 310, 320
SMGW, 81, 193
SMQ1, 114
SMQ2, 116, 234
SMQS, 114
SNRO, 64
SOAMANAGER, 378, 380
SPRO, 88
SPROXY, 92, 357, 358, 376
SSO2, 44
SSTRUSTSSO2, 45
ST05, 82
ST22, 81
STRUSTSSO2, 40, 43, 56
SU01, 63
SU02, 64
SWO, 82
SWO1, 82, 118, 127
SXMB_IFR, 349, 367
SXMB_MONITOR, 371
WE20, 288, 310
WE30, 87, 273
WE31, 87, 272
WE42, 289
WE81, 86, 275
WE82, 275
WSADMIN, 91, 314, 316, 334
WSCONFIG, 91, 314
Transaction code, 19

Transaction Control Protocol (TCP), 20
Transaction ID (TID), 79
Transaction model, 174
Transaction
  SE80, 376
Transport binding, 325
Transport object, 325
Trust, 35
Type handle, 170, 196

U

UDDI, 319
UME, 36
UME Persistence Manager, 36
Universal Description and Discovery Interface Service, 319
UNIX daemon, 76
Update
  Module, 67, 103
  Table, 28
  Work process, 23, 28
User, 17
  Context, 19
  Interface, 68
  Master record, 17
  Name, 17, 19
  SAPJSF, 36
  Session, 16, 19
User datastore, 37
User Management Engine (UME), 36
User mapping, 46, 260

V

VA, 39, 253
Variable
  SECUDIR, 54
Vendor purchase order, 58
Virtual Interface (VI), 324, 330, 331
Visual Administrator (VA), 39

W

Web container, 31
Web Dynpro
  ABAP, 69
  Java, 31, 69, 338
Web module project, 337
Web service, 311, 378, 387
  Adaptive, 334
  Binding, 324
  Endpoint, 312
  Home page, 91
  Interface, 313, 324
  Operation, 312
  Runtime, 325
  With J2EE, 326, 330
  With Java, 323
  Wizard, 312
Web service client, 389
  With C#, 342
  With Java, 326, 333, 340
Web Service Definition (WSD), 324
Web Service Description Language (WSDL), 91
Web Service Navigator, 331, 378
Windows Service, 76
Work process, 22
WSD, 324, 331
WSDL, 91, 314, 320, 334, 343, 379, 381
  Binding, 325
  Document style, 316
  RPC style, 316

X

X.500 (ISO standard), 36
XI SOAP, 92, 356
XML, 306
  Message, 311
  Schema Definition Language (XSD), 315
XSLT, 306, 354

All about fundamentals, technologies, and practical solutions

Covers the usage in online and offline scenarios

With examples of Adobe Document Services, Adobe LiveCycle Designer, ISR Framework, Web Dynpro Integration and many more

Jürgen Hauser, Andreas Deutesfeld, Stephan Rehmann, Thomas Szücs, Philipp Thun

SAP Interactive Forms by Adobe

The book adopts a classic structure: A general introduction explains what Interactive Forms are and how they are implemented. It then illustrates the creation of print and interactive forms by the usage of technology (Adobe Document Services), via tool (Adobe LiveCycle Designer) and interface call (Web Dynpro, web service). The level of complexity of the described approaches successively increases. According to the product idea, the book covers all topics comprehensively and holistically.
Basic knowledge in the areas of ABAP and Web Dynpro are, however, taken for granted.

624 pp., 2009, 79,95 Euro / US$ 79.95
ISBN 978-1-59229-254-7

\>\> www.sap-press.com

www.sap-press.com

Explains all steps from ID creation to custom development

Shows test tools, confirmations, user exits, update technologies, serialization, and much more

Provides numerous recommendations and tricks for the practical programming experience

Sabine Maisel

Practical Guide to IDoc Development for SAP

This book enables you to program and extend IDocs yourself by describing all details of IDoc development on the SAP side. The focus is on that part of the extension technologies that are relevant for IDocs, but the book also discusses methods that are not specifically designed for an IDoc type. Moreover, you learn about special features such as the workflow connection or the confirmation of IDoc status values. Numerous code examples and screenshots illustrate all solutions.

approx. 250 pp., 69,95 Euro / US$ 69.95
ISBN 978-1-59229-332-2, Dec 2009

>> www.sap-press.com

SAP PRESS